THE
PRUNE
B·O·O·K

THE
PRUNE
B·O·O·K

THE 100 TOUGHEST
MANAGEMENT AND
POLICY-MAKING
JOBS IN
WASHINGTON

JOHN H. TRATTNER
THE CENTER FOR EXCELLENCE IN GOVERNMENT

Madison Books
Lanham • New York • London

Library of Congress Cataloging-in-Publication Data

Trattner, John H.
The prune book.
Includes index.
1. Government executives—United States. I. Title.
II. Center for Excellence in Government (Washington, D.C.)
JK723.E9T72   1988   353'.074   88–8253
ISBN 0–8191–7000–3 (alk. paper)

CONTENTS

INDEX TO ORGANIZATION CHARTS

FOREWORD

As individuals with prior government service now in private sector leadership positions, the Principals at The Center for Excellence in Government know how good and--sometimes--how bad federal government service can be, depending upon the leadership it gets. We undertook to raise the resources, find the author and provide the support to complete this book as a practical contribution toward improving the performance of that institution within which many of The Center's Principals committed some portion of their professional lives.

For those talented people who make an honorable career in public service, for elected officials who must guide and judge the performance of federal institutions, and for citizens who live with the results of it all, the individuals who serve in the sub-cabinet jobs can make a critical difference. It is not just their intelligence, good intentions, and support of the administration that matters-- important though they are. A match between skills and experience and the needs of the job are key ingredients to good outcomes. We hope the jobs we describe here will have stronger incumbents as the result of these efforts, and we further hope this book stimulates a broader effort to insure the right talent in other important jobs.

A project of this scope does not just occur. Resources must be raised. Particularly important to this were the efforts of Frank A. Weil, whose special foreword appears below, and John R. Stevenson. These two Center Principals not only directly raised foundation funds, but were instrumental in the work of others toward the securing of sufficient funds, and served on The Center's Steering Committee for the project, which Jack Stevenson chaired. Without the support of Frank and Jack, this book would not have been written.

The Center wishes to gratefully acknowledge the support of the

Andrew W. Mellon Foundation, the Mary Reynolds Babcock Foundation, the Hickrill Foundation, the Norman Foundation, and the Commonwealth Fund--foundations without whose help the project could not have been done.

We also pay tribute to the assistance of Principals who served as team captains to select the jobs and assist the author in his research, including Dale E. Hathaway, Stanley J. Marcuss, Philip A. Odeen, Christopher T. Cross, Alvin L. Alm, Suzanne H. Woolsey, John K. Freeman, Heather L. Ross, Robert A. McConnell, William H. Kolberg, John R. Stevenson, Thomas J. Healey, Theodore C. Lutz, and Edward G. Sanders.

Money without talent to use it wisely would avail little. The Center, however, had the great good fortune to make common cause with John H. Trattner, the experienced and talented author of the volume. Writing is tough enough work on its own; but to accomplish the research and writing in the complex management structure needed for the project required special skill and tolerance. Perhaps his own government service helped prepare him for the chore. And we are not in doubt that the able assistance of Katherine C. Cowan and M. Catherine Faint aided in the successful completion of this project. Nonetheless, John's perseverance and capabilities have proved more than equal to the task.

No accounting of The Center's work is, however, complete without full recognition of the unflagging enthusiasm, energy, and inspiration which The Center's Executive Director brings to all its products. Mark A. Abramson beckoned or, where needed, pushed us all from the beginning to completion and made it happen.

William A. Morrill
Chair
The Center for Excellence
in Government

SPECIAL FOREWORD

What is more important to governing than getting the best people into the key jobs? In my own experience in government I found too few talented people well cast and often wondered how a vehicle could be created better to match talent to jobs. Thus, when Mark Abramson first mentioned the idea of a book that would collect the bi-partisan experience of prior incumbents of the toughest managerial/policy jobs in the federal government--a book to be produced in time for a new administration in January 1989--I was immediately moved to support it by the possibility of a triple play.

1. **For the Executive Branch** - the tool itself contains some new and useful information and its very existence suggests that it may be used by others to judge personnel selections in a new goldfish bowl.

2. **For the Senate** - the process of advise and consent can be better informed and thus perhaps more demanding in the case of some of those positions that have remained in the shadow of anonymity.

3. **For the Press** - which generally only has reported on exceptional and/or controversial appointments, there now can be more attention to key positions which could lead to an even more discerning Senate and even more substantive White House personnel process.

If anything resembling the interaction suggested by the triple play occurs, The Center for Excellence in Government will have contributed a lasting device in the process of striving for better governance.

The credit for this volume goes to John H. Trattner, without whom the laborious and complex process of compilation and writing would never have been accomplished, and to those who assisted him so ably. Mark Abramson, the tireless networker, wove the fabric that binds this volume among many supporters and doubters.

My suggestion of naming this *The Prune Book* sprang from the notion of a wizened and wiser plum book. For those who still think that was a lousy idea, I accept full blame. If that title helps spread the book's fame, Mark and John deserve the credit because a title without good content won't go far for long.

Let us all hope that the next administration will use *The Prune Book* and make it the first in a long line of many useful editions.

> Frank A. Weil
> Member, Management Council
> The Center for Excellence
> in Government

ACKNOWLEDGEMENTS

Many people, of different skills and talents, made this book possible.

Bill Morrill has already cited the indispensable support given the project by other Center Principals and by private foundations. Bill's own hard work also deserves emphatic mention and thanks. As chairman of The Center, he provided close and keen-eyed general oversight and, even more important, wise counsel of both practical and editorial value. I warmly second Bill's acknowledgement of the contributions of Jack Stevenson and Frank Weil. Jack, chairman of *The Prune Book* steering committee, was quietly responsible for obtaining substantial funding of the book. Frank, who conceived *The Prune Book* title, also sat on the steering committee, raised significant funds, and was a constant source of sound advice.

To the gratitude already expressed to the several foundations which assisted the project, and to the members of the teams which identified the positions in the book, I'd like to add my own. The book benefited greatly from the teams' conscientious and able work and from their vetting of the draft texts.

I'd like to pay special tribute to the staff of The Center for the essential parts they played in getting the book out.

When Mark Abramson, its executive director, discussed the writing of *The Prune Book* with me 15 months ago, the organization and research alone seemed extensive enough projects to soak up all the available time, before writing could begin. But Mark is a person of tough-minded determination and energy. His knowledge of the federal government and of Washington, personal familiarity with the Principals of The Center, and deft management of The Center's information and technical resources proved fundamental to the project. He deserves great praise as The Center's driving force and spirit.

Kathy Cowan is the talented associate director of *The Prune Book* project. A skillful and tireless interviewer, thoughtful and resourceful organizer, and perceptive and persistent editor, she was irreplaceable in both her substantive and day-to-day management roles. For much of the period of the book's incubation, especially when the writing of it began, she was effectively supervising the project. I relied on her for many a judgment call, unflinching criticism, and countless feats of memory. Her contributions to the book were impressive and invaluable.

Cathie Faint is another crucial figure in the production of this book. Though she had many other responsibilities at The Center, no amount of workload could disturb her calm, flexible and thorough approach to the immense technical tasks involved. Complicated though these were, however, they did not distract her from useful attention to content. Her suggestions and reminders, and her unflagging support in a dozen other ways, were of great assistance.

It is a privilege to have been associated with three such worthy colleagues. I am also indebted to four others: Tamar Osterman, Clyde Linsley, Deanna Peel and Tim Lynch, who worked on various stages of the project, and provided important help.

Finally, I am grateful for the strong support and critical editorial eye of my wife. Her strong belief and steady encouragement, in this as in everything, were unstinting and inestimable.

J.H.T.
Washington, DC
July 22, 1988

1

INTRODUCTION

In the end, it is good people who make good government. That truth is what drives this book.

Between the pinnacle of the executive branch of government, chosen by election, and the broad ranks of career servants, chosen by competitive selection, there is a thin layer of leadership chosen by Presidential appointment. The people in this small group are critical actors in the life of any administration.

Hardly anyone challenges the necessarily political character of the appointments of these senior managers and policymakers, though ample room exists for reasoned argument about how many there should be and which of them a President should fill in this way. Political appointments are part of the American political system, one of the abiding imperatives of successful democratic government.

At the same time, it is neither naive nor foolish for late 20th-century Americans to expect their government to be led by people who are not just politically attuned to their administrations but professionally competent to do the jobs to which they are appointed.

The world of the 1990s is unlikely to become less complicated and demanding than we find it today. It will confront Americans with the need to make important changes, just to stay even--to preserve our present economic prospects, physical health and creative and scientific achievement, hang on to our current place and role in the world, and continue to embody the ideals and principles the nation is supposed to stand for.

As the nation moves to meet this future, particular roles of the federal government may grow, shrink, or change. But the future will also demand that government play its part with skill and distinction. There is no shortage of ideas about the political, economic and social directions we should take, or of people who would lead the way. Yet we spend too little time and energy devising the means to reach the objectives we choose and intelligently shaping the government's role in reaching them. Governance is not solely a matter of policy choices. It is also the world of effective management.

What credentials should a person appointed to high public office bring to the job? Many people respond with the obvious: competence, experience, management skills and relevant background and training. It's one of those truths to which most of our leaders and many of the rest of us can easily subscribe in the abstract. And, just as easily, we ignore it in reality, even as events regularly remind us of the consequences of doing so.

The Prune Book underlines the reality. It is an attempt to improve the selection of the men and women who fill the crucial-- but often vaguely understood--senior positions in the critical management and policy-making area just below Cabinet level. Like the more visible figures above them who gather regularly around the Cabinet table, these assistant secretaries and administrators also burn the lights late, not only along the wide boulevards of Washington but in some of the capital's more remote, less accommodating quarters as well. Their faces are less familiar, but they make the critical decisions and deliver the services that are the real work of government.

What skills do these people need, what are the details of their work, and why is it important? Those are three of the questions *The Prune Book* tries to answer. Some of the others concern the environments these executives work in, the people they work with, how their jobs fit into the structure of their agencies, and the problems and challenges the immediate future holds.

Such information has been unavailable in any organized form. Its absence may have contributed to the failure by every administration, in varying degrees, to pay sufficient attention to the quality of the people needed for positions of management and policy leadership. That ignorance can sap the vitality of administrations, reduce their achievement, and lower the quality of services and their delivery. In extreme form, such shortcomings have pushed administrations to the brink of their own disasters--or beyond.

For some time, this way of doing business has been proving itself an outdated luxury. Government is getting a devalued return on the investment of its citizens in an age when, literally and otherwise, it can no longer afford it at home or abroad. The United States finds itself today with a political appointments system that can be dangerously haphazard and happy-go-lucky. The circumstances contributing to this situation won't be moderated or balanced over-night, if ever. Nonetheless, those given responsibility to manage the appointments process must begin doing so with far more under-standing and efficiency.

It would be reassuring in this respect to have tangible evidence, in primary and general election campaigns, that the contenders see the recruitment issue as a prime element in a successful philosophy of governing, one to which they are giving serious attention. If they do and if they are, however, they say little about it beyond generalities. Normally, right up to the Presidential election itself, not much is known publicly about the candidates' efforts and views in this area.

There are good reasons for that. Candidates don't like to seem presumptuous about their chances, and feel they must shield any such work from the public gaze. Moreover, potential choices about people, if known, create disappointment that can make unnecessary enemies during a campaign.

Yet thoughtful voters and the media already expect party nomi-nees to get a public head start on tasks like policy development and goal setting during their campaigns. They want to hear from them on the great issues of the day. But the country must also recognize the candidates' frank need for some advance planning in practical areas as well. They should be able to feel free in getting ready--openly and ahead of the election--for the job of running the government and finding the right people to help. A Presi-dent-elect should be prepared to take intelligent early action on key appointments and sustain it throughout his tenure.

We believe *The Prune Book* will provide help not only in the present way of doing things but in the better circumstances we hope will grace the future. If it improves even a few choices for the positions it discusses, the book will have justified the effort to produce it.

Why "Prune?" In the late fall of each election year an official publication called *Policy and Supporting Positions* appears in govern-ment book stores. It is a list of about 3,000 appointive positions throughout the federal executive branch, one line per job. More familiarly, people call it the Plum Book. The nickname echoes what users of the book think of the federal jobs it lists.

People thinking of seeking a federal executive job in a newly-elected or re-elected administration find it useful to browse through the Plum Book's inventory of positions, almost all of them outside the competitive civil and foreign services. As a new administration sweeps into office, it will fill these jobs with people of its choice.

Beyond the glancing analogy of their titles, the Plum and Prune books have almost nothing in common. The Plum Book tells the reader what appointive jobs exist. *The Prune Book* aims at improving the selection, quality and product of the individuals who fill the toughest of them.

Just as each book has its place and use, the imagery of their titles arises from the contrast between the plum's seductive surface but uncertain sweetness and the prune's wrinkled skin but reliable flavor. Since wisdom born of on-the-job experience and wear and tear is central to what the present volume offers, the prune analogy was inevitable.

Two kinds of prune wisdom went into this book. It came from the teams of Principals of The Center for Excellence in Government, who drew on their previous experience in government to select the positions in the book. It came also through the observations, advice and comments of the several hundred former occupants of the positions who were interviewed for the book.

In choosing people for these and similar positions in Washington, a new administration makes some of the most consequential and self-defining decisions of its tenure. This is true whether or not control of the White House changes hands or parties.

For the incoming team, finding, comparing, selecting and nominating what are assumed to be the best individuals for these positions is a formidable challenge, especially in the short time available. But getting it right is the genuine bottom line. No less can be said of the Senate's duty to confirm or reject nominees for most of the jobs in question.

The press, too, has a large and inestimably useful service to provide in describing the process and the nominees. As for the would-be holders of these jobs, they have a right to know whether they really want--and are able to handle--the jobs they have in mind. And, well ahead of time, those of them who manage to survive it all and win confirmation need more than just a notion of what they have gotten themselves into.

It is primarily for all those involved in this delicate, harried, imprecise and immensely important business, therefore, that this book is designed. We hope that many others will find value and insight in it as well.

2

FORCES SHAPING APPOINTMENTS

Transition and Timing

A newly-chosen President and close advisers must make many of the most important policy and job decisions, including sub-Cabinet positions, in the approximate ten weeks between the election and the inauguration. Within three months thereafter, they must complete the rest of the process if the new administration is to have its full complement of appointees confirmed and get off to a fast, coordinated and comprehensive start.

The November-January transition period is all too brief and chaotic a period for a new crew to examine the government they are taking control of. It must assess the structure and missions of departments and agencies, the senior jobs within them, and a staggering panoply of urgent issues which won't wait. A budget revision process must get underway. Conclusions must be drawn about the changes necessary to try to mold the vast federal establishment to the policies and objectives of the President-elect. Work on these tasks can be delayed or ignored only at the risk of piece-meal decisions made under the critical stare of the press.

In the last decade or so, candidates have made an effort to ease this situation by starting early, before the election. The nature of existing transition laws is among the reasons why this is a necessarily shrouded process, operating on scarce campaign funds or donated time and services. These self-imposed constraints on early starts handicap an already difficult task and make necessary a set of subterfuges arguably not in the public interest.

Legislation containing a provision for pre-transition funding passed the Senate in 1988 but as of this writing seems unlikely to go further. More probable is increased funding for the post-election transition that will do little more than stay even with costs.

Increased federal financial assistance for the pre-election period, however, would institutionalize and legitimize advance planning and bring it out of the closet. That in turn would broaden and strengthen the preparations a candidate can make for an enlightened beginning of a new administration. It would allow homework to be done, options defined, issues identified, and the appointments process established and initiated.

It's true that some policy choices would doubtless be delayed or announced after the election, and a candidate could properly decline to talk about early choices for appointment. But this kind of advance planning is likely to have the advantages of greater thoroughness and effectiveness. It would enable planners to answer last, not first, the question of whom to appoint to federal jobs-- and to begin that process with a thoughtful examination of how and where to find prospective nominees, how to evaluate them, and how best to balance off the forces which compete to influence and pressure that process.

Realistically, the transition will remain what a veteran of several transitions calls it--impossible to do perfectly, but possible to do well. All the advice about it from experienced hands centers on a few ideas: keep the transition staff small; concentrate on Cabinet-level appointments first; avoid trying to plan every policy initiative right away; and--easier said than done--keep job seekers off the transition team.

Political Contexts

The Prune Book does not proceed from any notion that one can appoint people to positions of authority and influence in the federal government in isolation from the realities of the American political system. No President can base all appointments on sheer merit alone. Political compatibility is important. There are political promises to honor, and supporters to recognize. Moreover, if these jobs are vital cogs in the business of running a government well, most of them are also trophies in the power game, symbols of achievement, and vehicles for broadening professional skills and horizons.

As such, they are prizes to be fought for and won, not only by those who would occupy the positions but by those with something to gain if individuals of their preference are appointed. No surprise, then, that the appointments counselor and staff of an incoming

President are quickly overwhelmed in a barrage of resumes and inquiries from seekers after the most desirable jobs.   No surprise, either, that they also find themselves at the center of a crossfire of demands, pleas, and proposed trade-offs from other quarters.

There is another, more important political reality which the appointments process must manage.   Nearly every President takes office with some set of ideas about where the country should go and what the government should do to take it there. History judges the correctness of those views.   But no administration can mobilize its policies effectively unless the people it puts into high-level management and policy positions are basically and substantially in accord with the President's intentions.

At this point of truth, however, an administration's approach to its political appointments runs the greatest risk of breaking down.   Time is short; the pressures are great; the President's strongest supporters, and the country, are waiting.   At such a time, political affinity can become the big measuring stick; if a prospective appointee qualifies on that score, the unexamined assumption is that competence in the job follows naturally--and that, if competence is obviously lacking, affinity alone will carry the day.

It is The Center's fundamental argument, however, that political compatibility need not conflict with professional competence in filling important senior positions in government.   A more careful match between jobs and qualifications would enable a President to place loyal supporters with specific skills in positions where they can be especially useful. Making those matches means understanding what the positions require.

Organizational Contexts

While political compatibility and professional competence can consistently be recruited in single individuals, it is not always possible to find individuals who are equally strong in every dimension of the complex leadership positions in federal agencies.   "Water walkers" come in limited quantities.

The effective response to this standard problem is to maximize the strength of the department or agency team by appointing individuals with complementary skills and strengths in closely related positions.   Perhaps the most common combination is a department secretary with strong policy identification with the President, and a strong internal manager in the deputy or undersecretary position. Other combinations, however, have also proved successful.   For example, a department with a very heavy Congressional workload might try to concentrate that work in the number two job to help the secretary avoid spending excessive time on the Hill.

Because everybody does not do everything equally well, the wise appointment process will consider at least the top two appointments together and probably more. For example, if the second-ranking position is deeply involved with Congressional work, the interaction and complementary skills and personality of the assistant secretary for legislation need to be considered.

More generally, effective department and agency performance will depend in important ways on the level of cooperation and coordination among its appointed leaders. While a very strong department secretary may be able to commandeer such collaboration no matter who fills the subordinate senior jobs, an appointments philosophy which takes the coordination factor into account is more likely to satisfy the President and prove beneficial to the country.

Further, the effective matching of talents is possible at the second and third levels of the departments and agencies in both staff and line positions to produce successful combinations of intellectual capabilities, communication and interpersonal skills, and managerial experience. Without such matching, Presidential and departmental policies and initiatives may never travel beyond the rhetorical state to implementation and action.

Appointments--First Round and Beyond

While some Presidential candidates may narrow down the choices or decide a few Cabinet appointments before election, few have gotten serious at that point about the many other selections to be made. For the small staff that will manage Presidential appointments, election day marks a shift from relatively tranquil to storm-tossed waters.

In the avalanche of mail, telephone calls and other more subtle probing of job possibilities that marks the first transition weeks, an appointments staff steers a course basically marked out by the President's wishes. In addition, the appointments office hears continuously from members of the Congress, campaign staff, campaign contributors, the President's own intimate circle, newly-designated Cabinet secretaries and agency heads, and groups in every sector of U.S. business, professional and working life.

It requires organization and discipline to navigate this storm while remaining consistent with the administration's political philosophy, program objectives and the substantive needs of individual jobs. It takes firmly and carefully established procedures for developing appointment proposals, conducting investigations and clearances, making and appealing decisions, and handling announcements of nominations.

There has to be provision for reference, if necessary, to the President or senior aides at every stage. Flexibility has to be built into the process. Above all, the appointments office has to stay in control. A former appointments counselor lays down one basic rule as a guide to effectiveness: "Control the process of selection, not whom you're choosing." None of those who have done this job, and whom we interviewed, disagree.

What constitutes a good process? Finding people is scarcely a problem, though finding the best is always uncertain. The process should begin at the top of a department or agency to give its leader a role in the selection of subordinates. The investigation of skills, reputations and potential conflicts of interest is relatively straightforward and absolutely essential. Short-cutting those procedures in any way could be as devastating as the plague.

The balance of power between department heads and the White House represents a long-standing battleground in the winnowing and selection process. All recent experience suggests that neither side should win or lose completely. A Cabinet secretary with carte blanche appointments power might take a department into unwanted adventures with a group of cronies who lack connection or loyalty to the President. Conversely, a Cabinet secretary whose key subordinates are imposed without consultation may understandably not feel accountable if they perform poorly. The best route seems to be one in which the department or agency head always takes part in decisions about that organization's positions, with strong disagreements resolved even-handedly by the President.

While names may abound for most jobs, the dragnet for suggestions should be broad. Presidential personnel staffs should turn regularly to other sources. Examples of these are law groups, trade associations, and other organizations representing professionals like former career diplomats. To be sure, such groups are not disinterested observers of the process. However, their institutional, less personal nature and longer-term perspectives lend steadiness and balance to their ideas for potential job candidates and to their counsel about proposed nominations. Another source of candidates is the ranks of the Senior Executive Service.

A different, but important consideration in the selection process should include a mutual set of expectations about tenure in office. Almost all observers suggest that less than two years of tenure produces little value for the time and confidence invested in the individual. While progress has been made on longer retention in some positions, the average time continues to decline. In its own best interest, the new administration in 1989 should devise a plan to reverse this trend.

Whatever is done about lengthening tenure, the appointments process of course continues beyond the first round and, in less hectic fashion, throughout the life of an administration. But its procedures should remain the same as during the initial transition. Subsequent appointments occur in an environment where considerably more development of administration objectives has occurred, and thus closer matching can occur between needs and candidates. These later appointments can also be used to fill gaps in an organization's aggregate talents and should be viewed from that perspective.

Finally, we note a variety of unwillingness in the past on the part of both incoming and outgoing appointment staffs to accept or offer assistance in a transition. We lament these missed opportunities which we think can provide some genuine and valuable help.

3

PUTTING THE BOOK
TOGETHER

Identification of Positions

To do the work of selecting the federal positions this book discusses, The Center chose 54 individuals, most of them its own Principals, to examine Cabinet departments and independent agencies. These men and women were chosen for their experience in executive positions across the many institutions of the federal government.

The Center formed them into 14 teams, each of which considered one or more departments and agencies relevant to the experience of its members. That experience had to be of sufficient stature and length to give team members vantage points and substantive exposure at upper levels of their departments. Only such background permits the overview, perceptions and detailed knowledge needed to identify the positions to be described. The teams, their leaders and members, are listed in Appendix III.

From the 1984 edition of *Policy and Supporting Positions* (the Plum Book) and other source documents, The Center developed the raw list of positions with which the teams began their work. The list included both line and staff positions, with a flexible bias toward line jobs. Staff positions in some agencies have distinct and substantial management dimensions that add up to line responsibility; the teams were asked to consider this factor in their overall deliberations.

Federal politically appointed positions divide into four categories--Presidential appointment with confirmation by the Senate, Presidential appointment not requiring confirmation, Senior Executive Service positions (of which political appointments are limited to ten percent of the total), and Schedule C jobs, appointments not requiring action at the Presidential level or confirmation. Working from The Center's basic list and using organization charts of departments and agencies, teams were asked to look at positions for *The Prune Book* based on their importance, not on the type of appointment a position called for or whether, in the SES category, a career or non-career person occupied it.

The teams began identifying positions to be described by *The Prune Book* in the late summer and fall of 1987. Ultimately, they chose only Presidentially appointed positions with Senate confirmation, and a few SES positions. Their list included both line and staff jobs.

The Center gave the teams a set of carefully designed criteria as a basis on which to compare the positions they were considering. The overarching requirement was that the positions chosen be those in which the making of policy and the implementation of policy intersect.

Specific criteria addressed the nature and level of a position's responsibilities; the size and scope of its management tasks; its supervisory duties; the position's Congressional and public visibility; and, most important, the consequences of failure to perform effectively in it. A team could recommend any number of positions for the book, bearing in mind that for practical reasons all could not be included. While the book may not speak to each of the criteria in its discussion of the positions, they were useful measurements with which to assess the jobs and match them against one another.

When *The Prune Book* was only an idea, the intention was to describe a hundred positions. The earliest draft title of the volume included that figure, and it has remained. But the selection teams identified fully 185 positions in their first cut. This was a total well beyond the deliberately conceived scope of the book. In the final cut, 116 positions remained on the list. To reduce that number further would have required illogical and undefendable distinctions. More important, it would have artificially distorted the true total picture as the teams perceived it.

Exceeding what its title promises, therefore, this volume in fact describes 116 jobs. It also lists the other 69 (in Appendix I) as a reminder that they, too, deserve special attention and care in the selection of those who take them on.

Exclusions

Readers of *The Prune Book* may ask why certain management and policy-making positions which eminently qualify for inclusion are not described or listed. These fall into several groups. Most obvious are the Cabinet-level jobs. In addition to secretaries of Cabinet departments, this group embraces such positions as the White House Chief of Staff, the Director of the Office of Management and Budget, the President's Assistant for National Security Affairs, the U.S. Trade Representative, and the Director of the Central Intelligence Agency. It would make little sense to repeat information that is readily available elsewhere about positions like these which are substantially more visible and familiar than those in this volume.

Further, choices at this level are much more closely related to a President's personal preferences than any others. In selecting Cabinet members, Presidents are identifying individuals whose abilities and particular qualifications they recognize and need as extensions of their own authority, and with whom they are politically and personally comfortable. Processes like these are intimately linked to the Presidential personality and prerogatives and, as such, defy consistent characterization of necessary experience and skills.

Similar observations apply to other positions, such as that of Chairman of the Federal Reserve Board or Director of the Federal Bureau of Investigation, that are appointed for terms not co-terminus with those of Presidents. They, too, are well-known posts to which an incoming administration needs few guidelines. There are also positions--Director of the National Security Agency is a good example--whose required degree of technical specialization is so great that, in the opinion of several who know the job well, they should be continued as career jobs.

Another category of positions excluded from the book are certain which, in the most recent administration, have become less prominent or important. Although they have historically been critical and might become so again in a new administration, the book must look primarily at what is, not at what might be. The science advisor to the President is a notable example of such a position. Increasing national concern with productivity, competitiveness abroad, and the need to combine innovation with fiscal restraint could push significant technical and scientific choices to the White House level in the 1990s. If the debate centers on the extent of the federal government's investment in the country's future technological health, the science advisor could become a crucial figure.

Finally, there are the chairmen, directors or presidents of independent federal agencies whose mission is entirely or almost entirely regulatory. On this list are such institutions as the Consumer Product Safety Commission, the Federal Communications Commission, the Federal Deposit Insurance Corporation, and the

Securities and Exchange Commission.

Responsibilities and requirements vary among the leadership positions of the regulatory agencies. Our analysis of these important jobs concluded that they deserve attention even though they fall into a different category in terms of *The Prune Book's* objectives. They are therefore included in Appendix I.

Research

The Prune Book is non-partisan, and has no agenda. It rests squarely on the comments, observations and advice of people who have held the positions it discusses. This group includes individuals who now hold many of the jobs and their predecessors in administrations of both political parties going back to January, 1969.

Several rules guided the detailed interviewing of these people and the analysis and assembling of the results. Where former incumbents of the jobs are concerned, we put together as thorough a mix of individuals from each party as circumstances permitted. Allowance was made for such factors as selective memory, subjectivity, evolution in the scope and responsibilities of jobs and, especially with current job occupants, the natural tendency to accentuate the positive.

Our objective in all interviews was to focus on positions, not politics. In publishing the book, our purpose is to discuss those positions, not to engage in political debate, take sides, or find fault. At the same time, the book is a product of real-world experience and perception. If the observations and views it cites in some sections collectively suggest the existence of certain systemic problems, past or present, it is because the book could not ignore them and remain useful or instructive.

The Center conducted, or commissioned an opinion research firm to conduct, interviews with almost 350 present and former occupants of *The Prune Book* positions, and followed up a number of them with clarifying or elaborative discussions with respondents. These were both Principals and non-Principals of The Center; a list of them identified as such can be found in Appendix II.

Center staff also held an additional 50 interviews with persons whose present and/or previous positions qualify them to discuss many of the positions in the book. Typically, these individuals are associated with Congressional committees and constituent groups affected by the decisions and activities of departments and agencies. Their work gives them special insights and different points from which to view the book's jobs. We valued their comments in getting a fix on the jobs, and as validation of or contrast with what we were hearing elsewhere. The organizations these interviewees represent are listed in Appendix II.

The Center contacted all interviewees by letter ahead of time to inform them of the book's purpose, secure their agreement, and provide a sampling of what would be asked. The interview document itself was designed to draw out both facts and comment. Its questions framed a job in terms of its structural relationships in and outside the agency or department, its purpose and the nature of its responsibilities, the experience and skills its occupant must rely on, the problems that individual can expect to encounter, and the consequences of incompetence.

The interviews are the exclusive source of all direct quotes attributed to incumbents and former occupants of the positions discussed in the book or to individuals with special knowledge of them. Direct quotes attributed by name were verified with and authorized by the respondents. In a few instances, the book draws on supplementary material published by former occupants of the positions or about the positions.

Each position description provides a list of those who have held the job and their current affiliations where known, from the incumbent back to January 1969 or to the year in which the position was established, if later than 1969. The Center compiled these lists from its own files and from many other sources, and cross-checked them against the records of the departments and agencies concerned.

Notes on Position Descriptions

Obviously, certain personal skills and talents are basic to senior executive positions in government or anywhere else. Nearly everyone interviewed for *The Prune Book* mentioned some of them. Rather than citing them in the discussion of each position, it is more useful to stipulate them in advance, as generic to all positions.

Reality dictates that few candidates are likely to possess all of these credentials, or to score at the top of the scale in those they do have. But reality also requires that every candidate qualify in at least a majority of them:

o   An informed and flexible intellect. Respect for the facts, including a readiness to discard inaccurate preconceptions and pet theories.

o   The ability to absorb large amounts of information quickly, discern its essentials, and identify workable solutions among conflicting views and currents.

o   Functioning political instincts and a robust skepticism. The courage of one's own convictions, but the wisdom to know when compromise is the better, or only, road.

o   Skill in getting acceptable and timely results from colleagues and staff.

o   Personal integrity.

o   Friendships or working contacts in upper echelons of the professions, business, government, education or journalism.

o   Experience in public speaking and handling the press.

The precise nature of many positions in the book often depends significantly on the relationship established between the occupants and their immediate superiors. It's another generic point, one which applies to working relationships in the private sector as well, and which cannot be stressed too often. As various discussions in the book make clear, nowhere is it more true than at the very top of departments and agencies, where what the deputy secretary or equivalent second-ranking individual actually does is a function of what the head of the agency wants that individual to do. It's worth noting as well that many of these same comments apply to relationships between assistant secretaries and the heads of departments and agencies.

These are fluid relationships in which the tasks change day by day. They work best when the two individuals operate within a framework they both agree on from the start. Hardly anyone we talked to about these jobs failed to mention the necessity of such an understanding; they use terms like "two-way street," "open door policy," and "direct access" to make it clear. But there is a larger point as well, one made earlier--that these leadership teams have a far better shot at effectiveness if the person who is to lead has some influence in the selection of the deputy.

Most of the positions described in the book have a Congressional dimension. This usually involves testimony; it almost always requires regular, often frequent contact with the members and staffs of Congressional committees who have oversight responsibility. For this reason, although the book usually addresses these Congressional aspects in the body of its discussion of a job, it normally does not indicate them in listing the job's external relationships. Similar considerations apply to many positions which entail varying amounts of informal contact at different levels of the White House and at the Office of Management and Budget.

Each position description lists regular contacts outside the federal government. This is meant only as an indication of the kinds of organizations and constituent groups with which the job's occupant deals. It is in no sense a comprehensive list.

No set of interviews, or amount of research, or careful drafting, is perfect. The book does not pretend in every case to have captured all the wisdom of its interviewees or to have distilled it faultlessly. Nor is the intention to offer, in its position discussions and chapter introductions, a detailed examination of jobs, departments and agencies. The book's goal, rather, is to enable those involved in federal political appointments to get a better grasp of the essentials of each job--its responsibilities, requirements, working environment, and challenges.

The Prune Book is a first effort. The Center would like to think that it is not the last. We believe the book underscores a continuing need for the kind of information it presents, perhaps with larger numbers of positions discussed at greater length, and supported by greater resources. It is a project whose time has come.

4

DEPARTMENT OF AGRICULTURE

This department is among the most diverse. Taking all of its 20 agencies into account, and stretching a point here and there, Agriculture could be said to have its own army and air force (Forest Service rangers who can carry weapons and fly aircraft), its own housing program (Farmers Home Administration), social service programs (Food and Nutrition Service) and its own diplomats (Foreign Agricultural Service). This mini-government has the fourth largest cabinet department budget, at $59.9 billion in fiscal 1988, and more than 100,000 people work for it. It has agricultural extension and stabilization offices in almost every county in the country.

Farm income and survival, particularly for small and medium-sized farms, have climbed back to some extent from one of the steepest declines in decades in the mid-1980s. But the damage was real, and extensive, and the farm economy will indefinitely remain a sensitive core concern for those in power in Washington.

In bad times and good, the offices of Small Community and Rural Development and International Affairs and Commodity Programs --with community development services and multiple forms of assistance to farmers that range from ownership and commodity loans to drought assistance and crop insurance--play fundamental department roles. Another component, the Marketing and Inspection Services, operates at the heart of the farm-to-market chain and carry out indispensable health and nutrition functions.

The sale of American agricultural products abroad has long since been an essential element of the U.S. farm economy, and is important in the trade deficit picture. The same decline in the dollar's international value that recently helped begin the reversal of farm fortunes will reportedly result in a $12 billion U.S. agricultural trade surplus in 1988. Farm exports, however, are subject to the notably stubborn trade practices of individual nations and of economic groups like the European common market. The subsidization, tariff and other habits of U.S. trading partners in this area have been slow to yield in international negotiating efforts. The Agriculture department promotes U.S. farm exports and is directly involved in the current Uruguay round of trade talks under the General Agreement on Tariffs and Trade.

With its strong grass-roots orientation, and with constituent groups of long experience and skill in mobilizing Congressional support, the department needs leadership that knows the issues. Many of these are local in scope and not particularly partisan. The current Senators from Iowa, for example, may differ politically on many issues, but not on corn. The problems of farm programs tend to match Presidents, with tight budgets to negotiate, against the Congress, rather than one party on the Hill against the other. Individuals who take senior Agriculture jobs need enough political astuteness to anticipate Congressional reactions and respond effectively to Congressional concerns.

DEPARTMENT OF AGRICULTURE

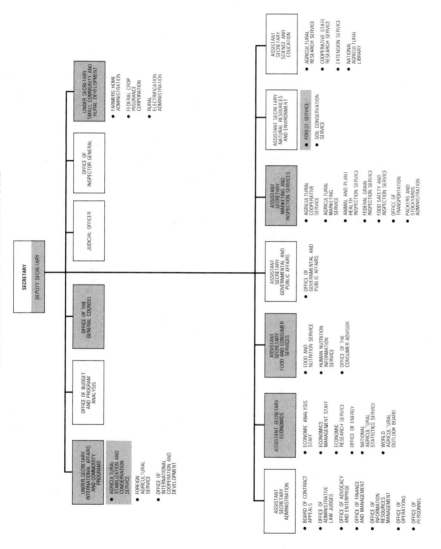

Shaded areas were selected as Prune Book positions

DEPUTY SECRETARY

Level II - Presidential Appointment with Senate Confirmation

Major Responsibilities

o   Serve as the department's chief managing executive. At the same time, assist the secretary in formulating policy and bringing it to bear on department operations. Function when required as acting secretary.

o   Oversee budget development, and lead budget negotiations with Office of Management and Budget and the Congress. Play a principal role in the department's Congressional relationships, especially in the area of appointments to positions in the department's large state and county structure.

o   Coordinate the work of the department's component agencies and offices, and represent it in high-level interagency proceedings. Provide necessary administrative oversight.

Necessary Background, Experience, Personal Skills

A talented, resourceful and energetic manager, one who has run a large organization and knows the agricultural scene, is the best bet for this post. But--important point--the position doesn't need a "farmer's image." While the deputy secretary must clearly know the issues and how they affect day-to-day operations, whoever fills the job also needs a knowledge of government and the Congress. An ability to interpret the evolving policy-budget context and keep the individual components of a large and far-flung organization working effectively together within it is critical.

Insight

Other than the Secretary of Agriculture, says the executive director of a leading farm association, "this is the key job in the department, the individual who really runs the place on a day-to-day basis." For example, the occupant of the position puts together the budget for the department, takes it through its OMB and Congressional tests, and represents the department and, on occasion, the secretary in the steady beat of interagency meetings where the details of policy are decided and its implementation coordinated. That's one reason why this office is a key consumer of in-house economic research and analysis.

The deputy secretary does much of Agriculture's senior-level business on the Hill, a portfolio which includes the filling of department positions at the state and county level throughout the country. Given that the Congress takes a natural and abiding interest in these political appointments, and that Agriculture carries more such Schedule C jobs on its rolls than any other agency, the deputy secretary can expect to invest significant time in this area. A key dimension of this effort is a sort of political balancing act between the competing priorities of members of Congress and the White House. The position is also a major contact point for the department's many constituent interest organizations.

In its relationship to the secretary's position, this job differs little from most equivalent positions in other agencies. Like colleagues in those jobs, this deputy must try to nail down at an early stage the general responsibilities and specific subject areas the secretary wants to assign, and what kind of assistance is expected in the policy and leadership duties of the senior job.

James H. Williams, who held this position from 1979 to 1981, came to it from a career that had included service as a Florida state senator and lieutenant governor, and some time in the cattle business. It had kept him "close to agriculture all my adult life." Without claiming that such a background is the best or only preparation, he stresses the value of certain kinds of working experience. "Either the secretary or deputy needs a knowledge or at least an interest in agriculture, and a working knowledge of government itself." In addition, "someone in one of those two slots needs legislative experience. It would be tragic if neither has it. You just don't know what it's like until you get there."

Embedded in the personnel oversight responsibilities of the job is one of its more difficult concerns, a continuing civil rights question on which the department has been legally challenged. The problem focuses on the staffing of the department's enormous regional structure at the state and particularly the county level. At issue is whether the field has been sufficiently responsive to department directives on minority hiring.

The department's densely populated but widely-dispersed structure doubtless contributes to such management challenges. "It's a huge department," Williams says. "It was impossible to get caught up." But he praises the senior career staff of the department--

"extremely dedicated, non-partisan, outstanding"--and the support it gave him, and would recommend the job. "You've got to like people and problem-solving," he cautions. "That's what this job is all about."

Key Relationships

Within the Department

Reports to: Secretary

Outside the Department

Assistant to the President and Executive Secretary, Domestic Policy Council
Director, Office of Management and Budget
Associate Director, Natural Resources, Energy and Science, OMB
Secretary and Deputy Secretary, Department of Energy
Chairmen, Senate and House Appropriations and Budget Committees

Outside the Federal Government

American Farm Bureau Federation, National Farmers Union, The Agribusiness Council and other groups representing farmers, agribusiness, and processors; National Association of State Departments of Agriculture and individual state agricultural officials; International Trade Council and other trade associations and commodity export groups; consumer advocacy organizations

Deputy Secretaries of Agriculture Since 1969

Administration	Name and Years Served	Present Position
Reagan	Peter C. Myers 1987 - Present	Incumbent

Reagan	John R. Norton III 1985 - 1986	Chairman and CEO J.R. Norton Company Phoenix, Arizona
Reagan	Richard E. Lyng 1981 - 1985	Secretary Department of Agriculture
Carter	James H. Williams 1979 - 1981	President River Groves, Inc. Ocala, Florida
Carter	John C. White 1977 - 1978	Washington, DC
Ford	John A. Knebel 1975 - 1976	Senior Partner Baker and McKenzie Washington, DC
Nixon/Ford	J. Phil Campbell 1969 - 1975	Watkinsonville, Georgia

UNDERSECRETARY
INTERNATIONAL AFFAIRS AND
COMMODITY PROGRAMS

Level III - Presidential Appointment with Senate Confirmation

Major Responsibilities

o   Direct the development and execution of policy for marketing American farm products overseas. Coordinate it within the department, and correlate it with other agencies responsible for general U.S. foreign trade policy. Oversee the operations of the Foreign Agricultural Service, and of the Office of International Development and Cooperation, providing technical agricultural assistance to underdeveloped countries.

o   Supervise the Agricultural Stabilization and Conservation Service in administering commodity, land use, indemnity, conservation and other programs to assure stable markets and prices and improve farm income. Serve as president of the Commodity Credit Corporation.

o   Maintain close contact and work with the Congress in support of these programs. Oversee budget development and negotiation.

Necessary Background, Experience, Personal Skills

All of those we talked to who have run this job agree that it needs an individual from an economic and--especially--an agricultural trade background. As the present undersecretary expresses it, candidates must have "practical experience in trade and know the people in it and how they operate." They should know the issues in agricultural trade policy and how domestic and international markets for farm products work, and have run a large organization. The position also requires an understanding of U.S. farm programs, particularly in the commodities area. It doesn't hurt to have some mediating, negotiating and political skills, or to be familiar with the Congress.

Insight

An experienced observer in the Congress thinks this job has two of the three high-profile issues in the Agriculture department --trade and commodities. That can't be far off the mark, considering that this undersecretary (1) manages export policy and foreign market development for all U.S. agricultural products, and (2) presides over the Commodity Credit Corporation, a body whose mission is to stabilize markets and protect farm income in principal agricultural staples from corn and cotton to milk and mohair.

Richard W. Goldberg, acting undersecretary since 1987, could be speaking for every federal executive involved in foreign trade matters in emphasizing that "domestic and trade issues are linked" and that "what happens in one affects the other." That explains why his job has an important voice in both, where agriculture is concerned. "This office," he says, "is really concerned with how the programs operate and how we can create a better market for sales and distribution."

One string to the undersecretary's bow as chief of agricultural trade promotion and development is supervision of the Foreign Agricultural Service. FAS' 100-member overseas team and its analysts and marketing experts in Washington represent U.S. agricultural interests in more than one hundred countries. It provides information on American products to foreign traders and governments and operates as a global intelligence and reporting system on agricultural conditions, crops, and weather.

Other parts of the international side of the job involve the undersecretary regularly and closely with the work of the U.S. Trade Representative, and with senior officials at State, Commerce and Treasury with related responsibilities. The undersecretary sits on the Trade Policy Review Committee, and chairs interagency groups on food assistance and sugar. The office runs exchanges of technical agricultural assistance teams with less developed countries, keeps track of the agricultural and trade policies of 75 other nations, and assists independent exporters who want to sell to them. The FAS also manages the department's responsibilities under the first three titles of Public Law 480 (Food for Peace Program).

On the domestic side of this job, the weekly meetings of the Commodity Credit Corporation are a principal channel through which the federal government fine-tunes its mandate to provide the American farm community with dependable markets and prices and assure a balanced flow of farm products and their orderly distribution. CCC's eight members get their authority from Presidential appointments confirmed by the Senate. With the secretary an ex officio chairman, the undersecretary, as president, runs the operation. The CCC is capitalized at $100 million; its borrowing authorization runs to $25 billion. Commodity loan and purchase decisions are carried out by the ASCS, and the CCC disposes of the commodities it buys mainly through sales and donations.

Goldberg shares testimony on the Hill about trade and farm legislation with the administrators and deputy administrators of the various programs under his supervision. "It depends on which committee it is," he says, "and whether it's a policy or a program issue."

While a wide acquaintance within the agricultural export and farm communities can be a useful two-way street, Goldberg also says "it can work against you. People assume you are their friend, when you need to be even-handed and fair." Clarence D. Palmby, who held these responsibilities as assistant secretary in 1969-72, recalls "questions, complaints and recommendations" from constituent groups as the most burdensome problem. "There are always problems regarding specific commodities and it's very time-consuming," he says. He thinks the department today has been "influenced too much by specific commodity interest groups, and actions have been taken that are only short-run answers to the problems." Elsewhere in the problem department, Dale E. Hathaway, undersecretary in 1979-1981, mentions what he remembers as "a constant struggle for policy control" between the two larger agencies in the undersecretary's domain--the Foreign Agricultural Service and the Agricultural Stabilization and Conservation Service.

The job has "an enormous high visibility factor," Goldberg says. "Constituents are all around you. Almost all the mail addressed to the secretary comes through this office, and almost all the mail to the President on agriculture comes here, too."

Key Relationships

Within the Department

Reports to: Secretary

Works closely with:

Deputy Secretary
Assistant Secretary for Economics
General Counsel

Outside the Department

Undersecretary, Economic and Agricultural Affairs, Department of State

Undersecretary, International Trade, Department of Commerce

U.S. Trade Representative

Associate Director for Natural Resources, Energy and Science, Office of Management and Budget

Assistant Secretary, Economic and Business Affairs, Department of State

Assistant Secretary, International Affairs, Department of the Treasury

Outside the Federal Government

National Farmers Union, American Farm Bureau Federation, The Agribusiness Council and other farmers, processors and agribusiness groups; National Association of Wheat Growers, National Association of Sugar Cane Growers and other agricultural exporters; National Cattlemen's Association; American Dairy Products Institute; state farm producer organizations; Futures Industry Association and other trade groups

Undersecretaries for International Affairs and Commodity Programs Since 1969

Administration	Name and Years Served	Present Position
Reagan	Richard W. Goldberg 1987 - Present (Acting)	Incumbent
Reagan	Daniel G. Amstutz 1983 - 1987	Special Ambassador for Agricultural Negotiations Office of the U.S. Trade Representative
Reagan	Seely G. Lodwick 1981 - 1983	Commissioner International Trade Commission Washington, DC

Carter	Dale E. Hathaway* 1977 - 1981	Vice President The Consultants International Group,Inc. Washington, DC
Ford	Richard E. Bell** 1976 - 1977	President Richland Foods, Inc. Stuttgart, Arkansas
Nixon/Ford	Clayton K. Yeutter** 1974 - 1976	U.S. Trade Representative Office of the U.S. Trade Representative
Nixon	Carroll G. Brunthaver** 1972 - 1974	President Sparks Commodities, Inc. Memphis, Tennessee
Nixon	Clarence D. Palmby** 1969 - 1972	Marcell, Minnesota

*   From 1977 to 1979, served as the Assistant Secretary for International Affairs and Commodity Programs, prior to elevation of job to Undersecretary for International Affairs and Commodity Programs.

**   Served as Assistant Secretary for International Affairs.

UNDERSECRETARY
SMALL COMMUNITY AND RURAL DEVELOPMENT

Level III - Presidential Appointment with Senate Confirmation

Major Responsibilities

o   Provide policy and administrative direction to national credit and insurance services designed to strengthen and improve the functioning of American small farm and rural agricultural communities.

o   Set goals for these operations in accordance with administration policy, and monitor progress.   Make budget recommendations in support of them, and supervise budget preparation and negotiation.

o   Represent small and rural community development policy and programs in the interagency coordination process, at the White House, and to the Congress and constituent interest organizations.

Necessary Background, Experience, Personal Skills

Because the undersecretary oversees a "quasi-financial institution," as a former incumbent calls it, the job requires some financial, preferably banking, background, a general knowledge of the problems of the U.S. farm community, and strong general management experience.   It also calls for substantial past exposure to small town and rural environments--to what they are and what they need.

Insight

This is a critical job for rural America because it plays an important part in deciding the resources to be directed toward that sector of the American community.   Discussing the responsibilities involved, an interested and knowledgeable source in a national housing assistance advocacy organization asserted to us that the rural United States has a disproportionate share of American poverty, lacking the kind of existence which urban areas take for granted. The undersecretary's job therefore "becomes important in that it helps determine whether a lot of rural areas make it or in fact fall by the wayside."

What is the structural set-up for this work? The undersecretary runs a three-part operation whose activities generally reflect policy guidelines set by its chief and others at the top of the department. The Farmers Home Administration, the key agency, administers credit in about a dozen categories, from running a farm to owning one, from surviving natural-disaster losses to conserving and developing land resources. FmHA loans reach into water and sewer services, community facilities, housing, rental and repair programs, and fire prevention ("if one house burns you can lose a whole community," says an authority on the FmHA).

A sister agency, the Rural Electrification Administration, dates from mid-depression 1935 when it was part of a larger program to soak up unemployment. Today, REA supports the continued extension and upgrading of rural telephone and electric power service by helping utilities to secure financing. The Federal Crop Insurance Corporation, whose reach the Congress significantly expanded in 1980, now extends to more than 40 crops in almost every state. It covers production losses stemming from weather, pests, plant disease, fire, and earthquakes.

To Frank W. Naylor, Jr., undersecretary in 1981-86, the essentials of the job--"making loans and managing loan portfolios"--were "much like a commercial bank. You carried out the managing half of a bank and insurance services, and executed administration policy." He "functioned as a chief executive officer would in the private sector," providing only general supervision of daily office routine. As with others who have held the job, most of the time and energy goes into decisionmaking--matters like designing or revising the objectives and incentives of the various loan programs or decisions on specific loan and insurance questions. In addition, there are staff meetings with the secretary, budget duties inside and outside the department, coordination sessions with other agencies on specific projects, gatherings of the Cabinet council on economics at the White House, and now and then attendance at a Cabinet meeting. Within the department, Naylor feels that the "weakest link" was the information reporting from the agencies he directed. "Sometimes I didn't have enough information to monitor progress, other times I had too much."

In the past, notes the housing group source mentioned above, some elements of the housing and community development operations that belong primarily to FmHA could also be found in certain other agencies of government. While a number of such activities have been eliminated in recent years, this source says, "FmHA has a lot of good friends in the Congress, and even though the levels of funding have been cut, the programs are still intact. They can get combined with state programs, for example, that float bonds for mortgage assistance, and some communities are prepared to give tax abatement and other kinds of breaks. Those combinations are really what works. But from a federal standpoint, for rural areas it's really the Farmers Home Administration that's still hanging in there."

In this view, the top three priorities in rural assistance are health, jobs and housing. "[FmHA] has that whole array of programs which, if coordinated and run well and given sufficient resources, could make a big difference in many parts of rural America. It's making a difference now; it could make a bigger difference if resources were more plentiful and if the people in policy positions emphasized that this is what we want people to be doing."

Key Relationships

Within the Department

Reports to: Secretary

Works closely with:

Deputy Secretary
Undersecretary for International Affairs and Commodity
    Programs
Assistant secretaries

Outside the Department

Assistant to the President for Political and Inter-
    governmental Affairs
Associate Director, Natural Resources Energy and
    Science, Office of Management and Budget
Assistant Secretary, International Affairs and Energy
    Emergencies, Department of Energy
General Deputy Assistant Secretary, Housing,
    Department of Housing and Urban Development

Outside the Federal Government

National Rural Electric Cooperative Association, Independent Bankers Association of America, Housing Assistance Council, Farm Credit Administration, Rural Housing Coalition, National Farmers Union

Undersecretaries for Small Community and Rural Development Since 1969

Administration	Name and Years Served	Present Position
Reagan	Roland R. Vautour 1987 - Present	Incumbent
Reagan	LaVerne Ausman (Acting) 1987	Deputy Undersecretary, Small Community and Rural Development Department of Agriculture
Reagan	Frank W. Naylor, Jr. 1981 - 1986	Chairman Farm Credit Administration McLean, Virginia
Carter	Alex P. Mercure 1977 - 1981	Partner Hicks, Mercure and Associates Albuquerque, New Mexico
Ford	William H. Walker, III 1975 - 1977	Not Available
Nixon/Ford	William W. Erwin 1973 - 1975	Bourbon, Indiana
Nixon	Thomas K. Cowden 1969 - 1973	Not Available

ASSISTANT SECRETARY
FOOD AND CONSUMER SERVICES

Level IV - Presidential Appointment with Senate Confirmation

Major Responsibilities

o   Administer food and consumer programs which provide coupons to raise food purchasing power, distribute food and commodities in general and supplemental services, carry out nutrition research, and advise consumers.

o   Work closely with the secretary in making and adjusting food services policy. Correlate the formation and execution of policy with other agencies involved or concerned--chiefly the Department of Health and Human Services. Maintain close consultative and advisory relationships with the Congress and with interest groups.

o   Take a leading part in articulating food programs policy in any of these contexts, and publicly. Oversee budget and administrative functions of the office of Food and Consumer Services.

Necessary Background, Experience, Personal Skills

This job has several times been filled by experienced Congressional staffers. Service on committees concerned with agricultural affairs builds a knowledge of federal farm programs, budgets and problems, and a workable familiarity with those in the Congress and elsewhere with roles to play on the food and consumer services scene. It also develops general Hill skills. But "there's nothing about the programs that can't be learned" on the job, says a recent assistant secretary. "Having a feel for it does help. It's more important to be attuned to the needs of the poor than to know the food programs. I would be most concerned about the person's philosophy and management skills. Someone from the state level or the private sector could do it." Alternatively, look for prior service at a senior level in this department or in a closely-related federal program, in either case with exposure to the Congress.

Insight

The Food and Nutrition Service (FNS), which is by far the biggest element of food and consumer services, oversees the delivery of food assistance benefits to low-income citizens. This job consequently has what one of its former occupants, Mary C. Jarratt (1981-85), calls "tremendous interface at the state and local levels with officials across the board--be they state welfare agencies, commodity distribution agencies, school food service providers, child care centers."

Food stamps, which Jarratt terms "basic assistance to low-income persons," is the largest program in dollar terms. In fiscal 1989, 18.8 million people will participate in it each month, at a cost of $13.4 billion. FNS also supplies financial assistance ($4.8 billion in 1989) to school lunch and breakfast programs; distributes food and government-owned surplus commodities, much of it to children in school and camp; and oversees the provision of supplemental feeding packages to needy women, nursing infants, and children.

The FCS position also sees to the development of dietary guidance information for the "healthy" U.S. population, and runs a two-way consumer complaint and advice operation on matters across the total spectrum of USDA responsibility.

Although FNS takes the lead in developing policy, other agencies play a role and, as noted, work with FNS in implementation as well. The Office of Management and Budget also figures in the policy process, of course, and the Congress has great interest in projects like food stamps. In part, making policy in this position is an exercise in the balancing of interests--deciding, for example, which foods to use in the programs and how that decision affects both the farmer-producer and the needy consumer.

Management of the programs is a large part of the job, embracing functions that run from development of budget, legislative initiatives and regulations to contract review, and personnel decisions. FNS also has a good deal of business with the State Department and Agency for International Development in international food assistance efforts. The assistant secretary oversees the work of about 3,000 employees in Washington and seven regional offices. It's a small force relative to the budget. Carol Tucker Foreman, who had the job in 1977-81, warns, in fact, that "with a small staff, you must be fanatical in attention to detail. It's a controversial position."

That description inevitably attaches to a job among whose principal concerns are hunger and adequate nutrition. A constituent group member terms it "probably as difficult a spot as there is in the department. You get caught between the interests of the farmers and ranchers on one side, and the welfare people on the other. If you walk in there and don't understand who's doing what to you and where all the various pressure points are, you'll be murdered. There's a great deal of emotion in that area, probably more than anywhere in the building. You've got to have a skin about 18 inches deep, but project a humane image."

Budget matters are also sensitive. "You want to deliver the benefit in the most cost-effective way," Jarratt says, "and you want to make sure that everyone who is eligible and needs help gets it." The definition of "needy" has been a core question, one that is highly charged politically. In her view, this is a question that "has to be worked out in accommodation with the public, the Congress and the administration."

Key Relationships

Within the Department

Reports to: Secretary

Works closely with:

Deputy Secretary
Assistant Secretary, Marketing and Inspection Services
Assistant Secretary, Science and Education
Assistant Secretary, Governmental and Public Affairs
General Counsel

Outside the Department

Assistant Secretary for Health, Department of Health
and Human Services
Assistant Secretary, Planning and Evaluation, HHS
Commissioner, Food and Drug Administration, HHS
Director, National Institutes of Health, HHS

Outside the Federal Government

American School Food Service Association; Women, Infants and Children Directors Association; advocacy groups in health care, hunger, consumer and women's affairs; organizations representing the elderly; American Farm Bureau Federation; Food Marketing Institute, National Cheese Institute, Public Voice for Food and Health Policy and other agricultural and general food marketing associations

Assistant Secretaries for Food and Consumer Services Since 1977*

Administration	Name and Years Served	Present Position
Reagan	John W. Bode 1985 - Present	Incumbent
Reagan	Mary C. Jarratt 1981 - 1985	President Jarratt and Associates Washington, DC
Carter	Carol Tucker Foreman 1977 - 1981	Chevy Chase, Maryland

* In 1977 the position of Assistant Secretary for Marketing and Consumer Services was split into Assistant Secretary for Food and Consumer Services and Assistant Secretary for Marketing and Inspection Services.

ASSISTANT SECRETARY
ECONOMICS

Level IV - Presidential Appointment with Senate Confirmation

Major Responsibilities

o   Direct data gathering and research services that provide information on the U.S. agricultural economy important in assisting farm production, maintaining orderly markets, administering agricultural programs and developing agricultural policy.

o   Work with the secretary and other senior department officers in the effective use of this information for the agency's objectives. Share with and interpret the information for the Congress. Take part in interagency consultations on such matters as commodity programs and immigrant farm labor.

o   Supervise the administrative management of the offices and services managed by the position.

Necessary Background, Experience, Personal Skills

Filling this position effectively means looking for individuals who understand data collection and analysis and also have farm production or general agribusiness experience. The job requires some training in economics. A knowledge of the international agricultural economy and management skills are excellent complementary credentials.

Insight

"This office is a stabilizing force in the debate over the agricultural economy to the extent that we can provide accurate information and good policy advice," says Ewen M. Wilson, assistant secretary since 1987. "It's a political job in the sense that this office has to be sensitive to political forces, but at the same time the agencies that report to me have a reputation for doing unbiased analysis. As long as they continue to do that, people will be willing to listen to what they say. In some instances, we'll provide analysis that the secretary may not want to hear, but if in my judgment that analysis is unbiased, then I have a responsibility at least to present it." But he cautions that the "fundamental difficulty" in the position lies in the unpredictability of commodity markets due to weather and economic conditions in the rest of the world. "For example, we have projections on what wheat exports will be but we don't know for sure. There's an awful lot of uncertainty in our estimates."

Three agencies report to the assistant secretary. The National Agricultural Statistics Service measures such key farm activities as grain crop sizes and yields (each month during the season) and hog production (once a month). The data it collects is prime information for the markets, and its periodic reports--generally written behind locked doors in the small hours of the morning--are released after the markets close.

The Economic Research Service produces data and policy analysis designed to assist farmers, processors, marketers and consumers, but also to support the development of policy and of legislation in the agricultural sector. This latter activity is important because American agriculture, a highly regulated industry, requires complicated policy constructions that need regular legislative overhaul.

The World Agricultural Outlook Board is an intelligence gathering and coordinating operation which reviews and coordinates domestic and foreign commodity and other agricultural and weather data, and provides guidelines for estimating and forecasting world agricultural production and conditions. It chairs the interagency commodity committee and develops a consensus that becomes the department's official estimate. Final responsibility for this rests with the assistant secretary.

About 20 percent of the time in this job goes into work with the Congress. "In many instances, we are going up there and using our analysis to urge some caution," Wilson says. "Often the members see a solution to some problem. Often when they enact the regulations there are unintended side effects. Our job is to provide the economic analysis."

There is substantial press attention to the work of the office, and public affairs activity, especially speechmaking, is a regular feature. Interest group contact is constant; where once the department primarily served farmers, it now looks out on a broad agribusiness constituency with an intense focus on what Washington is doing. That, in fact, forms part of what one former assistant secretary sees as the department's big challenge today. In the view of Don Paarlberg, who held the position from 1969 to 1977, it is to "weed out what is no longer relevant" and create new programs to handle the changing shape and requirements of U.S. and world agriculture.

Key Relationships

Within the Department

Reports to: Secretary

Works closely with:

Deputy Secretary
Undersecretary, International Affairs and Commodity
Programs
Other assistant secretaries
General Counsel

Outside the Department

Assistant Secretary, Economic and Business Affairs, Department of State
Director, Bureau of Economic Analysis, Department of Commerce
Assistant Secretary, Land and Minerals Management, Department of the Interior
Commissioner, Immigration and Naturalization Service, Department of Justice

Outside the Federal Government

American Farm Bureau Federation and other farm organizations, such as The Agribusiness Council, Agriculture Council of America, National Council of Farmer Cooperatives, National Dairy Board; commodity producers and trading associations, such as International Trade Council, North American Export Grain Association; consumer groups; counterparts in state governments, such as National Association of State Departments of Agriculture; research institutions, such as Agriculture Research Institute, Rodale Research Center

Assistant Secretaries for Economics Since 1969

Administration	Name and Years Served	Present Position
Reagan	Ewen M. Wilson 1987 - Present	Incumbent
Reagan	Robert L. Thompson 1985 - 1987	Dean School of Agriculture Purdue University West Lafayette, Indiana
Reagan	William G. Lesher 1981 - 1985	President Lesher and Associates, Inc. Washington, DC
Carter	Howard N. Hjort 1977 - 1981	Food and Agriculture Organization Rome, Italy
Nixon/Ford	Don Paarlberg 1969 - 1977	Professor Emeritus Purdue University West Lafayette, Indiana

ASSISTANT SECRETARY
MARKETING AND INSPECTION SERVICES

Level IV - Presidential Appointment with Senate Confirmation

Major Responsibilities

o   Direct a seven-part program providing regulation and inspection of agricultural food products; marketing services, advice and research to agricultural producers of food and commodities; and protection services for animals and plants.

o   Oversee administrative support for these operations. Supervise the budget in its preparatory and negotiating phases. Make the principal personnel assignments.

o   Speak for the administration on policy issues involving farm product inspection and marketing services.

Necessary Background, Experience, Personal Skills

The occupant of the position needs a background in agricultural production that includes familiarity with safety regulations and procedures involved in bringing products to market. This individual should also understand the concept of support for genuine competition and fair trade in farm markets, and of protection for producers and consumers against carelessness and fraud. More generally, look for management ability and experience and Congressional exposure; the current assistant secretary devotes about a third of his time to the Hill.

Insight

Most of the seven operations supervised from this position render services important to some part of the long process by which agricultural food products get to the marketplace. Grain farmers need protection from plant disease and pests. Their output needs weighing, inspecting, grading and handling in compliance with regulations set by law. Meat producers require control and eradication programs against communicable disease, and inspection of their products for safety and correct labeling. These and all other farm producers need support through mechanisms like regular market advisories, orderly market conditions, and safeguards against deceptive practices.

"The assistant secretary has a lot of line jurisdiction," a Congressional observer says, "in terms of marketing orders, important issues like food safety inspection services, and grain inspection services. From a bureaucratic standpoint, a lot of people are out there doing that sort of thing. But the high profile issues are not in that area." Still, says C.W. McMillan, who held the post in 1981-86, "you need experience lobbying or as a Congressional staff member" and a workable sense of the political realities to handle the job. "Evaluate the priority of the various functions going on," he advises. "Just because a program was successful 50 years ago doesn't necessarily mean it's needed now." Another veteran of the job thinks he became effective in it only when he understood that "making sound business decisions and understanding the political problems go hand in hand."

In regulatory policymaking--a significant part of this job-- McMillan says that, while major decisions went to the secretary, he made a substantial number of others on his own. That kind of flexibility "moves government quickly and smoothly," he points out. "Don't agonize--get the information, make the policy decision, and move on."

Kenneth A. Gilles, who has held this job since 1987, says "the mechanics of operations" levy the greatest demands on his time. "There are a lot of dockets to go through for the rule-making process" and a great amount of time goes into the health and safety area of his responsibilities--meat, poultry and grain inspection. The agencies he supervises in these sectors are the largest of the seven, employing more than 10,000 people. Most of them work in some 7,000 packing plants across the country, or handle the inspection of 11 grains and oil seeds and some 300 processed grain products. "We've got some very good professional people and we rely on them," Gilles says. The chiefs of his component services--"seven key players"--are a mixture of career and appointed officials. "I think there's merit to that," he asserts. "It's difficult to find people with the technical expertise and experience to bring in for short-term assignments."

In addition to the Food and Drug Administration, this job's regular working relationships include two other elements of the Department of Health and Human Services--the National Institutes of Health and the Centers for Disease Control--and the Environmental Protection Agency. The assistant secretary also sits on a number of interagency coordinating committees in such fields as biological science. It's also worth noting that this job takes its occupant into regular meetings with counterparts in the governments of Central America, and that fluency in Spanish clearly raises the quality of these contacts. "It improves relations," McMillan told us, "if you don't need to use an interpreter."

Robert H. Meyer, who held the job in 1977-78, has some critical comments to offer about bureaucratic life in general and what he feels is its tendency to frustrate initiative and original thinking because of daily political considerations. But he calls his time in this particular post "probably the most broadening experience of my life. It gave me the greatest overview of my area of interest, not just nationally but internationally." It "cost me dearly, both financially and personally," he says. "But I'd do it again."

Key Relationships

Within the Department

> Reports to: Secretary

> Works closely with:

> > Deputy Secretary
> > Assistant Secretary, Science and Education

Outside the Department

> > Assistant Secretary, Fish and Wildlife, Department
> > of the Interior
> > Administrator, Food and Drug Administration, Depart-
> > ment of Health and Human Services
> > Commissioner, U.S. Customs Service

Outside the Federal Government

> > Associations grouping growers of principal commodities, such as American Soybean Association, North American Export Grain Association; cattlemen and meat packer groups, such as National Cattlemen's Association, National Meat Canners Association, American Farm Bureau Federation; dairy cooperatives; horse breed-ers; flower growers, such as Floral Trade Council;

marketing associations; consumer organizations, such as American Council on Science and Health, Consumer Federation of America

Assistant Secretaries for Marketing and Inspection Services Since 1969

Administration	Name and Years Served	Present Position
Reagan	Kenneth A. Gilles 1987 - Present	Incumbent
Reagan	C. W. McMillan 1981 - 1986	President McMillan and Farrell Washington, DC
Carter	P. R. Smith 1978 - 1981	Winder, Georgia
Carter	Robert H. Meyer 1977 - 1978	La Jolla, California
Ford	Richard L. Feltner* 1974 - 1977	Louisville, Kentucky
Nixon/Ford	Clayton K. Yeutter* 1973 - 1974	U.S. Trade Representative Office of the U.S. Trade Representative
Nixon	Richard E. Lyng* 1969 - 1973	Secretary Department of Agriculture

*   Held this position as Assistant Secretary for Marketing and Consumer Services.

GENERAL COUNSEL

Level IV - Presidential Appointment with Senate Confirmation

Major Responsibilities

o   Function as chief legal officer of the department. Provide legal advice to the secretary, other principal officers and heads of component agencies in the formulation of policy.

o   Represent the department in litigation. Perform necessary coordination with other government agencies in legal matters involving the responsibility or interests of the department.

o   Oversee the proper handling of the legal aspects of department legislation. Manage legislative contacts in this regard and appear in testimony when required.

Necessary Background, Experience, Personal Skills

The lawyer appointed to this position needs a strong background in administrative law, in terms both of the federal law process and of litigation. Negotiating experience, and a working knowledge of legislative procedure are also required. Previous government service adds a highly useful resource.

Insight

In this position, as in certain equivalent legal jobs elsewhere in government, the comments of some who have served in them occasionally reflect just a hint of a wish to have been more actively involved in policymaking, or to have been more a part of the team. While generalizations about such matters can easily overstate the case, this situation--when and where it exists--deserves mention.

On paper, the chief legal positions in government departments are almost invariably staff, not line, jobs. Of itself, that distinction presents no real barrier to the informal but effective deployment of the top lawyer in a decision-making as well as a support role. But there seem to be other, less evident, reasons why some departments tend not to bring their legal counsel consistently into the

senior circle of deliberation or use their legal offices as extensively as they could. Sometimes it stems from simple failure to recognize
fully the value--or necessity--of legal input into policy or operational decisions. Sometimes it flows from a subconscious or deliberate desire not to be told, at least at the outset, that a proposed
action is inadvisable or impossible from a legal standpoint.

Thus we hear a former general counsel at Agriculture, Daniel
Marcus (1979-80) speak of "a tradition to view the general counsel
as a lawyer, not one of the policymakers." And, while traditions
come and go in government agencies, this lawyer thinks it important for a general counsel interested in policy to establish close
relationships at the top of the department and "be somewhat aggressive in getting involved in policy matters."

The general counsel exerts management authority along four
main lines of responsibility: International affairs, commodity programs and food assistance; community development and natural
resources; regulatory and marketing affairs; and legislation, litigation, research, and operations. There is a substantial amount of
interagency work--rural health care or food safety issues with the
Department of Health and Human Services, for example, or resource
conservation projects in which Agriculture and the Department of
the Interior share interests and concerns.

Most of the legal staff works in the main Washington office,
the rest in regional field offices. Asked what challenged him in
the job, A. James Barnes, general counsel in 1981-83, says it was
"bringing to bear the talent and experience of a group of lawyers
to aid the policymakers in meeting their objectives within the
framework of the law, and to facilitate the process by working
with other attorneys throughout the government structure."

Key Relationships

Within the Department

Reports to: Secretary

Works closely with:

Undersecretary, International Affairs and Commodity
Programs

Undersecretary, Small Community and Rural
Development
Assistant secretaries

Outside the Department

Assistant Attorney General, Civil Division, Department
of Justice
Assistant Attorney General, Land and Natural Resources
Division, Department of Justice
Associate Director, Natural Resources Energy and
Science, Office of Management and Budget
Solicitor, Department of the Interior
General Counsel, Department of Health and Human
Services
Chief Counsel, Food and Drug Administration

Outside the Federal Government

Consumer Federation of America, National Grain and
Feed Association; National Farmers Union and other
farm organizations

General Counsels of Agriculture Since 1969

Administration	Name and Years Served	Present Position
Reagan	Christopher Hicks 1986 - Present	Incumbent
Reagan	Daniel Oliver 1983 - 1986	Chairman Federal Trade Commission
Reagan	A. James Barnes 1981 - 1983	Deputy Administrator Environmental Protection Agency
Carter	Daniel Marcus 1979 - 1980	Partner Wilmer, Cutler and Pickering Washington, DC

Carter	Sarah C. Weddington 1977 - 1978	Washington, DC
Ford	James D. Keast 1975 - 1977	Partner Carmody, McDonald, Hilton and Wolf St. Louis, Missouri
Nixon/Ford	John A. Knebel 1973 - 1975	President American Mining Conference Washington, DC
Nixon	Edward M. Shulman 1967 - 1973	Not Available

ADMINISTRATOR
AGRICULTURAL STABILIZATION AND
CONSERVATION SERVICE

Senior Executive Service*

* (Occupant of this position is also Executive Vice President of the Commodity Credit Corporation, requiring Presidential appointment with Senate confirmation.)

Major Responsibilities

o Administer commodity purchase and loan programs designed to improve farm income, encourage voluntary adjustments in farm production, and stabilize commodity markets and prices. Manage land-use projects to conserve soil and water resources.

o Serve as Executive Vice President of the Commodity Credit Corporation.

o Supervise development of the Agricultural Stabilization and Conservation Service budget and its representation on the Hill. Oversee hiring of agency personnel.

Necessary Background, Experience, Personal Skills

It's difficult to imagine assigning this job to an individual who lacks familiarity with agricultural commodity production, specific knowledge of federal farm programs, and good contacts within the national farm community. Whoever fills the position will also find prior government service and experience in running a large-scale organization to be important resources.

Insight

To handle this position effectively, says Everett Rank, ASCS chief from 1981 to 1986, "you need to know what the problems are at the local level and to have lived through them." That comment seems supported by the close-knit state and county structure through which ASCS operates around the nation. At the state level, a committee appointed by the Secretary of Agriculture supervises the activities of the state office, whose director the secretary also designates. Second, in each of 3,000-plus agricultural counties a committee of locally-elected farmers and producers oversees a county executive director and staff who handle day-to-day activities. From Washington, five regional directors administer this multi-layered operation. Required by law, this way of doing business permits the making of many decisions at the local level by elected officials, and renders the administrator's job at once more difficult and more interesting.

Perhaps the major responsibility and activity of the ASCS administrator is the proper implementation of decisions of the Commodity Credit Corporation (CCC), the principal mechanism by which the United States tries to manage the decades-old problem of stabilizing farm production and maintaining and improving farm income. CCC programs cover most of the commodity terrain, making purchases and loans, as well as payments to growers. As executive vice president of the CCC, the administrator handles the agenda for its weekly decisions meetings, publishing it a week ahead of time. Sunshine laws are a factor here. "We had to be sure we did not meet too much in private or it could be taken as conspiring," says Ray V. Fitzgerald, administrator in 1977-81.

In the area of resource conservation, the principal ASCS operations focus on the most erodable farm land to protect and improve soil and water and to share the costs with farmers of operations to conserve timber and water assets.

In addition to CCC and interagency meetings and budget and personnel tasks, the administrator spends a fair amount of time on the road. There are state agricultural gatherings, consultations with state and county committee members and staff, and public affairs events such as television and radio interviews, speeches and ceremonial duties. Fitzgerald saw his responsibility in all of this work as making the service "as responsive as possible," and one aspect of this was "making the field people able to deliver programs to the farmers." Overall, he defines the key goal as making certain "that the programs are administered for their primary recipients, the farmers, and not for unintended beneficiaries--agricultural businesses." In this respect, says another previous administrator, "the person who becomes administrator has to know how to say no and be able to stand up to the pressures of the Congress and the commodity groups."

Key Relationships

Within the Department

Reports to:

Undersecretary, International Affairs and Commodity Programs

Works closely with:

Assistant Secretary for Economics
Administrator, Farmers Home Administration
Administrator, Agricultural Marketing Service
Administrator, Foreign Agricultural Service

Outside the Department

Assistant Administrator, Food for Peace and Voluntary Assistance Bureau, Agency for International Development
Deputy Assistant Secretary, Trade and Commercial Affairs, Department of State

Outside the Federal Government

Commodity producer associations and major agribusiness groups, such as The Agribusiness Council, Futures Industry Association, National Council of Farmer Cooperatives, U.S. Beet Sugar Association, National Farmers Union, American Farm Bureau Federation, National Farmers Union; bankers groups, such as American Bankers Association

Administrators for Agricultural Stabilization and Conservation Services Since 1969

Administration	Name and Years Served	Present Position
Reagan	Milton J. Hertz 1986 - Present	Incumbent

Reagan	Everett Rank 1981 - 1986	Fresno, California
Carter	Ray V. Fitzgerald 1977 - 1981	Falls Church, Virginia
Carter	Victor A. Senechal 1977 (Acting)	Not Available
Nixon/Ford	Kenneth E. Frick 1969 - 1977	Not Available

CHIEF
FOREST SERVICE

Senior Executive Service

Major Responsibilities

o   Manage the federal leadership role in protecting and conserving the nation's public and private forest resources. Advocate these causes within the administration, and in their Congressional and public contexts.

o   Direct the U.S. Forest Service of more than 50,000 employees nationwide. Oversee the service's budget process and personnel affairs.

Necessary Background, Experience, Personal Skills

The forest service itself offers almost the only framework in which the expertise in natural resources and the technical skills necessary for this job can combine with the agency management and political experience also required. For these reasons, those who fill the position normally come from within the agency.

Insight

For 15 years ending in 1987, the forest service had only two chiefs, both of them veterans of the agency before taking the top job. From their viewpoint, such longevity brings clear advantages. "This job transcends administrations," says R. Max Peterson, who led the service from 1979 to 1987. "It doesn't turn over with administrations, and there's a tendency to respect that." Because appointees average only two years in the assistant secretary slot to which the forest service chief reports, they spend much of their time learning on the job. It is up to the chief to help educate them on both problems and opportunities. More than that, Peterson points out, it's important to "know how to deal with initiatives from a new administration that may not work well or need modifying, explaining why some things may not be a good idea, and still stay open to trying new ones."

As head forester of the United States, the forest service chief has responsibilities in twin domains. First comes management of better than 150 national forests, about 20 national grasslands and 17 land use programs occupying almost 200 million acres in all but six states. The basic object is to assure the outflow of needed and replaceable natural resources--not merely wood, but water, wildlife, fish, animal forage, and outdoor recreation--and deploy an array of effective programs which support their conservation and replacement. Second, through state agencies and private forestry projects, the service assists non-federal forest owners, operators, and forest product industries in a wide variety of maintenance and improvement activities. The agency's forest research program serves all of these efforts in both sectors.

"The service is in a crisis these days, and recognizes it," the chairman of a prominent environmental group told us. "It's not making any of its constituencies happy anymore, whether on the industry or on the environmental side." In this view, the problem turns mainly on the management of the nationally important issue of timber sales, in which the multiple-use standard for federal lands has not been "even-handedly" applied. A three-cornered contest continues between these two parties and the service itself, with the service wanting to "hold on to control at all costs and write prescriptions according to its lights." Traditionally, this observer continues, the service has treated timber sales as technical, rather than political issues, and hasn't been sufficiently adroit in the political sense "in trying to balance attending interests. There's a sense that when the parties get together away from the service, they can find a better solution than the service can."

Still according to this source, there is "very much a battle for the soul of the agency" taking place. The "stubbornness of people down the line who don't want to accommodate"--for example, by developing unrealistic alternatives in a forest plan with which neither environmentalists nor the industry can identify, is "the real problem." In some ways this "is a fight between generations in the agency. I think some honest efforts at reform are going on." The key question is where the next chief of the forest service comes from. "It may be time to go outside the agency for leadership."

Whoever gets the job will still have to live with the familiar problem of short resources, declining staff, and increasing work load. To cope, Peterson took such steps as organizing task forces to "look ahead several years" and, by cutting down on instructions from the top, tried to encourage more flexibility and use of judgment at lower levels of the service.

The job involves an expectably steady round of staff and

interagency meetings, testimony on the Hill and less formal encounters with Congressional members and staff, budget consultations at the Office of Management and Budget, and discussions and exchanges with more than 50 constituent interest groups. Public speaking, ceremonial duties and some international travel complete the picture.

"What happens on the land is important to the country and around the world," Peterson says. "Much of the work in developing countries is based on what was done here. It's a long-term contribution."

Key Relationships

Within the Department

Reports to:

Assistant Secretary, Natural Resources and Environment

Works closely with:

Chief, Soil Conservation Service
Administrator, Agricultural Research Service
Administrator, Animal and Plant Health Inspection Service

Outside the Department

Department of the Interior:

Director, National Park Service
Director, Fish and Wildlife Service
Director, Land Management Bureau
Director, U.S. Geological Survey

Administrator, Environmental Protection Agency

Outside the Federal Government

Timber, wood products and building supply industries; railroads; foresters' associations, such as American Forestry Association, National Forest Products Association; conservation and environmental groups, such as

Coastal States Organization, National Parks and Conservation Association, National Wildlife Federation; scientific societies, such as National Association of Environmental Professionals; state government officials

Chiefs of the Forest Service Since 1969

Administration	Name and Years Served	Present Position
Reagan	F. Dale Robertson 1987 - Present	Incumbent
Carter/Reagan	R. Max Peterson 1979 - 1987	Fairfax, Virginia
Nixon/Ford/ Carter	John R. McGuire 1972 - 1979	Falls Church, Virginia
Nixon	Edward P. Cliff 1969 - 1972	Deceased

5

CENTRAL INTELLIGENCE AGENCY

In the words of a former member of CIA's leadership, the Iran-contra matter has once again given the agency "the problem of the public image and relations with Congress." To that gentle understatement one could add lowered self-confidence and morale. These are problems not confined to the CIA among government agencies. There is much room for improvement.

But, amid general agreement that such calamities must not recur, particularly of this disastrous kind, one reality of day-to-day intelligence work needs to be kept in mind. Iran-contra aside, it can be argued that image and Congressional difficulties seem destined always to trouble the CIA to some degree, like a dormant but ineradicable virus. Almost by definition, they are part of the territory for an intelligence agency in a democracy like this one. That is especially true if a certain level of covert activity is a part of the mandate, as it properly must be.

Any discussion of what the CIA needs most, however, must plainly and certainly include words like integrity, principled and experienced leadership, and further fine-tuning of Congressional oversight--a process in which the agency can avoid ultimate grief only if it genuinely understands the purpose and supports it fully. That requires renewed adherence to the concept, stressed by those interviewed for this book, that the function of intelligence organizations is to gather and provide the facts but not to participate in the policy decisions.

In an era when the tempo of change in international relationships and in the politics and policies of individual nations has risen, the CIA's role will inevitably change more rapidly. The agency will need greater expertise in the technological aspects of its mission, for example in the verification of existing arms reduction and control agreements and those which may be coming. It will also need leadership that is more articulate, more skilled diplomatically, and more enlightened in its approach to people and the conduct of programs.

DEPUTY DIRECTOR

Level III - Presidential Appointment with Senate Confirmation

Major Responsibilities

o   With the director of Central Intelligence, the deputy--as second in command with full authority to act for the director when required--has responsibilities as intelligence officer for the President, as principal spokesman to the Congress on intelligence matters, and in the allocation of resources to all intelligence agencies.

o   Serve as the agency's chief operating officer. Oversee its administrative and personnel functions.

Necessary Background, Experience, Personal Skills

The Deputy Director of Central Intelligence should be a career professional civilian or military intelligence officer, with a detailed knowledge of the intelligence community. Qualified candidates will be completely familiar with intelligence collection systems and have working relationships with the intelligence services of friendly foreign countries. The deputy should also know the Congress and be able to work productively with members and staff concerned with intelligence activities. Last and clearly not least, the job calls for an inclusive grasp of international affairs.

Insight

Some view this job as in some ways more difficult and impactive than that of the director. First, the deputy nominally runs the agency day to day for the simple reason that the director, as chief of the entire U.S. intelligence community, must develop persuasive and objective views about intelligence goals and projects. That means taking generic positions, not positions specific to the CIA. Second, the deputy job tends to exert greater impact on present and proposed programs. To members of Congress, this job represents more substance by nature of the deputy's management responsibilities and the deputy's responsibility to inform the Senate Select Committee on Intelligence on substantive matters. Third, as deputy, the individual in this job is also second in command of the intelligence community, but must also understand intimately how the CIA works.

Directors and their deputies ideally should complement, not duplicate, each other in knowledge and personal skills. The deputy needs to understand the implications of particular programs for particular countries, and to counsel the director about their legal, political and covert dimensions.

Most important, the deputy director has to understand what the mission of intelligence is--to provide facts, not influence policy. "It's a difficult role for both the director and the deputy," says an informed and experienced former CIA official. "They must interact in a political arena, but cannot influence policy in terms of decisionmaking. The CIA cannot advocate a particular agenda, and this is difficult when the people around the President, and the President himself, are very ideological. It's the same on the Hill. This is a tough job for someone who's trying to present a position and let it stand on its own."

Former deputy director B.R. Inman (1981-82), who believes this job must be filled with a career intelligence veteran, says that, while "good broad-scale knowledge" certainly helps, "there's no substitute for experience. It's not training, it's experience." He also believes this kind of strength serves the deputy well in dealing with strong professionals inside the agency. While support from below is sufficient, the deputy director "is going to need to rely on his knowledge. They could by-pass you easily if they didn't think you were important to their success," Inman says.

It's a fast-moving scene. Inside the agency, a typical day might find the deputy responding to breaking developments, making decisions on resource allocations, and hearing out differing viewpoints in order to discern the right direction to take on a given problem. The deputy handles evaluation and long-range planning tasks, and "makes the wheels go around day by day," as former deputy director E. Henry Knoche, who held the job in 1977, puts it. This entails, for example, oversight of all scientific and technical agency functions and systems acquisition. It involves promotion panels and other personnel decisions.

On the outside, the deputy director's regular rounds are extensive. One major stop, as already seen, is the Hill--a sizeable time investment in hearings and other briefings that in Inman's tour embraced all CIA activities except those related to covert activity. Others include Cabinet meetings, National Security Council deliberations, senior interagency sessions like the President's Intelligence Oversight Board, and visits to foreign counterparts and agency elements abroad.

A special concern for the deputy, in Knoche's view, is that, on the one hand, he needs to exercise good supervision and control in order to guard against excesses. At the same time, he wants to develop "a creative and innovative work force" which "an overly zealous approach will chill." Another, more familiar problem relates to substantive and jurisdictional battles within the intelligence community which the deputy can be called on to mediate. This, says Inman, is "chronic and daily." And an "amazing number of people," he adds, "are willing to hold your coat while you go out and fight their battles."

While one of the agency's big continuing problems remains its "public image and relations with Congress," Inman comments, he and Knoche feel this position offers the chance to help develop thoughtful foreign policy initiatives. Knoche believes the choice for the position must be "non-political" if its occupant is to be effective. He recounts his own selection and confirmation process and his first meetings with members of the Congress. "In the entire process, no one ever asked me what my party affiliation was. That is the way it should be in this position."

One point which the deputy more than anyone in the agency must grasp thoroughly is the increasing role of technology in intelligence, as opposed to the role of clandestine operations and analytical methodologies. We were reminded, for example, that the signing of arms reduction agreements means a newly important role for technology in verification. "This is no longer a pencil-pushing operation," our source commented. "Technology will have a significant impact on our ability to monitor the arms agreement. There will be some tough decisions and, although the director and deputy get a lot of advice, the advice conflicts because people pursue their own agendas. You have to be a bright person, but you also have to be able to understand the issues at a level just below the surface."

Key Relationships

Within the Agency

Reports to: Director

Works closely with:

Functional deputy directors

Outside the Agency

Deputy Secretary, Department of Defense
Director, Defense Intelligence Agency, Department of Defense
Director, National Security Agency
Associate Director, National Security and International Affairs, Office of Management and Budget
Assistant Chief of Staff for Intelligence, Department of the Air Force
Deputy Chief of Staff for Intelligence, Department of the Army
Director of Naval Intelligence, Department of the Navy

When acting Director of Central Intelligence:
Assistant to the President for National Security Affairs
Secretary, Department of State
Secretary, Department of Defense

Outside the Federal Government

Counterparts in foreign intelligence services

Deputy Directors of the Central Intelligence Agency Since 1969

Administration	Name and Years Served	Present Position
Reagan	Robert M. Gates 1986 - Present	Incumbent
Reagan	John N. McMahon 1982 - 1985	Executive Vice President Lockheed Missiles and Space Company Sunnyvale, California
Reagan	B. R. Inman 1981 - 1982	Chairman of the Board Westmark Systems, Inc. Austin, Texas
Carter	Frank C. Carlucci 1978 - 1981	Secretary Department of Defense

Carter	E. Henry Knoche 1977	Denver, Colorado
Nixon/Ford	Vernon A. Walters 1972 - 1976	Ambassador to the United Nations New York, New York
Nixon	Robert E. Cushman, Jr. 1969 - 1971	Deceased

GENERAL COUNSEL

Level IV - Presidential Appointment with Senate Confirmation

Major Responsibilities

o   Assist the director in regulating the conduct of a highly scru-
tinized agency.   Ensure CIA adherence to existing law and
executive orders.

o   Formulate CIA legal positions.   Defend the agency in court.
Assist in statute revision and the shaping of new legislation.

o   Direct the activities of the agency's legal staff, whose 100
members include about 40 lawyers.

Necessary Background, Experience, Personal Skills

The position calls for an experienced lawyer who can move
with confidence in tax, corporate, contract and international law.
The right candidate ought to be equally at home in the courtroom
and on the Hill, with some knowledge of the federal government
and a reasonable grasp of world affairs and administration foreign
policy.   A former general counsel thinks age should be a factor in
the selection--"you want a savvy, smart lawyer who's been around."

Insight

Stanley Sporkin, CIA general counsel in 1981-86, thinks this
legal position comes closer than any in government to resembling
the general counsel job in a large corporation.   But it also carries
all the responsibilities of any other senior government legal officer,
providing advice at all levels of the agency and in most operational
areas.   It has some special aspects as well.   For example, "you have
many employees all over the world who need advice quickly," as
Sporkin says, somewhat enigmatically.   He notes, too, that the
general counsel assists in the cases of certain CIA employees who,
"because of their undercover status, have difficulty retaining outside
counsel."   And the general counsel has to deal with "people trying
to graymail the government" with threats to go public with secret

information.

When we asked him what this job is mainly about, Daniel B. Silver, who held it in 1979-81, replied with a nutshell summation: "Keeping the CIA out of trouble." Doing so most effectively, he believes, means not changing general counsels each time the administration changes hands. In his view, appointment to "a job of this sensitivity" should be "non-political," with a strong effort to keep individuals in it longer and not follow the rhythm of the election cycle. It is also important, Silver says, in an agency where the career staff is "very suspicious of outsiders," to "win their confidence, and be known as a help, not an adversary."

On this subject of effectiveness, Sporkin makes two points. First, the job needs "someone who has the confidence of the director." This is particularly important, he explains, because at times of conflict between legal advice and the views of the substantive people, "you need someone who's going to back you--you can't be losing those decisions." Second, reflecting Silver's view to some extent, he says a new general counsel must understand that "you can't really impose yourself on others." With the exception of areas he felt obliged to get into on his own initiative, Sporkin waited for others to come to him. Ultimately, "they were going to have enough confidence in you, or gain enough confidence, to bring you in." From a rather lonely beginning, he recounts, "when I was ready to leave, I had to shut down the phone because they were bringing in all kinds of things to me. So this business of being a Doctor No (being perceived as usually advising against a decision or an action)--I don't think necessarily it has to happen." When the general counsel does have to turn something off, "if people understand why you're shutting it down, they'll appreciate it because they'll know they are not going to get into trouble."

Naturally, there is more than one legal way to skin a CIA cat. Finding the alternatives, Sporkin believes, depends on the degree to which the general counsel supports the mission of the agency and believes it must be carried out. "But it has to be carried out according to the legal structure." He recalls being faced with one situation in which "the easy solution would have been to say no." Because he felt that lives were at stake and didn't want to be second-guessed later on, he permitted the agency to "go yes," making clear at the same time that he would tell the Congress what was happening and "give them an opportunity to tell me no." Although the committees gave him a hard time initially, they did not ask Sporkin to change his counsel, and reflected it in later statute revision. "So there, I was able to accomplish my mission," Sporkin says, "do what the agency wanted to do, and do it legally."

Clearly, it is this kind of situation which both Sporkin and Silver have in mind in asserting the need to anticipate problems and take preventive measures before, not after, they explode. "Always be prepared for the unexpected, and be ready to deal in every branch of law," says Lawrence R. Houston, who spanned an eventful generation as general counsel from 1947 to 1973. "And if you have to seek outside help and none is available, you had better be ready to learn how to deal with it yourself."

With Silver, Sporkin sees this position's key challenge in "making sure the agency is abiding by the letter and spirit of the law so that it will not get distracted from its ultimate mission." Related to this is one of its biggest frustrations--the CIA's "tremendous amount of oversight" which in his view goes nearly to the point of micromanagement. "A lot of the time you spend trying to justify your existence to the Congress. There's a lot of wheel spinning and distrust." As in any job, he says, "you'll find yourself with a lot of things you don't like to do."

Key Relationships

Within the Agency

Reports to: Director

Works closely with:

Deputy Director

Outside the Agency

Attorney General, Department of Justice
Deputy Attorney General, Department of Justice
Assistant attorneys general, criminal and civil divisions, Department of Justice
Legal Adviser, Department of State
Director, Defense Intelligence Agency, Department of Defense
General Counsel, Defense Intelligence Agency, DOD
Presidential Intelligence Oversight Board

Outside the Federal Government

American Civil Liberties Union, Association of Former Intelligence Officers

General Counsels of the Central Intelligence Agency Since 1969

Administration	Name and Years Served	Present Position
Reagan	Russell Bruemmer 1988 - Present	Incumbent
Reagan	David P. Doherty 1986 - 1988	Senior Vice President Division of Enforcement New York Stock Exchange New York, New York
Reagan	Stanley Sporkin 1981 - 1986	U.S. Judge Federal District Court District of Columbia Washington, DC
Carter	Daniel B. Silver 1979 - 1981	Senior Partner Cleary, Gottlieb, Steen, and Hamilton Washington, DC
Ford/Carter	Anthony A. Lapham 1976 - 1979	Partner Shea & Gardner Washington, DC
Nixon/Ford	John S. Warner 1974 - 1976	Tucson, Arizona
Truman-Nixon	Lawrence R. Houston 1947 - 1973	Washington, DC

6

CENTRAL MANAGEMENT AGENCIES

Office of Management and Budget
Office of Personnel Management
General Services Administration

As with the running of any huge enterprise, government needs specialized mechanisms to bring resource allocation into congruence with administration policy and objectives, to hire, train, assign and support the work force, and to assure efficient, across-the-board administrative support for operations. While no formal structure groups together the agencies performing those tasks, they perform management functions that, by definition, require them to be in overall coordination and to cooperate on many specific actions.

At the heart of the executive branch, the Office of Management and Budget wields the policy and budgetary arm of the President. The heavyweight of the central management agencies, it runs the show at one of the most important inner crossroads of government, managing the dialogue between the politicians of the White House's West Wing and the appointed leadership of the bureaucracy. Through that dialogue, an administration stamps its purposes and political faith onto the direction and momentum of the departments and agencies in terms of programs, plans and money--or tries to.

The key product of that process is the President's annual budget document, one of official Washington's chief frames of reference and a recurring political and economic event in the life of the capital. In the words of a former senior OMB official, the budget "is an agenda-setting policy statement and must be used to introduce productive tension into political and policy debate." And whatever the nature and degree of any budget's ultimate impact, the budget function remains an energizing procedure with broad significance for all three branches of government and well beyond.

To midwife this dreadnought into existence each fall, OMB begins at the beginning, with the budget submission of each element of the executive branch. After painstaking internal review and ensuing discussion with the department or agency, it identifies desired changes to bring submissions into consonance with administration policy. These recommendations for change travel as far up the OMB and White House decision-making ladders as particular cases might require. Revised submissions then go back to the agencies, with a period for appeals, and become part of the President's final budget document. The entire process unfolds amid a psychology of near-chronic federal budget deficits and under the extra workload imposed by Gramm-Rudman-Hollings deficit reduction requirements.

The nature of these operations gives OMB a tangible role in the shaping and adapting of policy itself, as do its important current responsibilities in implementation and clearance. Working with the departments and agencies, it sees that their principal legislative proposals--reflecting the budget--rest on a workable strategy that takes the administration where it wants to go. Here and at other pressure points, including the area of regulatory reform, it thus manages the execution of policy as the budget has defined it.

Managing the merit system for federal employment is the central assignment of the Office of Personnel Management. Beyond its immediate broad responsibility to recruit, train and support federal career employees from first job through retirement, however, OPM would seem to have a fundamental part to play in resolving an ominous long-term problem. This is the decline in government's credibility and attractiveness as an employer, something touched on in interviews not only with former OPM directors but with numbers of other former federal executives. Arising from perceptions in the career service of a variety of inequities and unfulfilled intentions, this long-building situation has led to a decline of morale within the career ranks and helped to lower the appeal of government service.

As manager of the government's property, records, communications, supplies, transportation and stockpiles, the General Services Administration is part of the life of every department and agency. At the same time, the nature of these responsibilities may lie near the root of what one of its previous administrators alleges is a past agency reputation "for waste, fraud, abuse and inefficiency." One of the staggering burdens of this agency is trying to keep government equipped and updated with the same kinds of technology and systems that the private sector is exploiting, and which government needs just as much--or more. A former boss of GSA recommends that, in this and other respects, GSA should stop what he describes as "delegating" its work to other agencies.

DEPUTY DIRECTOR
OFFICE OF MANAGEMENT AND BUDGET

Level III - Presidential Appointment with Senate Confirmation

Major Responsibilities

o   Assist the director in management of the agency. Function as acting director when necessary. Represent OMB in consultation with the Congress on such matters as budget reconciliation, and in testimony as required.

o   In consultation with program associate directors, resolve or recommend decisions by higher authority on key issues raised in the agency's principal responsibility for government-wide budget development and implementation. Work with associate directors to assure that the programs, activities and legislative requests of federal departments and agencies remain consistent with budget precepts and obligations.

o   Oversee government financial and administrative practices with respect to reducing costs, controlling paperwork, increasing uniformity and raising efficiency.

Necessary Background, Experience, Personal Skills

Former deputy directors believe an analytical background, knowledge of economics or political science, and government experience best serve this position. A knowledge of accounting helps. An observer familiar with OMB thinks the job needs a tested manager from the private sector or someone who has successfully handled senior administrative responsibilities in a federal agency. Candidates will preferably have spent enough time in activity relating to the Congress to move comfortably on the Hill.

Insight

"This job can be whatever the director and deputy director want it to be," recalls Edwin L. Harper, Deputy Director in 1981-1982. He sees such flexibility as "the opportunity to participate in those things which are most important and challenging to achieve national objectives."

At certain times in the past, the director of OMB has been known to spend significant amounts of time on non-budgetary activity. In such circumstances, says a Congressional staffer who knows both jobs, the deputy can become extensively involved in overseeing development of the budget and its execution out in the federal vineyards. In any case, the major decisionmaking inherent in the budget process goes directly through the deputy's office, the deputy participates in the director's review function, and has responsibility in the clearance of administration testimony.

But a good part of the position's focus in recent years seems to have been on the management side of OMB. Substantial effort has recently gone into improving the administrative operations of the executive branch in the interest of efficiency and economy. OMB has always had important responsibilities in this area, but chronic large budget deficits have long since brought home the advantages of increased economy and efficiency in the vast expense of running the government. An improved cash management system offers a good example of this reform. Without incentive to do otherwise, some agencies and departments were making little short-term use of cash collected in various operations--in an era when even the overnight invested value of cash in such volumes represented big potential savings. Reduced telephone costs, new telecommunications installations, and consolidated payroll and accounting systems are further instances of the kinds of administrative reform which fall in the deputy director's management portfolio.

The varying dimensions of the job mean that the deputy gains by having a "clear understanding" with the director on the allocation of responsibility, a previous occupant points out. "Establish the relationship of being an alter ego" to the director, he advises, and adds: "I didn't anticipate the heavy political character of what we were doing. You are in the White House, which is political, and you must remember that you are effectively the objective policy advice person and not the political advisor."

In the constant dialogue between OMB and the Congress, only the deputy director and his chief normally appear in actual testimony on behalf of the agency. Recently at least, the deputy has also helped in representing administration positions on fundamental budget issues to the Hill. As described by the staff director of a House committee, "the deputy director is in charge, not of the policy, but whether the changes in policy add up to X dollars in savings. In effect, he became sort of the arbitrator of the budget summit (of December, 1987)....He had to see whether specific steps would in fact save the money that the summit said that our committee and the Senate committee were obligated to save. So (the deputy director) had to have a more substantive knowledge about the targets we were obligated to meet." In this observer's view, the deputy director's position has "great influence...on the give and take between Congress and the executive branch."

"OMB is a wonderful place to be," declares Paul H. O'Neill, Deputy Director in 1974-1977. "Every important issue of government goes through it. You get to be a player in most of the important problems of the world." And, while all this can happen, Harper offers this more sobering reflection: "There is no end to the number of hours you will put in to get up to speed with the program. The occupant needs to give specific thought to what impact this will have on his family."

Key Relationships

Within the Agency

Reports to: Director

Works closely with: Associate directors

Outside the Agency

The President
Secretaries and deputy secretaries of federal depart
   ments and agencies
Senior White House staff
Economic Policy Council
Domestic Policy Council
Deputy Assistant to the President for National Security
   Affairs

Outside the Federal Government

Urban affairs, civil rights, business, commerce, law, banking, and labor groups and many other organizations, such as AFL-CIO, The Agribusiness Council, American Bar Association, Center on Budget and Policy Priorities, Naitonal League of Cities, U.S. Business and Industrial Council, U.S. Chamber of Commerce

Deputy Directors of the Office of Management and Budget Since 1969

Administration	Name and Years Served	Present Position
Reagan	Joseph R. Wright 1982 - Present	Incumbent
Reagan	Edwin L. Harper 1981 - 1982	Senior Vice President & Chief Financial Officer Campbell Soup Company Camden, New Jersey
Carter	John P. White 1978 - 1981	Chairman and CEO Interactive Systems Corp. Santa Monica, California
Carter	James T. McIntyre, Jr. 1977 - 1978	Partner McNair Law Firm Washington, DC
Ford	Paul H. O'Neill 1974 - 1977	Chairman and CEO Aluminum Company of America Pittsburgh, Pennsylvania
Nixon	Frederic V. Malek 1973 - 1974	Executive Vice President Marriott Corporation Washington, DC
Nixon	Frank C. Carlucci 1972 -1973	Secretary Department of Defense
Nixon	Caspar Weinberger 1970 - 1972	Of Counsel Rogers & Wells Washington, DC

ASSOCIATE DIRECTORS
OFFICE OF MANAGEMENT AND BUDGET

ECONOMICS AND GOVERNMENT
HUMAN RESOURCES, VETERANS AND LABOR
NATIONAL SECURITY AND INTERNATIONAL AFFAIRS
NATURAL RESOURCES, ENERGY AND SCIENCE

Senior Executive Service

(Because these four associate directors manage the same kinds of responsibilities for different sectors of government, they are considered here as a group rather than individually.)

Major Responsibilities

o   Manage the development of the President's annual budget by the departments and agencies in the associate director's assigned areas of responsibility, reviewing individual submissions within OMB and in discussions with the leadership of the departments and agencies.

o   Participate in the development of major administration policy in the assigned area.

o   Oversee department and agency preparation of legislative proposals in accordance with the final budget message and administration policy.   Coordinate this function within the executive branch, consulting or negotiating with relevant legislators and Congressional committees as necessary.   Work with departments and agencies to see that their decisions, actions and day-to-day operations remain consistent with the content and direction of both policy and budget.

o   Clear legislative submissions and all administration testimony and other statements which have reference to, or policy implications for, the assigned areas of government activity.

Necessary Background, Experience, Personal Skills

Candidates for these jobs should demonstrate substantial,

hands-on experience in the operations of the federal government, preferably sharpened at the management level. In this respect, a previous associate director feels that "it is almost more important to understand the mechanisms of the government than the statutes." The positions require a strong sense of how policy is formed, framed in dollars-and-cents terms, and executed in a public sector context. They demand a comfortable grasp of economic principles. Beyond these, the associate director with the national security portfolio needs a firm grasp of foreign policy issues and international economic development, and should understand intelligence policy and procedures. Many occupants have had prior, first-hand experience in Congressional staff positions. One of them also recommends that future associate directors have advanced degrees in the social sciences, which "lend prestige to their decisions and clarity to their thinking." Finally, no one can assume these responsibilities without understanding thoroughly where the administration is coming from --and going.

Insight

One of the ironies of life at OMB, suggests a veteran associate director, is that "everybody thinks these jobs are wonderful, a terrific place to be, wonderful career enhancement. What they don't realize is that, if you're doing your job well here, you'll probably never get another one. Because you're not in a position where you can be doing favors and nice things for people--which is the way this town works." It doesn't work that way at OMB, she says. "There's a tension between doing your job well and making all these friends. You can't have it both ways. That's not what this agency is all about."

OMB can hardly ignore the political counterpoint that embroils agencies, interest groups and Congress, or the stakes and stakeholders involved. It deals constantly with all of them. Former director Bert Lance (1977-78) reflects this in calling the agency "the heartbeat of policy and the administration." But OMB works for the President in an important sense that the rest of the executive branch does not. It is answerable to the White House only. Its singleminded attention and energy focus on producing an annual budget shaped in the image of the administration's goals. And whatever the inevitable effects of political, fiscal and economic reality are on the development of the document and its final impact, OMB must see that government operations reflect the mandates laid down by the budget as a basic expression of policy and intent.

Each of the four "PADs" (program associate directors, to distinguish them from other associate directors) carries budget development and implementation responsibility for roughly a quarter of the federal departments and agencies. With individual staffs of about 70, they take the budget submissions of their agencies through the entire gamut--initial review, "passback" to the agencies, and final approval. In the implementation phase, they oversee their agencies' development of legislation and their adherence through the year to approved policy/budget directions. They clear testimony and other enunciations of policy relevant to their areas, wherever in the government they may originate.

The job entails regular consultation with department and agency leadership, normally at the level of head or deputy head or chairman; with OMB superiors; and with various elements in or associated with the executive office of the President. PADs find themselves in constant coordination, negotiation and mediation within the administration and with the Hill. "Most of my time," a former associate director recalls, "was consumed in very seriously addressing policy issues, either with my staff, or inter-agency meetings, or intra-White House meetings."

Daily decisions can easily number in the hundreds. Most are taken on a PAD's own authority; these can range from public service employment to State Department security to routine regulatory questions. More significant decisions go up the line as high as necessary; the budget of the Department of Housing and Urban Development, for example, might present the policy question of whether to approach the shortage of low-income rental housing through continued housing assistance payments and subsidizing of construction, or to move further toward the voucher method.

"I think the job is even more impossible now than when I had it because of the budget crunch," says Suzanne H. Woolsey, an associate director in 1977-80. "Clearly, the person needs a lot of endurance. You deal with a set of endemic problems that have to do with conflicts in values, and conflicts between doing good and having no money. The difficulty is to get people to look at the issues with sharp, analytical skills, to stop thinking about things in the same old way. These are incredibly tough issues, and I'm personally convinced that the only way you deal with them is to turn them on their side and look at them from a new angle."

Another perspective comes from Constance J. Horner, an associate director from 1983 to 1985 who now directs the Office of Personnel Management. "You have to understand what policy debate is like," she asserts, "and how the players function in it, so you can recognize when people feel or don't feel strongly and--most important--so you can recognize when an issue gets to the heart of how people believe politically, and when it's merely superficial. It's the capacity to know when to hold them and when to fold them, as the old country and western song says. You have to know when to push a policy very hard, and when to move off it because the array of political forces is such that it's just inadvisable to persist."

PADs thus need at least a good sixth, if not almost a seventh, sense about the flex and sway of the political landscape. In giving policy its shape, direction and momentum within the budget framework, however, do they ever make policy in their own right? "It's not written down anywhere that OMB can involve itself in pure policy issues," Horner points out, "but historically it has, and continues to do so. If an issue has a budgetary impact, this of course is an explicit power; otherwise, it's an informal power which rests upon the knowledge of the agency in question that people at OMB are closer than agency people are to people in the West Wing. That's not always the case, but enough of the case that the agencies are willing to share policy decisions with OMB, as a rule."

Former PADs speak enthusiastically about OMB's "superb" career staff, "the best in government." The six dozen or so professionals assigned to an associate director labor under large and increasing workloads with which the necessary extra resources have not kept pace. Asked how much the Gramm-Rudman deficit reduction exercise has added to this burden, a onetime PAD replies simply, "Oh, my God." Discussing staff, another says "they will do or die for any President. But they need to be appreciated, brought into important meetings and have their work valued and recognized. Since the associate director is so heavily reliant on the staff, that staff had better be pulling for the associate director. By and large, they will do that out of institutional loyalty, but it's very helpful if they can also develop personal loyalty."

What particular qualities of character and mind does it take to do these jobs? Those who have held them or know about them from close observation have a lot to say. Samples (all from former PADs, except where noted):

> "The most important criterion is really the willingness to be strong and not to cave....A lot of people are not willing to be unpopular, and the way to have people like you is to let the agencies do anything they want. It's very easy to be captured by these...pressures. But you should never forget that you work only for the

Presidency. You're the one who is supposed to pass along the tough decisions the agencies don't like to make....This agency's job is to look over their shoulders. You are the front line, the one who is giving instructions to agencies about how to go about getting there, what's going to move them toward the objectives and what isn't....The staff can give you a lot of advice...but the tough political calls are not their function."

"A very strong intellectual grounding in policy. I would not put anyone in that position who had not spent time on policy issues affecting the nation. That doesn't mean someone has to know particular policies. That's not relevant. What's relevant is the capacity to think in policy terms. It's very desirable to have someone...who's conversant with the history of policy debate even if it's in a non-related field."

"...There are two types of people who can succeed in this job--someone who is very politically sensitive and knows how to deal with the Hill and the agencies, or someone who is very analytic. The best is a combination of both. You have a pretty high-powered staff throwing a lot of information and data at you and trying to push you into a position usually against the agencies, and you have to be able to look at that critically." (Senate Appropriations subcommittee staffer)

"One of the keys to success...is to understand and account for the goals and interests of OMB as a career organization while at the same time representing the President and his policy and budget desires."

"Stress is a large concern. Not just any old person can make it. You have to be willing to give up your own life. You have to have a very strong sense of self, a lot of self-confidence....OMB is the place everybody loves to hate, everybody's whipping boy....It takes a very special person to be willing to do it."

Still another previous associate director, not cited in any of the foregoing, effectively mirrors such strains with this wry aside about life at OMB: "My husband is a lobbyist in Washington. He has told me that he is very glad I never took his name in marriage."

Key Relationships

Within the Agency

Reports to:

Director
Deputy Director

Works closely with:

Assigned career staff
Other associate directors

Outside the Agency

Economic Policy Council
Domestic Policy Council

Associate Director for Economics and Government:

Heads or deputy heads of the Departments of Justice, Treasury, Commerce, Transportation, and Housing and Urban Development; chairmen of several financial regulatory and other agencies.

Associate Director for Human Resources, Veterans and Labor:

Heads or deputy heads of the Departments of Agriculture, Health and Human Services, Labor, Education, and the Veterans Administration; and the heads of about 20 smaller agencies.

Associate Director for National Security and International Affairs:

Vice President, White House Chief of Staff, heads or deputy heads of Departments of Defense and State, National Security Council, Central Intelligence Agency, U.S. Information Agency, Arms Control and Disarmament Agency, and International Development Cooperation Agency

Associate Director for Natural Resources, Energy and Science:

Heads or deputy heads of Departments of Agriculture, Energy and Interior, Environmental Protection Agency, National Aeronautics and Space Administration, the Nuclear Regulatory Commission and other agencies

Outside the Federal Government

State and local officials and a broad range of private and other public sector organizations in most areas of U.S. society.

Associate Directors for Economics and Government Since 1973*

Administration	Name and Years Served	Present Position
Reagan	Carol T. Crawford 1985 - Present	Incumbent
Reagan	Constance J. Horner 1983 - 1985	Director Office of Personnel Management
Reagan	Annelise Anderson 1981 - 1983	Senior Research Fellow Hoover Institution Stanford, California
Carter	Roger Schlickeisen 1979	Not Available

Carter	Frank D. Raines 1978 - 1979	Managing Director Lazard, Freres and Company New York, New York
Carter	Dennis O. Green 1977 - 1978	General Auditor Ford Motor Company Dearborn, Michigan
Ford	Daniel P. Kearney 1976 - 1977	Principal Aldrich, Eastman and and Waltch Boston, Massachusetts
Nixon/Ford	Walter D. Scott 1973 - 1975	Professor of Management Kellogg Graduate School Of Management Northwestern University Evanston, Illinois

Associate Directors for Human Resources, Veterans, and Labor Since 1969

Administration	Name and Years Served	Present Position
Reagan	Jay Plager 1987 - Present	Incumbent
Reagan	Debra Steelman 1985 - 1987	Partner Epstein, Becker and Green Washington, DC
Reagan	John F. Cogan 1983 - 1985	Senior Fellow Hoover Institution Stanford, California
Reagan	Kenneth Clarkson 1982 - 1983	Not Available
Reagan	Donald W. Moran 1981 - 1982	Vice President Health and Sciences Research, Inc. Washington, DC

Carter	Gilbert S. Omenn 1980 - 1981	Professor and Dean School of Public Health University of Washington Seattle, Washington
Carter	Suzanne H. Woolsey 1977 - 1980	Partner-in-Charge Coopers and Lybrand Washington, DC
Ford	Dan L. McGurk 1975 - 1977	Private Investor Newport Beach, California
Nixon	Paul H. O'Neill 1972 - 1974	Chairman and CEO Aluminum Company of America Pittsburgh, Pennsylvania
Nixon	Richard P. Nathan 1969 - 1971	Professor Woodrow Wilson School Princeton University Princeton, New Jersey

Associate Directors for National Security and International Affairs Since 1969

Administration	Name and Years Served	Present Position
Reagan	L. Wayne Arny 1987 - Present	Incumbent
Reagan	Alton G. Keel, Jr. 1982 - 1986	Ambassador to NATO Brussels, Belgium
Reagan	William Schneider, Jr. 1981 - 1982	Not available
Carter	Edward R. Jayne II 1977 - 1981	Vice President Strategic Program Development McDonnell Douglas St. Louis, Missouri

Ford	Donald G. Oglivie 1974 - 1977	Executive Vice President American Bankers Association Washington, DC
Nixon	B. A. Bridgewater 1973 - 1974	President Brown Group, Inc. St. Louis, Missouri
Nixon	Kenneth W. Dam 1971 - 1973	Vice President IBM Corporation Armonk, New York
Nixon	James R. Schlesinger 1969 - 1971	Counselor in Residence Center for Strategic and International Studies Washington, DC

Associate Directors for Natural Resources, Energy and Science Since 1969

Administration	Name and Years Served	Present Position
Reagan	Robert K. Dawson 1987 - Present	Incumbent
Reagan	Randall E. Davis 1985 - 1987	Partner Jones, Day, Reavis, Pogue Washington, DC
Reagan	Frederick N. Khedouri 1981 - 1985	Managing Director Bear Stearns and Company Washington, DC
Carter	Katherine Schirmer 1980 - 1981	Not Available
Carter	Eliot R. Cutler 1977 - 1980	Partner Cutler and Stanfield Washington, DC

Ford	James L. Mitchell, II 1975 - 1977	Not Available
Nixon	Frank G. Zarb 1974 - 1975	Managing Director Lazard, Freres and Co. New York, New York
Nixon	John C. Sawhill 1973 - 1974	Partner McKinsey and Company Washington, DC
Nixon	William A. Morrill 1972 - 1973	President Mathtech, Inc. Princeton, New Jersey
Nixon	Donald B. Rice 1970 - 1972	President The RAND Corporation Santa Monica, California
Nixon	Maurice Mann 1969 - 1970	Chairman and CEO Pacific Stock Exchange San Francisco, California

*   The position of Associate Director for Economics and Government was created in 1973 as a result of a reorganization. The position assumed some responsibilities previously held by the Associate Director for Human Resources, Veterans and Labor and the Associate Director for Natural Resources, Energy and Science.

DIRECTOR
OFFICE OF PERSONNEL MANAGEMENT

Level II - Presidential Appointment with Senate Confirmation

Major Responsibilities

o   Function as chief personnel officer of the executive branch. Advise and consult with the President and his staff on government-wide personnel matters and, with them, design the key tenets and directions of administration personnel policy.

o   Develop detailed policy and apply it throughout the government's personnel management structure, making the major overall decisions in such areas as employee recruitment, examination, and training, and in performance standards, pay, and benefits.

o   Seek desirable legislative and other changes permitting the improvement of personnel policy and administration in the interests of better recruitment and greater productivity, economy, and employee satisfaction.

o   Speak for all facets of personnel policy to federal employees, the Congress and the public.

Necessary Background, Experience, Personal Skills

Candidates for this position need extensive knowledge of personnel administration, including senior-level work in benefits, compensation, recruitment and labor relations. General management background in large organizations would also be a useful additional qualification.

Insight

From more than one direction come predictions and advice about what the next director of OPM will face. The "major problem," in the view of a Congressional authority in this area of government, "is re-establishing some credibility with the work force." Federal employees are looking for "predictability" and "adherence to some kind of model," this observer says, "instead of saying 'we don't have any money so we're going to give you a two percent raise.'" Regardless of political party, the new director will have a "tremendous job" in restoring morale, because the work force has too long been seen "as a bunch of over-compensated, under-worked, pampered kids. The new director will have to show that this isn't the attitude any more." Alan K. Campbell, who directed OPM in 1978-81, agrees that the agency has "lost credibility with federal civil servants" and "must find a way back." He would undertake programs and policies which enhance the future of career employees. Further, he says, "the full potential of the Senior Executive Service has not been realized. Ways and means must be found to induce these senior career executives to assume ownership of the career system and provide leadership not only for the SES but for the promotion and improvement of the federal career system." Campbell would also "pay more attention to developing the bonus system through better performance evaluation."

At first glance, OPM's operations might seem to bear a certain resemblance to those of the industrial relations division of a large corporation. It is a service organization that handles personnel administration from the recruitment and training stage to retirement, with all the familiar accompanying concerns--labor relations, compensation schedules, benefit structures, grievance procedures, and special added features like overseas personnel management. But in administering the federal government's personnel system, additional considerations weigh in. OPM's director lives and works in a political climate unlikely to characterize private-sector personnel management. It's a context which has relevance for some of the significant decisions the director must make. Salary schedules and the money to pay them depend not very much on productivity and not at all on corporate profits, but on decisions by the U.S. Congress that sometimes interconnect with matters having little or nothing to do with federal employees. Other factors intrude, such as employment investigations that normally go well beyond similar processes outside of government. And, obviously, there is the sheer size of the federal work force.

Despite these notable differences between public and private sector personnel management, each can learn from the other. In particular, says Campbell, "the federal government needs to look at what the private sector has done in reducing the size of the work force and still retaining effectiveness." Future directors must also concentrate, he says, on some unfinished business addressed by the Civil Service Reform Act of 1978. "The CSRA attempted to de-emphasize the agency's regulatory role and makes its central mission the provision of service. That role change is still to be accomplished."

The regular work routine of this job takes the director into meetings around the government--with cabinet secretaries, assistant secretaries handling administrative and personnel responsibilities in the various agencies; with various legislative task forces; and with the cabinet council on management, the President's Council on Integrity and Efficiency, and the Emergency Preparedness Board, to name a few. The director mediates when an agency has an unusual or overriding personnel problem, and supervises OPM responses to Congressional queries about jobs for constituents. Among other recurring tasks are budget preparation and review, senior-level appointments within OPM, speeches, award ceremonies, and regular contact with labor unions representing federal employees.

No description of this job should omit mention of one further duty, simply because it can generate a lot of public attention and is frequently a tough call. When snowstorms or other severe weather conditions hit the capital, OPM must decide whether special report-to-work and dismissal hours for Washington's immense federal work force are necessary. Such decisions must be neither premature nor too late. If the guess is wrong, the price--in money and criticism--is high.

Key Relationships

Inside the Federal Government

Reports to: President

Works closely with:

Director, Office of Management and Budget
Director, Presidential Personnel
Administrative chiefs of departments and
agencies

Outside the Federal Government

Government employee unions and associations, such as American Federation of Government Employees, National Association of Retired Federal Employees; life and health insurance carriers, such as GEICO Corporation; insurance provider and consumer associations, such as Health Insurance Association of America, National Committee on Public Employee Pension Systems; minority groups

Directors of the Office of Personnel Management Since 1978*

Administration	Name and Years Served	Present Position
Reagan	Constance J. Horner 1985 - Present	Incumbent
Reagan	Donald J. Devine 1981 - 1985	Chairman Citizens fo America Washington, DC
Carter	Alan K. Campbell 1978 - 1981	Vice Chairman ARA Services, Inc. Philadelphia, Pennsylvania

* This position was created by the Civil Service Reform Act of 1978.

ADMINISTRATOR
GENERAL SERVICES ADMINISTRATION

Level III - Presidential Appointment with Senate Confirmation

Major Responsibilities

o   Direct a large, dispersed organization in the management of all federal property, records and communications systems.

o   Advise and assist the President and staff on significant policy issues arising in these areas, and recommend actions when necessary at those levels.

o   Manage the GSA administratively, including budget development and defense and key personnel decisions.

Necessary Background, Experience, Personal Skills

While well-tested business skills--in contracts, procurement, real estate and logistics management, labor negotiations, and accounting--provide good general grounding for this position, anyone taking on the assignment should also have run a big organization effectively or handled a senior management job. Some background in real estate acquisition and disposal helps.

Insight

A former GSA administrator calls the occupant of this job "the business manager of the government." As with the head of the Office of Personnel Management, there are rough comparisons with similar posts in the private sector. To some extent, the responsibilities of GSA's chief resemble those of the senior administrative executive in a large national corporation with a widely dispersed physical plant, complex telecommunications, vast supply requirements, hundreds of contracting relationships, and many thousands of employees.

"I expected a real challenge, and it was," says Ray Kline, who had the job during the Carter-Reagan transition in 1981 as well as in 1984 and knew its scope from previous career service in

GSA and NASA. In the policy-making area, his responsibilities extended to virtually everything GSA does--"property and information resources management, telecommunications, travel and procurement regulations, the archives program, management of the national stockpile (of strategic materials) and all the regulations attendant to those programs." There were some problems with procurement and with constraints on resources, he recalls, as well as in "dealing with the bureaucracy across the government" but he also makes the point that "the organization was generally very supportive in what we wanted to do." Another former occupant who had prior GSA experience and knew what to expect says simply that "someone from outside really knows nothing of what they're getting into."

In addition to its Washington headquarters, GSA operates through almost a dozen regional offices and through field activities nationwide. Four chief components, each with its own commissioner, provide GSA's key services. The Public Buildings Service designs, constructs, operates, maintains and protects several thousand federally-controlled buildings in the capital and around the nation. Correct use and disposition of these properties is the job of the Federal Property Resources Service, which also handles the stockpile of strategic and critical materials necessary to national defense. Everything from the rugs on a federal office floor to the trip of a federal official to Capitol Hill or Katmandu comes under the control or supervision of the Federal Supply Service. Finally, the Information Resources and Management Service coordinates federal purchase and use of data processing and telecommunications systems, and tries to improve the government's information management and record keeping.

Gerald P. Carmen, who ran GSA from 1981 to 1984, asserts that "you have to know the total goals of the agency and understand the limitations of cost frames and time frames." On this score, he says, "the training system is ineffective" and describes "difficulty in assigning targets within budget and time limitations and carrying them out" as a persistent GSA ailment. "Every problem seems to require a budgetary request, so the government ends up budgeting failures and starving successes." The right prescription, he thinks, "is the concept that money is finite, forcing you to set priorities."

One of those who has run this organization regrets that "GSA is not an agency which is on top of the priority list," a situation that makes it "difficult to get problems resolved." But another says "when I needed help, I got it. It's a matter of taking the reins and doing the job with a complete reliance on yourself." On managing GSA generally, Carmen remembers that "it took me a while to figure out that anyone can take a simple problem and make it

complex, but it's much harder to make a complex problem simple."
As administrator, he thinks he made a dent in such situations, but
warns that "the lesson is not in what we've done but how far
we've got to go. You really can't manage correctly without a
dream, an idea. Anything less than that and you become a trades-
man in an average job."

Key Relationships

Inside the Federal Government

Reports to: President

Works closely with:

Cabinet secretaries and agency directors and
administrators
Assistant secretaries for administration in departments
and agencies

Outside the Federal Government

Business and industry across a wide range, among
them real estate, construction, telecommunications,
management information systems and data processing,
contracting, office supply, office furnishings, and
security; AFL-CIO; American Subcontractors Association; Associated General Contractors of America;
Computer and Business Equipment Manufacturers
Association; Computer and Communications Industry
Association

Administrators of the General Services Administration Since 1969

Administration	Name and Years Served	Present Position
Reagan	John E. Alderson 1988 - Present	Incumbent
Reagan	Terrence Golden 1985 - 1988	Washington, DC

Reagan	Ray Kline (Acting) 1984	President National Academy of Public Administration Washington, DC
Reagan	Gerald P. Carmen 1981 - 1984	President & CEO Federal Asset Disposition Association Washington, DC
Reagan	Ray Kline (Acting) 1981	President National Academy of Public Administration Washington, DC
Carter	Rowland Freeman 1979 - 1981	Not Available
Carter	Joel Solomon 1977 - 1979	Deceased
Ford	Jack Eckerd 1975 - 1977	Clearwater, Florida
Nixon/Ford	Arthur Simpson 1972 - 1975	Deceased
Nixon	Robert Kunzig 1969 - 1972	Deceased

7

DEPARTMENT OF COMMERCE

Smallest of the cabinet departments in budget ($2.4 billion in fiscal 1988), Commerce is large in scope, diversity and in the impact it has on a great variety of people and institutions. While its most visible work may be in the areas of trade, oceans and atmospheres, and the census bureau's many studies of national life, the department's programs in other fields--such as communications and information--should not be underestimated.

Whichever party controls the administration, trade policy is certain to be near the top of the agenda, with the Commerce department centrally involved. Developing trade strategy, however, should be more than merely steering a course between the chief protagonists of the trade scenario--protectionists, free traders, supporters of an aggressive attack on the trade restrictive practices of other nations, and those who fear that this could damage valued foreign relationships. Tough as it is to try to reconcile such opposing views, the designers of successful trade policy will have to intensify their consideration of other factors as well.

For example, moving the trade problem toward solution also means carefully-thought-out, long-run education and labor policies that boost competitiveness, and trade negotiators whose longevity, accumulated experience and language skills begin to match those of their counterparts in other countries. It means a reduction of the debt of third-world countries--especially in Latin America--that, in strengthening their economies, allows them to buy more from the United States; and export control rules for dual-purpose technology that don't unnecessarily harm U.S. sales.

In an administration intending to address these various objectives in a coordinated way, the Department of Commerce should expect to find itself in closer collaboration with the departments of the Treasury, State, Labor, Education, Agriculture, and Defense, and with the U.S. Trade Representative and the White House.

Internally, the department and the administration will probably be forced to examine at some point in the near future whether a vital component like the National Oceanic and Atmospheric Administration would be better off in another department, or conceivably as an independent agency. Engaged almost entirely in scientific work, NOAA may be misplaced and undersung within a department of 38,500 employees whose basic roots are in trade and commerce. Two other highly important agencies, the Bureau of the Census and the Patent and Trademark Office, are reported to need better operational relationships with the department's leadership and better physical facilities.

DEPARTMENT OF COMMERCE

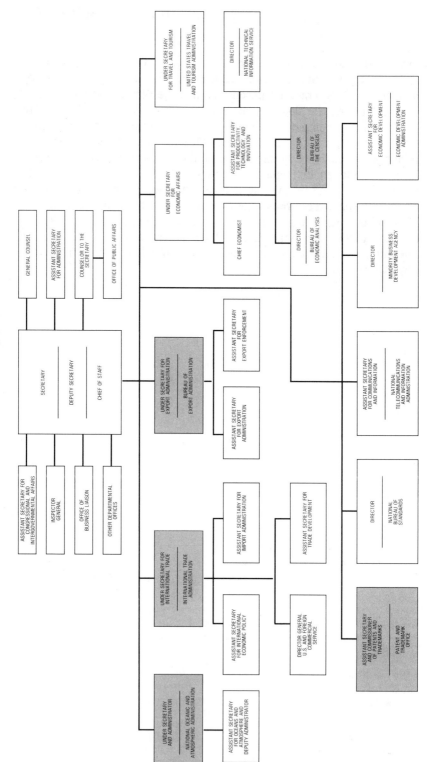

Shaded areas were selected as **Prune Book positions**

UNDERSECRETARY
EXPORT ADMINISTRATION

Level III - Presidential Appointment with Senate Confirmation

Major Responsibilities

o   Formulate and administer U.S. export control policy and the laws to carry it out, in accordance with the requirements of U.S. national security and foreign policy and with national economic needs. Enforce policy against trade boycotts.

o   Counsel the secretary in the design of policy, and coordinate it and its implementation within the department, at senior interagency levels, and with foreign governments. Consult with and advise the Congress.

o   Manage the interagency export control decision-making process with full recognition of the need for consensus in an environment where the principal agencies involved often hold strong and differing views that, unless fully reconciled, can weaken any decision.

o   Provide administrative, budget and personnel oversight to trade administration components.

Necessary Background, Experience, Personal Skills

This position needs experience and skills across a broad front. They include a knowledge of international economics, a background in international security affairs and foreign policy, and training in the law. Political skill and familiarity with Washington, a strong technical background, and management ability complete the list. "A good solid corporate chief operating officer could do it," says a qualified and interested source, "but he would also have to have Washington political background as well." This undersecretary will have to make export control decisions on matters that involve highly technical issues from the point of view of engineering and the physical sciences, and deal effectively with experts in those fields.

Insight

Establishment of this position in the fall of 1987 recognized the high degree of responsibility required by the management of export controls and the enforcement of anti-boycott law. It also marked the practical necessity of giving those responsible for these functions sufficient rank to make them at least the formal equal of their counterparts in other agencies. Before 1987, these duties were handled at the level of deputy assistant secretary and senior deputy assistant secretary.

Paul Freedenberg has been this new position's only incumbent to date. He defines export control policy in terms of three fundamental objectives. One of these, in the foreign policy area, is essentially the withholding of U.S. exports to modify the international behavior of foreign governments. "The squeeze that we put on Noriega, though it is not formal foreign policy control," was the best recent illustration of this kind of effort. Other steps have been the blocking of the Soviet gas pipeline to western Europe in order to influence Soviet behavior in Poland, and the ban on high technology products for oil and gas exploration to get Moscow to change its behavior in Afghanistan.

A second type of export control action, and the least often employed, aims at preventing "short supply." It ensures that the United States does not run short, or run out, of products and materials it needs to remain economically healthy.

By any measure, however, the national security area is the main operating arena for this undersecretary. At stake is the control of certain high-technology exports, based on the premise that much high-tech has a dual use, military as well as civilian. A good example is the supercomputer which can help build a better car, but also a better tank, missile or bomb. Since the days of the Cold War, the United States has led NATO and other high-technology producing countries in an effort to deny dual-use items to the Soviet Union and eastern European countries and, on a different level, to China.

The informal 16-nation international committee which discusses and decides on overall export control strategy and many individual export licensing applications is known as COCOM (Coordinating Committee on Multilateral Export Controls). "Dual-use technology needs careful watching and we need a very serious licensing program," says Freedenberg, who estimates annual U.S. individual validated export licenses at 100,000. He adds that 60% of American exports to western Europe are licensed, something not aimed directly at these U.S. friends and allies but rather to have a paper trail, to identify the organization or individual who was the initial recipient of an item if later it turns up in unintended hands.

According to a representative of a leading business and industrial association with whom we talked, 40% of all U.S. exports "need some kind of prior approval" before leaving the country. "That's $70 billion worth of trade." Thus, this observer feels, the undersecretary holds "a really critical job." Next time around, "business will pay a lot of attention to who the candidates are." In this view, whoever takes on the job will encounter a good deal of legitimate debate on the question of what constitutes a strategic export. Technologies once critical no longer are, but remain on the list because "people in charge didn't have the power and standing to act." Doubts about whether something could go out without a license were therefore semi-automatically resolved in favor of licensing it. Now, at a time when exports are starting to boom, the next administration should generate "sensible policy to deregulate products that are no longer strategic" and appoint an undersecretary who can accomplish this and not engage in a "crusade against the Russians using American business essentially as the lance."

Individual license matters get a lot of discussion at the technical level, in Washington and at COCOM in Paris, where one or another member of the Washington staff can be found almost continually. It might be machine tools one week, computers the next, fiber optics the week after. The undersecretary goes to Paris if major issues require it and, in any case, for regular COCOM meetings about twice yearly. While the State Department takes the diplomatic lead in such activity, the undersecretary in this job negotiates with other governments to get cooperation in enforcing the controls, both bilaterally and through COCOM. "It's very rare," says the manufacturing group source quoted earlier, "that you'll have people making high-level policy that can understand the technological issues involved. It's astounding, the decisions that have to be made at (those levels) with very, very limited knowledge of what those technologies are."

In Washington, coordination of export control policy is an extensive, complicated, time-consuming exercise. Freedenberg currently spends a third of his working life in this interagency effort, which he calls "the real hard thing" about the job. It is "very much an interagency system" and because export administration is "a very sexy subject," everyone wants to get into the act. Although Commerce is clearly the lead agency, he says, "it still has constant turf battles to keep that lead and to keep the policy flowing. Frequently policies are more difficult to negotiate within the U.S. government than outside."

It's a wry complaint heard often in agencies with foreign policy involvement. In this case, it means that the undersecretary must earn the respect of counterparts and of experts in various technical disciplines, and defend positions inside and outside the department in acceptable terms of reference. An inability to do so makes a drift of authority elsewhere inevitable.

In export control, State and Defense are the other big players; Freedenberg rates State not as "turfy" as some other agencies, and Defense as "constantly kibitzing the process." He has had to play a "fairly big role in reconciling our differences. That is not inherently bad. It just means that the process is somewhat adversarial, but we move along." How this typically happens was sketched by Walter J. Olson, Jr. deputy assistant secretary for trade and export administration in 1983-86. A company in New York might come in with a specific license application for export, say, to the People's Republic of China. "They're saying, look, we're going to lay off 100 people if we can't get this through," Olson says. "It would come into us, we would have to go over to Defense for coordination, maybe to State, and then over to COCOM for review. You're looking for ways to speed up that application, to see whether, if Defense does not buy off on it, for example, there are some alternative conditions they could live with. So you're negotiating back and forth on these things."

When not engaged in this kind of two-continent coordinating duty, Freedenberg spends his time managing--"in which the bureaucratic day-to-day side is just getting your people to do the job they are hired to do"--and trying to improve such internal systems as the computerization of licensing data. The job's often controversial nature, he says, also means substantial work with the Congress. As for international travel and meetings, he does less than his predecessors ("because I have just had to do more managing") but they still take 15-20% of his time.

What are the risks in this job? Freedenberg sees several. One is the danger of perceived conflict of interest, if the undersecretary seems to favor business interests at the expense of national security. "Your job is national security, but Commerce's natural constituency is the business community, so you must be careful not to speak just for business. You must be ready to say no when it's appropriate." Related to this is the possibility of too-great restriction of profitable and efficient companies which "lose their international markets because you have over-regulated them." Another risk is "naivete--not knowing the ball game." Here, Freedenberg explains, the problem is frequent turn-over in positions like his. "You need to know that most of your foreign counterparts...have been around for a long time," in one key instance for 30 years. Finally, there is a risk "that any bureaucracy can overwhelm its administrator if he does not know what he is doing."

One of his predecessors has the final word on risk, however: "It's a job that could kill you, but from a substantive point of view, it was very interesting."

Key Relationships

Within the Department

Reports to: Secretary

Works closely with:

Deputy Secretary
Undersecretary, International Trade

Outside the Department

U.S. Trade Representative
Deputy Undersecretary, Trade Security Policy, Department of Defense
Deputy Secretary, Department of State
Deputy Assistant Secretary, International Trade Controls, Department of State
Assistant Secretary, International Security Policy, Department of Defense
Assistant Secretary, Defense Programs, Department of Energy
Commissioner, U.S. Customs Service, Department of the Treasury

Outside the Federal Government

Individual international and U.S. corporations and industry associations in such sectors as aerospace, data processing systems, health and communications; trade associations, such as American Association of Exporters and Importers, Council of Defense and Space Industry Associations, Computer and Communications Industry Association, American League for Exports and Security Assistance, American Businesses

for International Trade; and trade and diplomatic
officials of other countries

Undersecretaries for Export Administration Since 1987*

Administration	Name and Years Served	Present Position
Reagan	Paul Freedenberg 1987 - Present	Incumbent

Held Position of Deputy Assistant Secretary for Export Administration**

Reagan	Vincent F. DeCain 1986 - 1988	Deputy Assistant Secretary Technology Transfer Control Department of State
Reagan	Walter J. Olson 1983 - 1986	President Walter J. Olson & Associates Washington, DC
Reagan	Bohdan Denysyk 1981 - 1983	Senior Vice President Global USA Washington, DC
Carter	Eric L. Hirschhorn 1980 - 1981	Bishop, Cook, Percell & Reynolds Washington, DC

Held Position of Deputy Assistant Secretary for Export Enforcement**

Reagan	William V. Skidmore 1987 - Present	Deputy Assistant Secretary Export Enforcement Department of Commerce

Regan	Theodore W. Wu	Partner
	1982 - 1987	Lewis, D'Amato,
		Brisbois & Bisgaard
		Washington, DC

Held Position of Deputy Assistant Secretary for Trade Regulation**

Carter	Stanely J. Marcuss	Partner
	1977 - 1980	Milbank, Tweed, Hadley
		& McCloy
		Washington, DC

Held Position of Director of the Office of Export Administration**

Nixon/Ford	Rauer Meyer	Not Available
	1969 - 1977	

*   This position was created in 1987 by a statutory provision in the Export Administration Act of 1985.

**   Prior to the creation of the Undersecretary for Export Administration, the primary responsibility for the export function in the Department of Commerce was lodged in these positions. These positions reported to the Undersecretary for International Trade position which held responsibility for both the export and import functions in the Department.

UNDERSECRETARY
INTERNATIONAL TRADE

Level III - Presidential Appointment with Senate Confirmation

Major Responsibilities

o   Manage federal programs grouped under the International Trade Administration (ITA) to assist the development of non-agricultural U.S. international trade, and to apply anti-dumping and counter-vailing duty laws and certain other import controls.

o   Supervise continual ITA monitoring and analysis of world economic conditions and of international markets, and advise on the development and execution of U.S. international economic and trade policy.   Coordinate closely with the negotiating efforts of the U.S. Trade Representative.   Administer the activities of the U.S. and Foreign Commercial Service through its director general.

o   Oversee budget functions of the International Trade Administration.   Work with the Congress to explain and promote administration of international economic and trade policies.

Necessary Background, Experience, Personal Skills

The best-equipped candidate for this position is likely to be a senior executive in a large company, probably its chief executive officer, with significant international background.   One qualified outside observer partly summarized this requirement as "experience selling things overseas."   While lawyers can perform well in the job, one former undersecretary warns that they usually lack the requisite management and leadership skills developed in a corporate career.   Another, however, would lean towards a lawyer because of "the importance of the regulatory issues."   Familiarity with the federal government and ability in a principal foreign language are excellent, though not essential, assets.

Insight

Until the fall of 1987, the responsibilities of this undersecretary included licensing and enforcement authority in the export of sensitive technology, such as dual-purpose computers. The job also had oversight of anti-boycott compliance rules. These export functions are now the province of the Undersecretary for Export Administration. In revising the structure, the Congress was persuaded that a single individual could not simultaneously try to promote U.S. sales in foreign markets and defend national security interests through export restrictions.

This split in responsibilities, says Bruce Smart, ITA undersecretary from 1985 to mid-1988, "adds another critical relationship that must be managed" in this position. That's because both undersecretaries must coordinate policy so that one will not be restraining U.S. exports to a country where the other is attempting to open up or expand U.S. markets. Other effects of the 1987 reorganization are felt by U.S. exporting industries, which no longer have what Smart calls "one-stop shopping on trade issues," and by the department's trade staff overseas, which now must serve two bosses.

The undersecretary oversees ITA activities in four substantive areas, each run by deputies at the assistant secretary level. The Office of International Economic Policy divides the world into four regions, examining trade and investment issues and collecting market and other economic data in each, on a region-wide and country basis. The information thus gathered and analyzed assists the development of U.S. economic policy toward individual nations as well as in multinational contexts.

Second, in the area of trade development, ITA aims at strengthening the ability of U.S. business and industry to sell its products around the world. It conducts a trade development program that among other services offers industry-by-industry analysis and promotion advice. This office houses several other trade responsibilities. It is the source of data and analysis on U.S. industry, on U.S. trade, and on foreign investment in the United States. Through individual industry advisory committees, the trade development office monitors U.S. industry views on trade and trade negotiation issues that, for example, help to form U.S. positions in periodic multilateral trade negotiations such as the current "Uruguay" round.

ITA's third basic assignment is to administer laws governing the import of manufactured and agricultural imports sold at prices that put domestic producers at a harmful disadvantage, or which could damage industries essential to national security. The softwood lumber dispute with Canada, involving about $2 billion in annual imports to the United States, is a good recent case in point. ITA was heavily involved in investigating complaints by the U.S. lumber industry that Canada was subsidizing its exporters. Robert E. Herzstein, undersecretary in 1980-81, believes this "very technical regulatory function" should be a "central concern in looking at people to fill this job." Part of the undersecretary's task in this area, he thinks, is to shield staff members who handle import cases from "excessive political pressures" from various quarters that otherwise result in a politicized program which "loses its respectability for U.S. industry and foreign governments." This, in turn, destroys an important effort--"to demonstrate to the world that international trade can be conducted according to the rules."

Administering these anti-dumping and countervailing duty regulations can be complicated by the role of the U.S. Trade Representative. The Department of Commerce has clear authority in this regulatory area, but the trade representative has an obvious interest in major cases. If an issue is to be settled by international negotiation rather than unilateral decision, the trade representative, who has the negotiating responsibility, wants to be involved. A different sort of problem arises on the trade policy front. There, the trade representative is supposed to make decisions based on the conclusions of the Trade Policy Review Group, of which the undersecretary is a member. In developing and analyzing policy, the trade representative needs to use Commerce's considerably greater resources in areas like trade data and census statistics, but sometimes tends not to seek input at the higher, decision-making level. To maintain a role in trade policy, the undersecretary has to stay informed on when and why ITA staff are providing assistance to the trade representative.

For reasons like these, "there gets to be quite a bit of tension between the undersecretary and the trade representative," Herzstein says. He thinks this represents a "defect" in the system, and that there should be "one trade department." Meanwhile, it is essential in his view for the undersecretary to "interact gracefully but firmly" with the trade representative and staff.

The fourth area of ITA responsibility is operation of the U.S. and Foreign Commercial Service, which designs and distributes services and products geared to keeping U.S. exporters and the international commercial world supplied with updated marketing information. In activities linked to the goals of trade development, it promotes U.S. products and runs a number of similar supportive operations to advance U.S. trade, including fairs and exhibitions overseas. "Right now," says a senior official of a prominent national business association, the foreign commercial service "is probably underfunded. They still haven't got the kind of real-time computer linkages between the U.S. commercial and foreign commercial services, so that U.S. exporters with an interest can get real-time information about where there are potential markets."

Frank A. Weil, who served in 1977-79 in the then-existing position of Assistant Secretary for Trade and Industry, thinks previous federal government exposure is important for this job. Like others we talked with, he stresses "experience in running a large organization," which numbered 2,500 during his tenure. He and Smart both say they spent substantial time in regularly-scheduled meetings. In fact, Smart points out, the position is "very much oriented toward interagency coordination" in which the undersecretary's most frequent partners are the State Department's undersecretary for economics and assistant secretary for economic and business affairs and both deputy U.S. trade representatives. "You also have a very active role in the Trade Policy Review Group in coordinating the government's overall trade policy," he says. These relationships require "an immense amount of attention and work," Smart warns, as well as team players who are not "turf oriented" --qualities on which Weil and Herzstein also put a high premium.

To play the interagency game effectively, the occupant of this job "has to be able to grasp some complex issues--but quickly," says an informed representative of a manufacturing constituent group. "Once you get into the multilateral trade negotiations issues, and problems related to third-world debt and export credits, you need to feel at home. Otherwise, you'll get lost in interagency dealings, because the State and Treasury departments will know those issues."

Smart suggests that the next newcomer to this job get into full stride early. "People need to view you as a more-than-adequate second to the secretary or you won't have the necessary influence," something that is equally true with the Congress. "House members are usually delighted to have an undersecretary call them. Senators often want the secretary. But if you need a Senator, you have to figure out how to get to him and get him to deal with you." The manufacturing constituent group source mentioned earlier has similar advice for dealing with the business sector. "If businessmen don't feel they're being listened to, or that they're being talked to instead of talked with and not getting a fair hearing, they might go to the secretary or deputy secretary. And those guys' plates are full already."

This observer goes on to say that this "extremely important" job is the one federal position where U.S. industry would like to feel it has an advocate in the making of foreign policy. "It's our one shot into the sub-cabinet level where someone could be looking out for the concerns of domestic manufacturers."

The job is an unusually visible one, attracting more press interest than might casually be assumed. Further, a former undersecretary says, trade associations and foreign governments lobby the position hard. With big money at stake, they spend big money "protecting their interests," and "generating a lot of pressure that you cannot simply ignore." Remember, too, advises this veteran, that one of the "largest, most important and least represented" constituencies of the job is the American consumer, whose interests cannot remain neglected.

Key Relationships

Within the Department

Reports to: Secretary

Works closely with:

Deputy Secretary
Undersecretary, Export Administration

Outside the Department

Undersecretary, Economic and Agricultural Affairs, Department of State
Assistant Secretary, Economic and Business Affairs, Department of State
Assistant Secretary, International Affairs, Department of the Treasury
U.S. Trade Representative and deputies
Economic Policy Council, Executive Office of the President
Senior Director, International Economic Affairs, National Security Council
Undersecretary, International Affairs and Commodity Programs, Department of Agriculture
Undersecretary, Department of Labor
Assistant Secretary, International Security Policy, Department of Defense

Outside the Federal Government

All major trade and manufacturing associations, such as National Association of Manufacturers, American Textile Manufacturers Institute, American Iron and Steel Institute, Electronic Industries Association, American Association of Exporters and Importers; individual companies marketing products abroad; labor unions; and lobbyists of foreign governments

Undersecretaries for International Trade Since 1969

Administration	Name	Present Position
Reagan	W. Allen Moore 1988 - Present	Incumbent
Reagan	Bruce Smart 1985 - 1988	Upperville, Virginia
Reagan	Lionel Olmer 1981 - 1985	Attorney Paul, Weiss, Rifkind, Wharton and Garrison Washington, DC
Carter	Robert E. Herzstein 1980 - 1981	Partner Arnold and Porter Washington, DC
Carter	Frank A. Weil* 1977 - 1979	Chairman Abacus and Associates New York, New York
Ford	Leonard S. Matthews** 1976 - 1977	President American Association of Advertising Agencies New York, New York
Ford	Travis Reed** 1975 - 1976	Not Available

Nixon/Ford	Tilton H. Dobbin** 1973 - 1975	Owings Mills, Maryland
Nixon	Andrew E. Gibson** 1972	Not Available
Nixon	Harold B. Scott** 1971 - 1972	Not Available
Nixon	Robert McLellan** 1970 - 1971	Not Available
Nixon	Kenneth N. Davis, Jr.** 1969 - 1970	Not Available

*   Held position as Assistant Secretary for Industry and Trade.

**   Held position as Assistant Secretary for Domestic and International Business.

UNDERSECRETARY
OCEANS AND ATMOSPHERE

Level III - Presidential Appointment with Senate Confirmation

Major Responsibilities

o   Supervise the operations of the National Oceanic and Atmospheric Administration, a five-component agency broadly engaged in studying and reporting on the earth's marine waters and resources, its atmospheric, space and sun environments, and its weather. With the secretary, develop and articulate the policy guiding these operations.

o   Seek to assure the efficient and timely collection, analysis, and provision of data, and of predictive and commercially applicable information, about the fields under study. Maintain and improve the agency's computerized storage of information.

o   Testify on and otherwise represent agency policy, activities and resource needs to the Congress. Take the lead in developing and negotiating the agency's budget. Oversee administrative and personnel management.

Necessary Background, Experience, Personal Skills

A science, engineering or other technical background is critical in leading this scientific agency, as well as in understanding and giving shape and direction to its work. It lends credibility to the advocacy of the agency's interests and needs with the Congress and constituency groups, and helps in managing relationships with a wide array of scientists in industry, commerce, agriculture and research. The job also calls for considerable political skill, and for ability in analysis, management and public affairs.

Insight

Even a five-word summary of NOAA's activities--weather, satellites, research, fish and oceans--effectively conveys the sweep of its services, from the ocean floor to space and around the world.

On a given day, the agency might be found hatching turtle's eggs or measuring seawater pollution, studying environmental data from near-space or examining coral diseases, archiving some of the huge amount of data it collects or trying to figure out better ways to process and use it. In between, it might be pursuing the task of persuading Washington that its under-funded weather service needs help, or trying to improve itself on other scientific fronts where it needs better information to do the expanding job expected of it.

On an annual budget of about $1.5 billion, NOAA charts the world's oceans and U.S. coastal waters, profiles and maps sea floors, protects marine fisheries and other living resources of the ocean, predicts weather, and studies conditions in several environments which closely affect the earth. The consumers of the information it produces range from farmers, airline pilots and rocket booster manufacturers to sea bed mining engineers, fishermen, environmentalists and populations not only of American seacoasts but of countries everywhere.

The federal government itself is a key user of what NOAA produces. That is but one of the reasons why the undersecretary, among other duties, sits on interagency coordinating bodies in such areas as oceans and atmosphere, whales, and acid rain. Apart from that, the Congress takes more of the job's working time outside the office than anything else, especially on fisheries and commercial satellite issues. The undersecretary attends many substantive and ceremonial events of constituent groups, and is a frequent public speaker and lecturer; one of the most popular subjects is the weather.

In some respects, the most problematical of the several atmospheres NOAA deals with surrounds the agency itself. There are two aspects to this, political and organizational. The first, familiar to many senior federal executives, relates to conflicting views and objectives in the Congress about the diverse and economically significant areas of the undersecretary's responsibility. These opposing Congressional currents, of course, reflect the aims of constituent groups, the personal political inclinations of members--or both. Typical of this kind of situation, where the undersecretary's political dexterity can be severely tested, is the controversial issue of commercial whaling, where the Congress has been known simultaneously to consider one bill to ban it completely, and another to permit it for Eskimos. A variant on this sort of thing occurs when, in addition to Congressional positions, other agencies whose functions overlap some of NOAA's take different or opposing positions along the spectrum of a given issue.

"It can cause many conflicts when political philosophies on

the same subjects are different," says John V. Byrne, who held the job in 1981-84 when its title was administrator of NOAA. "The job," says Anthony J. Calio, undersecretary in 1985-87, "is politically a hot box," and required "more political sensitivity than I thought I needed." In many cases, he says, the undersecretary is put into difficult situations. That, he adds, however, goes with the territory and "if you can't stand the stress, don't take the job."

Organizationally, NOAA's problem as described by Byrne is a more particular one. "Prior to this administration," he points out, "NOAA was almost an independent agency. Now it is part of Commerce," where in his view it doesn't belong. "It's a science agency in a department whose primary function is commerce and international trade. That makes communication difficult." Byrne notes further that, on budget questions, NOAA officials negotiate with the economics and government section of the Office of Management and Budget, "when they should deal with the science people." In the existing situation, he thinks the undersecretary should try to give more systematic attention to educating the secretary and the department "about the value of NOAA in language they understand."

Key Relationships

Within the Department

Reports to: Secretary

Works closely with:

Deputy Secretary
Undersecretary, International Trade
Assistant Secretary, Congressional and
    Intergovernmental Affairs
Director, National Bureau of Standards
General Counsel

Outside the Department

Science Advisor to the President
Administrator, National Aeronautics and
    Space Administration
Assistant Secretary, Oceans and International
    Environmental and Scientific Affairs, Department
    of State

Administrator, Environmental Protection Agency

Outside the Federal Government

Green Peace, Sierra Club and other environmental and marine animal protective organizations; Coastal States Organization; National Ocean Industries Association, National Fisheries Institute, Agricultural Research Institute, Marine Technology Association and other groups representing fishing, farmer, agribusiness, oceanographic and meteorological interests; and scientific organizations in other disciplines

Undersecretaries for Oceans and Atmosphere Since 1969

Administration	Name and Years Served	Present Position
Reagan	William Evans 1988 - Present	Incumbent
Reagan	Anthony J. Calio 1985 - 1987	Senior Vice President Planning Research Corp. McLean, Virginia
Reagan	John V. Byrne* 1981 - 1984	President Oregon State University Corvallis, Oregon
Carter	Richard A. Frank* 1977 - 1981	President Population Services International Washington, DC
Nixon/Ford/ Carter	Robert M. White 1965 - 1977	President National Academy of Engineering Washington, DC

* Held position under title of Administrator of the National Oceanic and Atmospheric Administration.

ASSISTANT SECRETARY AND COMMISSIONER PATENTS AND TRADEMARKS

Level IV - Presidential Appointment with Senate Confirmation

Major Responsibilities

o   Supervise the examination and processing of patent and trademark applications currently totaling 138,000 annually, and the issuance of about 80,000 design, plant and utility patents and 56,000 trademarks each year.

o   Maintain a scientific library and public files available for application research. Manage other operations responsible for hearing appeals from applicants, compiling an official weekly notice of patents and trademarks issued, and selling printed copies. Take a leading role in U.S. cooperation with other nations in patent and trademark policy.

o   Direct the patent and trademark office, whose staff includes 1,450 patent examiners. Provide budget, personnel and other administrative oversight for the office.

Necessary Background, Experience, Personal Skills

The consensus appears to be that training and experience as a patent lawyer, and reputation in the field, are imperative for good performance and credibility in this position. At least one view holds, however, that candidates for the job should come out of industry, with "a lot of years of fairly heavy management experience" that a patent lawyer would lack. Finding a combination of these backgrounds might be difficult, but not impossible. It helps to have a familiarity with intellectual property law and the 35 countries and private organizations involved with it, as well as with the executive branch and the Congress. The assistant secretary's horizons should be wide enough to allow an appreciation of the relationship between patent and trademark procedure and the national economy.

Insight

Gerald J. Mossinghoff, who held this post in 1981-85, is certain the Senate would not have confirmed him in it if he had not been a practicing patent lawyer earlier in his career and an adjunct university professor teaching patent law at the time of his nomination. "Patent law is like a fraternity," he says. "You have to be a member to be accepted." Mossinghoff does suggest that--if it didn't prejudice a candidate's nomination--"you could sacrifice some patent law knowledge for experience in how the government works, because that is essential."

But Donald J. Quigg, the current assistant secretary (since 1985), feels strongly that a combination of patent law and solid management background is the most essential. With a staff of 3,500 and three labor unions in the picture, "there are management considerations here" to which a patent lawyer without corporation management experience is less attuned. And Mossinghoff himself makes some of these considerations clear. For him, two of the big management challenges were the budget process, "which is horrendous," and the patent examiners' union, "which is really strong." Telling an oft-heard story from the budget battlefront, he says the office would submit a budget to the Department of Commerce and the Office of Management and Budget, each of which would "tear it apart," requiring him to "go through the process of getting it back piece by piece. As for the examiners' union, it is not allowed to bargain on wages and fringes, and "likes to file grievances over small things," Mossinghoff says. The career staff, he adds, is "by and large, very good. They want to be led, they want some focus and direction," and they respond to a "hands-on manager."

A more general management problem for the patent office is clearly its antiquated system of filing by hand the approximately 28 million documents it stores and makes available to those researching prospective patent or trademark applications. About four years ago, work began on computerizing and automating the office, but this $400-500 million undertaking has run into problems and won't be ready, says Quigg, until 1994. It currently takes about 20 months to review and issue a patent, and much longer for proposals in specialties like biotechnology, where the first "transgenic non-human mammal"--a mouse--was patented in the spring of 1988.

One reason for such delays, says C. Marshall Dann, who ran the office in 1974-77 is "the continued problem of attracting high quality people as patent examiners." Their relatively low salaries have reportedly put a severe crimp in efforts to hire molecular biologists who can be schooled as patent examiners in the burgeoning biotechnology field. "It takes a long time to train them," Quigg says. As of spring, 1988 about 14,000 biotechnology patent applications were pending. The patent office has taken criticism about its processing delays, seen as significantly holding back U.S. progress in such promising but competitive areas.

"This office is a bit more independent than other agencies in Commerce," Quigg notes, "because what we do is so different." He concentrates on management, but attends "a lot of policy meetings," sees OMB regularly and, like Mossinghoff before him, spends "a fair amount" of time on the Hill. He does most of the testifying on intellectual property issues and, in most instances, thinks the relationship with the Congress is a good one. He does not get involved much with other agencies, but "we work a lot in the international field" in places like Geneva. The job also levies a sizeable public speaking requirement.

In 1995, the patent and trademark office's fees will cover 85-90% of its costs. If he were in the job at that point, Quigg would raise fees further to cover the remaining costs, persuade the Congress to establish the office as an independent government corporation, "get us out of the bureaucracy and have us operate as a business." This would bring several advantages, in his view. It would free the office from "micromanagement," allow the corporation to float short-term bonds to maintain the computerized data systems that are coming, and permit it to issue longer-term instruments to fund a "secure" headquarters. This would replace the 13 non-secure buildings which now house the office in a Virginia suburb of Washington.

Consequences of failure in this job? "Unless you carry out the objective of improving the quality of the products we put out," Quigg warns, "the patent system could go down the drain." He emphasizes that, in the 1960s and 1970s, many issued patents were contested in court and "very few were found to be valid." Litigation costs are "so extreme" that issuing patents without the strong probability that they can be sustained later "is a menace."

Without patents, Mossinghoff reminds us, "we would have no innovations, particularly in manufacturing and pharmaceuticals." In fields like medicine and intellectual property, there are "new developments all the time. The patent office is complex. You must really understand the issues from a legal and technical standpoint. It's a very important job." Dann takes the same view. The work is vital, he says, because "it fosters technical development. We have been falling behind technologically, and the patent office can help us get back to where we were."

Key Relationships

Within the Department

Reports to: Secretary

Works closely with:

Deputy Secretary
Director, National Bureau of Standards

Outside the Department

Assistant Attorney General, Anti-Trust Division,
Department of Justice
Administrator, Food and Drug Administration, Department of Health and Human Services
Deputy Assistant Secretary, International Finance
and Development, Department of State
Counselor, Multilateral Trade Negotiations, Office of
the U.S. Trade Representative

Outside the Federal Government

Inventors and inventor groups, such as Intellectual
Property Owners, Inc., National Patent Council; Patent
Law Division of the American Bar Association and
other bar associations; major manufacturing associations, such as National Manufacturers Association,
Pharmaceutical Manufacturers Association; consumer
groups, such as National Consumers League; and
patent law associations

Assistant Secretaries and Commissioners of Patents and Trademarks Since 1969

Administration	Name and Years Served	Present Position
Reagan	Donald J. Quigg 1985 - Present	Incumbent

Reagan	Gerald J. Mossinghoff 1981 - 1985	President Pharmaceutical Manufacturers Assn. Washington, DC
Carter	Sidney Diamond 1979 - 1981	Not Available
Carter	Donald W. Banner 1978 - 1979	Not Available
Carter	Lutrelle F. Parker 1977 - 1978 (Acting)	Not Available
Nixon/Ford/ Carter	C. Marshall Dann 1974 - 1977	Of Counsel Dann, Dorfman, Herrell and Skillman Philadelphia, Pennsylvania
Nixon	Robert Gottschalk 1972 - 1973	Not Available
Nixon	William E. Schuyler, Jr. 1969 - 1971	Not Available

DIRECTOR
BUREAU OF THE CENSUS

Level V - Presidential Appointment with Senate Confirmation

Major Responsibilities

o Lead the Bureau of the Census in activities designed to count and profile the nation's people and institutions accurately, objectively and cost-effectively.

o Provide this information to public and private institutions and organizations, including the Congress and components of the executive branch, for use in analysis, judgments, decisions and actions across an extremely broad range of economic and political activity.

o Protect the integrity of the bureau and its reputation for objectivity and reliability. Oversee administrative management of the bureau.

Necessary Background, Experience, Personal Skills

Good executive skills and sensitivity to the integrity of the statistics assembled by the census bureau are the primary requisites in directing it. While a statistical background is not strictly necessary, the job calls for good data skills. The director should have some experience in analyzing or using census products, understand their application to public and private decisions and use, and be able to explain them and discuss their merits and limitations. Business, government or education are all backgrounds where that kind of experience might have developed.

Insight

The world's first census apparently took place in China, well back in the B.C. era. In those days, census takers didn't rely on population samples. They tried to count *everyone*.

In 1990, in a much more complicated world with vastly greater populations, the United States will conduct its 21st consecutive,

Constitutionally-mandated ten-year census. That, too, will count everyone--actually, people plus housing characteristics. But it is only part of the contemporary census bureau scene. Nearing the 200th anniversary of the first U.S. census, the bureau counts and measures a great deal more, not only every ten years, but continually. Having pioneered the technique of sampling, the bureau collects detailed information on scores of subjects by surveying comparatively small and carefully chosen segments of society that depict the whole. Beyond population and housing, the bureau's component operations reach into U.S. society to look at such dimensions of the national existence as income, foreign trade, industrial growth, agriculture, and state and local government.

Surveys based on sampling are the building blocks of many of the approximate 250 bureau programs which the director now oversees. The programs vary widely in staff and funding--from 15 to 200 people, and anywhere from a million dollars to 20 or 30 million. Each requires a careful mesh of people, organization, a survey instrument, timing, data collection, compilation and reporting. The objects of these exercises range widely, from individuals, institutions, and businesses to farms, ranches and government entities. The sponsors vary from survey to survey, as do the quantity or quality factors being measured, and the sensitivities that each arouses.

Together, they provide an immense range of statistical and other informational products. Yet few people fully understand their importance for the political, economic and social life of the country, and to the countless public and private decisions made every day that affect every citizen. The list of consumers of bureau output is long and astonishingly diverse--city and regional planners, university and industrial researchers, developers, genealogists, marketing research firms, banks contemplating new branches, supermarket chains, churches, labor unions, and governments at all levels, to name a few.

Of all the programs headed by the bureau, the decennial census is the largest and most important. As current bureau chief John G. Keane says, "it provides the foundation for democracy in this country by allowing for truly representative government." Because of its importance in drawing the lines that make up Congressional and state legislative districts, the decennial census can be highly controversial on issues ranging from whom is counted and how, to the published results--which, after the 1980 census, were the subject of more than 50 lawsuits. Estimates of the cost of the 1990 census currently are running at about $2.6 billion, nearly a 50% increase from 1980 in current dollars. Of this and other bureau programs, Daniel B. Levine, who was acting director in 1979 and 1981 and deputy director in between, says the director must be sure to "produce effective statistics in anticipation of today's policy needs, not yesterday's, as well as think about tomorrow's."

Although the census takes place only every ten years, the bureau works on it constantly in the interim. Dress rehearsals for 1990 are just about completed, and a 21st century census planning group for the ten-year census already exists. Keane, bureau director since 1984, warns that the next director could be frustrated by his inability to shape this next census. "Not only are the decisions already made on the criteria and number of people, where they will be and what they will do and the processes already in place and running," he points out, "but the timing of the census is driven by Constitutional mandate. Congress can't stop it. The President can't stop it." He advises his successor to "be supportive and have faith in the institution" and its ability to carry out the census effectively.

Keane's view stems in part from the fact that, as director, he is the bureau's only appointed official. Everyone else on the staff belongs to the career service. This gives the bureau good institutional memory, durable expertise, and esprit de corps. It also makes it difficult to inject radical change from administration to administration. Keane thinks the first responsibility of the job is to "lead the organization thoughtfully and carefully," with a sense of the past and of the programs, and "an understanding of its role in the federal statistical system and the nation." While it is not as large as many government agencies, the bureau may be more complex than most, and Keane sees one of its main leadership challenges as realizing that "census bureau tentacles reach far and deep."

According to Keane, the bureau works "constantly" to improve its product. A principal avenue to that objective is the strategic planning efforts he introduced in 1984 and which the bureau is likely to continue after he leaves. This is a continuous process of environmental scanning to identify bureau strengths and weaknesses, define its function within the government and map out new directions for the years ahead. It has, Keane says, strengthened the organization's ability to integrate and streamline the various program sections and to link staff efforts more clearly to the bureau's long-term goals. It is also an additional and vital way to perceive and handle the bureau's changing environment. "I think strategic planning like this is enough in the blood stream of the bureau by now that the next administrator will continue it," Keane says. "I've tried to help ensure that by taking myself out of the process at this point. This plan is a product of the agency, not of mine."

The bureau works with virtually all of the departments in the federal government but perhaps most frequently with Labor, Agriculture, Education, Health and Human Services and, of course, its parent department, Commerce. Typically through interagency advisory councils, the director and his staff develop and track programs to compile the demographic, social, economic, and other pertinent data to try, as Keane puts it, "to describe [a particular] population in different ways."

Within the Washington and national political contexts, Keane believes the director "absolutely has to be non-partisan. It is critical because the data have to be legitimate. Luckily, most people in government seem to realize that this is a nonpartisan organization and don't attempt to put too much untoward political pressure on the director." But one of his predecessors recalls that the bureau "became a political football that Commerce assistant secretaries could kick with impunity." He also encountered "pressures to satisfy the demands of special interest groups" and "attempts to embarrass the bureau because of unpopular statistical programs." He thinks "it is important to develop an understanding of the political sensitivities of the bureau's programs."

He and Keane variously cite difficulties in integrating with the rest of the Commerce Department and with access to the secretary. The bureau's location several miles east of Washington doesn't help. Keane says the bureau is the second largest in the department, yet ranks only with organizations much smaller, is not a "free-standing agency," and the director does not attend senior staff meetings. "For the second-largest agency, that's frustrating. Without the chance to hear the discussion, it's hard to find out the gray of things." He recommends that future directors be included in senior level meetings.

In selecting the director, Keane thinks "it is essential to get someone in here who will stay. This is not a prestigious jumping off place for a career move. Choose someone who really knows and cares about the institution....There has been too much turnover here. You definitely don't want a political individual in here, someone who might be tempted to bend an ethic or shade a conclusion. You want people with integrity and some sensitivity to the role the bureau performs in the federal statistical system. Somebody who will speak for the bureau but who also doesn't have blinders on to its faults."

Keane and others note the ability to communicate that vision to the country as an essential quality in leading the bureau. The nation's people and institutions should view "the census bureau as a friend...and understand that the work [it] does improves our quality of life."

Key Relationships

Within the Department

Reports to: Undersecretary for Economic Affairs

Works closely with:

Chief Economist
Director, Bureau of Economic Analysis
Undersecretary, Economic Affairs
Deputy Assistant Secretary, Intergovernmental Affairs

Outside the Department

Commissioner, U.S. Customs Service
Commissioner, Labor Statistics, Department of Labor
Director, National Center for Health Statistics, Department of Health and Human Services
Director, National Institute on Aging, HHS
Director, Center for Education Statistics, Department of Education
Director, Bureau of Justice Statistics, Department of Justice
Director, Statistics of Income, Internal Revenue Service
Director, Information Management and Statistics, Veterans Administration
Administrator, Information and Regulatory Affairs, Office of Management and Budget
Chief, Statistical Policy Office, OMB

Outside the Federal Government

American Statistical Association, American Economics Association, American Marketing Association; public interest groups, such as Worldwatch Institute; American Planning Association, American Health Care Association; state and local government officials; agricultural organizations; National League of Cities, U.S. Council of Mayors; minority organizations; American Civil Liberties Union; polling organizations; teacher, academic and research institutions; urban and regional planners; genealogists and many other users of bureau products

Directors of the Bureau of the Census Since 1969

Administration	Name and Years Served	Present Position
Reagan	John G. Keane 1984 - Present	Incumbent
Reagan	Bruce Chapman 1981 -1983	Ambassador U.S. Mission to the United Nations Vienna, Austria
Carter/Reagan	Daniel B. Levine 1980 - 1981 (Acting)	Senior Associate Committee on National Statistics National Academy of Sciences Washington, DC
Carter	Vincent P. Barabba 1979 - 1981	Executive Director Market Research and Planning General Motors Corporation Detroit, Michigan
Carter	Manuel D. Plotkin 1977 - 1979	President M.D. Plotkin Research and Planning Company Chicago, Illinois
Ford	Vincent P. Barabba 1973 - 1976	Executive Director Market Research and Planning General Motors Corporation Detroit, Michigan
Nixon	George Hay Brown 1969 - 1973	Sea Island, Georgia

8

DEPARTMENT OF DEFENSE

Huge in size, labyrinthian in structure, Defense has been labeled everything from the biggest business in the world to a zoo. And most of these cliches are true.

With about 3.2 million uniformed and civilian employees on the payroll, the department is the largest employer of government agencies, and its budget of $320.1 billion in fiscal 1988 ranks second. The money it spends each year on acquisition exceeds the budgets of most nations of the world; just the operations of its advance research and development component approximate the annual expenses of the entire Department of Commerce.

Even Defense's apparent problems with its procurement procedures, which came to light with the extensive investigation announced in the spring of 1988, seem larger than life. They were not the first difficulties the department has encountered on this score, however, and some of its most vocal critics point out that acquisition on such a scale almost certainly means they won't be the last.

It would be difficult to fashion a complete list of future tasks facing the Defense department. Beyond the reform which will probably result from the procurement situation, the acquisition function also appears to offer another important challenge for the near future. This relates to the power and responsibility of the Undersecretary for Acquisition, a key position created as the result of earlier reform but which seems partly disabled by an unclear sharing of authority with the deputy secretary.

It will also continue to be important that the secretary and deputy are individuals with closely similar views on policy issues and a personally and professionally congenial relationship. The immense reach of the department's activities does not allow time for such bonds to develop on the job; the teamwork between the two will be put to an early, continual and exceptionally tough test by the veteran uniformed leadership of the department, with its own objectives, rivalries, and traditions.

Defense is yet another Washington arena where amateurs are unlikely to be effective, or even survive, in the leadership positions. In some cases, these jobs demand a detailed technical background; in many cases, they require an updated expertise in defense issues and the skill to handle Congressional relationships in the assigned area of responsibility; in most cases, they need management experience in government or the private sector, including a talent for running large projects within shrinking budgets and a knowledge of the defense community. And in every case, individuals appointed to these positions must have the ability at all times to place the administration's policy objectives and the national interest above more parochial concerns within the department.

DEPARTMENT OF DEFENSE

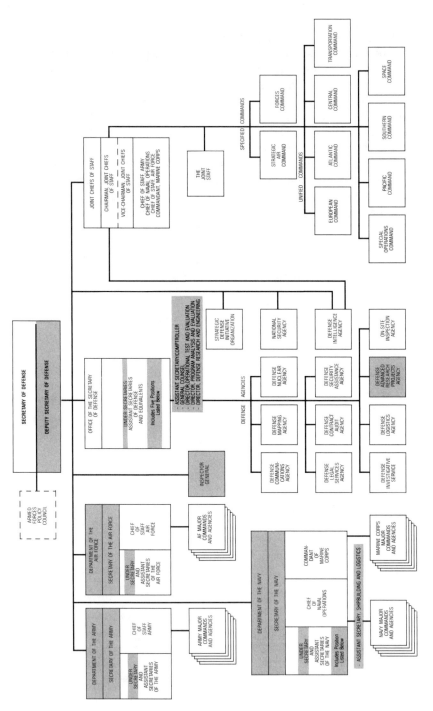

ARMED
FORCES
POLICY
COUNCIL

SECRETARY OF DEFENSE

DEPUTY SECRETARY OF DEFENSE

DEPARTMENT OF THE ARMY

SECRETARY OF THE ARMY

UNDER SECRETARY AND ASSISTANT SECRETARIES OF THE ARMY

CHIEF OF STAFF ARMY

ARMY MAJOR COMMANDS AND AGENCIES

DEPARTMENT OF THE AIR FORCE

SECRETARY OF THE AIR FORCE

UNDER SECRETARY AND ASSISTANT SECRETARIES OF THE AIR FORCE

CHIEF OF STAFF AIR FORCE

AF MAJOR COMMANDS AND AGENCIES

INSPECTOR GENERAL

OFFICE OF THE SECRETARY OF DEFENSE

UNDER SECRETARIES OF DEFENSE AND EQUIVALENTS
Includes Five Positions Listed Below

ASSISTANT SECRETARY/COMPTROLLER
GENERAL COUNSEL
DIRECTOR OPERATIONAL TEST AND EVALUATION
DIRECTOR, PROGRAM ANALYSIS AND EVALUATION
DIRECTOR, DEFENSE RESEARCH AND ENGINEERING

JOINT CHIEFS OF STAFF

CHAIRMAN, JOINT CHIEFS OF STAFF

VICE CHAIRMAN, JOINT CHIEFS OF STAFF

CHIEF OF STAFF ARMY
CHIEF OF NAVAL OPERATIONS
CHIEF OF STAFF AIR FORCE
COMMANDANT, MARINE CORPS

THE JOINT STAFF

STRATEGIC DEFENSE INITIATIVE ORGANIZATION

NATIONAL SECURITY AGENCY

DEFENSE INTELLIGENCE AGENCY

DEFENSE AGENCIES

DEFENSE MAPPING AGENCY

DEFENSE NUCLEAR AGENCY

ON-SITE INSPECTION AGENCY

DEFENSE COMMUNI-CATIONS AGENCY

DEFENSE CONTRACT AUDIT AGENCY

DEFENSE SECURITY ASSISTANCE AGENCY

DEFENSE ADVANCED RESEARCH PROJECTS AGENCY

DEFENSE LEGAL SERVICES AGENCY

DEFENSE LOGISTICS AGENCY

DEFENSE INVESTIGATIVE SERVICE

DEPARTMENT OF THE NAVY

SECRETARY OF THE NAVY

UNDER SECRETARY AND ASSISTANT SECRETARIES OF THE NAVY
Includes Position Listed Below

CHIEF OF NAVAL OPERATIONS

COMMAN-DANT OF MARINE CORPS

ASSISTANT SECRETARY SHIPBUILDING AND LOGISTICS

NAVY MAJOR COMMANDS AND AGENCIES

MARINE CORPS MAJOR COMMANDS AND AGENCIES

SPECIFIED COMMANDS

STRATEGIC AIR COMMAND

FORCES COMMAND

UNIFIED COMMANDS

EUROPEAN COMMAND

PACIFIC COMMAND

ATLANTIC COMMAND

CENTRAL COMMAND

TRANSPORTATION COMMAND

SPECIAL OPERATIONS COMMAND

SOUTHERN COMMAND

SPACE COMMAND

Shaded areas were selected as Prune Book positions

DEPUTY SECRETARY

Level II - Presidential Appointment with Senate Confirmation

Major Responsibilities

o   Assist the secretary in directing the operations of the U.S. defense establishment. Share leadership responsibilities and handle special assignments and other specific missions as the secretary requests.

o   Serve as chief operating officer of the Defense department. Function as acting secretary when the secretary is traveling. Seek and maintain a broad network of working relationships within the Congress for the articulation and support of administration defense policy.

o   Manage the formulation of defense programs covering acquisition, operations and a range of administrative activities. Direct the department's budget development process, and assist the secretary in negotiating and defending it within the administration and to the public. Appear on behalf of the budget before the Congressional committees of jurisdiction.

Necessary Background, Experience, Personal Skills

Management skills, acquired in government or the private sector, are the most important equipment by any measure. Some detailed exposure to the Defense Department and familiarity with the problems of weapons systems development and acquisition are highly useful in this job. In addition the deputy secretary must have a firm grasp of what roles the United States is currently playing in the military, political, and economic affairs of the world, and a complete understanding of the defense policies of the administration. The occupant of the job should move comfortably in the Washington political and Congressional environment.

Insight

The deputy secretary's position has substantial specific assignments, such as budget and--at present--a good share of the oversight of acquisition. It is also, and emphatically, a swing position. It requires not only flexibility but versatility, because the strengths, priorities and skills of the secretary largely define the deputy's job. The position needs an individual who can handle given tasks effectively, but who can also move with speed, skill and authority to respond to breaking developments across the immense expanse of defense issues and concerns.

In this, it is not unlike the secretary's job itself and, in fact, the deputy must often take over the secretary's role both inside the Pentagon and in the external domains which are normally the secretary's--speeches, testimony on the Hill, trips to the Oval Office, meetings with foreign defense officials, and much more. But the deputy secretary is primarily the internal manager of the department. "This means," says William H. Taft IV, who has held the job since 1984, "planning and programming the budget, supervising the execution of that program, and deciding the various issues that develop in the course of executing."

Little is possible in this area or any other, however, without a complete, mutual understanding and agreement with the secretary about operating procedures and assignments. In fact, in the absence of close cooperation between the two, the military services will play one off against the other, exploiting differences in their policy views. Thus W. Graham Claytor, deputy secretary in 1979-81, advises future occupants of the position to establish a "two-way street" with the secretary, adding that "a good relationship should be developed if it hasn't been before the appointment." Taft says "you've got to be very much in touch and in tune with the secretary, and you've got to be sensitive politically."

Elaborating on the budget responsibility, Taft says he runs "the process by which we decide what will be in our budget request and make all the trade-offs." He chairs the Defense Resources Board, which is "the mechanism through which, at the senior level, we make all the decisions regarding the programs. This is not only for weapons systems, but for operations as well, plus personnel issues, pay raises, military construction." Day-to-day managing also involves decisionmaking in two or three dozen other areas, a process which requires "making sure that the people who should be consulted are consulted" and that decisions are made when they need to be made.

That barely touches the surface of a job which, Taft says,

"is more like managing a corporation" than a government agency. The department is basically a service delivery operation with three million employees who run military installations; design, develop, test and use weapons; construct buildings; and move ships, aircraft, people and supplies.

In recent years this position has apparently focused particularly on the organization and oversight of the department's huge acquisition function, working at close quarters with the Undersecretary for Acquisition, a job established in 1987. Part of the reason seems to have been criticism, especially from the Congress, about how the acquisition process was being run. The 1988 investigations and other proceedings against reported Pentagon procurement scandals have, of course, greatly renewed the pressures on this front. It goes almost without saying that, whatever the deputy secretary's organic relationship to the acquisition function turns out to be in the future, the position will clearly have a good share of responsibility for developing and applying the corrective formulas that may result. In the phrase of the recent director of a large defense contractors association, that assignment should aim at repairing "reason, rationality and trust in industry-government relations."

Key Relationships

Within the Department

Reports to: Secretary

Works closely with:

Secretaries of the Army, Air Force and Navy
Vice Chairman, Joint Chiefs of Staff
All elements of the Office of the Secretary of Defense staff

Outside the Department

Deputy Secretary, Department of State
Deputy Secretary, Department of the Treasury
Deputy Secretary, Department of Commerce
Assistant to the President, National Security Affairs
Associate Director, National Security and International Affairs, Office of Management and Budget
Director, Central Intelligence Agency

Administrator, National Aeronautics and Space
Administration
Administrator, Environmental Protection Agency

Outside the Federal Government

Defense and related industries; foreign defense and
diplomatic representatives and military officials;
international organizations; military service associations and veterans groups; defense policy and research
organizations; and foreign affairs organizations

Deputy Secretaries of Defense Since 1969

Administration	Name and Years Served	Present Position
Reagan	William Howard Taft IV 1984 - Present	Incumbent
Reagan	Paul W. Thayer 1983 - 1984	Chairman ComputerBase Dallas, Texas
Reagan	Frank C. Carlucci 1981 - 1982	Secretary Department of Defense
Carter	W. Graham Claytor, Jr. 1979 - 1981	Chairman, President and Chief Executive Officer National Railroad Passenger Corporation Washington, DC
Carter	Charles W. Duncan, Jr. 1977 - 1978	Consultant Houston, Texas
Ford	Robert F. Ellsworth* 1975 - 1977	President Robert F. Ellsworth Company, Inc. Washington, DC
Nixon/Ford	William P. Clements* 1973 - 1977	Governor State of Texas Austin, Texas

Nixon	Kenneth Rush 1972 - 1973	Manchester, Vermont
Nixon	David Packard 1969 - 1971	Chairman of the Board Hewlett-Packard Company Palo Alto, California

* Held position simultaneously in 1975-1977. Second position of Deputy Secretary created by Public Law 92-256 in 1972 but only filled during this period.

UNDERSECRETARY
ACQUISITION

Level II - Presidential Appointment with Senate Confirmation

Major Responsibilities

o   Supervise the acquisition activities of the Department of Defense. Develop policy guidelines for acquisition strategy and approve the acquisition requirements of individual military service programs. Chair the Defense Acquisition Board.

o   Establish policy for the processes of acquisition--research and development, contracting, production, construction, logistics, security and distribution.

o   Formulate policy for the oversight of defense contractors, and serve as the department procurement executive.

Necessary Background, Experience, Personal Skills

The present undersecretary says "I don't see how you could do this job without being a very, very strong technical person." But prospective appointees to this job should also have broken out of their technology backgrounds to manage large organizations with broad-scope responsibilities and an international dimension. That view is widely shared among those who know this job well. One of them, a former senior Pentagon acquisition official, also believes the undersecretary should be oriented towards the development of weapons systems more than to procurement, and should know the department well through prior service in it or from experience with a defense contractor firm. The incumbent of the job agrees that the defense industry is one place to look for candidates, but warns of "the revolving-door problem," a situation that has attracted renewed attention with the investigation that began in mid-1988 into defense procurement procedures.

Insight

To understand this position is to recognize two fundamental

questions that surround it. One is basically operational, the other structural. Knowing what they concern is as important as knowing what the job is about.

The operational issue is short, if not simple. It relates to the investigations, announced by a U.S. attorney in May, 1988, into what the press subsequently reported as a broadly metastasized scandal within the procurement function of the Defense Department. At this writing, those investigations have not concluded. But it's probably reasonable to suppose that the extent of the transgressions under inquiry, if proven, will generate considerable further pressure to change the rules and regulations, and perhaps the management, of the procurement process. What kind of reforms, and whether they will have to await a new administration, must remain for the moment questions without answers. What does seem clear, however, is that the position of Undersecretary for Acquisition, itself the product of earlier reform, will be directly involved in whatever changes are made.

The second, structural, issue of this position is the relationship of the job to that of the deputy secretary and the adequacy of existing definitions of their respective responsibilities. One perception of this comes from the level of a former military department undersecretary. The problem has two basic roots, this onetime official says. First, it is impossible to have two individuals--the undersecretary and the deputy secretary--calling the acquisition shots. Second, trying to rationalize and discipline acquisition policy in an era of decreasing resources runs into trouble from the "inherent" fact that "the ultimate test is winning World War III." Deciding what one needs in order to do that, in this view, is always a risk judgment without easy or clear answers. The real problem thus becomes one "created by the statements of requirements." The undersecretary must therefore get involved in the requirements issues, areas jealously guarded by the military services.

This informed former insider views the undersecretary's job as ineffectually hung up somewhere between the department's political leadership, the joint chiefs and military services, and the technicians, "who believe everything should be driven by considerations of technical feasibility." As such, the assignment is not a "separable function," and the oversight of acquisition--a tough job under any circumstances--should be a responsibility of the deputy secretary. That, in any case, is where a substantial part of the responsibility seems to have been exercised in recent years, despite what was intended when this job was established in 1986.

But the comments of Richard P. Godwin, who served as the first undersecretary in 1987, run in the opposite direction. He believes the intent in establishing the undersecretary's job was "a cultural change" setting out a clear and separate authority in the management of acquisition, a step which to him is intimately bound up with how the overall defense mission itself should be managed. The Pentagon's leadership triumvirate, in his view, would consist of "someone who knows how to fight a war (chairman of the joint chiefs); someone who relationships with Congress and the White House, is the titular chief, and knows how to set the tone (the secretary); and somebody to run the biggest business in the world (the head of acquisition)." Such a set-up, he says, "forces you to define what the term acquisition includes."

Others, while not necessarily as revisionist as Godwin on this subject, also raise the problem of definitions, authority, and support from the top. One of them, who held the then-existing title of Undersecretary for Defense Research and Engineering, a forerunner of this job, says "the biggest management challenge is getting a consistent set of acquisition rules and regulations, not letting the service secretaries develop their own ways of doing business, having someone who is the keeper of the keys, the keeper of the department's view of the acquisition process." Another former ranking acquisition official warns that "either the secretary says you are my acquisition executive and you will make those decisions under my guidance, or you are the acquisition executive but you work for the deputy secretary. Those things have got to be understood beforehand....Without the trust and faith of the secretary, the undersecretary is not going to get anything done. He is going to be frustrated and beat his head against the wall."

An outside observer, formerly the executive director of a defense contracting association, points to "constant tugging" between the people who want to centralize acquisition authority in the Office of the Secretary of Defense (OSD) and the military services who have "rich, angry, volatile allies on the Hill" who can be summoned to battle "any effort coming out of the OSD to run the Pentagon." He adds: "Unless the phalanx is solid at the top of the Pentagon, [that effort] is already defeated."

On this subject of acquisition responsibilities at the senior levels of OSD, Godwin says "you have to be very precise as to what their various functions are; otherwise you get great turmoil.... Somewhere along the line, you have to say, are you responsible for acquisition or aren't you? Then you have to get a damned good definition of what acquisition means, of whom you report to, and who reports to you." Private industry, he points out, must do this or face a profit or loss situation, and "you know when you go broke in a hurry. But here, you don't know if you go broke or not."

Currently, he asserts, there is no way to obtain a timely, overall, comparative view of the status of various military service programs. Information must be sought from each service. "But it's not the same, there are different ground rules, and you always end up with mush. And you find out you're in deep trouble about a year after you're in deep trouble....We don't have enough commonality now. We develop the same thing twice, and sometimes three times."

Robert B. Costello, who has held this job since 1987, says he has worked to restructure the staff acquisition functions in OSD to establish policy and monitor the performances of the services as they manage their programs. Rather than discrete line-item management, the Defense Acquisition Board (which this job chairs) has laid down "a strategy, a mosaic of all the programs for all the services, to cover the parameters of all the needs a particular service has." As for the structural management problems outlined above, his advice is to "believe in and understand consensus management. There is no czar. I have direct authority over the services for acquisition matters, but that doesn't buy you anything. What you have to establish is a rapport with those people, have a level of credibility and trust, so you can talk about things openly. It's difficult, because the issues range so broadly."

So does the scope of the job, which Costello says is also "deeply involved in operations" as they relate to acquisition matters, with training, with a "very significant" contribution to policy, with foreign trade, foreign military sales, and technology exchanges with allies and other advanced nations. Further, Costello says he talks to the press "more than anyone else in the department except the secretary."

The job also has a concern for the health of the U.S. industrial base. That takes on added complications for the manager of defense acquisition, where other work must be found for losers of competitive procurement if specialized capabilities in an industry with few players are to be kept available for future competition or expanded workloads.

The undersecretary works directly with the armaments directors of North Atlantic Treaty Organization countries and some Pacific basin nations. "We're looking at a market place of which we're the largest piece," Costello says. But the United States "is no longer the citadel of world technology. There are other countries that have technology critical to what we want to do."

Despite the handicaps he sees, Godwin says that, "on the face of it, the present acquisition system works surprisingly well, considering the strains of the milieu in which it operates, with Congress sitting here, the White House here, contractors there."

Costello says "you know you can't change it overnight, but you can change it if you have well-defined goals. Take enough time to define them, announce them, commit yourself and your organization, and put a timetable on them so you can be monitored against the performance."

Key Relationships

Within the Department

Reports to: Secretary

Works closely with:

Deputy Secretary
Joint Chiefs of Staff
Undersecretary for Policy
Secretaries of the Air Force, Army and Navy
Assistant Secretary - Comptroller
Director, Program Analysis and Evaluation
Service Acquisition Executives

Outside the Department

Associate Director, National Security and International Affairs, Office of Management and Budget
Undersecretary, International Trade, Department of Commerce
Administrator, Federal Procurement Policy, Executive Office of the President
Undersecretary, Security Assistance, Science and Technology, Department of State
Assistant Secretary, Politico Military Affairs, Department of State

Outside the Federal Government

Defense contracting and high-technology companies and associations; trade groups; engineering and research and development firms and associations; armaments directors and other defense officials of NATO and other governments

Undersecretaries of Defense for Acquisition Since 1987*

Administration	Name and Years Served	Present Position
Reagan	Robert B. Costello 1987 - Present	Incumbent
Reagan	Richard P. Godwin 1987	Consultant Defense Group, Inc. Arlington, Virginia

* Position created in 1987 by a departmental reorganization resulting from the Packard Commission Report. Prior to then, the main acquisition function was performed by the then Undersecretary for Defense Research and Engineering.

SECRETARIES OF THE
AIR FORCE, ARMY AND NAVY DEPARTMENTS

Level II - Presidential Appointment with Senate Confirmation

(To a substantial degree, the civilian secretaries of the military departments carry similar responsibilities. The problems they wrestle with and the challenges they face originate in the same kinds of budget, procurement and operating situations. The discussion below examines these three positions together.)

Major Responsibilities

o Under the authority of the Secretary of Defense, direct the organization, activities and administration of--respectively--the Departments of the Air Force, Army or Navy, notably including the recruitment, training and equipping of their operating forces.

o Coordinate decisionmaking and implementation with the uniformed chief of staff of the military department. Represent the service to the Secretary of Defense and within the Department of Defense and the administration.

o Correlate decisions and actions through the Office of the Secretary of Defense and with the secretaries of the other two military departments on all matters affecting the operating forces of the service. Perform the same function as necessary with counterparts elsewhere in government in the areas of diplomacy, intelligence, national security, and international economic policy.

o Form and maintain close working relationships with members and staff of Congressional committees exercising jurisdiction over the department and defense matters in general. Advocate, explain and defend the service's mission, policies and budget on the Hill.

o Articulate these matters publicly, and with a broad range of constituent organizations. Follow a regular schedule of visits to the service's operating forces, bases and personnel within the country and overseas.

Necessary Background, Experience, Personal Skills

These positions call for individuals with extensive senior executive experience who can effectively manage organizations served by large numbers of people and fueled by some of the biggest budgets in Washington.

It is clear that a civilian perspective is critical to these jobs, especially in policymaking. They also require individuals who will be guided by a basic loyalty to the Secretary of Defense and to the intent and direction of administration defense policy. Candidates who meet these specifications, and who have some background in problem-solving environments like the law or management consulting, seem especially well-equipped.

Knowledge of the Congressional process and good working contacts on the Hill are other exceptionally important resources that are constantly in play. An understanding of procurement and the ability to handle big-money numbers greatly increases credibility and effective performance. Communications skill is essential.

Insight

Words like "anchors aweigh" or "into the wild blue yonder," famous calls to action from service academy anthems, denote more than just the beginning of the combat phase of military operations. They can also be said to symbolize the successful end of another phase--the continual, complex and unglamorous process of preparation that goes to the heart of operational effectiveness. That is what the jobs under examination here are about.

The armed services cannot march off, put to sea or take the air and expect to compete around the world without the sustained effective leadership of the three civilians who run the departments in Washington and of their undersecretaries. Whatever the ultimate impact of the reported procurement scandal that began rocking the Pentagon in June, 1988, successful performance in the field by the armed services today almost certainly means correct decisions about engineering and procurement made or approved by the individual service secretaries up to ten years ago, and perhaps more.

In the Pentagon it is, of course, not the service secretaries alone on whom success depends. The Secretary of Defense and the chiefs of staff, under the direction of the President, make and execute the decisions about where the armed forces of this country go, what they do when they get there, and about states of readiness and other operational matters. The civilian secretaries are not in that loop. They are responsible, instead, for equipping the Navy, Army and Air Force to follow those orders and carry out their missions.

Such assignments cover a good deal of supervisory responsibility, from recruiting and training the personnel to procuring the weapons and the supporting systems that get people and weapons into the right places and allow them to function. In the wake of investigations into the bribery and other reported misdeeds, the procurement aspects of these jobs may change dramatically. Either way, those developments will only add weight to the service secretaries' important task of gaining public understanding and acceptance of the role and needs of the services. More vital still, these positions require the political skill and personal qualities to secure the Congressional support without which nothing else is possible.

Generally speaking, the secretaries focus on the external dimensions of department leadership--the Congress, the upper reaches of the Defense Department, the press--and in their travel and public activities they are the face and voice of their services. Their undersecretaries concentrate on making the military departments run, and on special tasks. But the secretaries' role can be, and often is, a dynamic combination of both.

"It's a steel-bending job," according to J. William Middendorf II, Secretary of the Navy in 1974-77. Part of it involves the here and now--seeing that the service has what it needs on any given day in terms of equipment and people, making promotion policy and seeing that it works, responding to Congressional inquiries or to a call for a hurry-up crisis management meeting across town with high-level officials from half a dozen other agencies. And part of the job involves staring hard into the fairly distant future. Putting an aircraft carrier into the water, Middendorf points out, now takes ten years--"to float it through Congress, design it, construct it, christen it." The mission is not only to equip the service, he says, "it's to look ahead at our needs years hence. If there's a ten-year lead time involved, your imprint isn't even going to be felt until years later." The secretary's job is therefore "not always one of immediate satisfaction."

That's especially true when a long-planned weapons system--a jet fighter, a tank gun, an armored troop vehicle--overruns its predicted cost or, worse, falls short of its advance billing. Service budgets may be huge. But the service secretary still has to grapple with costs which put just as much pressure on scarce resources in the military as anywhere else in government, and require constant team work and coordination within the service. Looking back on his years as Army secretary in 1965-71, Stanley R. Resor says the right individuals for these jobs must "have a serious interest in national security and in force planning and the major issues arising from that, such as resource allocation. For that you need the cooperation of the chief of staff and the military professionals." With defense budgets currently on a downward track, this problem promises to grow tougher. Edward Hidalgo, Navy secretary in 1979-81, suggests that "programs in which progress is most necessary must replace those that are no longer urgent."

The long lead times on equipment mentioned by Middendorf also complicate the management of Congressional relations. While the Hill may have its favorite programs and elements, he says, they're elected every two or six years "and they don't necessarily like putting a lot of money into something that isn't going to show for at least five to ten years." Imperative as Congressional support is, however, Middendorf warns that "one of the first things you realize is that you're on your own. The department isn't going to sell these things for you, and neither will the Secretary of Defense, except in a broad-brush sense. In the final analysis, you've got to get up there. You've got to work with the staffs every day." In addition, service secretaries find it useful--and in any case necessary--to visit Congressional districts with significant military installations or defense contracts.

Committees and staff with whom the service secretaries regularly deal are knowledgeable and astute, and usually don't go for something quick and new. On the average, the secretaries can expect to spend 25% of their working time on the Congressional waterfront. Nonetheless, recalls Verne Orr, Air Force secretary in 1981-85, "Congress was my chronic problem. They want their friends favored over everybody else." Thomas C. Reed, who had the same job in 1976-77, complains of "interference by Congress" and "hundreds of different Congressmen with different views on what should be done" as a major headache.

Each branch of the armed forces, of course, has special tasks or must deal with particular problems presented by the military and foreign policy postures of the world's various alliances as well as of individual nations. These positions change, however gradually, and must be taken into account from a military standpoint. As only one example among many, the key mission of the Army secretary, according to Resor, "is to supply the ground forces for the defense of Europe." That mission could well change in the wake of the U.S.-Soviet accord, signed in the spring of 1988, to reduce intermediate-range nuclear missiles in Europe.

Not surprisingly, several individuals formerly in these jobs emphasize along with Resor the importance of building good relationships with the uniformed career men and women within the service. Robert F. Froehlke, Army secretary in 1971-73, recalls that "they actually run it for you in the first months," he says. "It's important to have a good relationship with them so that you can learn." Middendorf views the career service as "an established hierarchy" with "their own way of doing things. They're going to be there a long time after you're gone, and were there a long time before you got there. You've got to earn their respect, and when you move forward on a major program, you've got to have them a hundred percent on board."

In this--and all other responsibilities of these positions--care must be used to avoid co-option and manipulation by the service. A good sense of balance and proportion is essential. The secretary, while speaking for the service inside and outside the Defense Department, cannot allow advocacy of it to become the chief role, or permit service considerations to distort or override the policies and directives of the Secretary of Defense.

Part of the secretary's effort to establish good working relations with the uniformed service is a steady round of visits to the field --air bases, fleet elements, training camps, specialty schools, artillery and infantry installations and many more, inside the United States and overseas. It adds up to a sizeable investment of time. "You've got to find out what's going on," Froehlke says. "You can't just look at memos in Washington." "It's always good for morale," Middendorf adds, "when the Secretary of the Navy shows up and visits the boiler room." Or, as Hidalgo puts it, this kind of travel is an excellent way "to get in touch with reality."

But, in the view of a senior civilian official within one of the military departments, travel can be overdone. "You can't have a service secretary who squanders away time traveling around the world being popular with the troops," he warns. "You need people who are really capable in these critically important chief executive officer positions. The Secretary of Defense cannot be the only person running the place. He needs a corps of loyal lieutenants running those big subsidiaries."

Key Relationships

Within the Department

Reports to: Secretary

Works closely with:

Deputy Secretary of Defense
Undersecretary, Policy, Office of the Secretary of
Defense (OSD)
Undersecretary, Acquisition, OSD
Assistant Secretary - Comptroller, OSD
Deputy Assistant Secretary, Military Manpower and
Personnel Policy, OSD
Director, Program Analysis and Evaluation, OSD
Assistant Secretary, International Security Affairs, OSD
Chief of Staff of the service
Secretaries of the other military departments

Outside the Department

Chairmen and ranking minority members of the Senate
and House Armed Services and Appropriations
committees and subcommittees, and key staff members
bers
Senior officials of the departments of State, Treasury
and Commerce and of the Environmental Protection
Agency
Associate Director, National Security and International
Affairs, Office of Management and Budget

Outside the Federal Government

Defense and construction contractors; foreign military
and diplomatic officials; retired officers and veterans
organizations; state and local government officials;
journalists; citizens groups concerned with location
or relocation of bases

Secretaries of the Air Force Since 1969

Administration	Name and Years Served	Present Position
Reagan	Edward C. Aldridge, Jr. 1986 - Present	Incumbent

Reagan	Russell A. Rourke 1985 - 1986	President Epp Company Annapolis, Maryland
Reagan	Verne Orr 1981 - 1985	Pasadena, California
Carter	Hans M. Mark 1979 - 1981	Chancellor University of Texas System Austin, Texas
Carter	John C. Stetson 1977 - 1979	Partner Sullivan and Cromwell Washington, DC
Ford	Thomas C. Reed 1976 - 1977	Chairman River Oaks Agricorp Healdsburg, California
Nixon/Ford	John L. McLucas 1973 - 1975	Chairman of the Board Questech, Inc. McLean, Virginia
Nixon	Robert C. Seamans, Jr. 1969 - 1973	Senior Lecturer Massachusetts Institute of Technology Cambridge, Massachusetts

Secretaries of the Army Since 1969

Administration	Name and Years Served	Present Position
Reagan	John O. Marsh, Jr. 1981 - Present	Incumbent
Carter	Clifford Alexander, Jr. 1977 - 1981	President Alexander and Associates Washington, DC
Ford	Martin R. Hoffman 1975 - 1977	Not Available

Ford	Howard H. Callaway 1973 - 1975	President and CEO Crested Butte Mountain Resort Denver, Colorado
Nixon	Robert F. Froehlke 1971 - 1973	President and CEO IDS Mutual Fund Group Minneapolis, Minnesota
Nixon	Stanley R. Resor 1965 - 1971	Partner Debevoise and Plimpton New York, New York

Secretaries of the Navy Since 1969

Administration	Name and Years Served	Present Position
Reagan	William L. Ball III 1988 - Present	Incumbent
Reagan	James H. Webb, Jr. 1987 - 1988	Washington, DC
Reagan	John F. Lehman, Jr. 1981 - 1987	Managing Director Paine Webber New York, New York
Carter	Edward Hidalgo 1979 - 1981	Partner Vorys, Sater, Seymour and Pease Washington, DC
Carter	W. Graham Claytor, Jr. 1977 - 1979	Chairman, President and CEO National Railroad Passenger Corp. Washington, DC
Nixon/Ford	J. William Middendorf II 1974 - 1977	Chairman Middendorf, Ansary and Company Washington, DC

Nixon	John W. Warner	United States Senator
	1972 - 1974	State of Virginia

Nixon	John H. Chafee	United States Senator
	1969 - 1972	State of Rhode Island

UNDERSECRETARY
POLICY

Level III - Presidential Appointment with Senate Confirmation

Major Responsibilities

o   Under the direction of the secretary, manage the development of U.S. international defense policy and military strategy, including strategic deterrence. Take a leading role in correlating these with U.S. foreign policy and arms control objectives.

o   Assure that defense policy and strategy are fully taken into account in budget and other decisions affecting the department. Oversee certain defense intelligence activities and defense mobilization policy, and contribute to military contingency planning.

o   In testimony and other contacts, keep the Congress advised on policy questions reflected in defense authorization and appropriations legislation.

o   Serve as senior spokesman on defense policy matters within administration councils. Fill a similar role in the public arena as requested by the secretary.

Necessary Background, Experience, Personal Skills

Nothing less than a thorough immersion in military policy issues and a solid grasp of U.S. foreign policy is sufficient for this position. It calls as well for an understanding of international affairs, with emphasis on the military aspects. A wide acquaintance within the national defense community and with defense policy officials of other countries is important. Experience in the areas of arms control, national security, diplomacy and intelligence characterized the prior careers of recent undersecretaries. In addition, the occupant of this job needs substantial management talent, and an instinct for bureaucratic maneuver.

Insight

This position carries central impact on the development of the long-term U.S. defense effort. The undersecretary integrates defense policy, arms control strategy, and such regional involvements of the department as security assistance to other countries, military base negotiations, and relations between the U.S. and foreign defense leaderships. A large part of the responsibility involves Defense Department relationships with the other elements of the U.S. national security and foreign policy establishment--in particular, with the National Security Council, the State Department and the Central Intelligence Agency. Defense policy does not stand alone; it is fundamental to how the United States addresses its political, economic and security objectives within the international community, and to U.S. aspirations for continued leadership in world affairs.

One of the most difficult challenges of the job, says Fred C. Iklé, undersecretary from 1981 to 1988, "is to translate policies into real military systems and capabilities. You have to get the services to move in accordance with the policy you have drafted and the secretary has approved." But if the ability to drive the implementation of policy is critical, the secretary's backing is also required to get the job done. Even the secretary is somewhat hampered in implementation by the structure of power flow in the Pentagon, in which the armed services report to the Joint Chiefs of Staff, and the chairman of the joint chiefs reports directly to the President. "The services want to do things their own way," Iklé says. "They like to continue to do them the way they have been doing them before."

That's why the undersecretary's job needs a senior person who can see the horizon, and beyond. Another recent undersecretary calls this quality "creativeness, innovation, a broad gaze, understanding the ramifications of the problems encountered." If the undersecretary doesn't play this role, it's unlikely that anyone else will. The secretary has less than adequate time for it, and it clearly can't be left to a deputy. "You have to press against the entrenched positions of the services, who may have a different long-term view, in order to get a harmonious position" that accords with the policy of the President, Iklé says.

The occupant of this job serves the secretary in a very direct relationship. Iklé says he worked most closely with the secretary on policy issues, and with the deputy secretary on budget--a set-up which, of course, changes as incumbents change. "It depends on a self-chosen division of labor" between the two most senior jobs, he points out. The undersecretary's activities, in any case, are very heavily on the policy side of the house, and range widely across Washington and the world. The job, for example, may entail attendance at NATO foreign ministerial and Defense Planning Group meetings. In another area of responsibility--oversight of defense mobilization--the undersecretary guides preparations for industrial preparedness and mobilization planning. On the Hill, the undersecretary deals with issues like arms control, relations with the Soviet Union and Central American issues. "These are not big budget items for defense," Iklé says, "but I still spent a big chunk of time on it. The things the policy guy focuses on aren't correlated that closely with the money." Another former undersecretary notes, however, that he "insisted on being involved in the budget. I liked to make sure that whatever the department decided to do, it had adequate funding to do it."

He and Iklé take somewhat different positions on the question of the proper background for appointment to this job. On balance, this same undersecretary believes it should be filled by individuals with the experience that political appointees don't always have. "You need someone proficient in defense matters who also has talent," he asserts. "This job should not in any way be handled by someone who lacks the experience it so badly needs." Iklé feels the appointee should be "consonant with the political persuasion of the President and his perceived mandate. This is a job helping to shape policy." He notes that the undersecretary's position is "politically adversarial" on the broader issues, such as defending the Strategic Defense Initiative or the administration's policy in Central America. It is visible outside the government, he says, to groups interested in military strategy and arms control. How visible, he adds, depends on the secretary's own inclinations in the public affairs area.

Problems encountered by an earlier undersecretary included "inadequate talent or experience on the staffs, insufficient staff for systems analysis policy needs," and "inadequate flow of information upwards from large defense components such as the military departments." When he reached obstacles or hurdles, he says, he had to do it himself. He thinks these kinds of deficiencies remain. The department, he believes, "must insist on a better training program and a more qualified political staff."

Iklé suggests that future undersecretaries make an early-morning habit of reading worldwide intelligence reports, "not just the daily things" but longer-term information on trends in technology and foreign forces and the policies of other governments. "Then, spend time in understanding the military services systems, where those systems are going, where they do and don't fit with national security policy. You have to know whether there is a mismatch between what the services are going to build in the next seven years and what the Secretary of Defense has articulated as being policy."

Key Relationships

Within the Department

Reports to: Secretary

Works closely with: Deputy Secretary

Outside the Department

Assistant and Deputy Assistant to the President for National Security Affairs
Undersecretary, Political Affairs, Department of State
Director and Deputy Director, Central Intelligence Agency

Outside the Federal Government

Diplomatic and defense officials of other countries; arms control groups, think tanks, and campuses interested in defense issues

Undersecretaries for Policy Since 1977*

Administration	Name and Years Served	Present Position
Reagan	1988 - Present	Vacant
Reagan	Fred C. Iklé 1981 - 1988	Bethesda, Maryland
Carter	Robert W. Komer 1979 - 1981	Consultant The RAND Corporation Washington, DC
Carter	Stanley R. Resor 1978 - 1979	Partner DeBevoise and Plimpton New York, New York

* Position created by Public Law 95-140 in October 1977.

ASSISTANT SECRETARY - COMPTROLLER

Level IV - Presidential Appointment with Senate Confirmation

Major Responsibilities

o   Advise the secretary in the annual preparation of an integrated budget and a five-year financial plan for the department. Defend it within the Office of the Secretary of Defense, justify it with the Office of Management and Budget and present and support it before the Congressional committees of jurisdiction.

o   Assure that the current-year budget is properly executed. Collect and analyze information about the department's management of its resources for OMB, the Congress and the General Accounting Office.

o   Provide policy and operational oversight of the Defense Contract Audit Agency. Set policy for and oversee the management and acquisition of the department's automatic data processing systems.

o   Manage the activities of the Office of the Assistant Secretary-Comptroller.

Necessary Background, Experience, Personal Skills

Broad, senior-level knowledge of the federal budget process and the systems which support it is a requisite for this job. Preferably, a candidate with that credential developed it in a previous government financial management position, but service as the chief financial officer of a large corporation is also excellent training. This assistant secretary needs auditing, accounting and data processing experience, and should have developed a reputation for integrity.

Insight

The Defense department develops an annual budget currently running in the neighborhood of $300 billion. With numbers of this size, and given their impact on virtually every aspect of the national existence, this assistant secretary is hardly the dominant budget player in the macro sense. The budget is the largest and most complicated of its kind; the procurement function of the department alone is frequently described as the biggest business in the world. But the occupant of this job, as the senior financial manager of the department, organizes the budget process, is responsible for assembling the information, plays a leading part in all of its phases, and monitors its implementation.

To prepare it, close and regular consultation is necessary with each of the military departments, 18 separate Defense agencies, and the Secretary of Defense. Members of the Office of the Secretary and officials at the National Security Council and other agencies have contributions to make. The document goes through complex negotiations with the Office of Management and Budget, with the President a close observer, guide and ultimate decisionmaker. When the budget gets to the Congress, the assistant secretary is a key spokesman and advocate.

Vincent Puritano, who held the job in 1983-84, terms it "really a very elaborate, complex process. Some numbers you get from the President, the NSC and OMB. You work within those for the services and the functional areas. But that changes all year long as Congress does its finite management thing, and that's another part of the problem. You're planning a budget for one year, defending one that you presented previously [for the coming fiscal year], and executing a third year and then Congress makes radical changes at the very end of the process." All this takes place while the assistant secretary is also trying to project and draft a five-year plan.

Asked their views of the department's biggest problem from a resources point of view, previous assistant secretaries we talked with generally agree that the military services "expanded too fast and now they're getting cut back too fast and can't adjust," in the words of Jack R. Borsting, who held the job in 1980-83. Wrestling with these issues of what stays in and what goes out in the context of substantial budget cutbacks of the last three years, the secretary must have clear and objective advice about the relative merits of the department's hundreds of programs, operations, and plans. "The services will fight for their individual programs and be parochial about it," Puritano says. "But that's not surprising. You would expect the individual services to do that. You have to make your judgment across services lines in a comprehensive way and present it, regardless of where the chips fall." Underlining the importance of process, Robert C. Moot, assistant secretary in 1968-73, recalls that his approval of the budgets of the military departments "was the key to their success with the secretary."

Political considerations are something the assistant secretary cannot afford to be drawn into, or guided by. "His job," Puritano asserts, "is to play the straight game of taking the budget guidelines from OMB and the President and applying them in house, trying to be neutral and getting the product out. You have to answer questions from both sides of the [Congressional] aisle and from the staffs. It's not a political job. You have to be the guardian of the integrity of the numbers." That takes energy, a willingness to tangle with difficult issues, and the ability to make decisions.

The highly technical character of much of what the department does normally presents a key difficulty for an individual whose specialties and skills lie elsewhere. "I don't think anybody is ever going to get past that," Puritano warns about the weapons and electronic systems, the exotica of strategic defense plans, and the research and development activity whose essential nature the assistant secretary must try to grasp. "The staffs are broken down into the details," he says. "You really have to be able to synthesize one helluva lot of information and get the essence of the key issues, because you can't get into the details."

To Borsting, the challenge of this job "is to be the financial manager of a $300 billion business in a fishbowl where the public is looking at the agency all the time." For Moot, the value of a job managing resources of that order of magnitude is that "you see what is planned, you see how it happens, and you contribute to its happening. You are directly a part of history."

Key Relationships

Within the Department

Reports to: Secretary

Works closely with:

Deputy Secretary
Undersecretary for Acquisition
Director, Program Analysis and Evaluation
Secretaries of the Air Force, Army and Navy
Assistant Secretary, Force Management and Personnel
Assistant Secretary, Production and Logistics
Comptroller of the Air Force
Assistant Secretary of the Army, Financial Management

Assistant Secretary of the Navy, Financial Management
Chiefs of staff of the military services
Director, Information and Resource Management,
   Joint Chiefs of Staff
Financial officers of department agencies

Outside the Department

Associate Director, National Security and International
   Affairs, Office of Management and Budget
Counterpart, National Security Council
Comptroller General, General Accounting Office

Outside the Federal Government

Defense contracting firms and associations; Government Finance Officers Association, American Society of Military Comptrollers, Association of Government Accountants and other financial and accounting groups

Assistant Secretary - Comptrollers of Defense Since 1969

Administration	Name and Years Served	Present Position
Reagan	Robert W. Helm 1984 - Present	Incumbent
Reagan	Vincent Puritano 1983 - 1984	Vice President Government Affairs and International Trade Unisys Corporation Washington, DC
Reagan	Jack R. Borsting 1980 - 1983	Dean, School of Business Administration University of Southern California Los Angeles, California
Nixon/Carter	Fred P. Wacker 1976 - 1979	Not Available

Nixon/Ford	Terence E. McClary	Not Available
	1973 - 1976	
Nixon	Don R. Brazier (Acting)	Not Available
	1973	
Nixon	Robert C. Moot	Oakton, Virginia
	1968 - 1973	

ASSISTANT SECRETARY OF THE NAVY
SHIPBUILDING AND LOGISTICS

Level IV - Presidential Appointment with Senate Confirmation

Major Responsibilities

o   Oversee the Navy's procurement processes for ships, aircraft, weapons and supporting systems, and its maintenance, supply, distribution, transportation, construction and housing operations.

o   Work closely with the Secretary and Undersecretary of the Navy and with others in the department responsible for acquisition to make key procurement and resource allocation decisions.

o   Maintain effective relationships with the armed services and appropriations committees of the Congress. Assist in developing and supporting the naval procurement budget on the Hill.

Necessary Background, Experience, Personal Skills

The position calls for training and practice in engineering, manufacturing or another technical field, and considerable experience in military procurement. Candidates might come out of a management background in industry or government, but should be familiar with one or more phases of the military acquisition cycle--as in engineering, design, contracting, development, or testing. The assistant secretary must be able to walk into a shipyard or aircraft construction plant and understand the operations. The job also needs an individual who can develop and negotiate a budget and deal with Congressional interest and inquiries.

Insight

In the period since 1981, the emphasis in the procurement responsibilities of this job has been on the front end of the shipbuilding process. Traditionally, the job came into the picture at the stage when the product under acquisition was well enough defined to be written into production contracts. Even then, the position had some involvement with the engineering and design phases that precede the contract stage. Given the growing complexity of ship systems, however, including their weapons, and the Navy's increased role in defense strategy, this position was brought into the full cycle. Another contributing reason, of course, was the decision in 1981 to expand the fleet by 30 percent, and what was seen as the uncertain capabilities of U.S. naval shipbuilders at the time. But these perceptions and emphases are subject to change.

In defense acquisition, the lines between development and production tend to blur, because the product is always being changed. In fact, says George A. Sawyer, assistant secretary in 1981-83, "there is no such thing as a stable configuration." Adding significantly to this, in his view, is "the pressure of peacetime military life," which augments the tendency to change the product every year. "I don't think it is either necessary or good," he says. "I call it contractor pull, military push--a push/pull amplifier." Sawyer thinks there is no easy way out of this situation, among other reasons because of the "tremendous micromanagement" of the Congress. "And of course they represent these constituencies that [have no defense contracts], or those that [do] but want to make more money on a program."

Beyond shipbuilding, the assistant secretary has procurement responsibility for aircraft, other weapons systems and much of the rest of what the Navy needs in order to operate. On the logistics side, the job oversees the purchase of many kinds of support equipment, spare parts and supplies, the construction and maintenance of housing, the transportation of parts and supplies, and the operation of naval shipyards. The assistant secretary plays a central part in the planning and support of operations like those the United States has conducted in the Persian Gulf. And, as with procurement, the logistics responsibilities involve a great deal of contracting.

One of the talents the assistant secretary must bring to these duties is the ability to understand the language of industrial production. This means, for example, knowing what a quality incentive program is, how statistical quality control and statistical process control are performed, how to manage a payroll, how to apply a cost-plus or a fixed-price-incentive contract, and what the difference is between them.

The job also entails the productive use of personal relationships. These can be especially helpful if the secretary has trouble getting programs through the bureaucracy and the need increases for decisionmaking by consensus. Other, more tangible, problems of the job involve, first, the immensity of a procurement contract portfolio exceeding $30 billion a year, and second, overseeing a support organization of about 300,000 people. Further, Sawyer says, "you do not have hire/fire authority, none of the information systems are quite standardized or formalized and, most importantly, unlike private industry where you deal with a single criterion, in defense it is much more complicated. You are trying to manage four or five objectives. It isn't just defense of the free world. You've got Congressmen coming in with other issues. There are jobs. One guy gets a contract and the other guy doesn't. It can have major impact on an entire region. The politics are great, the stakes are high, and the objectives by which you manage are much more diffuse."

Goals to aim for in future administrations, Sawyer thinks, are to "bring the new destroyer and submarine programs through to fruition." These are big new ship projects that, he says, will "see the Navy through to the year 2030." In logistics, he sees the task as maintaining present commitments with less money.

Sawyer believes the major issue of the next administration at the Pentagon will be "restoring some sanity to the procurement process." He thinks it will be difficult, since "you can't really ever get order out of chaos."

Key Relationships

Within the Department

Reports to: Secretary of the Navy

Works closely with:

Undersecretary
Assistant Secretary, Research Engineering and Systems
Undersecretary, Acquisition
Assistant Secretary, Production and Logistics, Office of the Secretary of Defense

Outside the Department

Administrator, Maritime Administration, Department of Transportation

Outside the Federal Government

Shipbuilding and aerospace companies; electronics companies, such as International Business Machines and Raytheon; engine manufacturing firms, such as General Electric and United Technology; ordnance manufacturers; and naval architecture and engineering companies

Assistant Secretaries of the Navy for Shipbuilding and Logistics Since 1969

Administration	Name and Years Served	Present Position
Reagan	Everett Pyatt 1984 - Present	Incumbent
Reagan	George A. Sawyer 1981 - 1983	Laguna Beach, California
Carter	Joseph E. Doyle 1979 - 1981	Not Available
Carter	Edward Hidalgo 1977 - 1979	Partner Vorys, Sater, Seymour and Pease Washington, DC
Ford	John L. Bennett 1976 - 1977	Not Available
Nixon/Ford	Jack L. Bowers 1973 - 1976	Chairman of the Board and CEO Sanders Associates, Inc. Nashua, New Hampshire
Nixon	Charles L. Ill 1971 - 1973	Not Available
Nixon	Frank P. Sanders 1969 - 1971	Washington, DC

DIRECTOR
DEFENSE RESEARCH AND ENGINEERING

Level IV - Presidential Appointment with Senate Confirmation

Major Responsibilities

o   Manage the overall direction of department research and development programs, seeing that the evolution of U.S. defense technology serves the future acquisition requirements of the military services and supports basic defense policy.

o   Allocate funds for this purpose to the service departments, emphasizing technologies where the generic need is greatest. Seek to reduce duplication of effort through such means as the development where possible of multi-service weapons and support systems.

o   Support the research component of the department's budget request in the Congress. Provide concerned and interested committees with the information necessary to follow and understand the department's research and engineering efforts.

Necessary Background, Experience, Personal Skills

A sound technical background and a successful senior management record are vital in this position, but it also requires an understanding of the major weapons and other systems in use by or proposed for the military services. "The best place to look is industry," a former director asserts firmly. The job needs experience in resource allocation amid urgent and competing interests, and its occupant should know how to deal with financial numbers. As is usual in senior federal jobs, a knowledge of Congressional budget authorization and appropriation procedures is useful.

Insight

One of the missions of this job is to protect the technological base of the U.S. defense establishment. This means assuring that the capabilities in weapons, communications, and other areas that are crucial to successful defense in war are not eroded either by failure to advance along the major fronts of defense research and development or by inadequate funding for those efforts. At the same time, a solid technological base paves the most rational road to successive stages of modernization--that is, the constant effort of armed forces to remain contemporary in a fast-changing, high-tech military environment.

The Director of Defense Research and Engineering is a key figure in that effort, controlling and allocating funds for the purpose to the armed services. The occupant of the job, says Richard D. DeLauer, who directed research and engineering in 1981-84, "is the top technology person in the department--research and analysis, international programs, tactical warfare programs, space stuff." Essentially, it is the director's task to monitor the caliber of the department's technological strength as a whole--to measure its adequacy to the defense task, evaluate what each service believes should be its future directions and requirements, and decide how, when and where to spend a limited amount of money for the necessary research and development. Getting the budget to do that and justifying its use both currently and in terms of what is to be requested next time around is also part of the director's assignment.

A conversation with a former senior official in the department's acquisition process produced some reflections on the fundamental nature of this job. "Basically," he says, "there's a threat that we face. Everything comes from the perception of the threat. It involves being able to counter what's coming at you. That's how [decisions are made] on the technologies that should be followed. You look at the civilian world, at what's being developed, you look at what your threat is, and at what the defense industry is capable of. You have this pot of money, you [calculate] what can be done with it, and you go out with requests for proposals. There is an order, a logical sequence. The art of this business is understanding what that order is. You do that by going back to the beginning, by locating your threat and defining it."

Organizationally, the research and engineering function of the department has a fairly complicated recent history, and one which is intertwined closely with the position to which it now reports. The director is a lineal descendant of the former Undersecretary for Defense Research and Engineering, which in 1978 was also given overall department responsibility for acquisition. In 1985, those functions were split into two jobs. Research remained with the existing undersecretary; the acquisition functions went to a new job at the assistant secretary level, where they briefly remained until the deputy secretary took them on. Shortly thereafter, the secretary re-established the acquisition function separately in the new job of Undersecretary for Acquisition and placed the research and engineering position at the director level, reporting to the undersecretary. That is the way it stands today.

Tight constraints on resources present this position with some of its biggest challenges, says this former official. These are "making sure that your limited resources are spent on the technologies that need it the most; that the duplication between the services on how money is spent is somehow lessened; and coping with the micromanagement of the Congress."

When he had these responsibilities in 1973-77, Malcolm R. Currie believed that the steady support of the secretary and deputy secretary was imperative. He still does, asserting that "the power invested in this particular position is only valid to the extent that the bosses back it up." To that end, he spent time developing the relationships in the Office of the Secretary of Defense that are important to effectiveness. "It's a mind-expanding position," he says. "Four years experience equalled 40. It is an avenue for tremendous personal growth and, therefore, very attractive." But, he adds, "in these jobs we need the finest leadership, and those with the right background and experience. The jobs are becoming increasingly less attractive because of the restrictions on them. Sometimes the hassle just isn't worth it."

Key Relationships

Within the Department

Reports to: Undersecretary for Acquisition

Works closely with:

Deputy Secretary
Director, Operational Test and Evaluation
Vice Chairman, Joint Chiefs of Staff
Undersecretaries of the Air Force, Army and Navy
Undersecretary, Policy
Director, Operational Test and Evaluation
Director, Defense Advanced Research Projects Agency
Service acquisition executives
Service research and development executives

Outside the Department

Undersecretary, Department of Energy
Undersecretary, Export Administration, Department of Commerce
Associate Director, National Security and International Affairs, Office of Management and Budget

Outside the Federal Government

Research and development components of defense contracting companies; technology campuses and university science and technology departments; general manufacturing, engineering and R&D firms and their associations; defense research officials of other countries and of the North Atlantic Treaty Organization

Directors of Defense Research and Engineering Since 1969

Administration	Name and Years Served	Present Position
Reagan	Robert C. Duncan 1987 - Present	Incumbent
Reagan	Donald A. Hicks 1985 - 1986	President Hicks and Associates McLean, Virginia
Reagan	James P. Wade, Jr. 1984 - 1985 (Acting)	President Defense Group, Inc. Arlington, Virginia
Reagan	Richard D. DeLauer* 1981 - 1984	President Orion Group Ltd. Arlington, Virginia
Carter	William J. Perry* 1977 - 1981	Chairman and CEO H & Q Technology Partners Menlo Park, California
Nixon/Ford	Malcolm R. Currie 1973 - 1977	Executive Vice President Hughes Group Los Angeles, California

Nixon   John S. Foster, Jr.   Vice President
                  1965 - 1973   Special Projects
                                                  TRW Space and Defense
                                                      Sector
                                                  Redondo Beach, California

*   Held position as Undersecretary for Defense Research and
    Engineering.

DIRECTOR
OPERATIONAL TEST AND EVALUATION

Level IV - Presidential Appointment with Senate Confirmation

Major Responsibilities

o   Serve as principal assistant to the secretary in assessing the operational worthiness and readiness of newly-developed weapons and weapons systems for all military services. Set guidelines for the conduct of tests and evaluation in general, and for testing specific systems. Assure diligent compliance.

o   Coordinate this work closely with the leadership of department components, especially in the research, development, engineering and communications areas, and with the Undersecretary for Acquisition.

o   Direct the operation, improvement and modernization of principal test ranges. Manage joint test activities involving more than one military service.

o   Report to the secretary and the Congress on the operational capability of individual systems. Report annually on the test and evaluation status of major weapons programs. Engage in regular formal and informal contact with Congressional committee members and staff concerned with budgetary and operational questions relating to the test and evaluation function.

Necessary Background, Experience, Personal Skills

It would be difficult, if not functionally impossible, to handle this job without a sound understanding of the joint development of complex weapons systems by industry and government, and of the acquisition process. Almost certainly, that means training and experience as an engineer, a senior line manager in a defense con- tracting company, or a research and development director in that or a closely related field. Some previous experience in the depart- ment itself is also judged a requisite. With any of these back- grounds, a potential appointee must also demonstrate proven ad- ministrative skill and some political intelligence and sensitivity.

Ability in a European language is a useful resource.

Insight

In plain language, this director is the individual who steps into the early stages of the life of a new weapons system--one that has been discussed, authorized, designed, developed, and partly paid for--and sees what's right and wrong with it, and if it can be used or has to go back to the drawing board. Whether it works, or doesn't work and requires major overhaul, the evaluation report calls it as the director sees it. To the military department involved, the contractor, and other parties with a stake in a given system including the Congress, this role can sometimes be that of a bad news bear, and occasionally the traps are out.

There is, however, a fair amount of insulation which the designers of this job built into it. Selection of the director, for example, cannot by law be based on a candidate's political party or any personal connection with the administration. Only the President can remove a director, and must tell the Congress why. The test and evaluation function is supposed to operate independently of any individuals or institutions--a military service, a member of Congress, a contractor--with advocacy of a weapons system. The director signs an independent report to the secretary and the Congress on whether a system can do operationally what it is supposed to do. It's a report the Congress must receive before a military service can contract for full production of the system.

"We intercede in the acquisition process prior to full-rate production," says John E. Krings, director since 1985. "We're there because the user is never represented when the decision is made. In this independent role, all I care about is whether it works for the guy who needs it." He has a staff of 43. The office reviews, approves and oversees operational tests, but the military services operational test agencies actually perform them. The master plan for a testing process, Krings explains, "goes from the concept of a weapons system all the way out until you field it." Final approval of the plan rests with him, "so that I can ensure that the requirements are written, that the testing process is disciplined, and that there is a check and balance all the way through the acquisition life" of the system. "That's the management tool," he says. "You can shape a lot of things with that without writing a policy. You can start doing things to each program, and it evolves into an unwritten policy about how you do things."

Not unlike a number of peers around the Pentagon, the director manages a complex effort amid a large and complicated bureaucracy --a five-sided beehive of overlapping layers, duplicative procedures, and several power centers. Despite the intensely technical backdrop of this job, effectiveness in it seems to depend substantially on crafting productive personal relationships up and down the line.

Charles K. Watt, director in 1984, soon after the job was established, warns that "it is imperative that the individual in that position have informal networks that can work effectively within the bureaucratic process, as well as the formal channels." He emphasizes that "trust is an essential ingredient." The problems arise when confidence in the leadership and among the various parties to a project breaks down.

Inevitably, however, certain problems of other kinds also exist. In his experience, Watt says, the "timeliness of test events critical to decisionmaking" was not adequate. Planning procedures for such events were deficient. Among the office's principal deputies --in the areas of acquisition, strategic and naval warfare systems, tactical and land warfare systems, and facilities and resources-- rotation of duty among those in uniform was too frequent. Below them, substantive and support staff were too few. And, Watt adds, the basic problem in carrying out his responsibilities was "trying to get rationale and stability built into the budget process. The current process was cumbersome." Rationalizing and justifying the budget was more difficult because of the yearly budget cycle--in his view, too short.

According to Krings, "the only time we get 'pressures' from the contractors is if they've been hoodwinked." This situation occurs, he says, when a military service has given a contractor technical specifications which don't produce a product that can meet the operational requirements. "They make it totally according to specs, but then it doesn't work in the real world. So we are trying to educate the contractors, since they're the only ones who produce the products. If they don't make a profit, they won't be there...and we don't have a product. What I try to tell them is, make sure when you sign up for this thing you know what's going to be on the final operational exam, what the user requirements really are. Don't get led into something."

In addition to the test programs, the director is responsible for 19 major test ranges and for joint testing offices and activities, and establishes and enforces policy for all three. There are fairly regular range visits to observe test operations. Tests can be department- or industry-based. An annual budget of about $3 billion covers operation of the ranges, and the director has another several hundred million dollars to improve and modernize them. Joint tests, for example, of an aircraft for use in different versions by two or more of the military services, can last for several years. Three or four joint tests might be underway at the same time.

This is a job filled with meetings of many kinds--to hammer out policy guidance and enforce it, work towards complicated technical decisions, discuss budget problems on the Hill, or share information. The director is a member of the Defense Acquisition Board, chairs or sits in a wide variety of other meetings within the office of the secretary, the military service departments and the test and evaluation community, and confers with test range commanders and industry representatives. "Also," Watt adds, "I spent a lot of time answering questions from everywhere--the secretary's office, the undersecretaries, the Congress, and the press."

Krings divides the Congress into two groups--"the ones who are very helpful to us, think we're doing a fair job, and that want us to be involved, and then there are the killers, who only measure you by how many program managers' scalps you have on the wall, not how many Indians you've converted. They are bipartisan killers [who become infuriated if] they've got somebody in this job who's not a scalper."

"One should go in there with patience," Watt says. All decisions, he advises, need a solid rationale backed by the facts. "Be careful how you deal internally and externally," he says, "and have the informal channels in place." Be prepared, as necessary to bypass the formal bureaucracy. "I think that was typical of everyone in the higher positions. If it wasn't, they wouldn't last very long."

The most important quality in the job, Krings believes, is independence. It needs "somebody who really enjoys arguing, without being arrogant and picking fights, who's very confident and can tell somebody no without getting them mad at him." He likens working for the government to "working on another planet. You've got to learn how to survive on the moon, so if you think you're going up there and breathe regular air, I've got news for you....That doesn't mean the moon is worthless or the bureaucracy is worthless. It just means you'd like to perfect man's life on the moon without changing the atmosphere. It's not a rewarding, incentive-oriented planet. You've got a stick with no carrot on the end. So you hit them with the stick." He says his staff is "really exceptionally good. But we create an atmosphere where they can be that way."

Key Relationships

Within the Department

Reports to: Secretary

Works closely with:

Undersecretary for Acquisition
Director, Defense Research and Engineering
Deputy Undersecretary, Tactical Warfare Programs
Deputy Undersecretary, Strategic and Theater Nuclear Forces
Deputy Undersecretary, Research and Advanced Technology
Assistant Secretary, Command, Control, Communications and Intelligence

Outside the Department

Chairmen, members and staff of the armed services, budget and appropriations committees of both houses of the Congress
Undersecretary, Department of Energy
Assistant Secretary, Defense Programs, Department of Energy

Outside the Federal Government

Individual companies in the aerospace and related industries and their associations, such as the Electronic Industries Association and Institute of Electric and Electronic Engineers; Aerospace Industries Association of America, National Security Industrial Association, and American Defense Preparedness Association; space and scientific organizations; campuses and research institutes; state and local governments; counterparts in other governments, and in the North Atlantic Treaty Organization

Directors of Operational Test and Evaluation Since 1984*

Administration	Name and Years Served	Present Position
Reagan	John E. Krings 1985 - Present	Incumbent
Reagan	Michael D. Hall 1984 - 1985 (Acting)	Director Advanced Programs Department of the Air Force
Reagan	Charles K. Watt 1984 (Acting)	Director Systems and Technics Lab Georgia Tech Research Institute Smyrna, Georgia

* Position established in 1983 by the FY1984 Defense Authorization Bill.

GENERAL COUNSEL

Level IV - Presidential Appointment with Senate Confirmation

Major Responsibilities

o   Counsel the secretary on the legal ramifications of all Department of Defense activities and recommend the correct course where their legality is concerned. Undertake assignments as directed by the secretary to deal with special problems.

o   Direct or oversee all legal functions of the department on both the military and civilian sides. Integrate these functions, and their contribution to policy formulation, with the decisions and actions of other departments and agencies of the government, and at the White House. Supervise the department's representation in all legal proceedings in which it is involved. Maintain liaison with the Congress on defense legal matters.

o   Provide administrative supervision of the office of the general counsel.

Necessary Background, Experience, Personal Skills

Merely good general legal credentials won't cut it in this job. To be sure, it calls for someone with a superior legal education and lengthy, solid experience in the practice of law. But this individual must also have carried substantial private firm or corporate responsibility with distinction, and be recognized both for that and for professional and personal integrity. The general counsel must have strong dispute resolution skills and some background in commercial negotiations, must know criminal law, and "be able to write about anything under the sun on one page." In addition, handling the position requires a broad grounding in national security issues and a substantial previous exposure to the Washington political terrain, including the hills and valleys of the Congress. Finally, as a former general counsel says, "a great deal of the premium is on judgment, acquired by observing the mistakes of others."

Insight

In an organization which among other things spends $150 billion a year on procurement alone, has more than three million employees, occupies and uses facilities around the globe, and deploys nuclear weapons, the legal adviser and chief lawyer doesn't have to look for things to do. But perhaps the first point to keep in mind is the view of some who have occupied this job that dealing effectively with its considerable sweep of responsibilities depends crucially on the relationship with the secretary.

"A great deal of advice the secretary needs has to do with things that are usually the most difficult to deal with," says Deanne C. Siemer, general counsel in 1977-79. "The responsibilities of the general counsel depend on how the secretary wants to use his legal resources. You have exactly the amount of power as the relationship with the secretary allows. The level and quality of that relationship makes all the difference." Chapman B. Cox, who held the job in 1984-85, asserts that, "when people come to the secretary for a decision, only the secretary can be sure that the general counsel has input when necessary." The secretary must understand that a high proportion of matters have legal implications requiring general counsel input, and ensure that the people in his immediate office, especially the senior military advisor and special assistant, also understand it. Cox says he saw the secretary or deputy secretary several times a day, and "had input into any issue that involved legal questions or any proposal whose legality was questionable."

In the broadest sense, the general counsel keeps the secretary and the department's most senior officials in close touch with the legal aspects of everything they are doing and, in every instance, recommends the proper course from the point of view of the law. The job has direction of the Defense Legal Services Agency, which furnishes legal advice and services to the department. In an agency employing an estimated 6,000 lawyers, this position carries the department's senior legal authority and has oversight, or more direct control, over all legal functions. The general counsel bears ultimate responsibility for the legality of everything the Pentagon does, and of the actions of every uniformed and civilian individual on the payroll.

The most ready example of this--and in its way, the most illustrative--is the kind of problem, under the general heading of procurement practices, that began to come to light in June of 1988. But the general counsel's authority also extends to a myriad of other actions large and small, procedural and substantive--the soldier charged with illegal sales to civilians in Manila, or the alleged transgression of import privileges by a senior Navy officer returning from duty in the Caribbean, or the assignment of Marine Corps units to Lebanon. "You are one of three lawyers who knows whether the President is required to report to Congress under the War Powers Act," says Togo D. West, Jr., who held the job in 1979-81.

One of the products of exercising these responsibilities is a constant flow of decisions and recommendations from the general counsel's office. These are based on the review of procurement contracts, of proposed or revised international treaties, of the deployments of armed forces, of briefs and court transcripts, of speeches and Congressional testimony, of proposed legislation, of military agreements with other countries, and of documents in a dozen other categories of defense establishment activity. Scores of papers requiring concurrence, rejection or revision cross the general counsel's desk. "The department is a large paper factory," Siemer says. "There is an enormous number of things the general counsel must sign off on. The most daunting task is looking at your in-box. It's unreal."

As part of the process of reaching conclusions and acting on them, the general counsel sits in on an unusual number of multi-lateral meetings. These range from the secretary's daily inner-circle discussions to those of the Defense Policy Committee to the deliberations of a White House task force on national drug policy. In between are meetings with the general counsel's own staff, with the senior legal officers of the three services, with the general counsels of many other federal departments, and with legal officials at the White House. There are sessions with the judge advocates general, who oversee the functioning of military justice within the armed forces, presiding over what a former general counsel equates to "one of the largest criminal law firms in the world." Beyond this are frequent ad hoc interagency meetings and one-on-one encounters with opposite numbers around the executive branch and with Congressional members and staff.

The job has a public affairs component that varies between average and above-average for a senior federal official. It is characterized by a certain number of speeches, typically to bar associations or at military bases inside the United States and overseas, and ceremonial duties like ship christening. Cox, for one, thinks the general counsel, as a representative of the secretary, should avoid a lot of public pronouncements. "The job is to give good, confidential advice, and you can't do that if you're out speaking or running at the mouth."

One substantial factor complicating the decision-making process is, simply, the size of the department, something that Siemer speculates "is beyond the comprehension of most civilians." The secretary's "span of control," Cox notes, "is very great--a deputy, two undersecretaries, 11 unified commanders in chief, three service secretaries, the six joint chiefs, and 17 assistant secretaries." He believes it is too great, at least from the general counsel's standpoint. The accountability to the secretary of so many people "made it difficult to evaluate every option. There were so many decisions being made by so many senior executives that it was hard to have an input on all of them. Many were made before I even saw them." The job also has problems, he says, when "department officials rely on legal advice from other sources. Some claim they have a legal basis for their actions, but don't. Others try to avoid the general counsel because they suspect their proposal might not be legally sound, or they rely on other lawyers outside."

West thinks one of the job's challenges is developing the ability "to get facts out of a reluctant bureaucracy." He would advise the incoming general counsel to "get to the secretary in time to give advice that will help avoid a problem" and "remember that the position is advisory, not mechanical." For Cox, the challenges were "immense and broadening." As for the opportunity of the position, Siemer sees it as the chance "to get into a mega-sized world that you'll never see again anywhere else."

Key Relationships

Within the Department

Reports to:

Secretary
Deputy Secretary

Works closely with:

Undersecretary, Acquisition
Undersecretary, Policy
Assistant secretaries
General Counsels of the Departments of the Air
    Force, Army and Navy
Judge Advocates General of the three services

Outside the Department

General counsels or legal advisers of most other federal government departments and agencies
Assistant Attorney General, Civil Division, Department of Justice
Associate Counsel to the President
National Drug Policy Board (White House)

Outside the Federal Government

American Bar Association, American Association of International Lawyers, Federal Bar Association, Public Law Education Institute; defense contractors; organizations representing armed services members who are missing in action or prisoners of war; veterans groups; ethnic and women's rights organizations; Sierra Club and other environmental organizations

General Counsels of Defense Since 1969

Administration	Name and Years Served	Present Position
Reagan	Kathleen A. Buck 1987 - Present	Incumbent
Reagan	H. Lawrence Garrett III 1986 - 1987	Undersecretary of the Navy Department of Defense
Reagan	Chapman B. Cox 1984 - 1985	Partner Sherman, Howard Colorado Springs, Colorado
Reagan	William Howard Taft IV 1981 - 1984	Deputy Secretary Department of Defense
Carter	Togo D. West, Jr. 1979 - 1981	Partner Patterson, Belknap, Webb and Tyler Washington, DC

Carter	Deanne C. Siemer 1977 - 1979	Partner Wilmer, Cutler and Pickering Washington, DC
Ford	Richard A. Wiley 1976 - 1977	Partner Csaplar and Bok Boston, Massachusetts
Nixon/Ford	Martin R. Hoffman 1974 - 1975	Washington, DC
Nixon	Fred J. Buzhardt 1970 - 1974	Deceased

INSPECTOR GENERAL

Level IV - Presidential Appointment with Senate Confirmation

Major Responsibilities

o   Supervise the continual examination of department programs and operations for their legality and efficiency, through inspection, auditing and investigation procedures to prevent and detect fraud, waste and the abuse or violation of statutory law and regulations.

o   Develop and recommend to the secretary policy to guide these efforts. Inform the secretary and the Congress on their status, about problems and inadequacies encountered in administering them, and about requirements for remedial action.

o   Administer the Office of the Inspector General. Oversee the auditing and criminal investigation activities of each of the military departments. Serve as the principal department contact and liaison for the audit procedures of the General Accounting Office.

Necessary Background, Experience, Personal Skills

Legal, financial and accounting backgrounds are all good preparation for this position, as is specific experience in the auditing and investigations area. Management skills are essential. In an agency like Defense, says the present occupant of the job, previous service as an inspector general elsewhere in the government is invaluable; in fact, she doubts whether anyone coming in without prior, related government experience--a senior FBI or Department of Justice position, for example--could succeed.

Insight

The 1981 legislative provision which established this position conferred on it a reporting relationship to the Congress as well as to the secretary. This gives the job a considerable measure of independence in the sense that, unlike any other function in the

Pentagon, what the inspector general sends to the legislators is seen, but cannot be altered, by the secretary. The same principle applies to the scope of the IG's mandate. Except for time-sensitive operational plans, intelligence and counter-intelligence matters, and criminal investigations by another unit that are in progress, there are no areas or activities of the department that the secretary can shield from the IG's gaze. Reportedly, the secretary has never blocked an inquiry or investigation into these exempt areas. If that must occur, both the IG and the secretary are required to report it to the Congress.

The inspector general's criminal investigative organizations are participating in the investigation announced in June 1988 by a U.S. attorney into the department's procurement process. Once satisfied that information reported to it fell into the category of matters that are reported to the FBI, the IG's office contacted the agency and a joint investigation ensued. In the wake of the announcement, June Gibbs Brown, Inspector General since 1987, was meeting with the secretary as often as two or three times a day, although, as she said at the time, "I can't tell him a lot of what's going on because most of it is under seal." However, she was able to offer suggestions and make contributions to the secretary and his task force set up in connection with the investigation.

The IG normally sees the secretary at least six times a week in regularly scheduled staff meetings, and one-on-one with the secretary at any other time the situation requires. About the relationship between them, Joseph H. Sherick, inspector general in 1983-87, says "I didn't make elephants if they were really mice. But you have to keep [the secretary] alert to everything that's happening. The secretary knew what my job was, and he respected that and supported me." The IG also has regular contact with most of the assistant secretaries in the Office of the Secretary of Defense.

Basically, the inspector general's extensive domain is organized into inspection, investigation and auditing groups, as well as a special inquiry section, with an office staff numbering about 1,500. The IG also has policy and operational oversight of the audit and criminal investigation units of each of the military service departments, and of the Defense Contract Audit Agency and its 6,000 auditors. In addition, the inspector general sits on the President's Council on Integrity and Efficiency, an interagency body that groups principal federal departments. The office works closely with the General Accounting Office (GAO), the auditing and investigative arm of the Congress. One quantitative measure of the vast audit universe covered by Defense management and funding is Brown's estimation that, at any given moment, "there are about 300 GAO audits going on" at the department. Her office tracks and sees the resolution of all GAO recommendations.

Does the IG's office respond to events or take its own initiatives? It does both. An audit, of course, is planned well ahead of time in a lengthy process which surveys the programs or activities to be examined, obtains the views of the people involved and others within the department, and produces a written assessment. That process forms the basis for decisions on the audit plan for the next year and is coordinated with other auditing organizations, such as the GAO and military audit agencies, to avoid overlap or duplications. Inspections also get advance planning. The reactive side of the operation is driven chiefly by the office's "hotline," an alerting mechanism that produces more than a thousand letters and calls a months from individuals with apparent reason to believe a situation or activity bears looking into. "We look into all of them," Brown reports, "and about a third are significant enough to open some kind of inquiry." Since 1982, the hotline has rung more than 50,000 times.

Criminal investigations also have a reactive element, she adds, "but we have a lot of preventive activities, such as fraud awareness training." This has reached about 260,000 employees, who learn to look for and report factors like a high failure rate in certain equipment that might indicate a systemic problem requiring action by the inspector general. Criminal matters are always a priority, Brown says, "we're going to follow up any lead and devote the resources to developing the evidence." She would like to invest more resources in prevention, and is working on a voluntary procedure for contractor disclosure. The IG's office cooperates with thee Department of Justice to achieve criminal prosecutions.

Substantial political attention focuses on this job because of its special relationship with the HIll. The Congress can request an investigation or other action, and the inspector general tries to oblige in every case. Decisions must, however, be governed by practical considerations, such as evaluating the best use of the IG's limited resources. The Congress gave the IG, by statute, the discretion to determine what jobs will be scheduled, and made clear that the IG will not be appointed on the basis of politics. Moreover, great care is taken to assure that the results of the office's work are objective. "If a report happens to meet someone's political objective, that's coincidental," Brown emphasizes. "But as Congress contemplated, we cannot be used for political purposes."

On matters of general approach, operating style and relationships with the rest of the department in carrying out the job's responsibilities, Brown has these comments: "In order to build cooperation and assure the usefulness of our recommendations, the single most important thing is the quality of our work product. If there are meaningful findings and they're presented objectively, then there is pretty good acceptance. We coordinate with the components to be examined well ahead of time on inspections and audits so that they are aware of what we're going to do. They have to have confidence the office of the IG knows what it's doing, has the appropriate technical qualifications, and is fair, objective in identifying problems and recommending corrective measures to assure that the department operates in the best possible manner. Being nice, or being tough, is not the issue. OIG personnel must be objective, correct and professional."

The key problem of the job, Sherick says, "was the allocation of resources and managing our priorities while handling the priority jobs for the secretary." He thinks the job offers great challenges, "but the rewards are basically self-satisfying. It's not a thankless job, but if you don't get your own feeling of satisfaction and accomplishment, there's not much else that's going to come to you."

Key Relationships

Within the Department

Reports to: Secretary

Works closely with:

Deputy Secretary
Undersecretary, Acquisition
Assistant Secretary - Comptroller

Outside the Department

Assistant Attorney General, Criminal Division, Department of Justice
Assistant Attorney General, Civil Division, DOJ
Inspectors General in other federal departments and agencies
Comptroller General, General Accounting Office
Director, Federal Bureau of Investigation

Associate Director, Management, Office of Management and Budget

Outside the Federal Government

Association of Government Accountants and other accounting associations; auditing groups; legal and law enforcement associations

Inspectors General of Defense Since 1983*

Administration	Name and Years Served	Present Position
Reagan	June Gibbs Brown 1987 - Present	Incumbent
Reagan	Joseph H. Sherick 1983 - 1987	Annandale, Virginia

* Position established by Public Law 97-252 in 1982.

UNDERSECRETARIES OF THE
AIR FORCE, ARMY AND NAVY DEPARTMENTS

Level IV - Presidential Appointment with Senate Confirmation

(Like the secretaries of the military departments, the undersecretaries perform under similar mandates, with many of the same operating situations and problems. The following discussion examines them as a group.)

Major Responsibilities

o   Assist the secretary of the service in the management of its activities, acting under the secretary's direction as chief operating officer and focusing mainly on acquisition and general internal administration. Serve as acting secretary of the department when necessary.

o   Work closely with counterparts in the other services and with the uniformed leadership of the department. Establish productive relationships with the senior leadership in the Office of the Secretary of Defense, including the secretary.

o   Oversee the department's budget processes. Lead negotiations on the budget within the Defense Department and the administration. Support and defend it in the Congress.

o   Supplement the secretary's role as a public advocate and spokesman for the service's mission, activities and requirements.

Necessary Background, Experience, Personal Skills

Conversations with present and former undersecretaries indicate that the broad central requisites for these positions are (1) private-sector experience in managing a big organization and (2) technical background or training. But within those general definitions, the choices for the jobs need careful consideration. An incumbent of one of them, for example, would stay away from "big CEOs from corporate America" who are used to their perks and don't expect to stay late into the night. "I can't tell you," this undersecretary says, "how many CEOs or senior vice presidents, even those who are usually very successful, have come in here and left, having accomplished nothing and being completely frustrated." Where technical qualifications are concerned, a former Army undersecretary believes that a broad background is more valuable than being a specialist, and that it should include production experience, not merely pure science. In the Air Force context, a former undersecretary suggests, a senior engineering position in the aerospace industry is a good place to look.

Other backgrounds can be useful. One that some of these veterans raise is prior military experience; one of them thinks senior experience in the Pentagon itself is the "pre-eminent" qualification. Others mention law training or practice, which, says one, "enables you to pick out the trees" in the forest. There's no question that a knowledge of contract procedure, familiarity with the Congress, and some acquaintance with Washington's political byways and fairways all help immeasurably.

Insight

If the secretaries of the three military services manage a good deal of the outside business of their departments--by no means an unvarying definition--then the undersecretaries are the insiders, and in a big way. Although these jobs carry the responsibility to deal as required with the President, the public and the Congress (especially on budget matters), and to step into the shoes of the secretary when necessary, they focus primarily on day-to-day management, budget, acquisition of weapons and systems, and the bureaucracy.

The job of running the Department of the Air Force, says James F. McGovern, undersecretary since 1986, embraces "everything a corporate conglomerate encounters, and much more--managing and justifying to the Congress every item within our annual $100 billion budget." His list of these items and of the job's general duties is in fact descriptive of all three services: recruiting, training, motivating and retaining large numbers of military and civilian employees; procuring and maintaining exceptionally sophisticated defense systems; and every acquisition and environmental issue, airplane flying hour, and paper clip. "It includes a lot of other things you wouldn't normally think of that go along with running a Fortune 500 company," McGovern adds, such as "occupational safety and health issues, commerce-related issues, legal issues, labor issues and international sales, to name a few." It's a life "under the aegis or pall" of the office, says Robert H. Spiro, Jr.,

Army undersecretary in 1979-81. "It's all-consuming in the sense that you're available day and night."

One factor playing a determining role in the precise size, shape and nature of the undersecretaries' individual responsibilities is the relationship with their respective secretaries. One definition of this is offered by R. James Woolsey, Navy undersecretary in 1977-79. It is "whatever the secretary wants you to do," he says. "There was nothing in any regulation or structure that said I'd deal with research, engineering, intelligence or manpower, but that's what [the secretary] wanted me to do."

James R. Ambrose, Undersecretary of the Army in 1982-88, puts it this way: "The undersecretary is a creature of personalities, not of law or formal administrative procedure. Therefore, what it takes to fulfill the function is going to depend a great deal on his relationships and ambitions." Ambrose thinks the secretary and undersecretary should be chosen as a pair. "And," he says, "the pair, in my view, needs to be complementary." In Spiro's view, that pair must "be in sync as friends, on the same wavelength. But a good secretary will want dissent, he will want opinions."

They require up to half of the undersecretary's time. Considerable other time, particularly in the acting secretary role, is spent with the Secretary of Defense and the deputy secretary, and on the Hill. Testimony before a Congressional committee provides "a different kind of experience," says H. Lawrence Garrett, Navy undersecretary since 1987, "being grilled for six or seven hours on the minutiae within a $100 billion budget."

An important point to keep in mind concerning the Air Force undersecretary is that job's added responsibility for the management of highly technical intelligence-gathering systems that dwell in the deepest secrecy. This time-consuming mission demands strong technical and engineering background. Because of it, the occupant of the position normally spends less time in budget and personnel matters than the other two undersecretaries.

The interest and reach of the Congressional committees with oversight of the service departments go considerably beyond the purse strings they control. Many members and staffers have an in-depth grasp of the services' programs. They understand the acquisition process, and the issues which underlie it. "The way you level the playing field," Ambrose advises, "is just simply try to know as much or more than they do. Knowledge and forthrightness, integrity in dealing with them, have been largely the tools I used."

Amid the burgeoning investigations in mid-1988 of alleged bribery and other misdeeds in the Pentagon, trying to depict what the procurement responsibilities of these jobs are likely to be in early 1989 would be premature, to say the least. One or two generalizations may have continuing applicability, however. For one thing, it seems obvious that procurement on the Pentagon scale makes it difficult to centralize all authority in any one individual. "You can't run the research and procurement of the vast numbers of goods and services the military services require from your office," McGovern says. "You're just fooling yourself if you try." For another, says Garrett, acquisition means "spending a lot of money finding out if a widget is going to work. But there are so many wickets to go through, not just in the service but in the Pentagon. That's one of the reasons it takes so long."

To operate in this complex matrix demands an understanding of how the matrix works, who the players are, and how the many-layered decision-making process works--knowledge that cannot be acquired quickly. That means, as two who have had these jobs point out, an inevitable--if temporary--position behind the learning curve.

One key learning area is the bureaucracy, military and civilian. Some of those who have held undersecretary positions feel the uniformed military is not really equipped to handle standard procurement responsibilities. "Their primary job is to be ready to fight," says David S. Potter, Navy undersecretary in 1974-76. As Ambrose puts it, "military people are not selected or trained to fight these kinds of wars--the administrative, Congressional and budget priorities wars. So, until you get a transformation, which is difficult to accomplish, I think you need strong civilian support, not criticism or tearing down, but helping...." Another learning task, he says, is to understand the differences between the power and command structure of the military--where "planning and order-giving comes out of the staff"--and that in industry, "where staffs are advisers and the division managers have the boss and executive power."

Former undersecretaries give the career ranks credit not only as "highly intelligent people, highly motivated, and very articulate," but as "consummate warriors in the administrative as well as the military sense." They mention the usual battles over turf, and warn of "being run over unless you have strength" and of subordinates trying "to hide the ball from people at the top." One says he made himself "infamous for asking questions and not accepting [uninformative or evasive] answers."

In running bureaucracies like these, McGovern offers this prescription: "You've got to be in town to have an impact on the important issues; you've got to do your homework at night. You can't just sign memos and expect that, as with a private sector company, everyone will march smartly to carry out your orders. If your opponents disagree with your decisions, they have plenty of other opportunities to throw in roadblocks. You have to be a street fighter, be willing to put yourself at risk, and throw yourself at a lot of issues. That takes being here and having the program facts and the political savvy about how you get things done in Washington." He does not think an undersecretary can "command" consensus. "You clearly have to earn the respect of your subordinates. It takes a while and a few issues to do that." Garrett stresses the importance of clear and organized decisionmaking: "Anyone who comes into this organization who is not willing to fish or cut bait is really going to have a problem."

Future undersecretaries will "have to make up their own minds about priorities," Ambrose says. "The only way they can do that and make it stick is to know enough about the subject." His advice is to "immediately learn everything you can and, in particular, how to get reliable information promptly when you need it. Don't depend on the organized flow of information, because it could be misused and old. Establish relationships with the key military personnel and get calibrated by them." He would like to see appointments that last four years or more, without a view of the job as a stepping stone.

Potter agrees, saying he finds it "very discouraging to watch people use these positions for personal gain." And, given the conflict of interest laws now on the books, James W. Plummer, Air Force undersecretary in 1973-76, says "the ideal appointee would be someone who would do the job for four years, not just two, and then be willing to go home and sit in a rocking chair."

Key Relationships

Within the Department

Reports to: Secretary of the service department

Works closely with:

Undersecretary, Acquisition, Office of the Secretary of Defense (OSD)
Assistant Secretary - Comptroller, OSD
Deputy Assistant Secretary, Military Manpower and Personnel Policy, OSD
Director, Program Analysis and Evaluation, OSD

Assistant Secretary, International Security Affairs, OSD
Chief of staff of the department
Undersecretaries of the other service departments

Outside the Department

Chairmen, ranking members and staff of the budget
and appropriations committees of the House and
Senate
Counterparts at the departments of Transportation,
Treasury, State, Justice, Commerce, Labor, the
Environmental Protection Agency, and the Small
Business Administration
Deputy Director, Central Intelligence Agency (Air
Force undersecretary only)

Outside the Federal Government

Defense contractors in a very wide range; retired
officers and veterans associations; environmental
groups; state and local government officials; representatives of foreign governments

Undersecretaries of the Air Force Since 1969

Administration	Name and Years Served	Present Position
Reagan	James F. McGovern 1986 - Present	Incumbent
Reagan	Edward C. Aldridge, Jr. 1981 - 1986	Secretary Department of the Air Force
Carter	Antonio Handler Chayes 1979 - 1981	Chairman Endispute Cambridge, Massachusetts
Carter	Hans M. Mark 1977 - 1979	Chancellor University of Texas System Austin, Texas

| Ford | James W. Plummer
1973 - 1976 | Jacksonville, Oregon |
| Nixon | John L. McLucas
1969 - 1973 | Chairman of the Board
Questech, Inc.
McLean, Virginia |

Undersecretaries of the Army Since 1969

Administration	Name and Years Served	Present Position
Reagan	Michael P. W. Stone 1988 - Present	Incumbent
Reagan	James R. Ambrose 1982 - 1988	Atherton, California
Carter	Robert H. Spiro, Jr. 1979 - 1981	Chairman of the Board Sports 2000, Inc. McLean, Virginia
Carter	Walter B. LaBerge 1977 - 1979	Not Available
Ford	Norman R. Augustine 1975 - 1977	Chief Executive Officer Martin Marietta Corp. Bethesda, Maryland
Nixon/Ford	Herman R. Staut 1973 - 1975	Not Available
Nixon	Kenneth E. BeLieu 1971 - 1973	Not Available
Nixon	Thaddeus R. Beal 1969 - 1971	Not Available

Undersecretaries of the Navy Since 1969

Administration	Name and Years Served	Present Position
Reagan	H. Lawrence Garrett 1987 - Present	Incumbent
Reagan	James F. Goodrich 1981 - 1987	Washington, DC
Carter	Robert J. Murray 1980 - 1981	Director National Security Programs John F. Kennedy School of Government Harvard University Cambridge, Massachusetts
Carter	R. James Woolsey 1977 - 1979	Partner Shea and Gardner Washington, DC
Ford	David S. Potter 1974 - 1976	Santa Barbara, California
Nixon/Ford	J. William Middendorf II 1973 - 1974	Chairman Middendorf, Ansary and Company Washington, DC
Nixon	Frank P. Sanders 1972 - 1973	Not Available
Nixon	John W. Warner 1969 - 1971	United States Senator State of Virginia

DIRECTOR
DEFENSE ADVANCED RESEARCH PROJECTS AGENCY

Senior Executive Service

Major Responsibilities

o Consult closely with the science and technology managers of the individual military services on the high-technology requirements of service programs.

o Formulate and direct projects of basic and applied research which exploit very advanced technologies to meet these operational needs. Obtain department approval for the programs and guide them through the budget process within the administration and with the Congress.

o Recommend for the secretary's attention additional advanced research with the potential to move defense programs forward. Keep the Office of the Secretary of Defense (OSD), the Joint Chiefs of Staff and the military departments abreast of noteworthy scientific and technological developments emerging from the research effort.

Necessary Background, Experience, Personal Skills

A strong technical background is requisite--engineering or scientific training at the doctorate level and substantial experience in defense research--at some point in the acquisition spectrum. Skill as a manager, a general familiarity with the Defense department, and a knowledge of the missions of the military departments are all highly useful resources. The position benefits greatly from an entrepreneurial flair and the ability to take unconventional approaches to the problems at hand.

Insight

Former directors with whom we talked use slightly different words to characterize the basic mission of this job, but with the same eyes-on-the-horizon theme. Robert S. Cooper, who led the

Defense Advanced Research Projects Agency (DARPA) in 1982-84, says its challenge is "to appropriately determine the needs of the military departments and formulate engineering and scientific answers [that keep the country] ahead of our adversaries." To George H. Heilmeier, director in 1975-78, the agency's task is to "keep the United States in the forefront of defense technology." Stephen J. Lukasik (1972-74) thinks it is "to prevent technical surprises to the U.S. defense establishment."

DARPA is a separate agency within the Defense department. From an operational if not from a budget point of view, the organization has what amounts in some respects to a blank check to look into areas of advanced defense science that could bring benefits to one or more of the military services in carrying out assigned tasks. DARPA projects have their origins chiefly in the perceived needs of the services, are worked out in close consultation with them and with the OSD, and carried out jointly. But DARPA suggests to the defense establishment research ideas of its own as well; in this, it is usually out ahead of the services, which normally are more concerned with current technology or current technological solutions.

Lukasik recalls the agency as "a small group of managers, without labs or contract facilities, that worked with other parts of the department," with a special focus on technical ideas the rest of the department was not working on. In that sense, he says, DARPA was "like a big balance wheel." The agency's more or less open-ended mandate lends a venturesome tone to its undertakings. It has a "charter," Heilmeier says, to work "with high-payoff operations" in situations which also carry high risk with respect to the time and resources required. "You have to feel comfortable with taking risks." But just as in any executive position, "you must have the right kind of chemistry [with your superiors]. They gave me autonomy and flexibility, not day-to-day direction."

The director sits on the Defense Resources Board, rides herd on agency program and budget decisions, deals with the successive phases of the budget process, including the Congress, supervises the technical direction and execution of programs, and has a hand in personnel administration. DARPA operates on an annual budget of something close to $2 billion. "It's a small organization," Cooper says, "so you should have natural leadership qualities, be respected for yourself and your capabilities, and have integrity." The major strength of the staff, Heilmeier thinks, "is that they're very entrepreneurial." To keep it that way, "you have to bring in new people with new ideas all the time."

Doing so, however, is complicated by limited resources. Cooper found a problem in "not being able to bring in the most technically needed personnel" and Heilmeier calls the task of attracting good staff the agency's "major problem."

The very nature of DARPA's mission can also bring it opposition elsewhere in the department. "The conflicts come," Heilmeier warns, when DARPA "challenges the status quo, an approach that is characteristic both of the job and the agency." In coping with this, he says he acted "as any executive would--do the homework, meet the critics, and be straightforward."

Key Relationships

Within the Department

Reports to: Undersecretary, Acquisition

Works closely with:

Deputy Secretary
Director, Defense Research and Engineering
Director, Operational Test and Evaluation
Undersecretaries of the Air Force, Army and Navy
Director, Science and Technology, Department of the Air Force
Director, Research and Development, Department of the Army
Chief of Naval Research, Department of the Navy

Outside the Department

Deputy Director, Science and Technology Policy, Executive Office of the President
Associate Director, National Security and International Affairs, Office of Management and Budget

Outside the Federal Government

University engineering and technical departments; defense contractors; science, technology and defense organizations, such as National Academy of Engineering, National Academy of Science, and American Defense Preparedness Association; and military service associations

Directors of the Defense Advanced Research Project Agency Since 1969

Administration	Name and Years Served	Present Position
Reagan	Raymond S. Colladay 1988 - Present	Incumbent
Reagan	Robert C. Duncan 1985 - 1987	Director of Defense Research and Engineering Department of Defense
Reagan	Robert S. Cooper 1982 - 1984	President Atlantic Aerospace Greenbelt, Maryland
Carter/Reagan	Robert R. Fossum 1978 - 1981	Dean School of Engineering and Applied Science Southern Methodist University Dallas, Texas
Ford/Carter	George H. Heilmeier 1975 - 1978	Senior Vice President Texas Instruments, Inc. Dallas, Texas
Nixon	Stephen J. Lukasik 1972 - 1974	Vice President Northrop Corporation Los Angeles, California
Nixon	Eberhart Rechtin 1969 - 1971	Palos Verdes Estates, California

DIRECTOR
PROGRAM ANALYSIS AND EVALUATION

Senior Executive Service

Major Responsibilities

o   Serve as program planning adviser to the secretary, and as the secretary's personal assistant in other assignments involving multi-year defense programs, force structures and military capabilities.

o   Review the five-year program proposals of the military services in terms of their effectiveness in achieving assigned objectives and missions. Develop alternative issues and proposals for the secretary as necessary. Coordinate this review within the Office of the Secretary of Defense (OSD).

o   Manage the programming aspects of the department's annual planning, programming and budgeting cycle. Participate actively in the planning and budgeting phases of the department's five-year cycle, defining the defense policies and objectives and projecting the limitations on resources which together form the basis for the decisions made.

Necessary Background, Experience, Personal Skills

Economics as a discipline is good preparation for this position. It should be buttressed by experience with defense issues in industry or government, and perhaps by military service. The director does not need a heavy background in analysis or programming, but should understand both. Superior ability in written and oral communication is a must.

Insight

The director's key task is to advise the secretary on what directions the individual military services should take to meet the future requirements of U.S. defense policy. Essentially that means deciding what's right and wrong with the forward plans and programs of the services for that period of time, whether their plans for force sizes and weapons systems will do the jobs assigned, and what alternatives deserve consideration.

To reach these conclusions, the director leads an annual review of each service's program objective proposal, examining it in detail for such qualities as consistency with policy goals, cost effectiveness and coherence, and raising substantive questions for the consideration of the secretary. (Note that, in the past year, the department switched provisionally to a twice-yearly review to reduce work load and minimize turbulence; this approach may be continued in the future.)

A review might ask, as one of them did recently, whether the Navy's carrier-centered battle groups are too heavy on carriers and too light on the right kinds of escort and logistics vessels. Another example concerned the Air Force's mix of active and reserve forces--whether more pilots could be retained in the reserves and fewer on active duty, a move thought potentially useful in easing the pilot-retention problem and saving money. A third review focused on the utility of the Army's light divisions, given likely future threats, and how many of them are necessary.

In the review process, the director and the Undersecretary for Acquisition dominate within OSD. The undersecretary's interest is oriented toward hardware programs--weapons systems, development, and acquisition. The director's mandate includes some acquisition issues but has no boundaries, allowing the program analysis and evaluation office to look at any and all aspects of a service's program. Disagreements among the several players at the OSD level about a service's program proposal are discussed in meetings of the Defense Resources Board, of which this job serves as executive director, and are normally settled by the secretary or deputy secretary.

Effectiveness here means understanding what is important to the secretary and deputy secretary and how to get those issues in front of them so that they can see clearly what the choices are. Part of this requires the presentation of complex questions, and the alternatives available, in precise and objective fashion. At the same time, the director needs personal skill in maintaining working relationships with senior personalities in OSD and the services, some of whom may be envious of the director's prerogatives.

Beyond these functions, the director also takes on a range of special or personal assignments from the secretary, in studies and analyses, speeches and statements, preparation of a variety of reports, or as troubleshooter. To a considerable extent, this has also been true where the present deputy secretary is concerned.

The director and the comptroller, unimpeded by parochial interests, seem to be among the few department officials who are placed to understand the secretary's and deputy secretary's perspectives on the department's program as a whole. It is important to have a direct line to both. Obviously, however, these relationships change over time and succeeding administrations, and it is well to note that the precise breadth and character of the director's job depend to a considerable degree on the operating style of the department's two top jobs.

Given its loose mandate and close ties to the secretary, the role of this position often changes with shifts in circumstances and management philosophies. During the first half of the 1970s, for example, program analysis and evaluation was deeply involved in National Security Council studies.

By OSD standards, the director's staff is not a large one-- about a hundred people. A senior department official who knows this job well says the office needs "probing and inquisitive minds which can separate the wheat from the chaff. They have to demand enough detail from the services to really know what the services are doing." The essential quality in a director, this official believes, "is a broad-basis understanding of military affairs," not the quantitative skills of an analyst. "It's the kind of a team where, if you have good managers at the deputy or team leader level, you can spend more time working with the secretary." Also useful is "a good understanding of where the department fits in Washington, in relation to the Hill." But the director, while providing support to the legislative affairs office of the department, currently has little direct involvement with the Congress; when this has occurred, it was usually in low profile.

The Congress is considering a recommendation to establish this position as an Assistant Secretary at executive level IV. It would remain a staff position, in which the policy interests of the secretary are paramount. The director serves no other office or individual. "I think not being heavily partisan helps," the same official says. "It's really better to have somebody who is simpatico to the party in power but knows how to deal with the others, than to have someone who is viewed as an ideologue."

The job is difficult in the number and complexity of the problems it addresses, and in the organizational and institutional pressures on it. Looking at the department today, Leonard Sullivan, Jr., who held these responsibilities in 1973-76, thinks the next director of program analysis and evaluation should reverse "the trend of letting the services decide their own objectives." He recommends the appointment of "a strong, mature individual who can command respect from the generals, rather than a someone whose experience is limited to being an analyst. You can't bring in people who don't have the technical background or experience in dealing with some tough, dedicated military professionals."

Key Relationships

Within the Department

Reports to: Secretary

Works closely with:

Deputy Secretary
Undersecretary, Acquisition
Undersecretary, Policy
Assistant Secretary - Comptroller
Undersecretaries of the Air Force, Army and Navy
Chairman and vice chairman, Joint Chiefs of Staff

Outside the Department

Assistant Secretary, Politico-Military Affairs, Department of State
Director, Congressional Budget Office

Outside the Federal Government

Individual defense contracting firms; defense industry associations

Directors of Program Analysis and Evaluation Since 1969

Administration	Name and Years Served	Present Position
Reagan	David S. C. Chu 1981 - Present	Incumbent
Carter	Russell Murray II 1977 - 1981	Special Counselor House Committee on Armed Services

Carter	Edward C. Aldridge, Jr. 1976 - 1977	Secretary Department of the Air Force
Nixon/Ford	Leonard Sullivan, Jr. 1973 - 1976	Resident Consultant Systems Planning Corp. Arlington, Virginia
Nixon	Gardiner L. Tucker 1970 - 1973	Not Available
Nixon	Ivan Selin (Acting) 1969 - 1970	Chairman of the Board American Management Systems Arlington, Virginia

9

DEPARTMENT OF EDUCATION

Established only about ten years ago, this department has already survived an attempt to dismantle it. But the scars show-- in a nervous and rather dispirited bureaucracy, the absence of a steady direction for long-range policy, criticism from some of those formerly in its leadership, and a largely disaffected constituent community.

For about the last two years, opinion surveys have consistently shown education among the two or three domestic issues of greatest public concern. Raising the quality of American education at every level, and extending it to all who need it, is a resistant and visible national problem, and the Congress knows it. Education is popular on the Hill; the legislators have strong feelings about the federal role and how the Congress has supported it. Any incoming senior official of the department unfamiliar with these attitudes should make grasping them an early item of business. This is all the more essential because the reauthorization of higher education and special education legislation is due for action by the next Congress.

Another central issue which may confront those who guide federal responsibilities for education is vocational instruction. It has been treated, a national education group representative thinks, "as a categorical program," merely an option for students unable to compete in traditional educational programs. This has made vocational training unavailable for those who can compete, and has become "a threat to traditional vocational enterprise, which is big business." How to merge vocational education into the mainstream is a debate likely to turn "really ugly" before it's over.

To recover its footing and momentum in an increasingly charged and urgent educational climate, the department ($20.3 billion budget in fiscal 1988, and 4,500 employees, smallest of the federal agencies) needs to get a running start at the beginning of the next administration. Its first steps should be energetic and confident. It should send clear signals of an intent to be interactive, to place competence over political consonancy, to be more receptive to its constituencies and more attentive to their views. In short, the department must develop a greater sense of mission and of relevancy.

DEPARTMENT OF EDUCATION

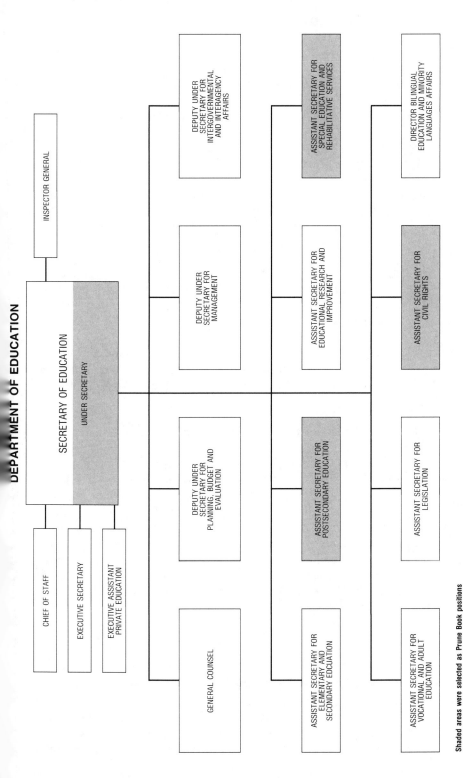

Shaded areas were selected as Prune Book positions

INSPECTOR GENERAL

CHIEF OF STAFF

EXECUTIVE SECRETARY

EXECUTIVE ASSISTANT PRIVATE EDUCATION

SECRETARY OF EDUCATION

UNDER SECRETARY

GENERAL COUNSEL

DEPUTY UNDER SECRETARY FOR PLANNING, BUDGET AND EVALUATION

DEPUTY UNDER SECRETARY FOR MANAGEMENT

DEPUTY UNDER SECRETARY FOR INTERGOVERNMENTAL AND INTERAGENCY AFFAIRS

ASSISTANT SECRETARY FOR ELEMENTARY AND SECONDARY EDUCATION

ASSISTANT SECRETARY FOR POSTSECONDARY EDUCATION

ASSISTANT SECRETARY FOR EDUCATIONAL RESEARCH AND IMPROVEMENT

ASSISTANT SECRETARY FOR SPECIAL EDUCATION AND REHABILITATIVE SERVICES

ASSISTANT SECRETARY FOR VOCATIONAL AND ADULT EDUCATION

ASSISTANT SECRETARY FOR LEGISLATION

ASSISTANT SECRETARY FOR CIVIL RIGHTS

DIRECTOR BILINGUAL EDUCATION AND MINORITY LANGUAGES AFFAIRS

UNDERSECRETARY

Level III - Presidential Appointment with Senate Confirmation

Major Responsibilities

o   Take an authoritative role in policy development for the department, in consultation with the secretary.   Function as chief
operating and administrative officer, and as acting secretary
as necessary.

o   Represent the department in relevant interagency consultations
and mediate differences in policy formulation and execution
within the administration.   Act as a principal spokesman for
the administration on education.

o   Manage the department's budget process, negotiate the budget
with the Office of Management and Budget and defend it to the
Congress. Represent the department in Congressional testimony.

Necessary Background, Experience, Personal Skills

To fill this position effectively, look for solid credentials in
the education or scholarly fields--a major university or a research
enterprise--that include more than a passing acquaintance with the
federal programs administered by the Department of Education.
Substantial experience in the management area should supplement
these qualifications.   As with several other senior positions in the
department, including its chief, the undersecretary position obviously
benefits if its occupant has developed constructive contacts at
various levels of the academic community.   Equally useful is familiarity with the Congress.

Insight

Echoing a general complaint of former officials elsewhere in
this department, some previous undersecretaries point to unclear
organization at the top as a principal problem they have encountered.
Though it is easy to overstate the case, their comments largely
agree about a flawed reporting structure, and one which in some

respects dates back a decade or more. The difficulty seems to center on parallel and sometimes conflicting reporting responsibilities to the secretary and on apparent overstaffing at certain other senior levels. "The problem," according to one veteran of the job, "was that the secretary had...people around him who would try to direct policy in directions not in the best interests of the secretary but in the better interests of themselves." He adds that "the secretary's personal staff should have no input, only a supporting role. They should not have any role in policy or personnel matters."

William C. Clohan, undersecretary in 1981-1982, reports that "there were almost too many people reporting to me (when in the capacity of acting secretary). "Be clear about the relationships you want, how you establish them and how you develop personal lines of communication to keep them open," advises Steven A. Minter, who held the job in 1980-81.

These considerations relate directly to a key task of the undersecretary--to discipline and improve the department's upward flow of information so that the secretary can speak and act with confidence and credibility. In this and other respects, it is important for the undersecretary to have professional credentials in the academic field. That is especially true if the secretary is not an educator.

Comments by former occupants of the job reflect its essential focus on policy development, day-to-day management of the department, work in the trenches and committee rooms of the Congress, and activity in the public sphere. The policy segment of these duties puts the undersecretary into regular and frequent meetings with the secretary and with counterparts in other agencies in the form of Cabinet council deliberations. Particularly in the absence of the secretary--but not only at such times--policy and other matters involve the occupant of this job in meetings and informal consultations at the White House.

As usual in the case of relationships between the top and second-ranking jobs in federal agencies, the best formula combines a logical division of workload between the two with the ability of the deputy when called on to take temporary command in an informed and efficient way. But Gary L. Jones, undersecretary in 1982-85, thinks that neither individual should get mired in routine management tasks. "You must look at the total picture and pull levers for the agency on a daily basis," he says. "You can't get involved in employee negotiations and administrative procedural matters which could impose never-ending time constraints upon you for months." He believes the department has been hurt over the years by a lack of day-in, day-out leadership. In his view, "the continuity of organizational leadership is an inherent problem in political organizations." He suggests that "the needs of students across the country" have suffered as a result of "separate and divergent agendas rather than a rigorous and continued emphasis on improving the quality of education." Two other former undersecretaries sound similar notes, expressing the belief that the department has developed a "credibility" problem, especially with interest groups whom its decisions affect most directly. A third previous occupant of the job says it needs "an executive mind, not ideological passion."

On that subject, a national education group representative feels that the undersecretary "has to be a person that folks regard as technically and politically in tune with the philosophy of the administration. I don't think the person can be completely separated from that kind of identity. When you work with professional and technical people and academicians you have to have enough credibility for them to value your involvement." That, in turn, strengthens the standing among educators and the broader community as well that the undersecretary needs to communicate effectively.

In the view of this observer, the occupant of this job must be "committed enough to the truth to be sure it gets said in the appropriate way to the appropriate people, so that when you have to make those aching compromises, you've left behind a trail of people who understand the battle has been fought and lost--or that this is a deliberate fall-back position enabling us to fight another day. There has to be enough mutual respect so that the debate is well-joined."

Key Relationships

Within the Department

Reports to: Secretary

Works closely with:

Deputy Undersecretary for Management
Deputy Undersecretary for Planning, Budget and Evaluation
Deputy Undersecretary for Intergovernmental and Interagency Affairs
General Counsel
Assistant secretaries

Outside the Department

Deputy secretaries and equivalents of other Cabinet departments

Associate Director, Human Resources, Veterans and Labor, Office of Management and Budget

Outside the Federal Government

State and local education groups, such as Council of the Great City Schools, National Association of State Boards of Education; state and local education officials; student, teacher and administrative organizations at the secondary level, such as National Education Association, National Association of Secondary School Principals, Student Loan Marketing Association, and American Association of School Administrators; and at the college and university level, such as American Association of University Professors, Association of American Universities, and Association of Independent Colleges and Schools

Undersecretaries of Education Since 1980*

Administration	Name and Years Served	Present Position
Reagan	Linus D. Wright 1987 - Present	Incumbent
Reagan	Gary L. Bauer 1985 - 1987	Assistant to the President for Policy Development The White House
Reagan	Gary L. Jones 1982 - 1985	Consultant Trinity IV Washington, DC
Reagan	William C. Clohan 1981 - 1982	Senior Partner Clohan, Adams & Dean Washington, DC

Carter   Steven A. Minter   President
                        1980 - 1981   The Cleveland Foundation
                                                    Cleveland, Ohio

*   The Department of Education was created by the Department
     of Education Organization Act, PL-96-88, October 17, 1979.

ASSISTANT SECRETARY
CIVIL RIGHTS

Level IV - Presidential Appointment with Senate Confirmation

Major Responsibilities

o   Assure adherence to civil rights laws protecting minorities, women, and the handicapped and disabled from discrimination by educational institutions receiving federal financial assistance. Closely monitor observance of these laws through the conduct of compliance reviews and the investigation of complaints and potential violations. Enforce compliance through the courts and by other remedial actions.

o   Advise and assist the secretary in policy matters relating to civil rights in education. Keep the Congress informed on administration policy and actions in this area and seek its support.

o   Maintain contact with groups and individuals concerned with federal civil rights policies, and work for their understanding and support.

Necessary Background, Experience, Personal Skills

Although this position does not require a lawyer, its occupant should have a grasp of judicial procedure, general legal precepts, and law enforcement. A background in civil rights, with knowledge of the current issues in that field, is highly desirable. It would also be useful to understand developments in U.S. secondary and post-secondary education, and to have some prior management experience.

Insight

LeGree S. Daniels, who has held this job since 1987, finds that the issues it deals with "are different in the 1980s." The general framework, she says, is "not as simple as it was in the 1960s. It's more person to person. The things we get now are more personal--harassment issues, for example." She thinks this represents a different set of issues which will require a different kind of commitment from the assistant secretary of the future. Though many people continue to think of civil rights generally in terms of race or national origin, she points out, the rights of the handicapped are the subject of most--54%--of the current complaints her office handles.

The chief activity of the Office of Civil Rights (OCR) is the investigation of individual complaints, which currently total about 2,000 a year. OCR refers most of these to the ten regional offices of the department which, after investigation, determine whether violations exist and, if so, what remedies must apply. Settlement of complaints takes place through voluntary compliance agreements, or in court. In the absence of voluntary agreements, OCR also has the option of setting a time period within which a violator must comply with the law or face a cut-off of federal funds.

"You're dealing with lawyers, advocacy groups, and Congressional staffs," Daniels says. She would advise an incoming assistant secretary to make early visits to each of the regional offices, which are the "backbone" of OCR. "They do the day-to-day job," she says, "dealing with the school boards and districts, and with the people who make the complaints." More than 800 people work for OCR, of whom 75% are in the field. Daniels rates the career staff highly and says "you can depend on those people and give them enough leeway to run their offices."

"Policy development is important," says Cynthia O. Brown, who held this job in 1980-81. "You have to define what discrimination is, and suggest remedies." Policy questions are a matter for consultation with the secretary but, Daniels notes, "we make decisions [based on it] independently." The assistant secretary sits on a number of interagency coordinating committees in which questions of civil rights in education are involved. On the Hill, OCR's activities are the concern chiefly of the committees on Labor and Human Resources (Senate) and Education and Labor Committee (House). Statutorily, OCR has some independence from the department in the sense that it operates on a separate budget and makes separate reports to the President and the Congress.

Brown remembers this position as "a very difficult management and policy development job." The agency operated in "constant controversy" and she was "constantly being criticized for doing too little or too much." Daniels agrees that it is "a hot political job." She says she has found an open-door policy helpful with advocacy groups, and says "if you're really trying to do the job the way Congress intended it should be done, it's not so hard." She adds: "Politics may have gotten you to the job, but when you walk in this door, politics has to step outside. You must vigorously enforce a law that covers everyone, and you can't do it from a political point of view." The real challenge for the 1990s, she believes, is "equal expectational opportunity, for want of a better phrase. We need to set our standards high and keep them up against the board. We're not a closed society anymore. If we're going to compete, everyone has to have a good education."

Key Relationships

Within the Department

Reports to: Secretary

Works closely with:

Undersecretary
General Counsel
Assistant secretaries

Outside the Department

Assistant Attorney General, Civil Rights Division, Department of Justice
Deputy Undersecretary, Employment Standards, Department of Labor
Director, Office for Civil Rights, Department of Health and Human Services

Outside the Federal Government

National civil rights and minority organizations, and groups representing the interests of the physically disabled such as the American Civil Liberties Union, National Association for the Advancement of Colored People, National Council on the Handicapped; teacher, parent and student associations; state and local education boards; university and college officials and attorneys; legal associations

Assistant Secretaries for Civil Rights Since 1980*

Administration	Name and Years Served	Present Position
Reagan	LeGree S. Daniels 1987 - Present	Incumbent
Reagan	Alicia C. Coro (Acting) 1986 - 1987	Director of Bilingual Education and Minority Language Affairs Department of Education
Reagan	Harry M. Singleton 1982 - 1985	Manager Harry M. Singleton & Associates Washington, DC
Reagan	Clarence Thomas 1981 - 1982	Chairman Equal Employment Opportunity Commission Washington, DC
Reagan	Fred T. Cioffi (Acting) 1981	Director of Management Improvement Initiative Staff Department of Education
Carter	Cynthia O. Brown 1980 - 1981	Director of the Resource Center on Educational Equity Council of Chief State School Officers Washington, DC

* The Department of Education was created by the Department of Education Organization Act, PL-96-88, October 17, 1979.

ASSISTANT SECRETARY
POST-SECONDARY EDUCATION

Level IV - Presidential Appointment with Senate Confirmation

Major Responsibilities

o   Design and implement policy for federal financial support of higher education through loan and grant aid to students, and assistance to institutions in the areas of instruction, resources, and construction.

o   Consult with and advise the secretary on setting policy goals and priorities.   Represent government higher education policy to the Congress and public.

o   Supervise the activities of the office of post-secondary education and its administrative operations.   Administer the White House Initiative for Historic Black Colleges and Universities.

Necessary Background, Experience, Personal Skills

The appointee to this position "must be rooted in the academic tradition," in the words of one who has held it, which really means experience running an academic institution, or service in a senior faculty or administrative position.   "Clear, recognizable credentials" is the term another uses.   Others agree, and also mention prior government and/or Congressional experience and some legal background as useful assets.

Insight

Those who have served in this job have little trouble identifying the opportunities it offers.   But they also find problems in a couple of areas that, until resolved, seem significant enough to make the opportunities potential rather than real.

One of the difficulties concerns structure and spirit.   "No one could enter the job with an accurate idea of its magnitude, its critical nature or its impact on students of higher education," says Edward M. Elmendorf, assistant secretary in 1982-86, who accordingly "expected to have more authority" but ran into "too many layers before decisions were finalized." One of his predecessors who coped with the same situation recommends streamlining the department's superstructure, now loaded with "too many assistant secretaries who have overlapping duties." Two other earlier occupants of the job report sagging morale among the career staff that one of them says has arisen from the elimination of senior career positions in the department. This in turn "affected productivity" which was "somewhat less than adequate." In the view of Edward L. Meador (1981), "it's of paramount importance to surround yourself with key staff--not 'yes men'--who are able to play hardball. It's fatal not to trust anyone--and not to be able to. Get yourself accustomed to finding, using and cherishing a good staff."

The other problem in the job--and an area where one of its former tenants sees definite recent improvement--is the absence of clear long- and short-term policy direction and the thinking that must go into it. "An awful lot was left to chance," Meador says. "There wasn't much carefully-thought-out strategic kind of stuff. I don't know if the agency was ever adequate in that department." "If I had it all to do over again," says another assistant secretary, "I would spend more time building relations between the department and the various academic institutions." Meador says "the reality is that the department is not accepted by the university community. What's needed is working with the academic community and avoiding unnecessary confrontation whenever possible."

The key focus of the position lies in its administration of student financial assistance. This covers many programs, among them Direct Loans to Students in Institutions of Higher Education, basic and supplemental Educational Opportunity Grants, and the Guaranteed Student Loan Program. Student aid programs make the department the biggest of federal loan collectors. Loan repayments and student defaults present one of the "usual problems of a grant-dispensing agency," notes a previous assistant secretary, who also says "I was not prepared for the forcefulness of some constituency groups; some felt they were first among equals, no matter what you did." He adds that "I piled my problems into two groups--panic and don't panic."

A qualified Congressional source familiar with the job points out that it "is one of the most difficult...because it is so technical." At the same time, "you have a lot of interest groups floating around. The research universities don't have the same interests as the community colleges. The community colleges don't have the same interests as the selective private colleges, and the selective private colleges don't have the same interests as the un-selective ones.

This position does have major policy elements."

The job should also be the center of debate, says a representative of one of the department's large constituent organizations, on fundamental issues like the assumptions underlying student loan assistance. One of the questions raised by this observer, for example, is why "proprietary institutions" (trade schools) seem to be treated on the same basis where loan aid is concerned as other institutions. "The effect of this on minority students, who are over-represented in proprietary schools, should be looked at."

In general, those who have held this job both perceive and support a federal role in post-secondary education, carried out within a revitalized department. As one of them puts it, "the opportunity remains for the federal government to formulate a policy that would help to build excellence in higher education."

Key Relationships

Within the Department

Reports to: Secretary

Works closely with:

Undersecretary
Deputy Undersecretary for Planning, Budget and Evaluation
Deputy Undersecretary for Management

Outside the Department

Fiscal Assistant Secretary, Department of the Treasury
Assistant Secretary, Science and Education, Department of Agriculture
Assistant Secretary, Indian Affairs, Department of the Interior
Director of the National Science Foundation

Outside the Federal Government

Major colleges and universities; post-secondary education associations, such as American Association for Higher Education, American Association of State Colleges and Universities, American Association of

Community and Junior Colleges, Association of Independent Colleges and Schools; National Association of Student Financial Aid Administrators, National Education Association; and student organizations

Assistant Secretaries for Post-Secondary Education Since 1980*

Administration	Name and Years Served	Present Position
Reagan	Kenneth P. Whitehead 1988 - Present (Acting)	Incumbent
Reagan	C. Ronald Kimberling 1986 - 1988	Executive Director Ronald Reagan Presidential Foundation Los Angeles, California
Reagan	Edward M. Elmendorf 1982 - 1986	President Policon Coporation Washington, DC
Reagan	Thomas P. Melady 1981 - 1982	President Connecticut Public Expenditures Council Hartford, Connecticut
Reagan	Edward L. Meador 1981 (Acting)	Springfield, Virginia
Carter	Albert A. Bowker 1980 - 1981	Vice President for Planning Research Foundation for City University of New York New York, New York

* The Department of Education was created by the Department of Education Organization Act, PL-96-88, October 17, 1979.

ASSISTANT SECRETARY
SPECIAL EDUCATION
AND REHABILITATIVE SERVICES

Level IV - Presidential Appointment with Senate Confirmation

Major Responsibilities

o Oversee and provide policy direction to programs of federal assistance to handicapped persons, as administered or supported by the Office of Special Education, the Rehabilitation Services Administration and the National Institute on Disability and Rehabilitation Research.

o Set priorities and resolve policy questions in considering about 30,000 annual proposals for formula and discretionary grant assistance under these programs.

o Provide administrative direction to the Office of Special Education and Rehabilitative Services.

Necessary Background, Experience, Personal Skills

Broad practical and technical experience in teaching and working with handicapped people is probably the best single credential. But to handle the position effectively, the assistant secretary must also understand the structure and efforts of state and non-governmental organizations in this field, and how states handle the distribution of federal assistance. An individual with these background elements should also have developed some authority and recognition among the specialized constituencies concerned.

Insight

"Many different federal agencies and programs impact on the lives of persons with handicaps," says Madeleine C. Will, who has held this job since 1983. "There is no one person or organization in the federal government coordinating all of the programs or funds. This makes it very difficult for persons with handicaps. The system is broken up into 40-odd programs, all developed piecemeal." Yet, she notes, the Office of Special Education and Rehabilitative Services (OSERS) enjoys a relatively rare condition as federal government organizations go: a basic continuum of programs dealing with handicapped individuals from birth to death which allows a measure of comprehensiveness in addressing their needs. "OSERS programs are also very popular," Will points out. "Congress is generally very supportive because of the huge increase in public awareness of the problem....As a result, they have maintained OSERS grant programs." She says the combined grant funds for the three major components of the office exceed $3 billion.

Through formula grants to state education agencies, and discretionary competitive grants to public and private agencies at the regional and state levels, OSERS supports a wide variety of programs to help handicapped children realize their full potential. In similar fashion, and with emphasis on the severely burdened, it supports rehabilitation services to expand the independence of handicapped youth and adults and increase their ability to lead productive lives. OSERS also coordinates and supports an extensive program of research and teacher training to strengthen the overall national effort. In 1986, the office took over program responsibility for three special institutions--Gallaudet University, the National Technical Institute for the Deaf, and the American Printing House for the Blind.

Critical comment on the degree of impact these programs are having comes from a member of the governmental affairs office of a prominent national education organization. "I don't think they've provided any leadership to the states in terms of how to accomplish a very complicated agenda," this representative says. "You have to have a commitment to the state structure," which is "kind of an advocacy base....This job could use a good manager who has had experience at the state level, or at the local level in a sizeable district....You have to find ways to encourage the participation of constituent groups in determining their own destiny and contributing to policy decisions, and also so that you have room for technical advice and consultation."

In grant-making, the assistant secretary often functions both as wide-ranging fact-finder and judge. Herman R. Goldberg, who headed OSERS in 1981, says that investigating grant proposals meant working closely with professionals in many fields, among them physicians, therapists, psychologists, special educators, engineers, and lawyers. Moreover, he recalls, "I had to conduct and testify at show cause hearings about why applicants didn't get grants. Sometimes we were able to settle disputes by adjudicating quasi-legal cases."

"The statutes governing this office are very complicated," Will notes. "You don't have to be a good lawyer yourself but you must have consistent, good legal advice." While the job deals with emotional issues, she advises, "you cannot include emotion in the decisions you make. There are political, statutory and practical realities that govern your decisions. It is essential that they be made clearly and with all the facts."

As for the personal appeal of this position, a former occupant says "you couldn't have it any better. The field is so big. There is sufficient money. It is not without its hurdles, but it's an opportunity to do very great things." "People need to understand the value of these programs to society," Will adds. "They are cost savings programs because they keep people out of benefit programs like welfare and make them productive, useful human beings."

Key Relationships

Within the Department

Reports to: Secretary

Works closely with:

Undersecretary
Assistant Secretary for Elementary and Secondary Education
Assistant Secretary for Vocational and Adult Education
Assistant Secretary for Civil Rights

Outside the Department

Administrator, Health Care and Financing Administration, Department of Health and Human Services
Commissioner of Social Security, HHS
Assistant Attorney General, Civil Rights Division, Department of Justice
Assistant Secretary, Fair Housing and Equal Opportunity, Department of Housing and Urban Development
Assistant Secretary, Employment and Training, Department of Labor

Outside the Federal Government

State education agencies and agencies associated with Medicaid funding; national associations for the blind, the deaf, and learning-disabled children, such as American Foundation for the Blind, Council on Education of the Deaf, National Association of State Directors of Special Education, National Council on the Handicapped, National Council on Rehabilitation Education, and United Cerebral Palsy Association

Assistant Secretaries for Special Education and Rehabilitative Services Since 1980*

Administration	Name and Years Served	Present Position
Reagan	Madeleine C. Will 1983 - Present	Incumbent
Reagan	Jean S. Tufts 1981 - 1983	Deceased
Reagan	Herman R. Goldberg 1981 (Acting)	President Ergo Associates, Inc. Bethesda, Maryland
Carter	Edwin W. Martin 1980 - 1981	McLean, Virginia

* The Department of Education was created by the Department of Education Organization Act, PL-96-88, October 17, 1979.

10

DEPARTMENT OF ENERGY

This department of just over 16,000 employees features the co-existence of programs to manage and regulate the national energy environment and programs responsible for the production of nuclear weapons and the material that goes into them. There is also an important function of research and development in energy technology.

If energy affairs and nuclear weapons seem an unlikely combination, the agency's genealogy provides an explanation, though perhaps not a rationale. The present department was created in 1977 in the merger of the Federal Energy Administration, other federal power agencies and functions, and the Energy Research and Development Agency, which itself had sprung from the former Atomic Energy Agency.

The agency's budget, which in fiscal 1988 ran to $10.8 billion, goes mostly into the agency's defense programs operation. But the need to manage a coherent national fossil energy plan effectively is probably more urgent than ever; the country's still-growing dependence on foreign energy sources, continuing trouble in the Middle East producer regions, and an inadequate Strategic Petroleum Reserve make that clear. It also weakens somewhat the argument that Presidential appointees are no longer necessary to head currently inactive department programs in the solar, wind, alcohol and other non-fossil energy fields--an issue for the next administration to consider. At the least, those programs probably need grouping under one senior official who, politically appointed or not, needs technical competence and experience with the issues.

In the majority view of those who have been on the inside, oversight of the big nuclear weapons production program is a fulltime responsibility in the agency. As indicated in more detail by the job discussions in this chapter, many people think the defense area should be the only assignment of the undersecretary, who now carries it in addition to other duties.

DEPARTMENT OF ENERGY

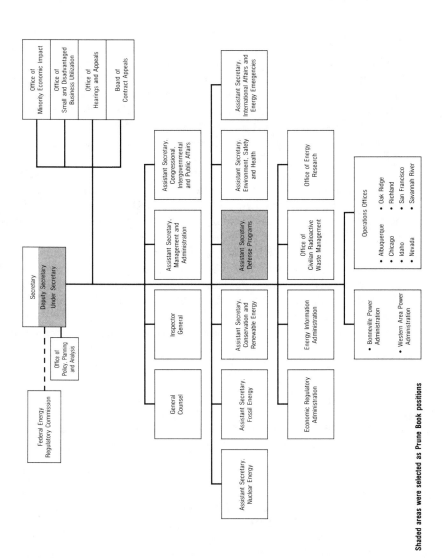

Secretary
Deputy Secretary
Under Secretary

Office of Policy Planning and Analysis

Federal Energy Regulatory Commission

Office of Minority Economic Impact

Office of Small and Disadvantaged Business Utilization

Office of Hearings and Appeals

Board of Contract Appeals

Assistant Secretary, Congressional, Intergovernmental and Public Affairs

Assistant Secretary, Management and Administration

Inspector General

General Counsel

Assistant Secretary, Nuclear Energy

Assistant Secretary, Fossil Energy

Assistant Secretary, Conservation and Renewable Energy

Assistant Secretary, Defense Programs

Assistant Secretary, Environment, Safety and Health

Assistant Secretary, International Affairs and Energy Emergencies

Office of Energy Research

Office of Civilian Radioactive Waste Management

Energy Information Administration

Economic Regulatory Administration

- Bonneville Power Administration
- Western Area Power Administration

Operations Offices

- Albuquerque
- Chicago
- Idaho
- Nevada
- Oak Ridge
- Richland
- San Francisco
- Savannah River

Shaded areas were selected as Prune Book positions

DEPUTY SECRETARY

Level II - Presidential Appointment with Senate Confirmation

Confusion has surrounded the sometimes overlapping responsibilities of this position and those of the undersecretary (discussed later in this section), and the relationship between them. In resolving it, a future administration has two alternative models to choose between, in the view of many who know the department well. The first model, favored by these observers, would assign the deputy secretary as chief operating officer of the department, and give the undersecretary oversight of the department's large defense programs operation and coordination of energy research and development programs. The second model would emphasize the deputy secretary's role as alter ego to the secretary and as a policymaker, and establish the undersecretary as chief operating officer while retaining the defense programs oversight.

In this book, discussion of these two positions follows the guidelines of the first model. If, however, model two is considered, the credentials of candidates for deputy secretary should stress a policy background, and a prospective appointee as undersecretary should be exceptionally strong in management, probably from a prior career in industry, with less emphasis in the science and technology area.

Major Responsibilities

o Assist the secretary in the direction of the department, acting as chief operating officer. Serve as acting secretary when required.

o Supervise preparation of the department budget, and its examination with the Office of Management and Budget. Support it and department policies in the Congress.

o Represent the department in interagency discussion of energy policy. Maintain effective relationships with constituent groups.

Necessary Background, Experience, Personal Skills

Most important for this job is general management experience and a knowledge of the federal policy and legislative processes, perhaps through working in another agency or on the Hill on domestic and international energy issues. Familiarity with technical areas--such as petroleum engineering--can be picked up, in the view of an experienced observer from a national industrial association. But "it is crucial that the deputy secretary knows the government process." Those who make the selection for this job, and the chosen individual, should understand its relationship to the positions of the secretary and undersecretary, as discussed here and in the examination of the undersecretary's job.

Insight

As suggested above, it's difficult to make a sharp distinction between this job and that of the undersecretary (discussed later in this section), whose responsibilities have a history of overlap and exchange. The department's organization chart doesn't help; it boxes both jobs together with the secretary's. There don't seem to be any answers in the 1977 legislation which established the department, and there are definitely no guidelines about the deputy's relationship to the secretary, though that is not unusual.

"It's unfortunate," says a former department official about this situation at the top. "There's more confusion between the roles of the deputy and the undersecretary than between either of them and the secretary. It would be much cleaner if you had a secretary, a deputy, and a panoply of assistant secretaries. Then you'd have the opportunity for a cleaner delegation of authority between the secretary and the deputy."

In recent years the deputy secretary has not really functioned as the chief operating officer of the department, as informed observers think the job should be run, and much the same way as e-quivalent jobs in other agencies are run. Like those jobs, the parameters of this one depend largely on the secretary's preferences or, as Danny J. Boggs, deputy secretary in 1983-86 puts it, "this job is very much what the secretary wants it to be."

But there's an important extra consideration here. The Department of Energy is heavily concentrated on defense production--designing and fabricating nuclear weapons. About four-fifths of its budget goes in that direction. The department's other chief mission covers the domestic energy field. In this improbable mix of unlike mandates, the deputy secretary currently serves as the secretary's alter ego and stand-in, and focuses mainly on policy, legislative matters, and budget. The undersecretary has complete oversight over the immense defense production task, and is also chief operating officer of the department--a schizophrenic spread of assignments that has sometimes proved burdensome and hard to manage.

Representatives of an energy industry association with whom we talked feel strongly that there should be a formalized functional division in these two positions "between domestic policy concerns and national defense concerns" that would still recognize "that there is a lot of overlap." On this subject, the former department official cited earlier thinks the operating problem actually begins "on the front end, when you get into these jobs." What has happened in the past, he speculates, is that recruitment for them took place without any clear idea of what the boundaries ought to be. "That's probably the cardinal thing that has to be done up front," he says. "Otherwise, a lot of confusion is created and it takes a long time to overcome that confusion once people are in their jobs."

From these conversations, one further point emerges about recruitment for the deputy secretary's job. It's a generic warning which applies to all such situations in the executive branch. If the White House selects the deputy, as has usually been the case at Energy, the secretary may choose to leave the deputy out of the department loop. If selection of a deputy is left to the secretary, however, the secretary might choose "a crony," as one of our sources puts it, adding that "it's probably a good idea to limit the secretary in that regard, because if the deputy is an old-time friend, he is less inclined to be open-minded to input from the outside."

Another observer comments that the coordination of these three officers at the top is no small task, and requires much skill. The dimensions of the problem can be reduced, he feels, "by a clear delineation, before the people are chosen. The Secretary and the White House should work closely together to select the deputy secretary and undersecretary."

This job manages the department and provides administrative supervision, including key personnel assignments. Policy direction and Congressional testimony and related activity also occupy much of the deputy secretary's working schedule. At least a dozen committees on the Hill have interest in or jurisdiction over some part of the energy portfolio carried by this job--international market prices, off-shore resources, regulatory matters, acid rain, the health of the oil patch, and more. The deputy secretary attends many cabinet council meetings and represents the department in the

Domestic Policy Council at the White House; develops and revises legislation; works out policy, budget and legislative questions with the Office of Management and Budget; and plays a policy role in management of the nation's Strategic Petroleum Reserve. The job calls for skill in outreach and coalition-building among constituent groups.

When oil prices came down in the mid-1980s, the department's and deputy secretary's role in the price-setting wars diminished. But U.S. dependence on foreign oil continues to increase. With domestic production declining and nuclear power not really a factor in energy production, the incoming deputy secretary will face the question of a potentially severe energy shortage, and contentious issues like the oil import fee sought by domestic producers and opposed by fuel-intensive industries.

The challenge will be to grasp and apply an understanding of the full range of implications for U.S. energy resources and the U.S. economy of the evolution of energy markets worldwide. It will be equally vital for the deputy secretary to understand thoroughly the impact of the federal government's interaction with the domestic industry. In addition, says one of those with whom we talked, the urgency of these matters "needs to be well understood and communicated."

Key Relationships

Within the Department

Reports to: Secretary

Works closely with:

Undersecretary

Outside the Department

Associate Director, Natural Resources, Energy and Science, Office of Management and Budget

Undersecretary, Department of the Interior

Undersecretary, Economic Affairs, Department of Commerce

Undersecretary, Economic and Agricultural Affairs, Department of State

Science Advisor to the President

Deputy Administrator, Environmental Protection Agency

Outside the Federal Government

Organizations, associations and individual firms representing the broad sweep of the energy and related industries, such as the American Institute of Chemical Engineers, the United States Energy Association, National Association of State Energy Officials, American Petroleum Institute, and the Edison Electric Institute; Natural Resources Defense Council, the Sierra Club and other environmental groups; energy officials of other countries; International Energy Agency and other international organizations with energy interests

Deputy Secretaries of Energy Since 1978*

Administration	Name and Years Served	Present Position
Reagan	William F. Martin 1986 - Present	Incumbent
Reagan	Danny J. Boggs 1983 - 1986	Judge U.S. Circuit Court of Appeals 6th Circuit Washington, DC
Reagan	W. Kenneth Davis 1981 - 1983	Consultant Bechtel Corporation San Francisco, California
Carter	Lynne R. Coleman 1980 - 1981	Partner Skadden, Arps, Slate, Meagher and Flom Washington, DC
Carter	John C. Sawhill 1979 - 1980	Partner McKinsey and Company Washington, DC

Carter	John F. O'Leary	Deceased
	1978 - 1979	

* Position created by the Department of Energy Organization Act, PL 95-91 in October 1977.

UNDERSECRETARY

Level III - Presidential Appointment with Senate Confirmation

(Note: Readers of this discussion should also refer to the comments at the beginning of the preceding examination of the position of deputy secretary.)

Major Responsibilities

o   Under the authority of the secretary, oversee the department's management of programs to design, produce, test, store and dispose of nuclear weapons for national defense. Develop policy to guide these activities. Act as leading spokesman for these programs within the department and the administration. Assure that the Congress has the information it requires about the policy, budget and operation of these programs.

o   Work closely with other agencies concerned in the production of nuclear weapons.

o   Coordinate the department's research in biological and physical sciences.

Necessary Background, Experience, Personal Skills

With oversight of nuclear weapon production as a major respon-sibility, this position calls for deep experience in research and development, and in its implementation. An individual with that background might come out of a national laboratory working in that field, or have run a large research and development organization. Management skills are a requisite. The undersecretary should, in addition, be able to bring to bear some Congressional and political skills.

Insight

This book's description of the position of Deputy Secretary of Energy (earlier in this section) discusses at some length the lack of clear delineation that has existed between that job and this one. The two positions can, of course, be anything the secretary wants them to be. Knowledgeable individuals who have served in the department or work closely with it generally agree, however, on the need for something resembling an institutionalized distinction between them that would sharpen the lines of authority flowing from each. In particular, such a step would rationalize the responsibilities of the undersecretary, who currently must serve as day-to-day manager of the department while also supervising a large and complicated nuclear weapons production program.

"If you assume the premise that the undersecretary should be relieved of his administrative duties," an experienced observer told us, "then he should have a background in the defense industry and systems analysis." At the same time, says a former senior department veteran, the department does a lot of basic research in the biological and physical sciences. "It makes sense," he asserts, "to give the undersecretary responsibility for these civilian research activities as well as the defense activities."

At the Department of Energy, the big issues are national security issues. That's where most of the resources go. The defense area of the department's mission accounts for about 80% of the total budget of $20 billion. Overseeing it is only one of a dozen tasks on the undersecretary's plate, but it may be one of the major management challenges the U.S. government has to offer.

The breadth of this oversight is not well understood, even within the department. In 1981, says W. Kenneth Davis, a former deputy secretary (1981-83) when that position had oversight of the defense programs, "the defense part was about 50% of the budget, but people in the White House and in the government in general didn't seem to have any idea that the undersecretary had that level of responsibility. They were all mixed up into gasoline, oil, rationing and deregulation." This lack of awareness was less true when he left, Davis recalls, "but I think the department still struggles under the misconception."

Working through the Assistant Secretary for Defense Programs, who has direct management responsibility, the undersecretary really presides as chief executive officer of a sprawling research, development and manufacturing enterprise--with a difference. The Department of Defense and the National Security Council prescribe the guidelines, and decide the targeting function of a weapon and its requirements. The undersecretary does not get into defense policy, but rather manages the production function of a sensitive, controversial set of weapons whose specifications are created elsewhere. Doing so means bringing to the job the ability to understand and work with the Department of Defense, responding to its needs and explaining what is and isn't possible.

One challenge of this work is to maintain and motivate an important sector of the nation's research and development capability. The undersecretary, we were told, must "really understand that today's science is tomorrow's technology. He needs to have a vision about that." Another challenge lies in the evolution of relations between the superpowers. If substantial reductions of strategic weapons systems come along, the deputy secretary's assignment in this area may become retrenchment management--"what you do with fabrication and manufacturing capacity so that you don't destroy it forever but mothball it or put it on standby."

Key Relationships

Within the Department

Reports to: Secretary

Works closely with:

Deputy Secretary
Directors, Livermore, Los Alamos and Sandia National Laboratories

Outside the Department

Undersecretary, Economic and Agricultural Affairs, Department of State
Undersecretary, Political Affairs, Department of State
Assistant to the Chairman, Joint Chiefs of Staff, Department of Defense
Director, Defense Nuclear Agency, DOD
Assistant to the Secretary, Atomic Energy, DOD
Undersecretary, Department of Labor
Assistant Administrator, Environmental Protection Agency
Senior Director, Board of Defense Policy, National Security Council
Director, U.S. Arms Control and Disarmament Agency
Director, Central Intelligence Agency

Outside the Federal Government

Energy industry groups, such as American Nuclear Energy Council; engineering and aerospace firms, and defense contractors; environmentalists, such as Natural Resources Defense Council, Energy Conservation Coalition and Environmental Policy Institute; anti-nuclear weapons and anti-nuclear power groups; science and research institutes and laboratories, on and off campus; state and local governments

Undersecretaries of Energy Since 1977*

Administration	Name and Years Served	Present Position
Reagan	Joseph S. Salgado 1985 - Present	Incumbent
Reagan	W. Patrick Collins 1983 - 1985	Managing Partner SKC and Associates Washington, DC
Reagan	Jan W. Mares 1982 (Acting)	Senior Policy Analyst Office of Policy Development The White House
Reagan	Guy W. Fiske 1981 - 1982	President Fiske Associates, Inc. New York, New York
Reagan	Joe B. LaGrone 1981 (Acting)	Manager Oak Ridge Operations Department of Energy Oak Ridge, Tennessee
Reagan	Raymond G. Romatowski 1981 (Acting)	Albuquerque, New Mexico
Carter	C. Worthington Bateman 1980 - 1981 (Acting)	Not Available

Carter	John M. Deutch 1979 - 1980	Provost Massachusetts Institute of Technology Cambridge, Massachusetts
Carter	Dale D. Myers 1977 - 1979	Deputy Administrator National Aeronautics and Space Administration

*   Position created by the Department of Energy Organization Act, PL 95-91 in October 1977.

ASSISTANT SECRETARY
DEFENSE PROGRAMS

Level IV - Presidential Appointment with Senate Confirmation

Major Responsibilities

o   Direct the nation's nuclear weapons research, design, development and testing operations, and the production of nuclear weapons material.

o   Work in close cooperation with the National Security Council and the Department of Defense in drafting Presidential directives governing these programs, and in carrying them out. Develop support for them, and for their funding, with the Congress.

o   Maintain contact on these subjects with broad sectors of the U.S. industrial, environmental and scientific communities.

Necessary Background, Experience, Personal Skills

One of two alternative sets of credentials is basic to this position. The first is a strong background in nuclear technology at the executive level, and a wide acquaintance and reputation in that and related high-tech communities. The second is a federal government career with very significant management, defense and Congressional relations components. With neither, a prospective appointee would be ineffective. In practice, the job has seen several former military officers of flag rank.

Insight

This job takes its basic cue from the President's nuclear stockpile memoranda, documents which direct how the nation's nuclear weapons inventory is to be developed, managed and disposed of. With that mandate, this assistant secretary is responsible for the operations of the major industrial complex that is the U.S. nuclear production program.

It's a large, spread-out, and intensely high-tech program which represents the bulk of the Department of Energy budget. There are three components. Research and design takes place in the Livermore, Los Alamos and Sandia national laboratories. Testing is done at the Nevada underground site. Production is spread among seven fabrication facilities under government contract, and several reactors producing weapons-grade material. The entire operation is budgeted at about $8 billion a year.

Working closely with the Department of Defense within the framework of the stockpile memos, the assistant secretary develops broad guidance for what this complex should look into and develop, and seeks the approval of the administration and the Congress for the budget to support it. With that achieved, the next task is to design the implementing instructions and oversee their execution on schedule. Making the whole thing go is a staff of 500 in Washington and about 2,000 in the field. They oversee more than 50,000 contractors nationwide.

"The very heart of these programs lies in the field activities," says Sylvester R. Foley, Jr., assistant secretary in 1986-87. They are relatively autonomous, overseen by field managers day to day, and the contact with them is continuous. Many field managers have long years of service and tend to be, in Foley's words, "600-pound gorillas who don't like a lot of interference." It takes, he says, "a strong management style to bring these people into your vision, so that their vision concurs with yours. You have to convince them that you know what you're doing. You can't just sit in Washington and run it; you have to go out there so that you have a feel for what's going on."

We heard additional comment on this point from representatives of a national industrial association, who take the view that the assistant secretary can become the captive of the structure. "It's a big machine, and the most powerful people there are the ones that run the operations offices," one of them says. The process, as described by this observer, begins even before the assistant secretary has been confirmed in the job. While that is being awaited, the staff is busy making its pitches to the new boss for their various programs. "Since the learning curve is so steep, and the issues are so difficult and there's so much history to it, he really cannot work his own will, and the bureaucrats capture him." In this view, the job needs "a hard-nosed manager who can ask tough questions, work day and night, and doesn't see this as another salary to collect on top of his military pension." The assistant secretary needs "energy and smarts" because the attitude of the career staff is "we've been doing this since the Manhattan Project, while you people just come and go."

The difference between this job and many others in Washington, according to William R. Hoover, who held it in 1984-85, "is that you really do need to have somebody who understands technology and also the political and governmental workings in Washington." Foley agrees, suggesting that an assistant secretary without any experience in government or with the political sphere will fall behind the curve. Foley's military background enabled him "to get things done. I knew the Defense Department, and they couldn't steamroller me."

Surveying another sector of the management front, Hoover says that relationships with the three national laboratories are "part of the challenge of the program." Their directors, and other scientists of national stature, "certainly have independent entree to the secretary and many other places in Washington," where they can make their own views known. "So managing the laboratories is one of the difficulties of the program." On the same subject, Herman E. Roser, assistant secretary in 1981-84, found that "experience in levels of organizations is very important in being able to organize and run the three laboratories."

Foley estimates he spent 70% of his working time in the department. The rest was typically absorbed by working with the Defense Department and the National Security Council on budget priorities, talking with Congressional staffs about local problems in their districts and about arms control and defense issues, traveling inside and outside the country, or meeting with representatives of local communities which are host to production and reactor plants.

As a general rule of thumb, weapons costs are about 10% of a major defense system such as Minuteman or the MX. That means, Hoover points out, that "you get to be the tail wagging the dog." But the assistant secretary also gets wagged now and then, because there is always some uncertainty about big weapons systems--their funding, and how they evolve. "So one of the frustrations is trying to provide what people think they're going to require....We were in the position of trying to satisfy our customer. But you have to justify almost separately the kind of production complex, the amount of research and development, all those things you need to have to satisfy that customer." Yet, there is not always agreement between the Congress and the administration on whether the customer needs those things.

This process becomes more difficult because the authorization and appropriation of the DOE Defense Programs budget does not go through the same committees as Department of Defense programs. That exposes the budget to political trade-offs for energy programs, or to being used as a stalking horse for those trying to kill a defense program by another means--for example, by not providing funding for a missile warhead.

In producing what's needed, Foley says, "there's no redundancy, there are just these plants. The plants are old, you are getting more and more visibility and oversight, you've got a lot of messes on your hands, you don't get much good news, and you're going to get beat up. You can't be wrong--you're deciding which warheads to build. There's lots of testing for quality and safety; you can't compromise. If you don't want to be a strong hands-on manager who can make decisions, and if you want to be loved, forget it. You want to be smart, tough and wary."

Key Relationships

Within the Department

Reports to: Secretary

Works closely with:

Undersecretary
Directors, Livermore, Los Alamos and Sandia National Laboratories

Outside the Department

Assistant to the Chairman, Joint Chiefs of Staff, Department of Defense
Director, Defense Nuclear Agency, DOD
Assistant to the Secretary for Atomic Energy, DOD
Senior Director, Board of Defense Policy, National Security Council
Assistant Administrator, Air and Radiation, Environmental Protection Agency
Assistant Secretary, Politico Military Affairs, Department of State
Director, U.S. Arms Control and Disarmament Agency

Outside the Federal Government

Aerospace firms, defense contractors, industrial organizations such as American Security Council; environmentalists; groups opposed to nuclear weapons, such as SANE/Freeze; science and research institutes and laboratories, on and off campus; state and local governments

Assistant Secretaries for Defense Programs Since 1978*

Administration	Name and Years Served	Present Position
Reagan	Troy E. Wade (Acting) 1987 - Present	Incumbent
Reagan	Sylvester R. Foley, Jr. 1986 - 1987	Consultant Foley Associates Annapolis, Maryland
Reagan	Don Ofte (Acting) 1985	Manager Idaho Operations Department of Energy Idaho Falls, Idaho
Reagan	William R. Hoover 1984 - 1985	Executive Vice President Air Transport Association Washington, DC
Reagan	Robert L. Morgan 1984 (Acting)	Manager Savannah River Operations Department of Energy Aiken, South Carolina
Reagan	Herman E. Roser 1981 - 1984	Albuquerque, New Mexico
Reagan	Robert L. Morgan 1981 (Acting)	Manager Savannah River Operations Department of Energy Aiken, South Carolina
Carter	Duane C. Sewell 1978 - 1981	Not Available

Carter	Donald M. Kerr	Senior Vice President
	1978 (Acting)	EG&G, Inc.
		Wellesley, Massachusetts

*   Position created by the Department of Energy Organization Act, PL 95-91 in October 1977.

11

ENVIRONMENTAL PROTECTION AGENCY

This agency's problems with misdirected leadership in the early 1980s produced virtual unanimity that it needs in its senior positions, from the top down, individuals with two basic credentials. The first is experience in environmental issues and in government. The second is a sophisticated, realistic view of the importance of balance between the requirements of environmental protection and the economic impact of those requirements. Maintaining that balance is the EPA version of risk management. It is probably the agency's most important task.

One of the many responsibilities incumbent on EPA's leaders is oversight of environmental matters throughout the government. In the course of this, the agency does business with just about every other federal agency, but in particular with the Departments of Labor, Commerce, Agriculture and Health and Human Services and the Consumer Product Safety Commission. Communication between the tops of these agencies, especially when a new administration takes office, is crucial. That's because, while they have many objectives and interests in common, it's easy to fall into working at cross purposes. If, for example, two agencies try to regulate the same substance using different data, they will reach different conclusions that confuse the public and make the administration look incoherent. That can be costly in terms both of resources and public confidence.

There are also questions of overlap, as between EPA and the Nuclear Regulatory Commission, in which the commission regulates radiation within a power plant and the agency worries about it outside the fence. The same artificial line divides the Occupational Safety and Health Administration, which is concerned with harmful substances within the work place, and EPA, which regulates them everywhere else. A former EPA administrator points out that such coordination does not come naturally, won't occur unless someone takes the lead, and that nobody has a bigger stake in doing it successfully than the individual who runs this agency.

Problems like these are but a few examples of the scores of large and small challenges facing EPA. One of the latest is the accumulating, if not yet fully conclusive, evidence of global climate change. It presents yet another competing priority which EPA must balance against the rest and deal with in a manner consistent with the policies of the administration and the requirements of the Congress. The ability to handle that assignment, in the view of the staff director of a Senate committee with oversight of EPA, is a quality desirable in every senior individual in the organization.

ADMINISTRATOR

Level II - Presidential Appointment with Senate Confirmation

Major Responsibilities

o   Direct a large agency which operates federal programs nationwide to control and reduce pollution of the country's land, air and water by toxic substances, solid waste, pesticides and radiation, and to restore damaged resources to the extent possible. These programs entail investigation, standard-setting, design and revision of statute-based regulations, construction grants and contracts, technology transfer, research and development, oversight of state and local governments, and enforcement.

o   Assist and counsel the President in setting the directions for environmental protection policy. Inform, assist and advise the Congress in matters of necessary environmental legislation and on the policies and actions of the executive branch in executing protection statutes.

o   Consult on and coordinate at the senior levels of many other federal agencies, and with the states, the implementation of environmental protection law. Maintain liaison with a very wide spectrum of constituent groups.

o   Represent U.S. environmental policy and objectives in international organizations and cooperate with the governments of other countries pursuing environmental programs and research projects. Act as spokesman for U.S. environmental policy and for the agency's programs, playing a public educational role in explaining the nature of the current and future environmental protection task and of the alternatives for carrying it out.

Necessary Background, Experience, Personal Skills

Despite its complicated mission and unusual scope, it's clear in talking with former administrators that the requirements of this job are not easily categorized. Although technical credentials may not be strictly necessary, the administrator should feel comfortable with scientists and technicians and have "a sense for economics."

Training or experience in law, engineering, public management or regulatory policymaking are useful, but a previous EPA chief says "the job is bigger than any one professional background." In any case, there are some general considerations to keep in mind in filling this position that go beyond specific expertise. First, more than most jobs, this one needs the benefit of perspective--the ability to look at a number of issues across different programs and "put them together in a cohesive whole." Second, no individual can run this job successfully without genuinely grasping the inter-relationships with EPA's various publics--the Congress, the press, industry, environmentalists, the states, individual citizens everywhere. These widely varying audiences must be able to view the chosen candidate as objective, someone able to generate confidence in the business and environmental communities alike.

Insight

One of those we talked to about this job is a senior staff member of the Senate Environment and Public Works Committee. He believes that raising taxes and managing the environment are the two chief elements of government's long-term relationship with the public. Asserting broad recognition that "government is part of the equation in protecting the environment," he thinks the EPA administrator holds "one of the most important jobs in government in the modern era."

That is only one view, perhaps expectable from someone professionally attuned to environmental matters. Few will argue, however, that the administrator's job stands as one of the most impactive, visible and--in its way--controversial posts in Washington. "It's an incredibly complex, sophisticated, difficult job," says the head of one of the agency's biggest constituent interest groups. "A lot of big money is at stake, there is litigation, and things go on forever."

Similar descriptions apply to the agency itself, and it is not hard to see why. One reason is EPA's stature as "the biggest and most diverse regulatory agency in the government," as former administrator Douglas M. Costle (1977-81) calls it, and the fact that "it regulates any industry that produces waste--virtually anyone." Taking decisions and actions that cut across the entire economy, the agency's mission has enormous implications for the affected industries and their work forces. But EPA must also operate in sensitive emotional areas where health, lives, and livelihoods are at stake. In many such situations, almost every move takes place under the intense gaze of the media and the public, and with the promise that nothing the agency does is likely to earn unmixed approval.

Lee M. Thomas, who has headed EPA since 1985, thinks of its basic functions as standards-setting, enforcement, inter-governmental relations and research. It supplies fully half of all the regulations reviewed by the Office of Management and Budget, he notes, and has "very powerful tools to assure compliance." At the same time, however, he makes the important point (examined further on) that "you can't say we're going to protect the environment to the exclusion of economic development. You're walking a tense line on those two things."

EPA interacts with many, perhaps most, other federal agencies in the policy development sense because, as Thomas explains, environmental protection is often a component of policy. "In particular," says William D. Ruckelshaus, who was EPA's first boss in 1970-73 and also led it in 1983-85, "the agencies who manage risk in the same way EPA does need to be pulled together in a much more coordinated fashion." While they don't always need to draw the same conclusions about a given substance, there should be greater understanding of "the elements of risk management and what successful strategies are for managing risk in our society."

In the life of any administrator, the Congress looms large. "Be prepared for attempts by Congress to control your agenda," warns Costle. Thomas estimates there are "over 75 different subcommittees that feel they have some jurisdiction" and says it's a rare day without testimony or a policy briefing on the Hill by a senior official of the agency. Ruckelshaus thinks the Congress should consolidate the environment-related work of its committees to improve efficiency and save time. But the key, in his view, is to achieve "flexibility to do what is sensible" by revising and rationalizing the "stringent" statutes that govern EPA's work. Without such flexibility, he argues, the Congress will continue "making promises the administrator cannot carry out" and setting "more stringent deadlines and requirements and see how you do against those." It is, he says, "a terrible spiral." Thomas agrees, saying "a lot of your direction is set in the statutes you've got. As a matter of fact, it's set too finely in some statutes. It inhibits your ability to really deal with the job because of the prescriptive nature of what's there."

Rising above any of these considerations are two basic themes which run through the comments of former administrators about the administrator's role. They see it, first, as that of an educator. Costle, for example, speaks of the administrator as the "national spokesperson and educator" on environmental protection issues with "a heavy responsibility to be out in public, speaking on issues." Thomas says the administrator must not only look inward to running the agency, but outward to the public, "explaining what the agency is trying to do, and why." Ruckelshaus agrees that much more attention must go to the educative mission of the job, but with an important difference. Where straight advocacy of environmental protection was once the keynote, he thinks that is no longer suitable "at this juncture of our history," when a more balanced role is necessary. "If the country is going to manage risk more wisely," he says, "nobody has better access to the information and knowledge about what is going on and how we are currently trying to perform those tasks than the administrator of EPA." Unless the administrator can communicate effectively "about the nature of the problems we're having" and how we are currently organized to deal with them and what changes ought to be made, there is no way you are going to get change." With that in mind, the role of educator is therefore "a terribly important assignment."

The second overarching role seen for the administrator is as careful guardian of the crucial balance between the environment and the economy. "We had to be tough and pro-environment, and balance legitimate economic concerns as well," Costle says. "It's a delicate line--bring about change but in a way that doesn't kill the goose that laid the golden egg." Thomas elaborates it this way: "In this country we have to work on how economic development and environmental protection link. There's a tension between the two, and (the administrator) has to have a sense of that tension. Most importantly, he has to be able to lead a staff in the kind of really hard analysis--really good, sound, scientific research--that gives them the basis for making the decisions that walk that line." "You don't want to tilt in any one direction," Ruckelshaus says. Like Thomas, he thinks the answer lies in calling on agency expertise to assist the making of balanced, reasonable decisions. The nation has already seen, he adds, "what can happen when you put someone in this job who...leans severely to one side of the spectrum."

"Somebody once described the state of environmental science as akin to medicine when they were still using leeches," says the Senate committee staff observer quoted earlier. "A lot of this stuff is just brand new. It may be that we're making mistakes by going at certain priorities sooner than we should....We need somebody with the perspective to really have a vision, but not divorced from the nuts and bolts of how this stuff works. You don't want just an ideological environmentalist with a pristine vision of where we need to go with our ecology."

Day to day, running EPA is hardly a rest cure. "Seemingly

endless conflict," is how Russell E. Train, administrator in 1973-77 remembers it, "and the environmental and industry groups are never satisfied." There is a heavy media and public speaking schedule. Costle compares the job to "running a hundred chess games at once" and says "it's not so much the size of the agency as of the inherent complexity of the job the agency has to do." The administrator rarely goes to the President with good news, he adds, and is more often the bearer of bad news. "You almost never have a decision where many people applaud it," Thomas says. In fact, "if everybody's a little bit mad, it must have been a good decision."

One prescription which may help is a little *glasnost*. "It is a very visible job and should be run on this basis," Train suggests. Thomas advises "trying to be as open as possible, inside and outside the agency." Even though EPA is a regulatory agency, "you can open up your process for policy development, regulation development, far more than was done in the past. Try to bring to the table as many outside views as you can, and try to have the constituent groups take on more of the problem-solving and not just the problem-raising part of the equation."

It should be noted that EPA, through various of its programs, administers one of the largest construction programs in the federal government. Although, for many, the agency means standard-setting, rulemaking and enforcement, it also spends at least $4 billion a year in construction money to clean up hazardous waste sites and build sewage treatment facilities. That's a budget that surpasses the current funding level of the Army Corps of Engineers for civil construction. Outlays of that size, especially by an agency still relatively inexperienced in contract management, heighten its vulnerability to waste and fraud.

All of these factors seem to underscore the care that should go into filling this position. Ruckelshaus thinks the candidate must be "someone who is articulate, experienced and competent enough to speak out on these issues without abandoning the role or goal of the agency. The best place to look is prior federal administrations or state governments." And he warns against the error of leaning too far in one direction in an effort to compensate for what might be seen as a previous swing to the other side. Thomas says "the last thing this agency needs is another political appointee who has not given a lot of thought to how tough it is to be the administrator or an administration which has not thought about who it is they really want."

Finally, the administrator needs political support from the White House. The job is "almost impossible without the support of the President," Costle believes. In it, he says, "you have to tell everyone to do things differently. People don't want to change. Industry doesn't want to clean up. You've got to have political support, a political bank account, and like every other bank account, you draw it down every time you write a check. You need the President's support and you must work at those relationships with other key people as well, and manage them so you don't overdraw, so there's always credit in the account."

Are there any rewards in this position? A former administrator likens it to "beating a train across a grade crossing--if you make it, it's a great rush. If you don't, you're dead."

Key Relationships

Inside the Federal Government

Reports to: President

Works closely with:

Cabinet secretaries and agency heads
Council on Environmental Quality, Executive Office of the President
Associate Director, Natural Resources, Energy and Science, Office of Management and Budget
Administrator, Information and Regulatory Affairs, OMB

Outside the Federal Government

Regulated industries, as individual companies and through their associations; environmental organizations; directors of counterpart agencies in each state, plus state governors, health commissioners, attorneys general, and agriculture officials; counterparts in other governments; representatives of international organizations

Administrators of the Environmental Protection Agency Since 1970*

Administration	Name and Years Served	Present Position
Reagan	Lee M. Thomas 1985 - Present	Incumbent
Reagan	William D. Ruckelshaus 1983 - 1985	Partner Perkins, Coie, Stone, and Williams Seattle, Washington
Reagan	Lee L. Verstandig 1983 (Acting)	Chairman Verstandig and Associates Washington, DC
Reagan	Ann M. Gorsuch Burford 1981 - 1983	Arlington, Virginia
Carter	Douglas M. Costle 1977 - 1981	Dean Vermont Law School South Royalton, Vermont
Carter	John R. Quarles, Jr. 1977 (Acting)	Partner Morgan, Lewis, & Bockius Washington, DC
Nixon//Ford	Russell E. Train 1973 - 1977	Chairman World Wildlife Fund Washington, DC
Nixon	Robert W. Fri (Acting) 1973	President Resources for the Future Washington, DC
Nixon	William D. Ruckelshaus 1970 - 1973	Partner Perkins, Coie, Stone, and Williams Seattle, Washington

* Environmental Protection Agency was created by Reorganization Plan #3 of 1970.

DEPUTY ADMINISTRATOR

Level III - Presidential Appointment with Senate Confirmation

Major Responsibilities

o   Assist the administrator in overall direction of the agency and in development of policy, acting as chief operating officer. Assume the administrator's responsibilities whenever necessary.

o   Represent EPA in senior interagency deliberations involving the agency's mission or interests. Take on specific and special assignments as directed by the administrator. See to effective coordination between agency components in the execution of EPA programs.

o   Take a substantial role in maintaining effective agency relationships with certain committees of the Congress and with a wide array of interest groups on every side of every issue. Oversee budget development and represent EPA in budget review and approval with the Office of Management and Budget and on the Hill.

Necessary Background, Experience, Personal Skills

Demonstrated skill in management and experience in the federal government meet the central requirements. But the successful appointee should, further, understand the current problems and stakes involved in environmental defense, and know something about EPA's structure, programs, resources, and constituent interest groups. Experience in contract management is a particularly useful qualification. It helps if the deputy is familiar with Congressional attitudes and approaches on environmental issues, has some working contact among members and staff, and is tenacious and results-oriented.

Insight

The difference between the administrator's job and that of the deputy, a former EPA chief reportedly has said, is that the deputy gets to announce the bad news. It's a characterization, says former deputy Robert W. Fri (1971-73), that "is sometimes almost literally true," even though neither the administrator nor the deputy of this big, visible and often controversial agency finds much chance to be the bearer of glad tidings.

But the joke helps to point up a deeper, more important truth asserted by another former deputy administrator, Alvin L. Alm, who had the job in 1983-85. "EPA has been most successfully managed when the deputy administrator and administrator have played their complementary roles," he says. This means the administrator "stays on the outside"--sitting in the topmost policy-making councils, reporting to the President, and acting as the central face and voice of administration policy on the environment and of EPA itself--to the Congress, constituent groups and the public.

The deputy supports this outside role in a hundred unseen ways and must be ready to assume it in the administrator's absence. Whoever fills this post must know programs, constituent groups and people on the Hill. But the most essential assignment in this job lies inside the agency, running it day to day, pondering the options on scores of substantive decisions the administrator need not or--occasionally--can not make, and spurring greater efficiency and speed in handling the agency's multi-faceted, many-layered rule-making, investigatory and compliance duties. The deputy's office is an obligatory and determining way station for assistant administrators reporting to the boss. The deputy needs a bias for action--making certain the agency's administrative engine is cranking satisfactorily, running the budget, touring regional offices and staying in regular touch with their senior staffs, and getting involved in personnel decisions.

"Sort of the ultimate insider," a Senate committee staffer says of the deputy administrator, "who should be congruent with the administrator's vision of the future...and help translate those visions into the policies of the agency." The deputy should also be available, this observer says, to take on "important but not urgent" projects--"something like indoor air pollution"--or projects that are indeed important "but the agency's resources just aren't set up to deal with it." Such an assignment might arise from a problem simultaneously embracing several environmental "media"--air, water, land--that no other senior officer has the authority and latitude to tackle. Another potential area for trouble-shooting is the agency's extensive construction activity, in which EPA both enters into contractual relationships and administers grants. The size of these programs inevitably increases the possibility and potential damage of abuse, improper practices, and waste.

Key Relationships

Within the Agency

Reports to: Administrator

Works closely with:

Assistant administrators

Outside the Agency

Associate Director, Natural Resources, Energy and
Science, Office of Management and Budget
Deputies in the departments of State, Defense,
Energy, Agriculture, and Commerce, and at NASA

Outside the Federal Government

State governors and environmental, health, agricultural
and legal officials; environmental protection advocacy
groups; officials of other governments, and of the
United Nations, NATO and other international organizations; industrial associations and individual
companies representing many manufacturing and
business sectors, notably chemicals, petrochemicals,
electric power generation, waste management, and
pesticides

Deputy Administrators of the Environmental Protection Agency Since 1971*

Administration	Name and Years Served	Present Position
Reagan	A. James Barnes 1985 - Present	Incumbent
Reagan	Alvin L. Alm 1983 - 1985	President Alliance Technologies Corp. Bedford, Massachusetts
Reagan	John W. Hernandez, Jr. 1981 - 1983	Not Available

Carter	Barbara Blum 1977 - 1981	President & CEO Adams National Bank Washington, DC
Nixon/Ford	John R. Quarles, Jr. 1973 - 1977	Partner Morgan, Lewis, and Bockius Washington, DC
Nixon	Robert W. Fri 1971 - 1973	President Resources for the Future Washington, DC

* Environmental Protection Agency was created by Reorganization Plan #3 of 1970.

ASSISTANT ADMINISTRATOR
SOLID WASTE AND EMERGENCY RESPONSE

Level IV - Presidential Appointment with Senate Confirmation

Major Responsibilities

o   Oversee national programs to deal with existing hazardous waste sites and the environmental and human emergencies they cause, and to prevent or minimize creation of future sites through effective management of solid and hazardous wastes.

o   Manage programs to respond to hazards from underground storage tanks, and to promote state and local readiness to meet and mitigate the effects of chemical emergencies.

o   Develop, administer and enforce regulations or rules to achieve these objectives.   Work closely with the Congress to seek statutory changes as necessary and to explain and defend policies, programs, specific actions, and budget.   Maintain similar liaison with a broad spectrum of industry and consumer interest groups.

Necessary Background, Experience, Personal Skills

Success here depends on the overall ability to put together a coherent strategy that can cope with highly technical but emotional challenges under often fierce public and Congressional pressures. On the technical side, training and experience in one or more such areas as chemistry or construction helps.   But among those who know this job well, the feeling is strong that the more important qualities are proven skill in public management, policy formulation, communications and the political arena, and the extra sensitivity to handle people in high stress situations and constituency groups in high dudgeon.   The assistant administrator will need to begin with at least a basic grasp of the statutes which underlie most of the position's responsibilities, and have the intellectual breadth to expand that knowledge greatly, in detail, and quickly.

Insight

The frame of reference for this job rests on two statutes, one aimed at correcting the mistakes of the past, the other at preventing their repetition in the future. Those, at least, were the directions in which the Congress wanted to move in the 1976-1980 period amid the emerging horrors of toxic waste sites like New York State's Love Canal. And those ultimate goals have won reaffirmation and strengthened support in subsequent re-authorizing and amending legislation in the mid-1980s. Even so, these still amount only to first steps on a long road, and the effort to get from here to there provides a living case study in the complex challenges of contemporary society.

Of the two basic pieces of legislation, the better known is probably the Comprehensive Environmental Response Compensation and Liability Act, the Superfund law. Born in 1980 and renewed in 1986 for a further five years with expanded goals and a higher funding level ($8.5 billion), Superfund is basically an extensive hazardous waste site clean-up effort with enforcement teeth. "We come into the sites from two angles," says J. Winston Porter, assistant administrator since 1985. "If there are no responsible parties whom we can compel or force to do the clean-up, then we do it with the $8.5 billion and try to recover the money later."

It can fairly be argued that Superfund, given the social and political realities which have confronted it, still shows progress and promise. Since re-authorization, its activity has increased substantially. Spending, once at $300 million a year, is now at $1.6 billion. Staff has grown dramatically at 200 to 300 a year and now totals about 2,700 people--800-900 working at EPA headquarters and the rest in EPA's ten national regions. According to Porter the record shows, first, close to 1,200 short-term removal actions--disposing, say, of hundreds of old, porous and leaking barrels of toxic industrial waste--at hazardous sites around the country since 1980. Second, Superfund has inventoried 29,000 sites and has conducted preliminary assessments at 22,000 of these to determine whether longer-term and more costly remedial actions may be required. Responsible parties are currently handling about a third of the actual clean-ups; Superfund does the rest using construction and other kinds of contractors, and EPA is trying to improve the ratio.

All this is encouraging as far as it goes. But as of mid-1988 the national priorities list--those sites judged most in need of urgent remedial action, a central Superfund concern--contained about 1,180 final or proposed entries. Since Superfund began, work has been essentially completed at about 40 sites. Many sites require long-term maintenance and monitoring before they can be deleted.

Some measure of the enormity of the task and inadequacy of the resources comes through in Porter's comments. "You're talking very big costs, for example, to dig up everything at, say, a 40-acre site. You might spend $100 million on one site. Well, I've only got, in terms of construction, about $500-600 million. That would go to five or six sites--but we're working with 600 and something." Allocating resources in what Porter calls "frankly, a very emotional atmosphere at a lot of these sites, where people are scared to death about chemicals in this country and, I think, with some justification," is an imposing responsibility. The nature and intensity of a community's feelings about a given site and its real or potential dangers often helps determine what solution to apply. "They are very, very tough decisions," Porter says. "Just to mention a couple of numbers, the law directs us to start 175 constructions and 275 engineering studies in three years. It'll be tough, but we're going to meet them. The big trade-off is production--meeting those goals--versus deliberateness or carefulness at an individual site."

While Superfund aims at hazardous sites that can't be handled in any other way, the Resource Conservation and Recovery Act (RCRA) provides for the clean-up or ongoing management of other, more tractable waste sites. Even more important, it is a regulatory program that focuses on the continuing enforcement of preventive hazardous and solid waste disposal techniques. Amended in 1984, it is in part an extensive regulation-writing and "permitting" operation, specifying how many and what kind of allowable waste disposal activities can or must be undertaken by given dates. Though it spends far less money a year than Superfund, RCRA generally requires more of the assistant administrator's time. Of the 45 to 50 hearings that took the assistant administrator to the Hill in the last two years, the great majority were RCRA-related. The program is involved with some very hot issues--disposing of municipal solid waste, for example, or changing public and industrial habits and regulations to reduce the amount of waste generated to begin with --as well as with used oil disposal, recycling, and bans on chemicals used on land.

A well-informed former EPA official underscores the complexities surrounding the enforcement sides of both the Superfund and RCRA programs. In the early part of a new administration, for example, enforcement can be expected to get a lot more attention, for political reasons, than standard-setting. At individual

Superfund sites, industrial companies may have the Hobson's choice of paying for expensive corrective measures or being forced to do so by judicial action--well before the proper kinds of remedies have been studied and decided on. Adjusting this problem will involve the next assistant administrator in extensive dialogues with individual members of the corporate community. This observer also predicts that the Superfund and RCRA operations will write more regulations in the next few years than any others in EPA, and that "the cost of that rulemaking to American society in general, as well as to specific industries, will be measured in the billions of dollars." This will be especially clear as the Congress moves to satisfy "a growing environmental constituency" by enacting further standard-setting requirements instead of "dealing with environmental problems as it did in the 1970s by pumping money into the system for projects such as the construction grants/sewage treatment facility program."

Viewed as a whole, the assistant administrator position is "a pretty tough job in my judgment," Porter says, "in the sense that it's very substantive and very production-oriented." He was once in the engineering and construction business and did "a fair amount of planning and conceptual kinds of things, and a fair amount of production. This job has both, in spades. That's been the management challenge--how to allocate your time between the two."

In the recent past, it's worth noting, the job has also presented other kinds of challenges. One came in the wake of charges in the early 1980s of too-cozy relationships between a previous assistant administrator and some of the industrial companies affected by decisions and actions taken in the job. "We had to re-establish credibility for the program," recalls Jack W. McGraw, acting assistant administrator in 1985. "Any new job you walk into has problems, but this one had all of them."

For the future, says Porter, a significant goal in this job will be the next reauthorization of Superfund, which "runs out again in fiscal 1991. There will be a giant debate. They'll probably re-open all the issues--how permanent is permanent [what standards or measures to use in judging the completeness of a waste site clean-up], how to write clean-up standards, whether to change the enforcement provisions." He also reflects about the job's context and public attitudes about its mission. "The public wants certainty, and I don't blame them. They want to know if this site, with these chemicals and this ground or this ground water--is my child going to get cancer? Well, I can't tell them....It's very hard to explain it in percentage terms because everything in life is a little hazardous....What we're dealing with is probabilities. In these Superfund sites, I think we can clean them up, to the level of very low risk relative to almost everything else in society. But we cannot, in my judgment, get to zero risk."

Key Relationships

Within the Agency

Reports to: Administrator

Works closely with:

Assistant Administrator for Air and Radiation
Assistant Administrator for Water
Assistant Administrator for Enforcement and
Compliance Monitoring
General Counsel

Outside the Agency

Assistant Attorney General, Land and Natural Resources
Division, Department of Justice
Officials overseeing programs involving nuclear or
toxic substances at the Departments of Defense and
Energy

Outside the Federal Government

Chemical, petrochemical, and waste management firms and industry associations; environmental groups; state and local government environmental officials; scientific organizations

Assistant Administrators for Solid Waste and Emergency Response Since 1980*

Administration	Name and Years Served	Present Position
Reagan	J. Winston Porter 1985 - Present	Incumbent

Reagan	Jack W. McGraw (Acting) 1985	Deputy Assistant Administrator Office of Solid Waste and Emergency Response Environmental Protection Agency
Reagan	Lee M. Thomas 1983 - 1985	Administrator Environmental Protection Agency
Reagan	Rita Lavelle 1982 - 1983	Environmental Consultant Southern California
Reagan	Christopher Capper 1981 - 1982 (Acting)	Not Available

* This office was created after passage of the Comprehensive Environmental Response, Compensation, and Liability Act of 1980. Some of the responsibilities that belong to the current assistant administrator existed within EPA prior to 1980, and were administered largely out of the Office of Water. However, no position of equivalent rank existed prior to 1981.

12

DEPARTMENT OF
HEALTH AND HUMAN
SERVICES

Largest of the cabinet departments in budget ($428.2 billion in fiscal 1988), HHS also ranks third in staff size, with nearly 120,000 employees. Social Security payments make up almost 60% of its annual budget.

In addition to Social Security, the Department encompasses two other operations of core importance to most of the country's population, the Health Care Financing Administration and the Public Health Service, whose six agencies include the National Institutes of Health, the Centers for Disease Control and the Food and Drug Administration. The department's two other operating components are the Office of Human Development Services and the Family Support Administration, which provide social services touching millions of people.

To point out that HHS deals with some of this country's most intractable and politically unsavory problems is an understatement. They present the department with its biggest challenges for the 1990s. First, with acquired immune deficiency syndrome expected to infect many more people in the next few years than the total to date, two equal priorities are obvious. The first is to press further the development of an AIDS vaccine. Second is to invigorate and reinforce the leadership of national programs of assistance to victims and of preventive education. In the AIDS battle, it should be noted, the federal role to date has been charged by qualified critics, including the President's AIDS commission, with a sluggish and too-narrow response that has lagged behind that of other advanced nations.

Even given the size and nature of the AIDS threat, however, the funding to combat it will have to be dug out of a resource-scarce environment in which other equally serious problems compete for adequate attention. These, it is already clear, will afflict large sectors of American society well after the spread of AIDS has been stabilized and the disease reduced to manageable proportions. They include the aging of the population, the entrenchment of inner-city poverty, the rising rate of teen pregnancy, the continuing boom in health care costs, and the country's complicated, dangerous problem of drugs.

As HHS and the administration construct their approach to this agenda and the fiscal 1990 budget which they will request to fund it, the department will be assuming the extra tasks required by the Congress' decision to add catastrophic health insurance to the provisions of Medicare. In addition, the welfare reform bill already approved by the Senate will, if it becomes law, open another new and significant chapter.

Individuals who take senior positions in HHS should know what the policy alternatives are in their areas in order to understand where it's possible to yield to the realities of limited resources and where it is not. That requires, in turn, a grasp of what is most important about the agency's mission and the ability, as the director of a large HHS constituent group says, to stick with it. Decisions made with an eye only on the short term can leave no basis, further down the road, on which a program can move ahead. In this view, the department needs people who can match the need for short-term scalebacks with longer-term planning that can put programs back on track.

DEPARTMENT OF HEALTH AND HUMAN SERVICES

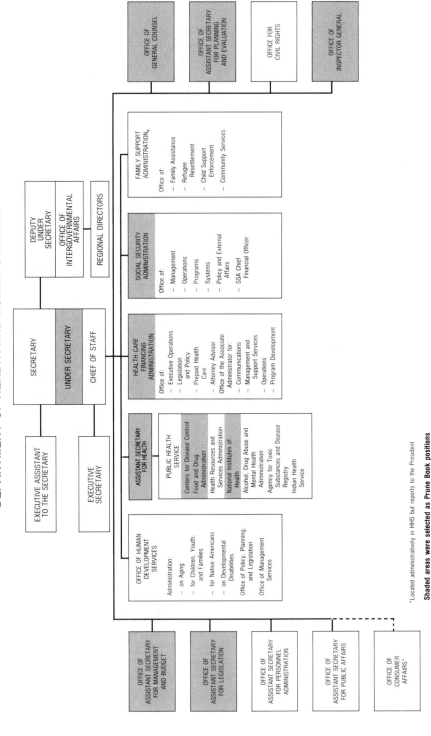

SECRETARY

EXECUTIVE ASSISTANT
TO THE SECRETARY

DEPUTY
UNDER
SECRETARY

OFFICE OF
INTERGOVERNMENTAL
AFFAIRS

UNDER SECRETARY

CHIEF OF STAFF

EXECUTIVE
SECRETARY

REGIONAL DIRECTORS

OFFICE OF
GENERAL COUNSEL

OFFICE OF
ASSISTANT SECRETARY
FOR PLANNING
AND EVALUATION

OFFICE FOR
CIVIL RIGHTS

OFFICE OF
INSPECTOR GENERAL

OFFICE OF HUMAN
DEVELOPMENT
SERVICES

Administration:
 – on Aging
 – for Children, Youth,
   and Families
 – for Native Americans
 – on Developmental
   Disabilities
Office of Policy, Planning,
and Legislation
Office of Management
Services

ASSISTANT SECRETARY
FOR HEALTH

PUBLIC HEALTH
SERVICE

Centers for Disease Control
Food and Drug
Administration
Health Resources and
Services Administration
National Institutes of
Health
Alcohol, Drug Abuse and
Mental Health
Administration
Agency for Toxic
Substances and Disease
Registry
Indian Health
Service

HEALTH CARE
FINANCING
ADMINISTRATION

Office of:
 – Executive Operations
 – Legislation
   and Policy
 – Prepaid Health
   Care
 – Attorney Advisor
Office of the Associate
Administrator for:
 – Communications
 – Management and
   Support Services
 – Operations
 – Program Development

SOCIAL SECURITY
ADMINISTRATION

Office of:
 – Management
 – Operations
 – Programs
 – Systems
 – Policy and External
   Affairs
 – SSA Chief
   Financial Officer

FAMILY SUPPORT
ADMINISTRATION*

Office of:
 – Family Assistance
 – Refugee
   Resettlement
 – Child Support
   Enforcement
 – Community Services

OFFICE OF
ASSISTANT SECRETARY
FOR MANAGEMENT
AND BUDGET

OFFICE OF
ASSISTANT SECRETARY
FOR LEGISLATION

OFFICE OF
ASSISTANT SECRETARY
FOR PERSONNEL
ADMINISTRATION

OFFICE OF
ASSISTANT SECRETARY
FOR PUBLIC AFFAIRS

OFFICE OF
CONSUMER
AFFAIRS*

*Located administratively in HHS but reports to the President

Shaded areas were selected as Prune Book positions

UNDERSECRETARY

Level III - Presidential Appointment with Senate Confirmation

Major Responsibilities

o   Exercise policy-making authority and carry out specific functions as directed by the secretary. Assume across-the-board duties as acting secretary when required.

o   Coordinate department activities when they involve several component agencies. Mediate jurisdictional questions. Take a leading part in developing and sustaining the department's relationships with state and local governments.

o   Supervise the department's budget preparation, and act as principal department representative in budget negotiations with the Office of Management and Budget and in consultations and formal presentations on the Hill. Oversee administrative management of the department and the selection of key personnel.

Necessary Background, Experience, Personal Skills

The key requirement is demonstrated success in managing a large, diverse and spread-out organization. Prior government service, familiarity with health care issues, technical skills in areas like accounting, financial transactions and contracts, and some exposure to the Congress--all help in getting a quick start and staying ahead in what can be a jack-of-all-trades situation.

Insight

An important consideration here--for both the undersecretary and the secretary--is the kind of working relationship and division of labor that they develop between them. This theme appears elsewhere in this book, in descriptions of equivalent positions in other departments. But the very size and diversity of HHS underline the importance of the principle, and make the comments of some who have held this second-ranking job worth an extra look.

One of them says "an understanding of who (secretary or

undersecretary) is going to do what" should be reached in the very early going. Such an agreement, this veteran thinks, should cover operational questions like these: Who will handle policy review and formulation? Who will oversee the execution of programs? Who will fill the senior spokesman role? Who develops and keeps an eye on "the long-range plan and strategy of control?" What about ongoing administrative details? And who supervises personnel recruiting and sees to the maintenance of morale?

Some of the answers may seem obvious. But this former undersecretary warns that "many of these things overlap and interrelate." Nonetheless it was "impossible" to get to the secretary, this veteran complains, and advises future undersecretaries to "get a clear understanding on the matter of access. You have to ensure there is an understanding on how you will communicate."

Relationships, of course, vary with the people conducting them. C. Hale Champion, undersecretary from 1977 to 1979, reports that he saw the secretary at lunch almost every day and that they operated together "as an office of the secretary. We had one common executive secretary. We divided the jobs and told each other what we were doing." As Champion points out, "in a large department with so much work to be done, the major responsibilities belong to the secretary but they play back and forth with each other. One or the other has to take the lead. (The undersecretary's job) is a subordinate position, but when carrying out policies or decisions, either can do it."

If comments like the foregoing have some meaning for relationships at the top of departments and agencies all over Washington, they also hint at the extremes that have characterized the secretary-undersecretary relationship at HHS itself. They tend to support the case for giving the secretary a role in choosing the most senior deputy, so that both can start off with some kind of personal and professional rapport. And that, too, may be a rule of thumb with validity across the government.

Key Relationships

Within the Department

Reports to: Secretary

Works closely with:

Assistant secretaries
Heads of HHS component agencies
General Counsel

Outside the Department

Equivalents in other departments

Outside the Federal Government

Medical, nursing and hospital associations, such as American Nurses Association, American Hospital Association, American Medical Association, National Health Council; retirement groups, such as American Association of Retired Persons; organizations concerned with major diseases, such as American Cancer Society; child and family associations; research organizations; state and local health agencies and officials

Undersecretaries of Health and Human Services Since 1969

Administration	Name and Years Served	Present Position
Reagan	Don M. Newman 1986 - Present	Incumbent
Reagan	Charles D. Baker 1984 - 1985	Professor General Management Group Northeastern University Boston, Massachusetts
Reagan	John A. Svahn 1983	Severna Park, Maryland
Reagan	David B. Swoap 1981 - 1983	Partner Franchette and Swoap San Francisco, California

Carter	Nathan Stark 1979 - 1980	Partner Kominers, Fort, Schlefer and Boyer Washington, DC
Carter	C. Hale Champion 1977 - 1979	Chief of Staff Office of the Governor Commonwealth of Massachusetts Boston, Massachusetts
Ford	Marjorie Lynch 1975 - 1977	Deceased
Nixon/Ford	Frank C. Carlucci 1973 - 1974	Secretary Department of Defense
Nixon	John E. Veneman 1969 - 1973	Deceased

ADMINISTRATOR
HEALTH CARE FINANCING ADMINISTRATION

Level IV - Presidential Appointment with Senate Confirmation

Major Responsibilities

o   Assist in shaping federal government policy on health care financing (basically, the Medicare and Medicaid programs), seek legislation supporting it, and explain it to the many and diverse national constituencies affected.

o   Manage, through contracting relationships, the claims payments processes of Medicaid and Medicare, which together serve more than 50 million people and currently take about ten percent of the federal budget.

o   Negotiate with states on behalf of the federal government to carry out the quality assurance provisions of the Medicare and Medicaid programs, setting standards and reviewing performance of carriers (Medicare, Part B) and intermediaries (Part A).

o   Through research and demonstration programs, explore and test new ideas for the provision of health care. Assess and improve the financing of federal health care, seek effective cost control, and evaluate coverage and benefits payments systems.

Necessary Background, Experience, Personal Skills

A solid grounding in the major public policy issues of health care heads the list. The right candidate should demonstrate an understanding of how health care financing and delivery systems interact, gained at a level that has provided the opportunity to show skill in managing large, complex operations. The context for this might have been an academic medical center or a large enterprise with a significant role in health care financing. Further, the continual dialogue which engages the administrator and HCFA's numerous interest-group constituents argues for someone who can combine a sympathetic approach with coolly objective judgment.

Insight

Consider some features of the climate and terrain which managers of federally-assisted health care must navigate in the years ahead:

o   Health care's biggest consumers, the aging population, will increase in number.

o   Health care costs will, by all experience, continue to rise.

o   Changes enacted and otherwise imposed on the federally-aided system in the last decade have made the job of paying hospitals and doctors much more difficult.

o   Administering the system will become a much larger responsibility with the decision of the Congress to expand Medicare to include the cost of catastrophic illness.

o   Whether and how to assist long-term home care of the elderly, as well as short- and long-term nursing home care, presents an increasingly sharp issue.

Heading into this challenging era, the federal government through HCFA already spends more than $100 billion a year on Medicare and Medicaid, more than 20% of what the nation as a whole spends on health care. Recalling her efforts to get ready to take on the job, Carolyne K. Davis, who held it in 1981-85, says "the three prior administrators I interviewed didn't really prepare me adequately for the breadth and scope of the position." "You're responsible for the biggest single piece of health care in the U.S.," another points out. "It's too big a job to get right in four years."

Specifically, some who have held the job remember these as its major challenges:

"The Office of Management and Budget wanted to second-guess our decisions on future directions. They should stop trying to micro-manage and let us decide how to spend the money." HCFA "should involve itself more in program goals than in budget matters."

"Constituent groups have to be dealt with and they all have very strong Washington lobbyists. I underestimated the importance of constituent groups and the influence of lobbying groups."

"Congress doesn't understand what is really necessary to make the programs work. We spend

money everywhere else but we couldn't invest
in these data systems."

The agency has "lost a lot of good staff and
recruiting people with the same competence is
difficult." The quality of operations and management staff is "mediocre." It's declined over time
"because the government hasn't been able to
hold on to them."

Nonetheless, one of its previous occupants finds the position
"unique" in its mix of "policy, the financing area and the managing
area." Where policy is concerned, he says, "you make the determination, seek the legislation and then you go yourself and do it." At
the same time, "it's a real management job, more like running a
factory. It's a big organization." This former administrator tried
to visit all ten regional offices once a year, went periodically to
see contractors and tour their facilities, and met health care agencies
and associations. He spent time on evaluations of senior personnel, hiring and firing decisions and the recruitment program. The
job also has a high public affairs component. Another previous
administrator sees communications ability as imperative for success,
adding "I even suggest taking a course on it." A colleague says
he averaged a speech a week.

Challenge and attraction of the job? In the collective view,
it presents (1) an opportunity to move toward real improvement in
the quality and extent of health care delivered to the nation's
elderly and indigent, by (2) effectively handling a big job in a
complicated and exacting management environment. "It's a very
high-stress job," reflects Leonard D. Schaefer, administrator in 1978-
80. "You're never secure--something's always going on out there.
Every day there's some unexpected problem in a state capital, a
hospital, or a research lab. Your priorities are always being juggled.
You have to be able to handle that. But you have tremendous
impact on the system."

Looking at this job from outside HCFA, two qualified interest
group analysts attach special importance to the kind of individual
selected for it and the primary tasks that lie ahead. "This is life
and death stuff," one of them says. "If the public gets the impression that you have an accountant there who isn't sensitive to the
social and moral aspects, it will really alienate people. There is
no more sensitive area where people feel or don't feel that government is doing right by them than health care....Medicare by virtue
of its position and size is more than a health program. It is also

the program that everybody copies and uses as a standard. The real role is as the leader of the health insurance industry."

The second of these observers thinks the HCFA position needs "someone who can look at health care creatively, for new ways to provide it." But, she points out, this "desire to explore alternatives" also needs "a bit of skepticism about new things, in order to work through them and put proper controls into place." She cites health maintenance organizations as an example of a promising new idea that took hold too fast. HCFA's research budget needs stepping up in her view--"it doesn't make sense to keep changing policy year after year and keep using the same old data." And the next administrator should review the kind of data HCFA does have to "find the holes in it, try to fill some of them in a systematic way. For instance, they know next to nothing about what's going on in ambulatory surgery right now, even though it is a field that is blossoming."

Key Relationships

Within the Department

Reports to: Secretary

Works closely with:

Commissioner of Social Security
Assistant Secretary for Health
Assistant Secretary for Planning and Evaluation
Assistant Secretary for Management and Budget

Outside the Department

Associate Director, Human Resources,
Veterans and Labor, Office of Management and
Budget

Outside the Federal Government

State Medicaid directors; American Hospital Association;
American Medical Association; National Association
of Retired Persons; American Nurses Association; AFL-
CIO

Administrators of the Health Care Financing Administration Since 1977*

Administration	Name and Years Served	Present Position
Reagan	William L. Roper 1986 - Present	Incumbent
Reagan	Carolyne K. Davis 1981 - 1985	Partner Ernst and Whinney Cleveland, Ohio
Carter	Howard Newman 1980 - 1981	Partner Powell, Goldstein, Frazier and Murphy Washington, DC
Carter	Leonard D. Schaefer 1978 - 1980	President Blue Cross of California Van Nuys, California
Carter	Robert Derzon 1977 - 1978	Vice President ICF/Lewin Washington, DC
Ford	Don I. Wortman (Acting) 1977	Project Director National Academy of Public Administration Washington, DC

* Position established under a departmental reorganization in 1977.

ASSISTANT SECRETARY
HEALTH

Level IV - Presidential Appointment with Senate Confirmation

Major Responsibilities

o   Direct the work of the Public Health Service and its constituent agencies in the fields of biomedical research, disease control, food and drug safety, health and health care resources, substance abuse and mental health, and protection from hazardous substances.

o   Develop and promote national health objectives, in cooperation with the states.   Maintain and expand international agreements and programs in areas related to health.

o   Advise the secretary in matters of national public health policy.

Necessary Background, Experience, Personal Skills

Asked about the requirements of this position, previous assistant secretaries speak with distinct accord on several points.   "I have M.D. and Ph.D. degrees, I've been trained in science and medicine," says one, "but if I didn't have management training in addition, it would have been extremely difficult to move this organization forward.   And if I hadn't had previous experience in government, I would have spent a year figuring out how it works."   A second: "A health or medical background--the most common is a physician"--plus "familiarity with health issues of the day and managerial experience at facilities with large-scale budgets."   A third cites the "combination of my being a trained surgeon and having good scientific background," adding that "you must understand health care delivery and have management experience in a hospital or university."

Insight

As chief of the Public Health Service, the assistant secretary oversees six agencies at the core of the country's health structure. They are the Food and Drug Administration, the National Institutes of Health, the Centers for Disease Control, the Health Care Financing Administration, the Health Resources and Services Administration and the Alcohol, Drug Abuse and Mental Health Administration. This and Congressional and public affairs responsibilities keep the assistant secretary out of the office and on the move nearly half the time. That includes communicating with nationally dispersed facilities and staff and managing and participating in regular contacts with state health agencies and officials. The occupant of this job presides over an annual budget currently exceeding $10 billion, developing and defending it inside the department and administration and on the Hill. "One is left with no time for reflection or planning," recalls a former assistant secretary, who refers only half in jest to "the urgent driving out the important."

The job appears to have a substantial policy role. Theodore Cooper, assistant secretary in 1975-77, uses the issue of medical liability insurance as an example. "We needed to take a position on it," he recalls. "The opportunity did exist to have a major input in major policy decisions." In a different policy dimension, James O. Mason, who had the job on an acting basis in 1985-86, discusses the setting of national health goals to reach in stated periods of time. Fifteen overall goals and 250 subgoals in areas such as heart disease and infant mortality were identified during his term for achievement by 1990. Mason thinks the incoming assistant secretary should emphasize attaining these objectives on time, and that goal-setting for the year 2000 should have already begun. This process should "say where the nation ought to be, and why we're succeeding in one area and failing in another."

In the policy area, among others, some former occupants of the position mention structural problems which, in varying forms over some 15 years, have at times hampered performance. As described, these extend in several directions. Upwards, one previous assistant secretary identifies the lack of regular, scheduled meetings with the secretary as an obstacle to getting timely discussion and decision on important matters. Another remembers "a large crew of special assistants assigned to various areas. This tends to get in the way. They do things the assistant secretary should do." In the downward direction, a third former occupant says "it's not a question of whether you had support from below. They will give you all the information you need. It's whether you are able to put together the organizational structure to enable them to do so." On this score, a previous tenant of the job feels, "you need to identify and outline what the responsibilities of those reporting to you are, who reports to you and whom you report to. There is frequently a breakdown."

As a result of some of these situations, a need for more clearly defined leadership in national health policy exists--for "coherent direction in policymaking," as a previous assistant secretary termed it. "There is a chance to consolidate the responsibilities and authorities by appointing the right person for this job," another adds.

Other kinds of obstacles, less severe and more commonplace, are typical of big administrative jobs with a large Congressional dimension, like this one. Former assistant secretaries include in this category the tribulations of "trying to change the orientation of people in the bureaucracy--people who are very competent but whose problems have become fixed," and "dealing with Congressional staffs who always assume their requests deserve a higher priority than any others."

To Julius B. Richmond, who held the post in 1977-81, "probably the most difficult problem is related to time allocation." In somewhat similar fashion to Mason's, he coped with it "largely by trying to have a conceptual roadmap of where I thought our programs should be moving for the next decade" and "thinking of daily pressures in the context of whether they were moving towards our long-range goals. I think that helps retain sanity."

Despite these differing kinds of problems, the job gets some good words from those once in it. One of these thinks it offers a broadening of perspectives on health issues and calls it "a learning experience." "The great opportunity in this job," another says, "is to have major influence on decisions affecting the health of the United States. In fact, that's the most important reason a person should be interested in this position."

Key Relationships

Within the Department

Reports to: Secretary

Works closely with:

> Other HHS assistant secretaries
> Commissioner, Food and Drug Administration
> Director, National Institutes of Health
> Director, Centers for Disease Control
> Administrator, Health Care Financing Administration
> Administrator, Health Resources and Services
>   Administration

Administrator, Alcohol Drug Abuse and
Mental Health Administration
Administrator, Agency for Toxic Substances and
Disease Registry
Surgeon General

Outside the Department

Assistant Secretary, Health Affairs, Department of
Defense
Assistant Secretary, Indian Affairs, Department of
Interior
Assistant Administrator for Solid Waste and
Emergency Response, Environmental Protection
Agency
Administrator, Agency for International Development

Outside the Federal Government

American Medical Association; American Hospital
Association; American Nurses Association; American
Public Health Association; state and voluntary health
agencies, such as National Association of Community
Health Centers; pharmaceutical industry and industry
groups, such as Academy of Pharmaceutical Research
and Science, American Pharmaceutical Association,
Pharmaceutical Manufacturers Association

Assistant Secretaries for Health Since 1969

Administration	Name and Years Served	Present Position
Reagan	Robert E. Windom 1986 - Present	Incumbent
Reagan	James O. Mason (Acting) 1985 - 1986	Director Centers for Disease Control Department of Health and Human Services
Reagan	Edward N. Brandt 1981 - 1984	Chancellor University of Maryland Baltimore, Maryland

Carter	Julius B. Richmond 1977 - 1981	Director, Division of Health Policy Research Harvard University Cambridge, Massachusetts
Carter	James F. Dickson III 1977 (Acting)	Senior Advisor Environmental Public Health Affairs Department of Health and Human Services
Ford	Theodore Cooper 1975 - 1977	Chairman and CEO Upjohn Company Kalamazoo, Michigan
Nixon/Ford	Charles C. Edwards 1973 - 1975	President Scripps Clinic and Research Foundation La Jolla, California
Nixon	Merlin K. DuVal 1971 - 1972	Senior Vice President Samaritan Health Services Phoenix, Arizona
Nixon	Roger O. Egeberg, M.D. 1969 - 1971	Washington, DC

ASSISTANT SECRETARY
LEGISLATION

Level IV - Presidential Appointment with Senate Confirmation

Major Responsibilities

o Advise the secretary in the development of legislation to support department programs and policy objectives.

o Establish and conduct working relationships with the chairmen, members, and staff of Congressional committees with jurisdiction over HHS programs.

o Present, explain, defend and negotiate the department's legislative initiatives and budget requests to the Congress, and evaluate Congressional approaches and reactions. Monitor and report all legislative developments relevant to HHS.

o Direct the activities of the legislative office and oversee the management of its administrative affairs.

Necessary Background, Experience, Personal Skills

The position would suffer fatally if managed without superior skills and effectiveness in Congressional relations. These might have developed through service on a Congressional committee or a member's personal staff, in a lobbying career, or in a similar liaison job elsewhere at the federal or state level. Analytical competence and legal or political science training are other useful strings for this particular bow.

Insight

Asked to characterize the role of the individual in this job, one of those who used to hold it answers with a one-liner: "The department's chief lobbyist." Depending on how one defines lobbying, that may or may not add lustre to the position. But it clearly captures an important dimension of this work, as confirmed by the view of two former occupants of the position that lobbying experience provides good preparation for it.

There are other dimensions to be considered as well. They go beyond the constant working of carefully-built relationships on the Hill to explain and solicit support for HHS policy and to gather insights into Congressional events and attitudes affecting HHS goals. The assistant secretary also manages and advises on the personal Congressional activities of the secretary, drafts testimony, supervises the two-way flow of Congressional correspondence, and handles Congressional inquiries on contracts, grants, and individual benefits sought by constituents.

Designing legislation probably takes as much experience and skill as anything else about the job. The department's huge entitlement programs affect the lives of millions of Americans, in many cases directly and centrally. Congressional action from year to year on the nature, funding, and operation of these programs determines their size and impact. This gives the legislative job at HHS unusual importance compared to its equivalents elsewhere in government. One of the key problems here, says Teresa A. Hawkes, who held the position in 1984-85, "is not having clear agreement between Congress, the White House, and the administration as to how much to spend....People want these programs until they realize they have to pay out of their own pockets. It will always be a chronic problem." With the assistant secretaries for planning and evaluation, and management and budget, she was part of a legislative team. Each of the three took responsibility for a piece of the action on a departmental initiative and for gathering and reading the echoes it evoked on Capitol Hill and elsewhere.

Other former assistant secretaries raise two additional problems. First, say two of them, the task of developing coordinated department legislative positions can often run into undue amounts of bureaucratic delay. Second, two others complain, component agencies of HHS have their own legislative liaison operations which at times parallel or conflict with the legislative assistant secretary's efforts. This, says Richard Warden, who had the job in 1977-79, "could be frustrating....People representing the offices were up on the Hill, doing their own thing....It made things difficult to hold together."

Stephen Kurzman (1971-76) ran into the same difficulty of "maintaining discipline among the agencies," adding that "I had little control of the way in which the agencies represented the secretary's position on legislative issues." While such situations vary from administration to administration, these comments illustrate a past, if not constant, hazard and one that can recur. To cope with such obstacles, Kurzman suggests, "enlist the agency heads, the other assistant secretaries, the general counsel, the undersecretary and the secretary. And, if possible, get hiring authority over your counterparts in the agencies."

Key Relationships

Within the Department

Reports to: Secretary

Works closely with:

Assistant Secretary for Planning and Evaluation
Assistant Secretary for Management and Budget
General Counsel
Assistant Secretary for Health
Assistant Secretary for Human Development Services
Commissioner of Social Security
Administrator, Health Care Financing Administration
Assistant Secretary for Public Affairs

Outside the Department

Counterparts in the Departments of Interior, Housing and Urban Development, Defense, and Labor

Outside the Federal Government

Associations of medical, nursing, hospital, and other health care deliverers, such as American Hospital Association, American Medical Association, American Nurses Association, American Public Health Association; retiree organizations, such as American Association of Retired Persons; medical research groups; pharmaceutical and medical equipment industries, such as American Society for Medical Technology, Health Industry Manufacturers Association, Pharmaceutical Manufacturers Association

Assistant Secretaries for Legislation Since 1969

Administration	Name and Years Served	Present Position
Reagan	Ronald F. Docksai 1986 - Present	Incumbent
Reagan	Lawrence J. DeNardis 1985 - 1986 (Acting)	Hamden, Connecticut
Reagan	Teresa A. Hawkes 1984 - 1985 (Acting)	Deputy Director Department of Health State of California Sacramento, California
Reagan	John F. Scruggs 1984	Not Available
Reagan	Thomas R. Donnelly 1981 - 1983	President The Pagonis and Donnelly Group Washington, DC
Carter	William B. Welsh 1979 - 1981	Booth Bay, Maine
Carter	Richard Warden 1977 - 1979	Legislative Director United Auto Workers Washington, DC
Ford	Thomas L. Lias 1976 - 1977	Associate Director Policy and Research ACTION Washington, DC
Nixon/Ford	Stephen Kurzman 1971 - 1976	Partner Nixon, Hargrave, Devans and Doyle Washington, DC
Nixon	Creed C. Black 1969 - 1970	Not Available

ASSISTANT SECRETARY
PLANNING AND EVALUATION

Level IV - Presidential Appointment with Senate Confirmation

Major Responsibilities

o   Assist the secretary in designing policies and related legislative proposals, and in their subsequent implementation. In this process, advise the secretary on the evolution of policy thinking at the top of the administration and in the Congress.

o   Ensure that the policies developed are consistent department-wide. Evaluate existing department programs. Oversee the department's economic and policy analysis. Assist in developing the regulatory aspects of implementation of legislation.

o   Analyze and assist in development of the department's budget.

o   When required, act as spokesperson for the department on policy matters.

Necessary Background, Experience, Personal Skills

Most occupants were economists until 1981, when the job got its first physician. Given the interactive and negotiating nature of the position, it helps to have a broad exposure to the governing process through experience on the Hill as well as in the executive branch. Professional training in economics or law, ability in mathematics, strong experience as a producer or consumer of analytical work, and skill in interpreting and synthesizing technical material are the other qualities which previous occupants stress.

Insight

This is one of those staff jobs with wide horizons. It provides the secretary with information, analysis and advice on the entire range of the department's substantive responsibilities. It has a main hand in shepherding program objectives through their design and legislative phases. These include Social Security, Medicaid and other entitlements which dominate the department's budget and for which the Congress sets policy. Congressional decisions in this area and the related policy-legislative functions at HHS thus drive the department's budget process and emphasize the program dimension of the assistant secretary's responsibilities. The position also acts as watchdog on budget adherence and on programs as they go forward. It must ensure that policy decisions are "coherent across all lines of the department," says William A. Morrill, who held the job in 1973-77, and that they are "taking us somewhere."

Occasionally the position can take its incumbent onto unaccustomed terrain, as with Robert J. Rubin, assistant secretary in 1981-84, who became public spokesman for the president's health plan; he appeared "frequently" on television and "regularly" in the press, far more exposure than he expected when he took the appointment. There is also substantial interaction with counterparts from other agencies where interests overlap, and with the Office of Management and Budget.

A veteran former HHS official feels that the nature of this position makes it the only place in the department where "creative tension" can develop. "It can help the secretary look objectively at what so-called experts elsewhere in the department are telling him," explains this observer, who thinks the right person in the position "can be a source of new ideas and new departures, and a trouble-shooter."

Policy formulation brings the assistant secretary into close association with the secretary, emphasizing the importance of a productive relationship there. In this advisory capacity he or she has to know where other major players (White House, Congress) stand on each specific issue in question. More important, in decisions at the top of the department on budget or program, he must translate and boil down complicated material--or as Morrill emphasizes, "see to it that the secretary knows what he is signing." When gathering information that can affect how a decision evolves, he thinks it vital "to amass the evidence that something is true, not just the conviction that it is."

Perhaps that is one reason why Morrill questions the degree to which his old job is involved with the Congress. He views it as primarily a position of evaluation, analysis and planning--activity which by definition requires the occupant to maintain objectivity. He spent more time "relating to Congress" than he expected to, and suggests keeping the job's Congressional exposure to a minimum.

Former assistant secretary Henry Aaron (1977-78) speaks of department-wide personnel and morale problems and sees a major staff rebuilding task ahead in which future incumbents should expect heavy duty. At the same time, he and his colleagues offer some bright descriptions of the job's potential: With the support of the secretary, says one, "the sky's the limit. You can do a whole lot of things." The challenge, in another's view, lies in dealing with a set of issues in depth and thinking them through--"tremendous issues for the country that have to be resolved. The opportunities are boundless." A third former occupant calls it "an elite analytic job (which) covers the whole political arena."

Key Relationships

Within the Department

Reports to: Secretary

Works closely with:

Other assistant secretaries
Heads of line agencies

Outside the Department

Associate Director, Human Resources, Veterans and Labor, Office of Management and Budget
Assistant Secretary, Tax Policy, Department of the Treasury
Special Assistant to the President for Policy Development

Outside the Federal Government

American Medical Association; American Hospital Association; Federation of American Hospitals; associations for the aging, such as American Association for Retired Persons, American Association of Homes for the Aging, National Association of State Units on Aging; organizations concerned with the low-income population, such as American Public Welfare League, The Urban League

Assistant Secretaries for Planning and Evaluation Since 1969

Administration	Name and Years Served	Present Position
Reagan	Robert B. Helms 1986 - Present	Incumbent
Reagan	Robert J. Rubin 1981 - 1984	President Health and Sciences Research, Inc. Washington, DC
Carter	John L. Palmer 1980 - 1981	Dean, Maxwell School Syracuse University Syracuse, New York
Carter	Benjamin Heineman, Jr. 1979	General Counsel General Electric Fairfield, Connecticut
Carter	Henry Aaron 1977 - 1978	Senior Fellow The Brookings Institution Washington, DC
Nixon/Ford	William A. Morrill 1973 - 1977	President and CEO Mathtech, Inc. Princeton, New Jersey
Nixon	Lawrence H. Lynn, Jr. 1971 - 1973	Dean, School of Social Welfare University of Chicago Chicago, Illinois
Nixon	Lewis H. Butler 1969 - 1971	President California Tomorrow San Francisco, California

COMMISSIONER
FOOD AND DRUG ADMINISTRATION

Level V - Presidential Appointment with Senate Confirmation

Major Responsibilities

o   Assure the safety and reliability of food, human and animal drugs, medical devices, food and food additives and cosmetics manufactured and/or sold in the United States.

o   Devise and implement procedures for the appropriate approval and distribution of consumer goods regulated by the agency.

o   Develop, secure White House (Office of Management and Budget) approval for, and administer a budget of $400-500 million.

o   Manage a large and geographically dispersed agency with a highly professional, scientific staff.

o   Communicate with the public, the Congress and other interested groups about the agency's purpose and goals, the rationale for its decisions and the impact on the lives of consumers of complex new products entering the market.

Necessary Background, Experience, Personal Skills

A thorough knowledge of science, including some medical or health care background, is critical. The occupant need not be a physician, but that is a plus. Other credentials mentioned: Literacy in scientific data, first-hand familiarity with research and statistical analysis, experience in running a large, highly dispersed organization, and communications skills, especially in television.

Insight

The occupant of this job finds himself in a continual crossfire between business and consumer groups, or liberals and conservatives, or lawyers, judges and scientists. "I was amazed," one former incumbent recalls, "by the scope of responsibility, the magnitude of the problems, the bitterness of controversies, and the attacks against the commissioner." "A lot of people," another says, wait for the commissioner "to misstep so they can capitalize on it...."

Also keenly engaged in this turbulent arena are members of the Congress with stakes in particular outcomes. Previous commissioners use words like "nasty," "terrorizing" and "crucified by an unfriendly Congress" in talking about some of their experiences on Capitol Hill. Mark Novitch, acting commissioner in 1983-84, describes the situation as "Congressional oversight that went beyond reasonable oversight," perhaps into what another bluntly labels the "heavy hand of politics." A third talks of the abuse of oversight responsibilities that can lead to "grandstanding at your expense."

None of this is really surprising, perhaps, for an organization which, one former commissioner claims, regulates about 25% of the products consumers spend their money on. In this situation, previous incumbents advise, a new appointee should realize well ahead of time that his decisions will never win any popularity prizes.

All agree, therefore, that this pressure position needs a self-confident, "people-oriented" individual--"the more charismatic the better"--and a manager skilled and articulate enough to "inspire" both the public and his own troops. A commissioner must "be squeaky clean, impeccably honest, with no sleaze factor attached." To those who have been in the job, these qualities are as mandatory as the thorough scientific and--if possible--medical training which they also stress. To a knowledgeable interest group member whose association deals frequently with the FDA, "you need someone with very sound judgment. These are really tough decisions. Some of them are scientific judgments and some are political or moral judgments. The job is in many ways like being a judge. It is a regulatory agency and you have to have someone whose judgment everyone has confidence in."

New products appear with a frequency that often outruns the availability of knowledge to evaluate them properly. A commissioner must frequently make decisions--in product labeling, food safety, drug approval, or a dozen other areas--on the basis of incomplete information. One who had to do so laments "the inadequacies of science" in this respect. It can prove tough, for instance--as Arthur Hull Hayes, Jr., who held this position in 1981-83 remembers--when "you are making decisions based on the greatest number of people who will benefit, or on a small number of people who have great need for a certain drug." The AIDS crisis, which will engage future commissioners for years, is a case in point. The kind of wisdom required by decisions under such conditions, says a onetime commissioner, "comes by slow freight."

Amid these pitfalls of politics and insufficient resources, former occupants firmly assert that a commissioner must keep overall goals in clear view. "You should be wearing the white hat," one of them advises. The goal to shoot for: "Preserve and protect public health without being anti-industry or anti-consumer." Ultimately, the agency must try to earn the public's trust and confidence so that it can begin achieving what another called its optimum state--"being left alone to do the job."

In this large and widely spread out organization, it is unusually important for a commissioner to have genuine access to the secretary of the department and in important relationships elsewhere in government. Unless he can demonstrate these connections, can "get through any log jam," and can "pay attention, discuss, defend and suggest on behalf of his staff," the next commissioner will probably fare no better with the agency's significant recruitment and personnel problems than his predecessors.

A former commissioner declares that running the FDA is one of the most difficult jobs he can think of--and adds that it is also "one of the most rewarding." Another speaks of the privilege of serving "the most powerful and influential public health organization in the world" which has, despite the rough road it travels, "a great deal of public respect." The job also earns praise as a "very good piece of work to do" that is "intellectually exciting" and "a very good pulpit."

Key Relationships

Within the Department

Reports to: Assistant Secretary for Health

Works closely with:

Secretary
Undersecretary
Director, National Institutes of Health
Director, Centers for Disease Control
Director, Alcohol, Drug Abuse and Mental Health Administration

Outside the Department

Administrator, Environmental Protection Agency

Administrator, Occupational Health and Safety
Administration, Department of Labor
Director, Food Safety and Inspection Services,
Department of Agriculture
Chairman, Consumer Product Safety Commission

Outside the Federal Government

Grocer and food producer associations, such as Association of Food Industries, Inc., National Grocers
Association, Food Marketing Institute; pharmaceutical
manufacturers, such as National Pharmaceutical Association, Pharmaceutical Manufacturers Association;
consumer organizations, such as Consumers Union of
the U.S., National Consumers League; heart, cancer
and other disease associations, such as American
Cancer Society, American Heart Association

Commissioners of the Food and Drug Administration
Since 1969

Administration	Name and Years Served	Present Position
Reagan	Frank E. Young 1984 - Present	Incumbent
Reagan	Mark Novitch (Acting) 1983-1984	Senior Vice President for Scientific Administration Upjohn Company Kalamazoo, Michigan
Reagan	Arthur Hull Hayes, Jr. 1981 - 1983	President and CEO EM Pharmaceuticals, Inc. Hawthorne, New York
Carter	Jere E. Goyan 1979 - 1981	Dean, School of Pharmacy University of California at San Francisco San Francisco, California
Carter	Donald Kennedy 1977 - 1979	President Stanford University Stanford, California

Nixon/Ford	Alexander M. Schmidt 1973 - 1976	Professor of Medicine University of Illinois Chicago, Illinois
Nixon/Ford	Sherwin Gardner (Acting) 1973	Vice President Grocery Manufacturers of America Washington, DC
Nixon	Charles C. Edwards 1970 - 1973	President Scripps Clinic and Research Foundation La Jolla, California
Johnson/Nixon	Herbert L. Ley, Jr. 1968 - 1969	Not Available

COMMISSIONER
SOCIAL SECURITY ADMINISTRATION

Level IV - Presidential Appointment with Senate Confirmation

Major Responsibilities

o   Take a principal role in formulating and publicly articulating social security policy for the administration, with a primary goal of ensuring continued financing of the special trust funds which support the program.

o   Oversee and ensure the timely and efficient monthly distribution of more than 50 million benefits payments, which currently total roughly 25% of the annual federal budget.

o   Manage a large service-oriented organization which remains labor-intensive (about 80,000 employees) and operates nationwide out of 10 regional offices, six service centers and about 1,300 local offices.

o   Revitalize and continue to upgrade the SSA's operating systems, particularly their computerization. Maintain work force morale and productivity.

Necessary Background, Experience, Personal Skills

Because of the size and dispersal of the organization and the extent of services it provides, the successful tenant of this job will bring to it strong managerial ability and proven leadership. Previous experience in technical areas, such as data processing systems, in the areas in which the SSA operates also ranks high in the recommendations of past commissioners. To this they add analytical ability and some savvy in public affairs--speeches, ceremonies, the press. Specific professional training in law or insurance (i.e., actuarial science) will help, but isn't essential.

Insight

Important challenges will continue to face SSA commissioners far into the future. First comes the continued soundness of the trust fund financing on which the system depends. When legislative and other adjustments become necessary to protect the integrity of this system, the commissioner works with the White House and the Congress to produce them. A considerable amount of time goes into the Congressional aspects of that effort. At the same time, he must also try to improve understanding of what it takes to keep social security programs strong and viable. This means a good deal of public visibility--explaining, persuading, image-building, acting as a "hands-on spokesman" in the words of one who held the job.

Two other challenges lie more in the realm of management, and one has some direct bearing on the other. For a population whose aging will steadily increase over the next generation, the agency already distributes about $250 billion annually in old age, survivors and disability benefits. It's a task requiring state of the art data processing and management. Though the SSA has long been working its way toward this goal through a familiar maze of budget and administrative constraints, it lags behind the curve. "I had no idea of the backlog and how outdated the computer system was," a recent commissioner says. Others formerly in the job echo this theme, as do outside observers. "What you need is a good administrator with a commitment, who is willing to stay there and see it through," says a member of a constituent group which follows SSA closely. "Turnover has been one of the main weaknesses....You need someone who can build up the morale of the agency and get the computer system in shape." Clearly, the SSA remains a labor-intensive operation which urgently needs to go high-tech.

Meanwhile, as the agency struggles toward that status, the commissioner will also have a work force of the present dimensions to communicate with and manage. Its very size complicates the process, perhaps leading former commissioner John A. Svahn (1981-83) to say "you have to run it like a military organization, give them a clear, direct order and they follow it." But morale is also a problem in an organization this big. Another previous commissioner complains of the "inability to convey policy accurately to the working level. Decisions from the top weren't the same when they reached the bottom." To help overcome these obstacles, the occupant of the job spends a lot of time meeting with employees in large groups, and making videotapes to instruct and encourage those he can't see face to face.

Communications difficulties can sometimes exist in other directions, too. Svahn feels he had trouble getting through to the top because others kept getting on his frequency; the Secretary "had a staff of 4,500 people who all thought they ran the department." A second, discussing relationships with the White House domestic policy staff and Office of Management and Budget, says he had to cope with the "very random and non-meritorious interest" these offices had in what the SSA was doing. A third, James B. Cardwell (1973-77), remembers the "chronic but not significant" problem that the SSA has its headquarters in Baltimore, not Washington. He dealt with this 40-mile gap by using his car as a mobile office for reading, drafting and telephoning.

Former commissioners agree that knowledge of how government works--whether gained inside it or outside--is invaluable in this position. It's a question of "knowing how to deal with the hierarchy and function in it," says Stanford G. Ross, commissioner in 1978-80, who adds: "The job doesn't carry the prestige of a cabinet post but does carry a great deal of responsibility. People who fill it have to have a lot of strength and dedication."

Three special issues of the future need mention. First, the trust fund financing solutions enacted in the 1980s are already generating surplus revenues to help cover the benefits now in place for the baby boom generation in the period beginning about 2010. In the short run, this will offer the temptation to "spend" these apparent surpluses with short-run political gains in mind, instead of making hard but necessary long-term fiscal choices.

Second, current pressures to cover the costs of long-term care of the elderly promise to become irresistible. With that prospect in view, guiding the likely changes along sound lines will be a significant extra assignment for future commissioners.

Third, proposals to make the SSA an independent agency will continue. Administrations of both parties have opposed this change, but its time may be near. The commissioner will take a key part in debating the issue, and in carrying out whatever decisions may result.

What all this means is that future administrators will have to struggle for equilibrium among vigorously competitive interests, in the government and in the country. A retirement association source, for example, thinks the commissioner will have to preserve the integrity of the program and fight off intrusions by future administrations and Congresses which consider social security a "ripe" target, as discussed above. Because that can place the person in "an adversarial position," he adds, "you need someone who appreciates and believes in the institutional importance of the program."

Key Relationships

Within the Department

Reports to: Secretary

Works closely with:

Assistant secretaries in HHS

Outside the Department

Secretary, Department of Labor
Secretary, Department of the Treasury
Director of the General Accounting Office
Administrator of the General Services Administration
Associate Director, Human Resources, Veterans and Labor, Office of Management and Budget

Outside the Federal Government

American Association of Retired Persons; American Bankers Association; Health Insurance Association of America

Commissioners of the Social Security Administration Since 1969

Administration	Name and Years Served	Present Position
Reagan	Dorcas R. Hardy 1986 - Present	Incumbent
Reagan	Martha A. McSteen 1983 - 1986 (Acting)	Legislative Counsel National Committee to Preserve Social Security Washington, DC
Reagan	John A. Svahn 1981 - 1983	Severna Park, Maryland
Carter	William J. Driver 1980 - 1981	Deceased

Carter	Stanford G. Ross 1978 - 1980	Partner Arnold and Porter Washington, DC
Carter	Don I. Wortman 1978 (Acting)	Project Director National Academy of Public Administration Washington, DC
Ford/Carter	James B. Cardwell 1973 - 1977	Executive Vice President Blue Cross and Blue Shield Atlanta, Georgia
Nixon/Ford	Arthur E. Hess 1973 (Acting)	Not Available
Kennedy/ Johnson/Nixon	Robert M. Ball 1962 - 1973	Visiting Scholar Center for the Study of Social Policy University of Chicago Chicago, Illinois

DIRECTOR
NATIONAL INSTITUTES OF HEALTH

Level IV - Presidential Appointee with Senate Confirmation

Major Responsibilities

o Develop and direct the mission of the National Institutes of Health--the conduct and support of biomedical research into the origin and cure of diseases. Determine the order of priorities as to society's immediate medical research requirements and those of the longer term. Make the key decisions about the nature and direction of extramural and intramural research and of training funded by NIH.

o Lead and defend the biomedical research community in public policy debate. Improve public understanding of its prospects and problems, challenges and requirements.

o Oversee preparation of individual budgets for NIH's 18 institutes and divisions, and defend them in their progress through the administration's review procedures and before the Congress. Nominate the directors of NIH's principal component units.

o Represent the positions and role of NIH within the administration and to the Congress, within national and international medical circles and to the public. See that NIH's activities and goals basically reflect the intent of the administration and the Congress.

Necessary Background, Experience, Personal Skills

No individual can provide effective leadership to NIH without the respect and support of the biomedical research community. To begin with, that kind of backing can only go to one of their own, who is both a successful medical scientist and a doctor with patient care experience. But the job requires additional qualities to handle the medical and public policy responsibilities involved. The director must not only understand, but champion, the role of scientific research in the continued health of society. Further, the right candidate should demonstrate sensitivity to the political aspects of scientific research. Professional and social credentials like these mean that the position needs what a former NIH director calls a "world class scientist."

Insight

What does NIH's role mean today, not just within the medical-scientific community, but for American society generally? One answer comes from author and scientist Lewis Thomas, president emeritus of the Memorial Sloan-Kettering Cancer Center. "I think the general public is aware that we are in the early stages of a genuine revolution in biological science," he told an interviewer several years ago, (as quoted in *Science Magazine*; see note). "We're beginning to understand at a deep level how living cells and tissues really work. The effects that this revolution is now having and will have in the years ahead on medicine itself are simply incalculable. All of this had its beginnings in the NIH, starting almost 40 years ago. All by itself NIH...stands as the most brilliant social invention of the 20th century anywhere."

In fact, the organization's ancestor laboratory began work in the 19th century (1887). Today NIH holds a position at the cutting edge of the breakthrough taking place on many medical and scientific fronts. Former NIH directors hold no illusions about the problems the agency must cope with. But the comments of these veterans--"it's very great to be in the forefront of one of the greatest periods of research" and "it's a great game that's for keeps"--reflect an equal awareness of NIH's attraction and potential.

NIH funding, and the Congressional appropriations that support it, have presented an encouraging picture in the last several years. In the view of current director James B. Wyngaarden, "biomedical research has strong champions in the executive branch, both houses of Congress and both parties. The appropriations committees in both houses are painstaking, farsighted, and supportive." Since the early 1960s, he continues, "the President's request for NIH has always been increased by the Congress...regardless of which party is in the White House and which party is in control of the Congress." This doubtless figures among the reasons why he says "the politics of the budgetary process is one of the first civics lessons to be learned by a new director."

Among NIH's chief concerns since 1982, Wyngaarden finds, have been the challenge of AIDS, the use of animals in medical research, and how far NIH's mission should extend in assisting U.S. industrial competitiveness in such areas as biotechnology. On the last point, he sees as the "dominant" view the feeling that NIH's most useful service would be to "continue to support basic research leading to discoveries that industry could translate into products, in other words to persevere in the kind of research that had given birth to the new biotechnology industry in the first place."

Lack of regular or easy access to more senior authority within the government seems at times to have presented a problem in this job. In the opinion of one of its previous occupants, "the executive branch does not have a good mechanism to evaluate a scientific organization." The Congress does have this capability, he explains, "because it exposes itself to lengthy direct testimony on scientific developments." He feels the NIH director needs access at the cabinet level or to the Science Advisor to the President. In this regard, it's worth noting the words of a knowledgeable former HHS executive about NIH: That it gives the Department of Health and Human Services and the administration generally "its window on the entire academic health community."

Managing NIH, says a former director, "is done through the grid system. It works very well because people want it to work. The director basically controls space. It's really a partnership, a collaborative management style. NIH is the protector of the research community, provides guidance to it as a whole, and represents it." Another who ran NIH calls it "basically, a fire-fighting job, constantly. Nothing is routine." He prescribes NIH's current goal as "continuity, because NIH supports many people, clinics and research organizations on a long-term basis and that support has to remain steady, and stable. It cannot suffer disruptions."

Some previous directors mention the usefulness of management skills in these tasks, but one points out that "the one director who had formal management training failed miserably. The theory of management doesn't work there. You need good common sense."

Key Relationships

Within the Department

Reports to: Assistant Secretary for Health

Works closely with:

Director, Centers for Disease Control
Director, National Center for Health Services Research
Commissioner, Food and Drug Administration

Administrator, Alcohol Drug Abuse and Mental Health
Administration

Outside the Department

Director, National Science Foundation
President, Institute of Medicine, National Academy
of Sciences
Assistant Secretary for Science and Education, Department of Agriculture

Outside the Federal Government

Research, health care, and disease prevention organiza-
tions and voluntary health agencies, such as American
Cancer Society, American Public Health Association,
National Health Council; universities and medical
schools, such as Association of American Medical
Colleges; medical and scientific associations, such as
American College of Physicians and Surgeons, Amer-
ican Medical Association; biotechnology industry;
animal rights groups, such as People for the Ethical
Treatment for Animals

Directors of the National Institutes of Health Since 1969

Administration	Name and Years Served	Present Position
Reagan	James B. Wyngaarden 1982 - Present	Incumbent
Reagan	Thomas E. Malone 1981 - 1982 (Acting)	Vice President, Research Association of American Medical Colleges Washington, DC
Ford/Carter/ Reagan	Donald S. Frederickson 1975 - 1981	Senior Scientist National Institutes of Health Department of Health and Human Services

Ford	Ronald Lamont-Havers 1975 (Acting)	Director, Division of Research Affairs Massachusetts General Hospital Boston, Massachusetts
Nixon/Ford	Robert S. Stone 1973 - 1975	Dean, College of Medicine Texas A&M University College Station, Texas
Johnson/Nixon	Robert Q. Marston 1968 - 1973	Professor Emeritus University of Florida Gainesville, Florida

(Note: Lewis Thomas quoted by J.B. Wyngaarden in "The National Institutes of Health in Its Centennial Year," *Science Magazine*, Volume 237, pp. 869-874, August 21, 1987. Copyright 1987 by American Association for the Advancement of Science.)

GENERAL COUNSEL

Level IV - Presidential Appointment with Senate Confirmation

Major Responsibilities

o   Provide legal advice to the secretary and deputy secretary and to the component agencies of the department.

o   Supervise the drafting of legislative proposals in support of department programs and the legal review of regulations.

o   Handle sensitive assignments for the secretary as requested.

o   Direct the operations of the department's legal staff, and supervise it administratively.

Necessary Background, Experience, Personal Skills

Only a trained and practiced lawyer can fill this position. If the general counsel can draw on a general understanding of current health care issues, or has substantial prior experience in the federal government, so much the better.

Insight

The general counsel job in this largest domestic department of government differs from equivalent posts elsewhere in the executive branch in the complexity of the statutory and regulatory structure it must deal with. As such, and depending on how the secretary wants to use the position, it can pack unusual clout.

Literally hundreds of funding programs managed by HHS produce great numbers of regulations to develop, analyze and apply. Difficult and contentious issues rise from many of these like steam from hot lava. This in turn generates mountains of lawsuits against the department. John B. Rhinelander, who held the position in 1973-75, puts the figure at 8,000-12,000 in that period. It was, he says, "an explosion of litigation," in which "we were deeply involved across the spectrum of a large and complex department, often in sensitive ongoing matters." What's more, he adds, "the time demand of litigation is much heavier now than when I was there."

The substance of these issues ranges widely--from civil rights and reverse discrimination to Social Security, welfare and food and drugs. At HHS, says another former legal counsel, "legal issues are the heart of it. The better lawyer you are, the better you'll be at doing this job. Being able to obtain the confidence of your client is very important."

The position has supervision of about 300 lawyers in nine divisions in the Washington/Baltimore area and in the 10 federal regions. As a group, this staff gets generally good marks from those who have led it. The general counsel has a big hand in assigning, and evaluating members of this staff, allocates the office's resources and handles justification of its budget.

Discussing the credentials a general counsel should bring into this job, one of its previous tenants understandably recommends "a strong attorney" with judgment and wisdom. "Wisdom is the most important," he says. But he also stresses that "a person serves the office and President best by the quality of his advice and his services rather than by the personal qualities he may have. It is critical that the person provide independent advice and stick to his positions even under political pressure."

Key Relationships

Within the Department

Reports to: Secretary

Works closely with:

Undersecretary
Assistant Secretaries for Health, Planning and
  Evaluation, and Legislation
Commissioner of Social Security
Administrator, Food and Drug Administration
Director, Office for Civil Rights

Outside the Department

Assistant attorneys general, Civil Division
  and Civil Rights Division, Department of Justice
Assistant Attorney General, Office of the Legal
Counsel

Counsel to the President

Outside the Federal Government

Hospital and nursing and physicians groups, such as American Hospital Association, American Nursing Association; voluntary health care agencies; associations of the retired and elderly, such as American Association of Retired Persons; lawyers representing these and other organizations across a broad spectrum

General Counsels of Health and Human Services Since 1969

Administration	Name and Years Served	Present Position
Reagan	Ronald E. Robertson 1985 - Present	Incumbent
Reagan	Terry Coleman (Acting) 1985	Principal Deputy General Counsel Department of Health and Human Services
Reagan	Juan A. Del Real 1981 - 1984	Chevy Chase, Maryland
Carter	Joan Z. Bernstein 1979 - 1981	General Counsel Chemical Waste Management, Inc. Chicago, Illinois
Carter	Richard I. Beattie 1979	Partner Simpson, Thatcher and Bartlett New York, New York
Carter	Peter Libassi 1977 - 1979	Senior Vice President, Corporate Communications The Travelers Insurance Companies Hartford, Connecticut

Ford	William H. Taft, IV 1976 - 1977	Deputy Secretary Department of Defense
Nixon/Ford	John B. Rhinelander 1973 - 1975	Partner Shaw, Pittman and Trowbridge Washington, DC
Nixon	Wilmot R. Hastings 1970 - 1973	Partner Bingham, Dana and Gould Boston, Massachusetts
Nixon	Robert C. Mardian 1969 - 1970	Phoenix, Arizona

INSPECTOR GENERAL

Level IV - Presidential Appointment with Senate Confirmation

Major Responsibilities

o   Conduct and supervise auditing, investigation and inspection procedures to protect the integrity of department programs and operations. Develop and recommend policy and remedial actions to increase their efficiency and cost-effectiveness and to prevent abuse and fraud.

o   Correlate the activities of the Office of the Inspector General with those of the General Counsel. Work with counterparts in other government departments on matters of common concern and interest.

o   Inform the secretary and the Congress on the work of the office and of measures necessary to correct defective situations and practices within department programs.

Necessary Background, Experience, Personal Skills

The position requires experience as an investigator, a knowledge of auditing procedures and government auditing standards, or substantial background in the field of program evaluation. The successful candidate should also have enough management talent to run an extensive operation. Individuals who have served in the federal government in an area closely related to the work of an inspector general would have an immense advantage, especially if it also brought exposure to the Congress.

Insight

In filling this position, it's important to understand that the technical experience it draws on is the most crucial quality to look for. The inspector general should begin with strength in one of three areas--auditing, investigation, or program evaluation. One factor to bear in mind is that government operations in these fields have developed specialties, especially where auditing is concerned, that often differ significantly from counterpart skills in the private sector.

Government auditing standards, as one example, are very complex. Auditing skills in the government differ greatly from, say, those of a certified public accountant dealing with taxes or cost accounting in the private sector. In the government, the focus is primarily on such areas as financial and program compliance audits.

For reasons like these, the incumbent inspectors general we talked to in two federal departments believe strongly that the most successful occupants of these jobs come from within the government itself. They cite the FBI, the postal inspection service, and the offices of inspectors general across the government as likely places to find such people. According to Richard P. Kusserow, inspector general at HHS since 1981, the less one knows about the technical areas cited, the more of a handicap it is. "If you look at the number of failures" in IG jobs over the years, he adds, "almost every one of them was somebody who was not a technocrat. The end result is that, probably in the last four years, there has been no one who has come from outside the bureaucracy." But he would not look, either, for someone from one of the program areas of a department like HHS. "They come with baggage...a vested interest in those programs," and therefore don't have the level of objectivity which is essential to the job.

The Office of the Inspector General (OIG) has three principal operations--the offices of Audit, Investigations, and Analysis and Inspections--and 1,300 employees. The programs they examine, ranging across all of HHS' operating divisions, cost an estimated $400 billion in fiscal 1988. The OIG also looks at overall departmental management functions like debt management and audit resolution. It oversees the auditing of government grantees by non-federal auditors, an activity that, according to the office's semiannual report of March, 1988, touches fully half of all federal funds granted to hospitals, colleges, nonprofit groups, and state and local governments. Where colleges and universities alone are concerned, the department has invested more money than any other federal agency in 96% of them, mostly in the field of biomedical research. This preponderant position means that the inspector general has what is known as "cognizant responsibility" to oversee the auditing of these institutions on behalf of the entire federal government.

Describing his basic operating arena, Kusserow says that "by and large, we deliver services." In the area of health, for example, this means the OIG examines contractors who provide health services, hospitals, medical suppliers, nursing homes, medical laboratories, biomedical research, medical scientists, and drug approval.

As with other such jobs in the federal government, this one by law has certain singularities. Kusserow points out that the occupant of this job cannot be dismissed without Presidential certification to the Congress that no political motive is involved. The inspector general also has the right to establish a general counsel function within OIG independent of the department's general counsel. Further, OIG has its own personnel authority separate from the department's, and the office's budget is an independent line item in the department's budget request. The inspector general presents the office's budget to the secretary, negotiates it with the Office of Management and Budget and defends it on the Hill. Finally, the inspector general is the only department official who can communicate directly with the Congress without going through the OMB clearance process; currently, the inspector general averages about a dozen Congressional hearings a year. The object of all such provisions, of course, is to protect the OIG from political pressure and permit it to operate free of the various internal pressures which might otherwise affect it.

From its establishment in the mid-1970s, the position has ranked as the department's senior assistant secretary, giving it what Kusserow calls a "confident relationship" with the secretary. In that responsibility, he says, he does not reveal "predecisional information" to which he has access, and avoids participating in policymaking, from which he is, in any case, barred by law. "But I'm there to advise where I think they can avoid problems in terms of wasteful spending or abuse, or opportunities to shut off vulnerabilities to fraud."

One of OIG's activities in the inspections and analysis area is the performance of certain studies that augment the quality of programs. For example, OIG discovered that the average age of smokeless tobacco users is ten, a fact that helped elevate the dangers of this form of nicotine to the same level of public awareness and warning as the others. In another area, the office reported that its study of hospitals' voluntary compliance with "Baby Doe" regulations showed a high rate of effectiveness, information that greatly assisted the fielding of Congressional questions on a subject of considerable public controversy. A similar effort produced useful findings on the issue of public attitudes toward the problem of youth suicide.

Thomas D. Morris, inspector general in 1977-79, says "the idea for [the Inspector General's] kind of responsibility grew in the 1970s. The function has proved its value. It's a very useful one as long as it's kept at a highly professional level." That stricture gets emphatic agreement from Kusserow. He puts great stress on the value of establishing and maintaining confidence within the department in the inspector general's personal approach to the job's responsibilities and the quality of OIG products. The only way an inspector general can function, he says, is to maintain objectivity, nonpartisanship, and neutrality, develop trust, and assure that the work of the office is credible and has no undertones or overtones of an "agenda."

"If you do that," he says, "then it's reasonable that employees who have a problem will turn to you, if they trust that you will treat the information they give with proper sensitivity. Fairness and objectivity and credibility is a critical mass."

Key Relationships

Within the Department

Reports to: Secretary

Works closely with:

Deputy Secretary
General Counsel
Assistant secretaries and heads of component administrations

Outside the Department

Inspectors General in the departments of Agriculture, Defense, Treasury, Commerce, Housing and Urban Development, and Labor, and in the Environmental Protection Agency and National Aeronautics and Space Administration
Assistant Attorney General, Criminal Division, Department of Justice
Assistant Attorney General, Civil Division, Department of Justice
Associate Director, Management, Office of Management and Budget
Comptroller General, General Accounting Office
Assistant Comptroller General, General Government, GAO
Assistant Comptroller General, Human Resources Programs, GAO

Director, Accounting and General Management, GAO

Outside the Federal Government

Professional auditors groups, such as Association of Government Accountants; accounting and legal associations; medical, nursing and hospital associations, medical groups, pharmaceutical manufacturers and other organizations in the health care field

Inspectors General of Health and Human Services Since 1977*

Administration	Name and Years Served	Present Position
Reagan	Richard P. Kusserow 1981 - Present	Incumbent
Reagan	Bryan Mitchell (Acting) 1981	Deputy Inspector General Department of Health and Human Services
Carter	Richard B. Lowe (Acting) 1979 - 1980	Judge New York City Criminal Court New York, New York
Carter	Thomas D. Morris 1977 - 1979	Bethesda, Maryland

* This position created in 1976, but not filled until 1977.

ASSISTANT SECRETARY
MANAGEMENT AND BUDGET

Senior Executive Service

Major Responsibilities

o Supervise preparation of the department's budget--reviewing the "wish lists" of individual component agencies and offices, adjusting them to fit overall budget parameters, and managing the appeals process. Submission and defense of the budget to Office of Management and Budget.

o Manage the department's administrative functions. Procure and maintain physical and technological facilities ranging from offices and furniture to data processing systems.

o Counsel the secretary on administrative and financial matters, especially with regard to the relationship between budget considerations and policy development.

Necessary Background, Experience, Personal Skills

Management experience and familiarity with budget procedure count heavily. Prior background in government and a knowledge of economics help. But a substantive knowledge of health and human services issues and--perhaps most important--good "policy sense" are also valuable assets, even in this basically administrative post. Its occupant should know the history of the programs offered by the department, and understand the scope of the needs they serve in order to channel the department's resources effectively.

Insight

All of the former assistant secretaries who discussed this job with us see a distinct dimension to it beyond the strictly administrative. "You have as strong a voice as most other people in the department about programs and policy decisions," a onetime assistant secretary says. "Management support to the secretary," in the view of another, "involved analyses of policy options, providing management structure and direction to the programs, and sharpening management practice within the department."

Most also think the position has an important responsibility for managing the work force efficiently that goes further than effective handling of payroll, office space allocation, or training programs. They speak of the need for "a high inclination for interaction with other people," of "the ability to get people motivated in the right direction on a continuing basis," of "getting the bureaucracy to see the larger picture, rather than individual pieces."

The occupant of the job gets some public exposure in speeches and media events and spends a considerable amount of time in Congressional testimony and budget encounters at the White House. Contact with interest groups absorbs a lot of energy, too. A former assistant secretary describes his only surprise in the job as "the extreme amount of penetration of interest groups into the department. They are very effective in getting what they want done. They can be very difficult to deal with and try to fragment policies at times." In fact, he continues, recalling the role of the Congress in department decisions, "you have to recognize the fact that you will have multiple bosses. There is no single core of authority."

Besides a general need to boost morale, some who have held the job identify departmental weaknesses that have presented management problems at one time or another over the years--such as personnel deficiencies in the facilities area and inefficient use of the analytical staff. Nearly all speak of what one calls the "tightened resource picture;" it has, he says, not only produced much more conflict with the Congress, but resulted in "more dominance of presidential staff in managing the agency," something that at least one former HHS secretary "would never have put up with." But John J. O'Shaughnessy, who held this position in 1983-86, while acknowledging that the shortage of resources has created a management problem for HHS today thinks that, "It is critical to conceptualize three things: 1) the role of the government in the economy; 2) the importance of the deficit in determining the size of the government; and 3) the relative shares of government spending to be allocated among departments."

Key Relationships

Within the Department

Reports to: Secretary
Undersecretary

Works closely with:

Assistant Secretary for Planning and Evaluation
Assistant Secretary for Health
Assistant Secretary for Human Development
Commissioner of Social Security
Deputy Undersecretary

Outside the Department

Associate Director, Human Resources, Veterans and Labor, Office of Management and Budget

Outside the Federal Government

National Association of County Officials; medical, hospital, and nursing associations, such as American Hospital Association, American Medical Association, American Nurses Association, American Public Health Association; health insurance organizations, such as Blue Cross and Blue Shield Association, Health Insurance Association of America

Assistant Secretaries of Management and Budget Since 1969*

Administration	Name and Years Served	Present Position
Reagan	S. Anthony McCann 1986 - Present	Incumbent
Reagan	John J. O'Shaughnessy 1983 - 1986	President Greater New York Hospital Association New York, New York

Reagan	Dale W. Sopper
	1981 - 1983
		Associate Commissioner
		  for Management, Budget
		  and Personnel
		Social Security
		  Administration

Carter/Reagan	Alair Townsend 1980 - 1981	Deputy Mayor for Finance City of New York New York, New York
Carter	Frederick N. Bohen 1978 - 1980	Vice President for Finance Brown University Providence, Rhode Island
Carter	Leonard D. Schaefer 1977 - 1978	President Blue Cross of California Van Nuys, California

Served as Assistant Secretary for Administration*

Ford	John R. Ottina 1974 - 1977	Vice President, Government & Education Management Systems Group American Management Systems Arlington, Virginia
Nixon/Ford	Robert H. Marik 1972 - 1974	President Cellular Radio Corporation Leesburg, VA
Nixon	Rodney H. Brady 1971 - 1972	President and CEO Bonneville International Corporation Salt Lake City, Utah
Nixon	James Farmer 1969 - 1971	Not Available

Served as Assistant Secretary, Comptroller*

Nixon/Ford	John D. Young 1973 - 1977	Falls Church, Virginia
Nixon	James B. Caldwell 1970 - 1973	Executive Vice President Blue Cross and Blue Sheild Atlanta, Georgia

Johnson/Nixon   James F. Kelly   Not Available
                  1965 - 1970

*   These two positions were combined in 1977 by a reorganization order of the Secretary, Health and Human Services, to create the position of Assistant Secretary, Management and Budget.

DIRECTOR
CENTERS FOR DISEASE CONTROL

Senior Executive Service

Major Responsibilities

o   Manage a national program to control and prevent communicable disease. Support this effort with research to improve and expand methods and means. Maintain active disease surveillance systems.

o   Consult with and assist federal, state, local and private health authorities and organizations in the control and prevention of disease.

o   Identify and define preventable national health problems and set priorities and goals for resolving them. Develop and direct prevention programs in the field of environmental health. Administer occupational safety and health programs.

o   Participate in international health programs and activities, with special attention to the developing world. Supervise the enforcement of quarantine regulations.

Necessary Background, Experience, Personal Skills

Those who have directed CDC in the past emphasize the importance of a director who can look beyond the strictly medical and scientific scope of this position to recognize the social framework in which it operates. Part of this, one of them says, has to do with being aware of social patterns and concerns, important "because the nature of disease is always changing." Part of it, says another, relates to approaching the job with the physician-patient relationship in mind, "and not as an administrator or agent." The position requires a medical doctor, preferably with a specific background in epidemiology. Also helpful: A better-than-average understanding of how state health departments operate, and some administrative experience.

Insight

Whether to combat legionnaire's disease, the many faces of influenza, AIDS or other communicable or toxic ailments, this job puts its occupant in the vanguard of the nation's anti-disease effort. This normally means a leading role in scouting out the problem, focusing on the pattern and meaning of new data, and marshalling the attack on a number of fronts. At the same time, the director runs a staff of doctoral and master's degree-level scientists in CDC's Atlanta headquarters that addresses a range of short- and long-term projects on a continuing basis. But CDC's chief must also find time for other imperatives. In a given week, these might involve Congressional testimony on the CDC budget or a particular health issue, attendance at a national or international meeting on health problems and disease control, or perhaps staving off pressure from various directions to modify a decision already made. The director spends time with state health offices (eight to ten meetings a year) and with national and international public health organizations (six to eight).

Specific activity in these and other directions reflect the director's wide array of responsibilities. Examples we heard about include a survey of disease-detecting scientific laboratories that uncovered major defects and led to state licensing requirements; the effort to see that support funds to state and local agencies remain in the communities they serve; development of immunization programs; and selection of the recipients of preventive health and health services grants.

Disease control being a high-visibility subject of wide and often intense interest, public speaking and other explanatory duties also take time. "The director is always being asked to interpret diseases," says William H. Foege, who held the job from 1977-83, "and there is the problem of conveying accurately to the public what a disease is." Another continuing difficulty, he remembers, "is to explain our scientific needs to non-scientific decisionmakers."

Looking at the job in its broad perspective, David J. Sencer, who ran CDC from 1969-77, asserts that it needs "a physician at that point in his life where he views the community as a whole as his patient, who thinks of himself as a manager, not a practicing physician. As diseases change, the targets become different, changing the technologies and priorities involved. But the goals remain the same."

Another former director finds one challenge of this position in "not getting sidetracked by what appears to be important to Congressmen and to the public at the expense of the broader goals."

Another advises that "CDC is not the place to go if you want a lot of thanks for what you're doing. You must keep developing the education of Congress and your own superiors so that disease prevention and cure remain better than thanks."

Key Relationships

Within the Department

Reports to: Assistant Secretary for Health

Works closely with:

Director, National Institutes of Health
Director, Health Resources and Services Administration
Administrator, Food and Drug Administration
Administrator, Alcohol Drug Abuse and Mental Health Administration

Outside the Department

Assistant Administrators, Air and Radiation, and for Pesticides and Toxic Substances, Environmental Protection Agency

Outside the Federal Government

State health departments, medical and hospital associations; World Health Organization; Pan American Health Organization

Directors of the Centers for Disease Control Since 1969

Administration	Name and Years Served	Present Position
Reagan	James O. Mason 1983 - Present	Incumbent

Carter/Reagan	William H. Foege 1977 - 1983	Executive Director Carter Presidential Center at Emory University Atlanta, Georgia
Nixon/Ford	David J. Sencer 1969 - 1977	Senior Fellow Management of Sciences for Health Boston, Massachusetts

13

DEPARTMENT OF HOUSING AND URBAN DEVELOPMENT

A key debate about the federal role in the national housing picture turns on the assisted-housing program. In one major view, the emphasis should be restored to unit-based rental subsidies, which involve federal assistance payments directly to the owners of low-income housing in a contractual relationship over a period of years. From the other side, the argument supports the current trend toward tenant-based subsidies, or vouchers, with which renters seek their own housing on the open market. It's one of several policy and operational questions on which the incoming administration will have to decide its own directions.

Another issue, less visible but acute, is low-income housing in rural areas. These regions often do not have the infrastructure, economies of scale and markets to provide builders and lenders with manageable risk and a sufficiently attractive return. Small communities usually also lack the tax base to qualify for mortgage-assistance bond issues. Without tax breaks or other inducements to neutralize such disincentives, small rural communities will continue to lag behind urban areas in adequate housing and, in some cases, the minimal amenities in utilities like electricity, water and sewage facilities. The programs both of HUD and the Department of Agriculture in this respect need thinking through.

Whatever the future administration's decisions on these basic issues, it will face a national problem of increasing ranks of the homeless and rising numbers of middle-class working families who cannot afford to buy homes. It will have to decide what to do about expiring unit-based assisted-housing contracts signed in the

1960s, where owners are tempted away from renewing those arrangements by the prospect of gentrifying their properties and selling or renting them at much higher returns. Acres of public housing in the HUD portfolio stand broken and abandoned, awaiting disposition. Although the roots of some of these problems stretch across several administrations, the department's current image for many constituent groups and other observers is one of quiet inactivism. From the available evidence, morale has suffered accordingly.

HUD is the sixth smallest cabinet department in terms of budget ($15.4 billion in fiscal 1988) and second smallest in terms of personnel, with 13,000 employees.

DEPARTMENT OF HOUSING AND URBAN DEVELOPMENT

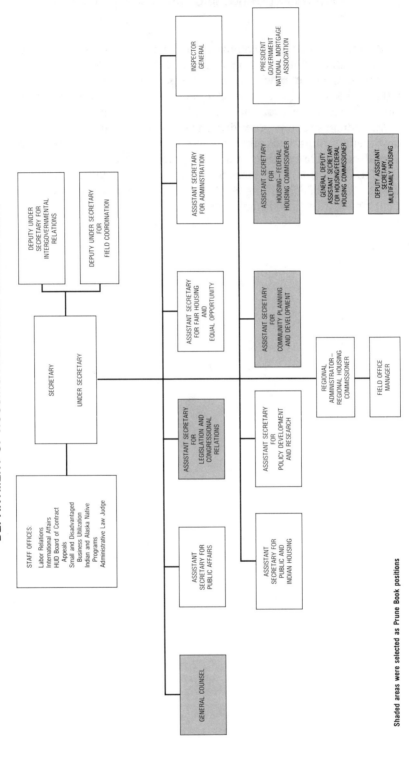

Shaded areas were selected as Prune Book positions

ASSISTANT SECRETARY FOR HOUSING/ FEDERAL HOUSING COMMISSIONER

Level IV - Presidential Appointment with Senate Confirmation

Major Responsibilities

o   Administer Federal Housing Administration (FHA) programs which:

-- Provide mortgage insurance and coinsurance for the purchase, building, refinancing and renovation of single- and multi-family housing, nursing homes, and hospitals.

-- Assist, through loans and rental assistance payments, the development and management of housing projects for the elderly and handicapped.

-- Furnish rental assistance payments directly and through public authorities to private owners for low-income housing in existing or renovated buildings.

-- Provide grants to cities and states to assist private developers in creating rental housing in areas where these facilities are in short supply.

-- Set and enforce federal standards for the construction and safety of manufactured homes, administer regulations governing land sales by mail, and dispose of property in the temporary custody of the Secretary of Housing and Urban Development.

o   Advise the secretary on federal housing policy issues. Represent federal housing programs to the Congress and public.

Necessary Background, Experience, Personal Skills

The critical requirement for this post is substantial experience in the housing industry--either as a contractor, developer, or housing manager, or as a banking official familiar with the technique of housing finance and the securement of mortgages. Supplementing that should be a knowledge of urban and suburban development issues, especially as they concern low- and moderate-income housing. It would be a clear advantage if exposure to these issues was gained through work at the federal, state, or local level of government. An ability to manage a large organization and perform resourcefully in the Congressional context are valuable personal skills.

Insight

This position is one of only three assistant secretaries in the department with line responsibility for program operations. "It deals with the primary mission of the department," says Lawrence B. Simons, who held the job from 1977 to 1981. Although there are 11 total positions at the same level, he suggests, "if you know what you're doing in this job you can find your way through the others and get a direct line to the secretary, because this is an important line operation job."

In it, the assistant secretary handles all policy and regulatory initiatives, keeps an eye on FHA's Congressional relations--legislative initiatives, appropriations and case work--and hears appeals and makes decisions in disputed cases. There are meetings around the country with FHA field representatives, attendance at White House economic and domestic policy discussions, budget encounters at the Office of Management and Budget, regular sessions with the agency's numerous interest groups, speeches, and television, radio and newspaper interviews.

Management is the key to the job. The sweep of Federal Housing Administration programs is wide. And, with the principal exception of assistance to cities severely short of rental housing, they are not grants, but federal operating programs. That means the FHA not only provides assistance to them, but oversees them as well.

FHA's basic lines of authority flow from the assistant secretary through a general deputy assistant secretary to deputies for single- and multi-family housing, and--in coordination with the Deputy Undersecretary for Field Coordination--to regional and field offices which, clearly, have a large part to play. Just as clearly, close two-way communication and direct contact between the field and the top of the department is, or should be, standard procedure. "This job is especially unusual because of the programmatic implementations that are necessary, and the national scope of it," Simons points out. "You need a uniform type of administration, with some sort of authority or ability for the assistant secretary to get down to his housing people." HUD continues to use this complicated system. Talks with present and former officials elsewhere in HUD indicate that it can be unwieldy and time-consuming.

Conversations with Simons and other former assistant secretaries convey a sense that those who receive FHA services should figure more importantly in how the system operates--that the agency's focus is somewhat nearsighted. Philip Abrams, who held the post in 1982-83, speaks of "too much concern for intermediaries"--those who provide the services--"and not enough for recipients of the programs." To a significant degree, that may reflect the fact, as he sees it, that "in Washington, no one represents home buyers or the undiluted housing problems of poor people." Abrams thinks subsidized programs should be targeted more to people who need it the most, particularly large families. "The emphasis should be on subsidies that are "people-based, not project-based."

Similarly, says David S. Cook, assistant secretary in 1976, "a lot more emphasis was put on budgeting than properly getting the job done. The unions had too much to say in what was favorable to them instead of to the people who need housing. The department is more involved with political matters than providing fair housing to the people of the country."

Both of these former assistant secretaries also point variously to "inertia," "nonrisktaking bureaucracy," and "inefficiency" as sources of some of the department's and FHA's problems. Simons and Abrams think getting priorities established in one's own mind, and with the secretary, is the first essential. Then, says Simons, "communicate it to the people who have to carry it out. The failings sometimes happen because there is no priority." Career employees are mostly "responsive to the policy you want," he says, "but they're not politicians. You have to tell them what you expect them to do, in order to be effective."

Simons advises those coming into this job to "be sure you have the freedom to choose your support staff," and to make appointments that reflect experience, quality, and ability, not political suitability. Two important Senior Executive Service appointments, he thinks, are the deputy assistant secretary in charge of policy and budget, and the general deputy assistant secretary, who should be "strong," someone "who can give you a feeling for what you have to construct and how to make that structure respond. If you're going to have to worry about how personnel moves and how paper moves, you're going to be overcome by it."

A major future policy issue for this job, and for the FHA generally, appears to lie in the assisted-housing programs, specifically in the relative merits of project-based and tenant-based rental subsidies. The FHA's move in recent years toward the tenant-based subsidy, or voucher, has brought criticism that focuses on the practicality of this approach. It's a debate which incoming FHA managers need to understand. Unlike Medicare, for example, tenant-based subsidies are not entitlements requiring appropriations to the limit of the need; they are programs with finite funding. Moreover, unlike rental assistance based on projects, the tenant-based subsidy is vulnerable to rent increases by landlords.

We heard two not entirely opposing perspectives on this issue, one from inside HUD, the other from a housing specialist in the government affairs department of a national retirement group. "Right now," says a HUD official, "it's a limited universe, not like Social Security or Medicaid. We want to maintain the current subsidy to everyone who's on it now and qualifies, but we'd like to add to the universe so that more people can get the subsidy. You need to strike a balance for budgetary reasons. We now have 4.3 million families on some kind of subsidy and probably two or three times that many who qualify."

In the view of our second source, the basic problem in housing is the existence of a poor population which needs housing but cannot generate demand. "So the private sector cannot respond. Strict privatization--in the sense that you turn the job over to the private sector and have the federal government step out--simply won't work. You need a federal program to take the lead. You need to encourage public/private partnerships. Obviously, you cannot make housing assistance an entitlement program in the same sense that medical care or welfare are. We could never afford it. At the same time, it's a cop-out to say that the problem is too big for the government to handle."

One positive fallout seen from the cutback on new federal construction of public housing since the early 1980s is the rising number of initiatives at the state and local level. This "creativity," says the retirement group expert cited above, presents an opportunity for the next administration. It needs to be fostered by "some tangible means of financial and regulatory support." Given the state of the federal budget, "we are not going back to the programs we had in the sixties and seventies and funnel billions of dollars to them. We are going to have to continue to rely on efforts at the state and local level to get housing built. This is another area where the new assistant secretary is going to have to be sensitive."

Key Relationships

Within the Department

Reports to: Secretary

Works closely with:

Assistant Secretary, Legislation and Congressional Relations
Assistant Secretary, Policy Development and Research
Assistant Secretary, Community Planning and Development
Deputy Undersecretary, Field Coordination
President, Government National Mortgage Association (Ginnie Mae)
General Counsel
Inspector General
Assistant Secretary, Administration

Outside the Department

Assistant Secretary, Domestic Finance, Department of the Treasury
Assistant Attorney General, Civil Rights Division, Department of Justice
Undersecretary, Small Community and Rural Development, Department of Agriculture
Associate Director, Economics and Government, Office of Management and Budget

Outside the Federal Government

Urban affairs, fair housing and city government associations such as Council of State Housing Agencies, Council of Large Public Housing Authorities, National League of Cities, Coalition for Low and Moderate Income Housing, National Low Income Housing Preservation Commission, National Center for Neighborhood Enterprise, National Housing Rehabilitation Association, National Association of Housing Cooperatives, and the National Urban League; mortgage banking, savings and loan, and real estate organizations such as the National Association of Home Builders, National Association of Realtors, Private Mortgage Insurers, Mortgage Bankers Association of America, and U.S. Savings and Loan League; groups representing the elderly, such as the National Council of Senior Citizens and National Institute of Senior Housing

Assistant Secretaries for Housing/
Federal Housing Commissioners Since 1969

Administration	Name and Years Served	Present Position
Reagan	Thomas T. Demery 1986 - Present	Incumbent
Reagan	Maurice L. Barksdale 1983 - 1985	Fort Worth, Texas
Reagan	Philip Abrams 1982 -1983	President Philip Abrams and Associates Englewood, Colorado
Reagan	Philip D. Winn 1981 - 1982	Ambassador to Switzerland Department of State
Carter	Lawrence B. Simons 1977 - 1981	Partner Powell, Goldstein, Frazer and Murphy Washington, DC

Ford	David S. Cook
	1976
		President, Director,
		  and CEO
		Buckeye Federal Savings
		  and Loan
		Columbus, Ohio

Ford	David M. deWilde 1975 (Acting)	Not Available

Nixon	Sheldon B. Lubar 1973 - 1974	Not Available
Nixon	Eugene A. Gulledge 1970 - 1973	Not Available

ASSISTANT SECRETARY
COMMUNITY PLANNING AND DEVELOPMENT

Level IV - Presidential Appointment with Senate Confirmation

Major Responsibilities

o   Administer national programs designed to further the economic and physical restoration of city communities and other urbanized areas. These programs operate chiefly through grants to assist rehabilitation and reconstruction and to encourage new economic development for depressed areas in partnerships with the private sector.

o   Formulate policy for these programs, under the secretary's direction. Develop regulations and program guidelines and make budget and administrative decisions.

o   Correlate policy and implementation with other agencies conducting related activities. Support policy, programs and budget before Congressional committees with jurisdiction.

Necessary Background, Experience, Personal Skills

This assistant secretary needs practical experience in or with state or city government in community development work. This might be in such areas as property acquisition, renovation of residential and non-residential buildings, utilities, construction contracts, or local economic development. Running this job entails constant contact "with the customers," as a veteran of the job puts it-- development directors, mayors, city councils, legislatures. An understanding of economic principles and their practical applications, and the ability to manage resources and people, are important.

Insight

The words "community planning and development" in the title of this job is, according to its current occupant, a misnomer. "It really is urban and state development--we're the UD in HUD," says Jack R. Stokvis, who took over the post in 1987 on an acting basis, and was nominated in June 1988 as assistant secretary. His office currently handles about $3.5 billion in assistance to cities and the urbanized areas of states. The biggest portion of that figure, $2 billion, takes the form of Community Development Block Grants, most of which goes to what are known as entitlement communities. The rest, about $900 million, goes to states under this program. In addition, about $225 million currently funds Urban Development Action Grants--a program which the Congress, as of June 1988, seemed likely to eliminate. The balance of the Community Development Funding goes into a number of smaller programs-- Rental Rehabilitation, Section 312, Emerging Shelter Grants, Secretary's Discretionary Fund, and Urban Homesteading and Neighborhood Development Demonstration. Stokvis says that 40% of the aggregate of these funds supports housing programs which include more housing rehabilitation than any other programs in the department.

Entitlement communities are cities with more than 50,000 population, central cities, and counties with more than 200,000. While they make their own decisions on what to do with grant funds they receive annually under a formula, their projects must, generally speaking, assist individuals of low and moderate incomes or aid in cleaning up or preventing urban blight. Non-entitlement areas get about 30% of the block grant funds, but don't receive annual grants and must apply under regulations established by the states. Fifty states, including Puerto Rico, have chosen to administer this money, with HUD managing. The program criteria are the same.

"This job has a lot of financial and staff management aspects," says Alfred C. Moran, who held it in 1985-86. "When budget priorities are set, you have to keep in mind the staffing needs to administer the programs." At present, the assistant secretary manages between 1,300 and 1,400 people, 265 of them in Washington and the rest in HUD's ten regional and about 40 field offices. But the department's operational anatomy makes it difficult to control them and the resources they handle. Field staff report to the regional administrators, who in turn are supervised from Washington by the Deputy Undersecretary for Field Coordination. In assigning field staff to a project, the assistant secretary must coordinate with the deputy undersecretary and 10 regional administrators. "It was a complicated situation," says Moran, "because the (regional) administrators took their orders from the deputy undersecretary, but the assistant secretaries developed the programs the regional administrators had to carry out. We overcame it by working together."

Stokvis has encountered the same problem. "It makes a very involved relationship with the CPD directors in the field offices," he notes. "In order to make sure my priorities are met, I have to spend a lot of time and energy to direct and lead people." He finds it "difficult to manage effectively or efficiently when you don't have control over the resources, when someone else sets the game rules. With the big issues, changing programs takes a long time. The system moves slowly."

Moran thinks the "overriding issue" is the "diminution of resources for the programs--trying to reconcile that with the delivery of services and trying to get cities to do more with less." Politically, he says, "it can be warm. The mayors are trying to get money, there's fierce competition for declining resources." On this front, Stokvis points out that the current emphasis is not so much on resources, but on greater efficiency. He says that, in 1981, "there was a lot of grantsmanship still around" and many city governments thought more money would solve the problems. "With much stricter budgets, cities have to look at how they're spending money and be efficient about it. They also have had to develop strong public-private partnerships. Neither the public nor private sector can do it alone."

As for suggestions for handling the job, Stokvis says good relationships with the Congress are important "because they make all the decisions on staffing, on money for programs. I deal with them a lot. The Office of Management and Budget is by nature a more adversarial relationship, because their aim is purely to cut budgets." He would also advise the next assistant secretary to learn to work closely with the career staff. "They are very good--and you can accomplish much by working with them. Properly articulate where you're going. It's a leadership position and people have to understand what you're trying to do."

Moran warns against coming in "with a cynical point of view." He thinks the job is a rewarding one. "It's got lots of pluses. You're doing a lot of things that will yield benefits to lots of people. The job is a very interesting and rewarding one...it's an interesting and educational place to be."

Key Relationships

Within the Department

Reports to: Secretary

Works closely with:

Undersecretary
Deputy Undersecretary for Field Coordination
Assistant Secretary for Housing
Assistant Secretary for Public and Indian Housing
Assistant Secretary for Policy Development and Research
Assistant Secretary for Administration
General Counsel

Outside the Department

Assistant Secretary, Economic Development, Department of Commerce
Administrator, Urban Mass Transportation Administration, Department of Transportation
Assistant Secretary, Conservation and Renewable Energy, Department of Energy
Assistant Administrator for Research and Development, Environmental Protection Agency

Outside the Federal Government

National Council for Urban Economic Development, National Housing Rehabilitation Association, National Trust for Historic Preservation, National League of Cities, U.S. Conference of Mayors, National Urban Coalition and other urban economic development, urban affairs, city government, and housing rehabilitation groups; retirement associations; urban planners

Assistant Secretaries for Community Planning and Development Since 1969

Administration	Name and Years Served	Present Position
Reagan	Jack R. Stokvis 1987 - Present	Incumbent

Reagan	Alfred C. Moran 1985 - 1986	Partner Barrett, Montgomery & Murphy Washington, DC
Reagan	Stephen J. Bollinger 1981 - 1984	Deceased
Carter	Robert C. Embry, Jr. 1977 - 1981	President The Abell Foundation Baltimore, Maryland
Nixon/Ford	David O. Meeker, Jr. 1973 - 1976	Deceased
Nixon	Samuel C. Jackson 1969 - 1972	Deceased

ASSISTANT SECRETARY
LEGISLATION AND CONGRESSIONAL RELATIONS

Level IV - Presidential Appointment with Senate Confirmation

Major Responsibilities

o   Take a leading role in getting department legislative and appropriations requests enacted. To this end, develop and strengthen personal and departmental relations with Congressional
committees of jurisdiction, and with individual members. Provide
services to the Congress relating to department programs.

o   Assist in developing required legislation. Examine and interpret,
for the use of the department and the White House, Congressional attitudes toward department policies and projected legislative requests.   Advise the secretary on proposed legislative
initiatives of the department, and on its Congressional relations.
Correlate legislative activities with other agencies with similar
and related responsibilities.

o   Oversee the maintenance of productive working and informational
relationships with state and city governments on housing issues
and questions.

o   Lead and supervise the budget functions of the legislative office.
Manage principal personnel assignments.

Necessary Background, Experience, Personal Skills

A strong substantive and procedural background in Congressional
affairs is the key to this job.   Service on a committee staff or
that of a member, or in a public or private sector position that
dealt in legislation, how it develops and what shapes it--these
represent the kind of experience this assistant secretary needs.
Some management and negotiating ability is helpful.

Insight

This job is mostly about the Congress. But it has a strong

responsibility as well for effective liaison between the department and state and local government officials, and for keeping a finger on the pulse of all those segments of society whose attitudes most affect, and are affected by, federal housing policy.

The assistant secretary's legislative role has several parts-- drafting legislation; working for its enactment; and assessing, analyzing and reporting individual and collective Congressional views and predispositions on HUD programs. Perhaps most vital to these functions is the ability to draw upon broad and active relationships among the members and staff of committees with jurisdiction over HUD programs and budget, and in a wider circle as well. This will be particularly true in the years immediately ahead, as HUD faces not only a likely redefinition of its role in the direction of greater activism but a changing and more demanding national housing environment. The ease and confidence with which the occupant of the position can move around the Hill has a lot to do with the credibility of the department's legislative program, and ultimately, its success or failure. It takes mobility, well-placed and substantive sources, and strong analytical powers backed by a detailed grasp of the issues.

Those, at least, must be the optimum goals and circumstances in this job. In practice, it may be harder and take longer. Stephen May, who held the position from 1981 to early 1988, finds it "difficult for most people in this position to have the time or ability to have a lot of influence on the shape of legislation proposed by the Department." In recent years, he says, most of this legislation has been small-bore, "the sort of thing the assistant secretary and his staff are somewhat better at putting together than someone who really needs to take a broader view in the Congressional affairs area." He strongly recommends a change in that situation. May also felt that the program assistant secretaries "tended to regard their subject matter as pretty much their own, and cross-fertilization is much easier said than done."

In this, his comments are similar to those of Dicken Cherry, assistant secretary in 1980-81. "Look out for program assistant secretaries who think they're also experts on Congress," he says. "They want to run their own Congressional show." Well-intentioned political appointees inexperienced in government, "often tend to think they are Congressional relations experts and go off on a tangent on the Hill" that is unhelpful to the department, May says. "This can be avoided if they are sensitized about it before going up there, or better yet consult about their plans with the Congressional relations office." Things broke somewhat differently, however, for Harry K. Schwartz (1977-78), who "had input in the development of the legislative program, and could say what could and could not get accomplished and be listened to."

Pretty clearly, the assistant secretary at the outset needs to establish firmly in the minds of the secretary and other senior staff the importance of the position. Also necessary, as May says, is getting them to coordinate their contacts with the Congress through the legislative office, "so that everyone is working from the same song sheet." In doing so, care is necessary to avoid strait-jacketing the informal contacts on the Hill, especially by career department staff, that are as vital as testimony or pre-arranged briefings. And, when the department is invited to give testimony, or plans a briefing on a policy matter, the assistant secretary needs to assure that the right individuals are chosen.

Part of Cherry's advice to upcoming assistant secretaries is to "watch the budget people. Your department's budget people are a part of a network of Congressional, department, and OMB budget people, and they're always doing business around you." He also notes that most of the department's Schedule C [politically appointed] jobs are located in this office, and "there is pressure from the White House to take people in. Be accommodating in terms of White House relations, but remember that you want quality people to run your office efficiently. You can make a plus out of it."

He believes that the entire department of HUD "is at a critical point in its history. The department has got to return to being the strong advocate inside the administration that speaks out for urban America. That's why it was created."

Key Relationships

Within the Department

Reports to: Secretary

Works closely with:

Program assistant secretaries
Assistant Secretary, Administration
General Counsel
Inspector General

Outside the Department

Counterparts in the departments of Interior, Labor,

and Treasury
Associate Director, Economics and Government, Office
of Management and Budget
Assistant to the President for Legislative Affairs

Outside the Federal Government

National Association of Realtors, National Association
of Home Builders, Mortgage Bankers Association of
America, National Association of Housing and Redevelopment Officials, Council of Large Public Housing
Authorities, Council of State Housing Agencies, U.S.
Savings and Loan League, National Low Income Housing Preservation Commission and other builder, developer, banking and housing groups and agencies;
groups advocating the interests of the elderly and
low-income populations

Assistant Secretaries for Legislation and Congressional Relations Since 1973*

Administration	Name and Years Served	Present Position
Reagan	Timothy L. Coyle 1988 - Present (Acting)	Incumbent
Reagan	Stephen May 1981 - 1988	Washington, DC
Carter	Dicken Cherry 1980 - 1981	City Representative National Center for Municipal Development Washington, DC
Carter	William B. Welsh 1979	Booth Bay, Maine
Carter	Harry K. Schwartz 1977 - 1978	Partner Lane and Edson Washington, DC

Nixon/Ford   Sol Mosher   Not Available
                      1973 - 1977

*   Position created at the assistant secretary level in 1973.

GENERAL COUNSEL

Level IV - Presidential Appointment with Senate Confirmation

Major Responsibilities

o   Function as chief legal official of the department, and legal adviser to the secretary.

o   Provide legal interpretations and services relating to department programs and activities, determining what procedures may be called for by the establishment of new departures or the revision of existing programs, and developing regulations as necessary.

o   Supervise and coordinate with the Department of Justice affirmative and defensive litigation to which the department is a party.

o   Assist in the formulation of the department's legislative initiatives. Establish working relationships with the committees of jurisdiction in the Congress concerning the legal aspects of department programs and actions.

o   Supervise the staff of the general counsel's office in Washington and furnish legal guidance for staff working in regional and field offices.

Necessary Background, Experience, Personal Skills

The position is that of a lawyer's lawyer. While some exposure to housing issues in their legal context is a valuable asset, it's even more important to bring substantial law experience to the job, and the kind of demonstrated skill and integrity that generates credibility and strengthens leadership.

Insight

This job resembles similar posts in other domestic program agencies where statutes and regulations drive the programs. At HUD, that means that the implementation of new programs or the revision of current ones must pass through the general counsel's office.

There, determinations are reached on whether a given proposal can legally fly within the existing statutory framework applicable to it. If the answer is yes, further conclusions are necessary about what that will take--an amendment to a regulation, a new regulation, or another form of administrative direction.

For example, a few years ago HUD decided it should eliminate the minimum property standards applicable to the construction of single-family homes eligible for coverage by Federal Housing Administration mortgage insurance. The department judged that the standards, which mostly duplicated local building code requirements, were no longer necessary and, more important, were adding to construction costs. Doing away with them required a decision whether the existing statutory authorities governing FHA insurance programs would permit it. After a decision that they did, the general counsel further ruled that a new regulation was necessary to effect the elimination, and developed the nature and terms of the new rule.

Requests for interpretation come to the general counsel from a variety of sources. The origin might be an individual case or a program staff wishing to change a policy. Much of the work in the position has budgetary as well as regulatory implications, and its occupant consequently deals often with the Office of Management and Budget. Especially if change in longstanding policy is at issue, but not only at such times, the general counsel spends time on the Hill, typically with the housing subpanels of the banking committees of both houses.

Interagency meetings to harmonize the content and implementation of new policy, and meetings with constituent groups are other regular features of the schedule. These groups usually apply less pressure in instances where they differ from the department on how they want an outcome to develop than when they seek something the department--or perhaps the Congress--opposes.

One of the job's challenges lies in the very nature of the decisions made. "An awful lot of things that people care a hell of a lot about come down to legal decisions," says John J. Knapp, who held the position from 1981 to 1986. The general counsel has a role, in his view, in maintaining HUD's credibility, of being seen as acting fairly, whether in its handling of applicants for program benefits or of those who have violated program regulations. While the job normally does not carry a criminal prosecutory role, the department does apply certain administrative sanctions to program participants--lenders under insured loans, or contractors, for example. It is also involved in a considerable amount of litigation in the areas of foreclosure and low-income assistance.

The general counsel is by definition a close advisor to the secretary and, in giving legal advice at that level as well as others, plays a policy role. Maintaining credibility and the acceptability of that advice are cardinal points to keep in mind. It's important to separate the legal and policy functions of the job and not confuse them deliberately or otherwise--to make clear when it is legal advice that is being provided and when it is policy advice, and to see that the legal staff is doing the same.

Knapp, who views the staff as exceptionally competent, warns that, unless they think the general counsel has that kind of professional integrity, "he's just not going to get anywhere. He won't be able to bring his people with him. The determinations the general counsel makes must be, and be seen as, legal determinations, not just arbitrary political determinations."

"The thing the general counsel has got to remember," Knapp believes, "is that this is primarily a lawyer's job. Unless he's perceived as viewing it that way, he'll be a political failure in the job. There are a lot more people who can say no than in a business environment. You're somewhat less in control."

Key Relationships

Within the Department

Reports to: Secretary

Works closely with:

> Undersecretary
> Assistant Secretary, Housing/Federal Housing Commissioner
> Assistant Secretary, Public and Indian Housing
> Assistant Secretary, Community Planning and Development
> Assistant Secretary, Fair Housing and Equal Opportunity
> Assistant Secretary, Legislation

Outside the Department

> Counterparts in the Departments of the Interior, Agriculture, Labor, Health and Human Services, Treasury and the Environmental Protection Agency

Assistant Attorney General, Civil Division, Department of Justice

Assistant Attorney General, Civil Rights Division, Department of Justice

President, Government National Mortgage Association

Administrator, Information and Regulatory Affairs, Office of Management and Budget

Associate Director, Economics and Government, Office of Management and Budget

Outside the Federal Government

National Association of Home Builders, Mortgage Bankers Association of America, National Association of Realtors, and other construction and banking associations; public housing authorities; urban affairs and city government organizations such as the National League of Cities and the National Urban Coalition; low-income housing advocates and other housing groups such as the National Housing Rehabilitation Association and the National Low Income Housing Preservation Commission; the National Housing Law Project; private fair housing organizations; groups advocating the interests of the elderly

General Counsels for Housing and Urban Development Since 1969

Administration	Name and Years Served	Present Position
Reagan	John M. Dorsey 1987 - Present	Incumbent
Reagan	John J. Knapp 1981 - 1986	Of Counsel Powell, Goldstein, Frazer and Murphy Washington, DC
Carter	Jane McGrew 1979 - 1981	Partner Weissbrodt, Mirel, Swiss and McGrew Washington, DC

Carter	Edward Norton 1979 (Acting)	Partner Bosbergs and Norton Washington, DC
Carter	Ruth T. Prokop 1977 - 1979	Partner Fortas, Prokop and Hardman Washington, DC
Nixon/Ford	Robert R. Elliot 1974 - 1976	Partner Elliott and Sugarman Washington, DC
Nixon	James L. Mitchell 1973 - 1974	Not Available
Nixon	David O. Maxwell 1970 - 1973	Chairman Fannie Mae Washington, DC
Nixon	Sherman E. Unger 1969 - 1970	Deceased

GENERAL DEPUTY ASSISTANT SECRETARY HOUSING/FEDERAL HOUSING COMMISSIONER

Senior Executive Service

Major Responsibilities

o   Assist the Assistant Secretary for Housing/Federal Housing Commissioner in administering federal programs which supply mortgage insurance and mortgage management covering a variety of operations in the single and multifamily housing field, among them purchases, construction and rehabilitation; provide loans to develop housing for the elderly and handicapped, and rental assistance payments to low-income families; and grant funds for state and local construction projects to alleviate rental housing shortages.   These programs also enforce construction and safety standards for mobile and prefabricated homes, regulate land sales by mail, and dispose of property in federal custody.

o   Supervise preparation of a daily regulations report.   Improve management procedures and communications with field offices and staff.   Provide administrative oversight for component offices of the FHA.

Necessary Background, Experience, Personal Skills

Substantial field experience in the housing industry, preferably as a developer or in construction, leads the requirements for this position.   The right candidate will also understand housing finance and know how government works.   On the latter point, some Washington exposure is best, but familiarity with state and city government processes also helps.   Because of the regulatory nature of the work, legal skills are valuable.

Insight

The responsibilities of this job duplicate those of the assistant secretary, and in current and recent practice the two split the work load between them.   Broadly speaking, that means the general deputy assistant secretary (henceforth "deputy," for short) oversees daily operations within the Federal Housing Administration (FHA), and the assistant secretary handles activities outside. As specific examples, the deputy runs program implementation, and the assistant secretary does most of the testimony on the Hill. But, when the situation requires it, the deputy must take over administration of the agency. And, says Morton A. Baruch, who held the position in 1977-80, "anything the assistant secretary could sign, I could sign."

The FHA manages close to 70% of the programs HUD is budgeted for, including $10 billion a year in subsidized programs--such as rental assistance and loans to developers of housing for low-income, elderly and handicapped occupants--on which the deputy signs off. The agency works through a structure in which a regional administrator will manage a given operation day to day, with field staff reporting to that regional office on a line basis. However, people in the field have a dotted-line link directly to the deputy and the assistant secretary which the current deputy, James E. Schoenberger (since 1987), calls "sort of an awkward relationship." Field staff, he says, "must come here for any kind of program guidance or interpretation of regulations." Thus, of HUD's 12,000 employees nationwide in ten regional and 80-odd field offices, the deputy supervises about 540 directly but has a good deal to say about what several thousand others do across the country.

Asked about management challenges in this job, Schoenberger attaches significance to a daily regulations report which lists "our highest priority regulations in terms of trying to put them out." The point is to get agency staff to recognize that regulations "are one of the most important things we do;" he says the practice has weaned staff "away from thinking that regulations are something it takes two years to put out." He also tries "to sit down with senior managers and focus on the priorities of the organization--to set them and not have too many. In essence, it's management by objective." The large number of FHA programs prompted the shift of the weekly staff meeting from a show-and-tell format to "common problem solving" in an effort to "get people more involved and moving in sync."

Schoenberger offers some points for an incoming deputy to keep in mind. "If you're not a lawyer, find one or two you can rely on and trust. Learn the key programs in a hurry." Mistakes show up down the road, he says, "particularly in insurance matters with projects that get into trouble. If you make a bad decision, it won't come out for years to come, but it can be very expensive." Overall, he adds, a new deputy should "within a month or so, set five or six big objectives for what you hope to accomplish, and keep it a manageable number." He thinks career staff "are an excellent resource....Keep an open mind and be prepared to work with them."

Key Relationships

Within the Department

Reports to:

Assistant Secretary Housing/Federal Housing Commissioner

Works closely with:

General Deputy Assistant Secretary, Community Planning and Development
General Deputy Assistant Secretary, Public and Indian Housing
Deputy Assistant Secretary, Administration
General Deputy Assistant Secretary, Policy Development and Research
Deputy Undersecretary, Field Coordination

Outside the Department

Assistant Secretary, Indian Affairs, Department of the Interior
Administrator, Family Support Administration, Department of Health and Human Services

Outside the Federal Government

National Association of Home Builders, National Association of Realtors, Mortgage Bankers Association, National League of Cities, and other construction, banking, and thrift associations; individual developers; National Low Income Housing Preservation Commission; National Council of Senior Citizens and National Institute of Senior Housing

General Deputy Assistant Secretaries for Housing
Since 1969

Administration	Name and Years Served	Present Position
Reagan	James E. Schoenberger 1987 - Present	Incumbent
Reagan	Silvio J. DeBartolomeis 1986	Real Estate Consultant Winn Group Englewood, Colorado
Reagan	Janet Hale 1985 -1986	Assistant Secretary, Budget and Programs Department of Trans- portation
Reagan	Shirley McVay Wiseman 1984 - 1985	First Vice President National Association of Home Builders Washington, DC
Reagan	W. Calvert Brand 1983 - 1984	Not Available
Reagan	Philip Abrams 1981 - 1982	President Philip Abrams and Associates Englewood, Colorado
Carter	Clyde T. J. McHenry 1980 - 1981	President Clyde McHenry, Inc. Washington, DC
Carter	Morton A. Baruch 1977 - 1980	President Morton A. Baruch and Associates Rockville, Maryland
Ford	David M. deWilde 1975 - 1976	Not Available

Nixon/Ford	Daniel P. Kearney 1973 - 1974	Principal Aldrich, Eastman & Waltch Boston, Massachusetts
Nixon	John L. Ganley 1972 - 1973	Not Available
Nixon	William B. Dockser 1971 - 1972 (Acting)	Not Available
Nixon	Woodward Kuigman 1970	Not Available

DEPUTY ASSISTANT SECRETARY
MULTIFAMILY HOUSING

Senior Executive Service

Major Responsibilities

o Under the direction of the Assistant Secretary for Housing/Federal Housing Commissioner, oversee federal mortgage insurance programs supporting the purchase, financing, construction or rehabilitation of multifamily housing.

o Manage national programs of subsidized rental and tenant assistance and insured loans and development loans for the multifamily housing of low- and moderate-income families and the elderly.

o Supervise the management and disposition of the department's inventory of multifamily real estate which, through housing project failure and other causes, is in the custody of the secretary.

o Provide personnel, budget and other administrative management for the Office of Multifamily Housing.

Necessary Background, Experience, Personal Skills

A knowledge of real estate and multifamily housing finance is the first qualification to look for, preferably developed through prior government service at the federal or local level, or in the housing industry. Equally important are management experience and leadership ability, especially a talent for handling people. In addition, one former deputy assistant secretary believes "you have to have done things politically before you go into this job. There are many times when you're forced to make decisions, people are looking over your shoulder, and you have to be careful." Public speaking and negotiating skills are handy assets.

Insight

"It's not an easy job from the perspective of someone just walking in," says Silvio J. DeBartolomeis, deputy assistant secretary in 1983-86. "There are so many parts that, to keep the whole thing moving in the proper way, it takes a bit of a master."

But, he adds, one learns a lot on the job. "You've got to go in there with an open attitude about what you need to learn, and about the people." Even a solid working knowledge of the subject doesn't always help. "The way you deal with not knowing about a particular area," DeBartolomeis says, "is be up front and say so."

The deputy assistant secretary promulgates, monitors and enforces a multitude of regulations covering the entire area with which the job deals--normally, an arduous task. But the opportunity to "put your fingerprints on policy" is there, as well as to "change what's happening in the administration of programs in a way that others do not," DeBartolomeis points out. For example, the department subsidizes somewhere between four and five million housing units, and "one decision about how you calculate the management fee will affect an entire industry." One point to keep in mind, he adds, is "the deputy assistant secretary's ability to really empower people." This means taking care that decisions "are not construed as favoritism toward a city, a public housing authority, or one industry to the detriment of another."

The job embraces some highly technical issues that can be difficult, but also intellectually stimulating. A lot of time goes into the "nitty gritty of properties"--the routine underwriting and servicing of loans; dealing with problematic projects and those that have failed and with the people involved; or restructuring a deal on a troubled property that will enable the developer to continue to live with it. There is a good deal of travel. "It's not that the job is that hard," a former deputy says. "You just have to be willing to make common sense decisions and back them up." A major problem for housing stems from the 1986 tax reform legislation which, by changing the depreciation schedules, eliminated important incentives for multifamily property investment. This comes down hard on areas of the country that are overbuilt.

Future deputies are likely to be increasingly preoccupied with subsidized housing problems arising particularly from the assisted-housing program. Under it, developers contract to build and manage low-income housing for tenants whose rental payments are subsidized by HUD. With many such contracts, signed 15 and 20 years ago, at or near the point of expiration, a sizeable number of owners want to charge rent at market rates and drop the HUD subsidy program. As the trend toward gentrification of low-rent neighbor-hoods increases, these landlords are tempted by the prospect of much greater income flowing from remodeling low-income housing for sale or rent at much higher prices. Either way, HUD's burdens--and those of the deputy assistant secretary--will increase.

The issues are "so many and so complex," DeBartolomeis says, that the deputy can't do it all. The relationship between this job and that of the assistant secretary bears greatly on how the work load is shared. "The country is getting larger," he emphasizes, "but the staff at HUD isn't getting any bigger. The private sector will have to take more of the processing role." The other big task, in his view, will be the management of "all those projects that had to be restructured due to tax reform."

Key Relationships

Within the Department

Reports to: Assistant Secretary for Housing

Works closely with:

Undersecretary
Deputy Undersecretary for Field Coordination
Assistant Secretary for Legislation
General Counsel
Inspector General
Deputy Assistant Secretary, Policy Development and
    Research

Outside the Department

Assistant Secretary, Domestic Finance, Department
    of the Treasury
Assistant Attorney General, Civil Division, Department
    of Justice
Deputy Undersecretary, Small Community and Rural
    Development, Department of Agriculture
Associate Director, Economics and Government, Office
    of Management and Budget

Outside the Federal Government

Mortgage Bankers Association, Institute for Real Estate Management, National Association of Homebuilders, Association of HUD Management Agents; individual real estate, construction and development associations, such as National Association of Realtors, National Association of Housing and Redevelopment Officials; minority and retirement groups; state and city housing officials; urban development officials and associations, such as National Multi-Family Housing Council, National Apartment Association

Deputy Assistant Secretaries for Multifamily Housing Since 1979*

Administration	Name and Years Served	Present Position
Reagan	R. Hunter Cushing 1986 - Present	Incumbent
Reagan	Silvio J. DeBartolomeis 1983 - 1986	Real Estate Consultant Winn Group Englewood, Colorado
Reagan	Maurice L. Barksdale 1983	Fort Worth, Texas
Reagan	Michael Karem 1981 - 1982	Not Available
Carter	Larry H. Dale 1979 - 1981	Senior Vice President, Multifamily Activities Fannie Mae Washington, DC
Carter	Marilyn Melkonian 1979 - 1980	President Telesis Corporation Washington, DC

* Position created through a departmental reorganization in 1979.

14

DEPARTMENT OF
THE INTERIOR

Because it has always managed a lot of federal land between the Mississippi and the Pacific coast--well over half the area of some states--this department from its birth in 1849 until 20 years ago historically looked west. That was the orientation of most of its staff, who knew the programs and problems of the big national parks, the millions of acres of federally-owned minerals, the waterways and dams, the wildlife refuges, and many of the Indian tribes.

Now there is an Interior presence in every state, and the department's outlook has been expanding accordingly. There are a number of reasons. The nation's recreation industry boomed, and not only in the west. With it came an enlargement of the parks system in the east, and department oversight of the recreation plans of each state. Regulation of surface coal mining broadened the department's eastern experience, as did an increasing emphasis on land and water conservation. Problems in the area of Indian affairs received national attention. Until the mid-1970s, federal off-shore oil and gas leasing on the outer continental shelf was limited to the Gulf of Mexico. Then came its extension to the Atlantic, the Pacific and Alaska.

These developments have given a national base not only to Interior's mission but, in a sense, to its problems. Off-shore leasing for oil and gas exploitation remains a confrontational issue, especially on the west coast, and is one of the department's principal future challenges. An informed Senate committee staff director thinks morale and professionalism in the Bureau of Land and Minerals Management and particularly in the Office of Surface Mining need rebuilding. Parks and fish and wildlife refuge programs, the object of conflicting recent policies, need to settle down.

Interior's fiscal 1988 budget was $5.4 billion, fourth smallest among cabinet departments. Its staff numbers 70,500.

The department's biggest overall assignment will be to strengthen its regulation of the competing interests of resource development and resource protection. Even in a country of continental dimensions, an expanding population and growing economy make that an ever tougher task.

DEPARTMENT OF THE INTERIOR

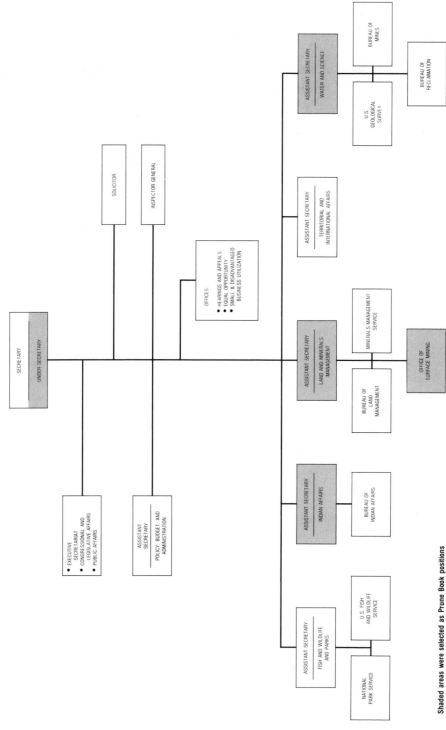

Shaded areas were were selected as Prune Book positions

UNDERSECRETARY

Level III - Presidential Appointment with Senate Confirmation

Major Responsibilities

o Support the secretary in developing policy and carrying out his responsibilities. Serve as acting secretary when required, with full secretarial authority.

o Function as chief manager of the department. Correlate the policy positions of component bureaus and offices. Represent department policy in senior interagency discussions and in Congressional contexts. Play a leading role in contact and exchanges with constituent groups, especially in the areas of Indian and territorial affairs.

o Oversee preparation and negotiation of the department budget and general administrative activities.

Necessary Background, Experience, Personal Skills

The occupant of this job needs a generalist's abilities, especially in management, negotiation, and public affairs. In filling this job, look also for some exposure to the land and resource management and conservation issues which are the department's central concern. Prior federal government service, familiarity with the legislative process, and effective communication and human relations skills are also important.

Insight

Versatility might be a key adjective describing what it takes to perform effectively in second-ranking federal department positions, of which this one is fairly typical. Another is the ability to grasp and keep perspective on the broad missions of the department, even while waging the day-to-day oversight and management battles that fill the day of a chief operating officer. Third, plainly, is the flexibility to mesh with the secretary's working style in a clear and effective division of labor at the top of the department, and to step smoothly into the acting secretary role.

Most descriptions of other deputy and undersecretary jobs in this book reflect those points to varying degrees, a result of the emphasis put on them by the people with whom we talked. Here are representative comments from James A. Joseph, Undersecretary of the Interior in 1977-81: "Any department is only as good as the relationship between the secretary and undersecretary....It all boils down to how the secretary uses the undersecretary's job." But, however that comes out, the undersecretary should secure a clear understanding at the outset of what the job's responsibilities are. In any sharing of assignments with the secretary, who does what must be equally evident. If that sharing is to be genuine, Joseph says, "there need to be areas in which the undersecretary has lead responsibilities and others where he has support responsibilities and these, too, should always be clear."

The undersecretary's job may also represent that level of the department where--in sum--policymaking and management meet on the most nearly equal footing. Joseph's feeling about the job seems to support this, as well as what D. Kent Frizzell, undersecretary in 1975-77, says about it. Asked how the position splits between policy decisions and execution, he says it was "taking decisions, acting on them, and making sure policy was implemented." At the White House for meetings of the Domestic Policy Council or with the Office of Management and Budget, he was in a policy mode; as an implementor, he talked regularly with department people in the field, took part in senior coordination sessions with other agencies, and testified on the Hill. In carrying special responsibility for Indian and U.S. territorial affairs, the occupant of this job is both policymaker and manager. And, when an open-minded undersecretary sits down with a constituent group in a dialogue about views and goals on both sides, a perceptive observer would see not only an aspect of implementation, but a bit of the raw material of policymaking as well.

The most vital challenge of this job is what Joseph calls "the conflict between resource development and environmental protection," or, to put it in slightly broader terms, "between competing users of natural resources." The Arctic National Wildlife Refuge project offers a good example of such a competition. As the referee of these conflicts the undersecretary performs what may be the most important service of the job, not merely for the department but for the nation. Interior offers a singular advantage in this highly impactive task because most, if not all, of the viewpoints on basic issues and specific projects are represented on the scene, in-house. The undersecretary thus can and should run what might be called an inclusive due process exercise which hears and considers every view.

Joseph and Frizzell see another key challenge in this position in the proper management and outcome of the sensitive federal responsibility in Indian affairs. Frizzell defines the problem in terms of balance in the trusteeship role--protecting Indian land, natural resources and civil rights and at the same time moving forward to Indian self-determination and self-government.

Key Relationships

Within the Department

Reports to: Secretary

Outside the Department

Counterparts in the departments of Energy, Commerce and Agriculture, and the Environmental Protection Agency

Special Assistant to the President, Domestic Policy Council

Associate Director, Natural Resources, Energy and Science, Office of Management and Budget

Outside the Federal Government

State government officials, users of federal lands resources, energy industry associations and individual firms, environmental groups, Indian tribal chiefs

Undersecretaries of the Interior Since 1969

Administration	Name and Years Served	Present Position
Reagan	Earl E. Gjelde 1987 - Present	Incumbent
Reagan	Anne Dore McLaughlin 1984 - 1986	Secretary Department of Labor

Reagan	Joseph J. Simmon III 1983 - 1984	Commissioner Interstate Commerce Commission
Reagan	Donald P. Hodel 1981 - 1982	Secretary Department of the Interior
Carter	James A. Joseph 1977 - 1981	President Council on Foundations Washington, DC
Ford	D. Kent Frizzell 1975 - 1977	Director, National Energy, Law and Policy Institute University of Tulsa College of Law Tulsa, Oklahoma
Nixon/Ford	John C. Whitaker 1973 - 1975	Vice President, Public Affairs Union Camp Corporation Washington, DC
Nixon	William T. Pecora 1971 - 1972	Not Available
Nixon	Fred J. Russell 1970 - 1971	Not Available
Nixon	Russell E. Train 1969 - 1970	Chairman World Wildlife Fund Washington, DC

ASSISTANT SECRETARY
INDIAN AFFAIRS

Level IV - Presidential Appointment with Senate Confirmation

Major Responsibilities

o   Develop and administer policies designed to strengthen Indian tribal capacity for self-determination and self-management. Provide resources and services consistent with statutes which support both that objective and Indian land, water, timber and civil rights.

o   Act as spokesman for Indian affairs within the executive branch and--to the Congress--for legislation in support of administration policy. Monitor Indian affairs, recommending necessary improvements to existing policy and law. Articulate and explain policy to the public.

o   Direct the Bureau of Indian Affairs (the largest employer in the department), setting budget goals, overseeing budget development, and supervising the operation and improvement of information management and accounting systems.

Necessary Background, Experience, Personal Skills

Most recent occupants of this job, including the incumbent, have been Native Americans with extensive experience in Indian affairs. This of course reflects a clear need for the thorough background, close and wide-ranging relationships and first-hand insights into the current state of Indian lives and aspirations that a tribal member, and preferably a tribal leader, can best provide. Two former assistant secretaries, and other observers, explicitly recommend the continuation of this practice. Given the amount of litigation currently involved in the Indian affairs area, some earlier tenants of the position also think that legal training helps.

Insight

The current assistant secretary in this job, Ross O. Swimmer,

states his view of its key goal succinctly: "Ultimate elimination
of the agency." This means removing the need for the Bureau of
Indian Affairs by achieving its purposes--by pursuing the intent of
federal law on Indian self-determination to its full, successful and
logical conclusion. Swimmer, who took over the position in 1986,
thinks his successors must concentrate on "moving the bureau away
from Indian country to empower tribes to develop their own initiatives, structure and philosophy." As things now stand, he says,
the government "is trying to do too many things to benefit too
many people." And he sees a paradox in the situation. The bureau,
he feels, should go on working to meet tough and urgent requirements like "credible systems of data collection" and "a better environment for Indian tribes to live in." But "it's hard, because
this agency should no longer exist. We should phase it out and at
the same time we're trying to improve it."

Meanwhile, the responsibilities of the job, some of them set
out in statutes like the Indian Self-Determination Act, translate
into three areas of activity. The first is to continue and broaden
the progressive turnover to the Indian tribes themselves of control
over their own destinies in developing and running many community
operations and programs, such as self-government and education.
Second, to support that goal and as general assistance, the bureau
provides resources and services to the tribes; further, it administers
federal trust obligations for Indian rights to land and natural resources, and works to advance Indian civil rights. Third, the assistant
secretary runs the bureau, sees legislation through all phases from
design and clearance to advocacy on the Hill, and oversees the
budget and personnel areas.

The job also puts its occupant into frequent contact with many
of the 310 tribes scattered through 25 states. This involves consultations, crisis management, speeches, and attendance at various forms
of ceremony and sport.

Operational problems vary. Former occupants of the job agree
on the need to establish and retain regular focus by the secretary
of the department on what the bureau is doing and trying to do.
That "requires a lot of personal contact and follow up on issues,"
one says. Still another mentions a "somewhat competitive" relationship with counterparts in other federal agencies about who has the
lead on a given issue. Another points to a lack of adequate information management in the bureau. Generally, former assistant secretaries cite an insufficient understanding of Indian issues in Washington and elsewhere. One of them says the bureau found more than
once, after the Congress designated new tribes, that "there were no
Native Americans" to represent them.

The sensitive nature of much of the bureau's work puts an unusual premium on genuine empathy for the people whose lives and problems it addresses. Morris Thompson, who headed the bureau in 1973-76, calls it a "human challenge" requiring a complete awareness of the "horrendous social and economic conditions" in which most Indians still live. He, too, stresses the importance of Indian self-sufficiency and lists some of the steps along the way: "Give tribes more autonomy. Generate economic development. Solve some of the social issues. Improve the quality of education and the educational attainment of Indian children."

Forrest J. Gerard, assistant secretary from 1977 to 1980, says "the bureau is a controversial agency. It operates under a complex budget system....Many of the Indian issues had an impact on broader constituencies, particularly in the West. I viewed my role as an advocate for Indian rights. You have to possess the ability to negotiate within the system on behalf of your constituents."

Key Relationships

Within the Department

Reports to: Secretary

Works closely with:

Undersecretary
Assistant Secretary for Land and Minerals Management
Assistant Secretary for Policy, Budget and Administration

Outside the Department

Director, Indian Education Programs, Department of Education
Director, Indian Health Service, Department of Health and Human Services
Assistant Secretary for Economic Development, Department of Commerce
Assistant Attorney General, Land and Natural Resources Division, Department of Justice

Outside the Federal Government

Indian tribal representatives and associations, such as American Indian Heritage Foundation, American Indian Higher Education Consortium, Americans for Indian Opportunity, Bureau of Catholic Indian Missions, National American Indian Council; economic development groups, such as National Rural Housing Coalition, Native American Rights Fund; foreign governments

Assistant Secretaries for Indian Affairs Since 1969

Administration	Name and Years Served	Present Position
Reagan	Ross O. Swimmer 1986 - Present	Incumbent
Reagan	John Fritz (Acting) 1985 - 1986	Not Available
Reagan	Kenneth L. Smith 1981 - 1984	President Ken Smith Associates Portland, Oregon
Carter	Forrest J. Gerard 1977 - 1980	Managing Director Tax Exempt Securities Division Morgan Stanley and Co. New York, New York
Nixon/Ford	Morris Thompson 1973 - 1976	President Doyon Ltd. Corporation Fairbanks, Alaska
Nixon	Louis R. Bruce 1970 - 1972	President Natmeamier Consultants Washington, DC

ASSISTANT SECRETARY
LAND AND MINERALS MANAGEMENT

Level IV - Presidential Appointment with Senate Confirmation

Major Responsibilities

o   Direct national programs for the management of public lands and the mineral resources they contain, for collection of royalties from federal mineral leases, and for enforcement of surface mining regulations and the reclamation of affected land areas.

o   Manage federal leasing of off-shore areas for mineral extraction and collect the revenues which result. Evaluate these areas as to mineral resource availability in the long term. Maintain effective collection and analysis of fossil fuel data.

o   Oversee the operations and administrative functions of the Bureau of Land Management, the Minerals Management Service and the Office of Surface Mining.

Necessary Background, Experience, Personal Skills

Veterans of the post to whom we talked agree that technical training and knowledge--in fields like geology, energy, and economics--is useful. Opinions vary, however, on whether it's essential. It seems clear in any case that this assistant secretary should have experience in resource management, and know how to marshal the individual staff skills and training which that specialty requires. Similarly, this individual must be able to listen to an unusually broad array of constituent organizations, and distill from their frequently opposing views the essential truths which help to produce correct decisions.

Insight

To a considerable extent, this assistant secretary is the resource manager for the federal government, presiding over about 700 million acres of public lands and 300 million acres of federally-owned minerals. Sixteen western states contain most of the public lands, which range from 47% of Wyoming to 87% of Nevada. All of it comes under the supervision of the Bureau of Land Management, one of three operations for which this job has responsibility. The Minerals Management Service handles federal off-shore oil and gas leasing on the outer continental shelf, and collects royalties on the extraction of federal minerals that total from four to ten billion dollars annually. The Office of Surface Mining (dealt with elsewhere in this chapter) controls the environmental impact of surface coal mining on both public and private land, enforcing prescribed operating and subsequent reclamation regulations. It collects taxes from coal operators to clean up abandoned mine sites.

Land management policy, says J. Steven Griles, assistant secretary since 1984, embraces the concept of "multiple use and sustained yield." That means putting the land into use on several simultaneous fronts as the number and level of its resources dictate, and doing it in a manner that permits the land to support such use "through history."

The assistant secretary sets policy in all three program areas, with authority to sign regulations covering them, and establishes day-to-day operational policy objectives and schedules. Discussing his work, Griles takes care to point out that "we are a resource and land manager; we are not in the development game." Thus, the Minerals Management Service (MMS) does not extract minerals itself. "It offers the private sector the opportunity to explore for and produce, if feasible, mineral resources of the federal Outer Continental Shelf, while protecting the marine environment and securing a fair market value for these resources for the American public. As part of this process, the public is provided the opportunity to review and comment on department programs and industry plans." The MMS enforces regulations protecting both the resource and the environment during extraction, and collects royalties on the products.

In some quarters one can hear the view that, in the last analysis, oil is what the Department of the Interior is all about, making this assistant secretary the focus of greatest attention and sensitivity on the part of the secretary. Wherever the truth may lie in this regard, it's clear that the off-shore drilling issue has been a prominently controversial one. It is also useful to note that the Minerals Management Service has attracted criticism for alleged slowness to collect royalties from on-shore coal, oil, and gas development and production on federal lands, and that royalties in the hundreds of millions of dollars remain, in fact, uncollected. In this situation, one such criticism charges, producers tend to structure operations to keep the royalties, with the result that the nation not only loses income, but that operators who do pay full royalties incur a competitive disadvantage.

Current MMS director William D. Bettenberg, whom we asked about this, cites two problems, one largely overcome, the other current. The first concerned inadequate data and information systems, which until about eight years ago were at the root of such severe inefficiency in royalty collection that they "almost bankrupted the operation." A comprehensive data base and auditing and accounting systems are now in place and in the final stages of completion, Bettenberg reports, adding that since the early 1980s, the MMS has collected $400 million in outstanding royalties and is litigating another $200 million. The second, tougher and more significant problem, he says, is that royalties collection laws, like those of income tax collection, are imprecise and nuanced, and thus vulnerable to interpretation by the companies in their own favor. This is a continuing problem that will face the next administration and the next assistant secretary.

"The public is very conscious of the environmental issues associated with these extractive industries," Griles says, but "I have a great deal of faith in the professionals in these three bureaus, that they understand what their job is and that they try to do it." How well they succeed can usually be measured, he thinks, in the regular contacts he tries to maintain with constituent groups around the country and in Washington, listening to and discussing their interests and concerns. Daniel N. Miller, Jr., one of Griles' predecessors, frames this dialogue in terms of the job's "responsibility to the public." It is important, he says, "to make sure these people are listened to and taken care of." Griles estimates he spends a third of his time out of the office--visiting these groups and the resources his office manages, and talking to his field bureaus. As for the Congress, he finds it more useful to invest less time in actual testimony than in informal talks with members and staff before and after hearings.

"The biggest thing we do in these positions generally is manage people," he says. "We're not technicians. I've got lawyers, economists, engineers, computer scientists working for me. What you need to be able to do is bring those people together in order to develop the information which will in fact result in a good decision."

Among the specific issues facing future assistant secretaries are the questions of what criteria will guide land management decisions in such matters as wilderness areas, and how the next administration will deal with the great amounts of continuing litigation related to control of surface mining and the effect of that litigation on federal-state relations in this area. There is also the question of whether to answer the depletion of domestic oil and gas reserves and rising U.S. dependence on foreign supplies with a decision to explore public lands.

Key Relationships

Within the Department

Reports to: Secretary

Works closely with:

Undersecretary
Assistant secretaries

Outside the Department

Assistant secretaries for Fossil Energy and for Environment, Safety and Health, Department of Energy
Assistant administrators for Air and Radiation, for Water, for Solid Waste and Emergency Response, and for External Affairs, Environmental Protection Agency
Commissioners, Federal Energy Regulatory Commission
Deputy Assistant Secretary, Installations, Department of the Air Force
Legal Adviser, Department of State
Commanding General, U.S. Army Corps of Engineers

Outside the Federal Government

State governors and officials responsible for land and mineral resources management and their associations, such as American Forestry Association, Western Governor's Association; cattlemen and wool growers associations, such as National Cattlemen's Association; oil, gas, coal, timber and electric power industries, such as American Gas Association, Western Fuels Association; environmental groups, such as National Parks and Conservation Association, National Wildlife Federation, Sierra Club; fishing, hunting, hiking and camping associations

Assistant Secretaries for Land and Minerals Management Since 1969

Administration	Name and Years Served	Present Position
Reagan	J. Steven Griles 1984 - Present	Incumbent
Reagan	Garrey E. Carruthers* 1981 - 1984	Governor State of New Mexico Santa Fe, New Mexico
Carter	Guy R. Martin* 1977 - 1981	Partner Perkins, Coie, Stone & Williams Washington, DC
Nixon/Ford	Jack O. Horton* 1973 - 1976	Not Available
Nixon	Harrison Locsch* 1969 - 1972	Not Available

* Held position as Assistant Secretary for Land and Water. In 1984, the functions of the Assistant Secretary for Land and Water and Assistant Secretary for Energy and Minerals were separated and recombined into the positions of Assistant Secretary for Land and Minerals and Assistant Secretary for Water and Science.

ASSISTANT SECRETARY
WATER AND SCIENCE

Level IV - Presidential Appointment with Senate Confirmation

Major Responsibilities

o   Develop and carry out economic and environmental policies, under the secretary's statutory mandate, to maintain and expand national water supplies and mineral resources and encourage their proper use. Direct the work of the U.S. Geological Survey, the Bureau of Mines and the Bureau of Reclamation in support of these goals.

o   Integrate the work of these bureaus with related responsibilities and efforts elsewhere in the government. Advise the secretary on scientific matters, and coordinate the department's scientific activities. Represent the department in working groups and interagency consultations and on official boards and committees which address water and mineral resource issues.

o   Administratively supervise the bureaus and oversee budget preparation and negotiation. Speak for administration national water and mineral policy. Maintain liaison with constituent groups.

Necessary Background, Experience, Personal Skills

Candidates for this position should know the resource issues whose effective management is this job's chief concern. An experienced source says the job needs a thorough legal and historical background of "water law practice" in the United States, and "some appreciation for science and land." The post also entails frequent exposure to the Congress in formal and informal settings.

Insight

Reflecting on his net impression of this job, James W. Ziglar, who has held it since 1987, expresses some uncertainty whether he is "sorely disappointed or pleasantly surprised." But one thing appears certain. "What I noted the most," he says, "is you're either willing to take on difficult issues or you're left hanging there without getting anything done." His perception of the goals involved, and the way he organized the 20,000 employees of the three bureaus under his management, "is to make sure that those bureaus are managed in a rational style." Specifically, Ziglar thinks the Bureau of Mines needs to continue to "re-orient and re-focus" its goals and that its research and development programs "need to be geared to take advantage of the explosive growth in high technology." It and the Bureau of Reclamation, he thinks, need to devote more resources to monitoring the environmental implications of their missions. All three bureaus are over-managed and suffer from inadequate funding--"we could use a lot more money for such things as research on better mining technology and research on contaminates in ground water." Other goals, as he sees them, are to energize the career staff and develop higher morale and a sense of direction. While "crisis resolution and conflict resolution are the things I deal with the most," he says, "I want to leave an organization that is well-tuned, focused and well-managed."

For western states, and especially those in and near the desert southwest, water supplies are the lens through which perceptions of this job are formed. Government officials with water and water-related responsibilities in these areas think the Bureau of Reclamation turned a significant corner in 1988 with the decision to turn away from new dam and irrigation construction and, instead, to emphasize greater efficiency in managing existing water systems. That means, an informed and experienced department official told us, a focus on better transfer of water from source to need, and improving power generation and water allocation. The Bureau took this step after assessing its current water management policy. It will not support proposals for funding any new starts.

From a managerial viewpoint, this policy change has several implications for the assistant secretary, who will have to oversee the Bureau's transition from a construction-oriented operation to one of environmental management. Personnel assignments will change, as will the general organizational structure. Current water laws and policy will have to be re-examined. Figuring importantly in the change-over will be the creation of new, non-federal institutional relationships in which municipal water districts will assume greater responsibility in managing and operating water systems.

Beyond the usual regular and numerous meetings at various department levels on policy, management or crisis matters, the occupant of this job works constantly with fellow assistant secretaries to resolve conflicts and overlaps and to provide mutual support. He represents the secretary or the department on the National

Critical Materials Council, the Trade Policy Review Group, the Emergency Preparedness Mobilization Board, and other interagency groups on Antarctic policy and acid rain. Appearances on the Hill, whether to testify or consult, come often. Speeches average four or five a month. Robert N. Broadbent, who served in the position in the mid-1980s, filled in for the secretary on a number of such occasions, and recalls Congressional meetings every week.

Ziglar says his deputy does most of the administrative and supervisory tasks and "the critical issues I deal with directly. I want to focus my energy on larger policy and management issues. The overall challenge lies in "moving an organization that is accustomed to doing things one way into a completely different way of doing things and looking at problems. This can be a very controversial job. You never will make everyone happy."

Key Relationships

Within the Department

Reports to: Secretary

Works closely with:

Deputy Secretary
Assistant Secretary, Land and Minerals Management
Assistant Secretary, Fish and Wildlife and Parks
Assistant Secretary, Territorial and International
    Affairs

Outside the Department

Assistant administrators for Water, for Pesticides and Toxic Substances, and for Air and Radiation, Environmental Protection Agency
Associate Administrator, Natural Resources Energy
    and Science, Office of Management and Budget

Outside the Federal Government

Water Resources Congress, National Water Resources Association, National Water Alliance; state and local water and sanitation officials, such as Association of Metropolitan Water Agencies, Association of State and Interstate Water Pollution Control Administrators; irrigation and hydropower groups, such as National Association of Water Companies, Irrigation Association, National Hydropower Association; consumer associations, mining and minerals firms and industry associations, such as American Mining Congress

Assistant Secretaries for Water and Science Since 1969

Administration	Name and Years Served	Present Position
Reagan	James W. Ziglar 1987 - Present	Incumbent
Reagan	Wayne N. Marchant 1986 - 1987 (Acting)	Principal Deputy Assistant Secretary for Water and Science Department of the Interior
Reagan	Robert N. Broadbent 1984 - 1986	Director of Aviation Clark County Department of Aviation Las Vegas, Nevada
Reagan	Daniel N. Miller, Jr.* 1981 - 1983	President I. W. O. Exploration Boise, Idaho
Carter	Joan M. Davenport* 1977 - 1981	Congressional Research Service Specialist Library of Congress Washington, DC
Ford	William L. Fisher* 1976	Director and State Geologist Bureau of Geology Austin, Texas
Ford	Jack W. Carlson* 1975	Not Available
Nixon/Ford	Stephen A. Wakefield* 1973 - 1974	Not Available

Nixon   Hollis M. Dole*   Deceased
                     1969 - 1972

*   Held position as Assistant Secretary for Energy and Minerals.
    In 1984, the functions of the Assistant Secretary for Land and
    Water and Assistant Secretary for Energy and Minerals were
    separated and recombined into the positions of Assistant Secre-
    tary for Land and Minerals and Assistant Secretary for Water
    and Science.

DIRECTOR
OFFICE OF SURFACE MINING

Level V - Presidential Appointment with Senate Confirmation

Major Responsibilities

o Set administration policy for national surface coal mining and reclamation programs in accordance with law.

o Act as chief representative of Office of Surface Mining(OSM) policy and actions to the Congress, as liaison with constituent groups, and as spokesman to the public.

o Provide substantive and administrative management of the activities of the OSM, which assists and monitors state execution of these programs. Review proposed changes to existing programs.

Necessary Background, Experience, Personal Skills

There is some difference of views about the background and training necessary to this position. One previous director was a lawyer with a mining engineering degree, another was an engineer, and a third had worked in public administration and management. A broad knowledge of the coal mining industry is very clearly indicated, however, and it helps if this extends to coal mining technology. Congressional exposure and past government service and political experience are, as always, important assets.

Insight

Congress established the Office of Surface Mining in 1977 with two primary environmental objectives. The office was to set up and run a national program to counter the harmful social and environmental impact of surface mining. Second, through reclamation, it was to assure the continuation of surface coal mining without permanent damage to land and water assets. In the ensuing period, many states have taken over primary responsibility for working toward those goals, in programs approved by the OSM and with the enforcement authority of OSM field offices. The director's chief current task is to make sure the states do it according to law and policy and to provide help when necessary. Where states don't fill the main role, the OSM handles it. Either way, the basic nature of the job is regulatory--and the basic responsibility for proper performance by the states is the director's.

When James R. Harris, OSM director in 1981-83, took over the job, many of the existing OSM regulations "had been based on design criteria, which often didn't work. So we changed from design criteria to performance standards." For example, the water coming off a mine property is put through a sediment basin and "the Environmental Protection Agency tells you what the water standards must be coming out the other side when it leaves the mine. If you tell [the engineers] how to design the [basin] and it doesn't do the job, they cannot meet EPA standards. We left it to the engineers and operators to determine how to build the thing and just told them what water standards to meet when the water left the property."

This is only one of the ways in which the position today differs from what it was when Walter N. Heine ran it in 1977-81 as the first OSM director. Then, his task was to build a new organization. "It's now ten years later and the bureaucracy is in place," he says. But other aspects of the work, like some of its Congressional dimensions, haven't changed. Heine recalls that "more than two-thirds of the Congress" supported creation of the office and the program, but that "many of them were very critical of the manner in which it was run." And one of his successors some years later complains that "some attacks on you personally, particularly by Congressmen, are simply for political purposes."

In surface mining, three types of situations exist. These are steep-slope mining in Appalachia, area mining in the Middle West, and mining in arid western states in which water supplies need careful protection. Each situation, says Harris, requires a different solution to the reclamation problem, and each state presents a different problem in terms of its economy or its administration. "This is the second-highest-profile environmental job in the federal government, next to the (administrator of the) Environmental Protection Agency," he says, and "a difficult management job." The OSM is represented by 22 field offices, and by two technical centers, and "you're working with so many different entities to get the program to work--Congress, OMB, mine operators and environmentalists and their associations, and the states."

Taking a different view of this job's visibility, an observer on the environmental side of mining issues thinks it lacks a high profile in "a very specialized field" and needs "revitalization" and "credibi-lity" and asserts that the reclamation and regulatory aspects of the OSM "have been watered way down." On the industry side, the government affairs director of a multinational company believes the job needs "someone who doesn't automatically exclude people," meaning all of the sometimes conflicting interests involved in surface mining. "In any natural resource program, you've got to come in wanting to deal in all instances with all sectors." On this score, administrations of both parties have been at fault, in the percep-tion of this commentator.

Harris says he took the job at a time when less than one percent of the nation's surface-mined coal was being produced in a state with an approved regulatory program. When he left, the figure was 99 percent. The oversight job remains a sizeable one for the director, he says, and "you have to have a good liaison situation and a good level of cooperation with the states. You probably spend at least a third of your time with the field offices and states, and two-thirds in Washington."

When Jed D. Christensen took over the position in 1986 (he held it until late 1987), he hoped "to turn the place around in a short amount of time." That was "a naive expectation," he remembers now. "It can take months, years, to find out what's already in place." He predicts the same for future directors, but describes a couple of operating methods that seemed to help meanwhile in getting the job done. First, by visiting state regulatory officials and meeting with various groups and associations in the industry, he received "a lot of feedback" about OSM positions and decisions. Secondly, he visited his own people in the OSM's dozen field and eight area offices. "You don't find a lot of initiative from the bureaucracy," he says. "I had to drive many activities or else they didn't get done. In the field, there needs to be a way to communicate ideas up and down the organization, so people know what's going on and what to do."

"It's terribly important that anyone going (into the job today) carefully choose the associate solicitor for surface mining," advises a former director. That position "primarily provides legal advice to the federal office," he explains, and "greatly influences what the OSM does." He also attaches special importance to selections for the office's Congressional liaison and public affairs jobs, areas in which the director himself invests considerable effort.

Key Relationships

Within the Department

Reports to:

Assistant Secretary for Land and Minerals
Management

Works closely with:

Director, Bureau of Mines
Director, U.S. Geological Survey
Director, National Park Service

Outside the Department

Solicitor, Mine Safety and Health Association, Department of Labor
Assistant Attorney General, Land and Natural Resources
Associate Director, Natural Resources, Energy and Science, Office of Management and Budget

Outside the Federal Government

Mining industry and individual mining firms, such as American Mining Congress, United Mine Workers; environmental organizations, such as American Council of the Environment, World Resources Institute; state legislators; Indian affairs groups, such as National American Indian Council, Native American Rights Fund

Directors of the Office of Surface Mining Since 1977*

Administration	Name and Years Served	Present Position
Reagan	Robert H. Gentile 1988 - Present (Acting)	Incumbent

Reagan	Jed D. Christensen 1986 - 1987	Assistant Executive Officer Fresno County Fresno, California
Reagan	John D. Work 1984 - 1985	Not Available
Reagan	James R. Harris 1981 - 1983	Consultant Dick Harris and Associates Evansville, Indiana
Carter	Walter N. Heine 1977 - 1981	President Walter N. Heine Associates Boiling Springs, Pennsylvania

*   This office was created by the Surface Mining Control and Reclamation Act of 1977.

15

DEPARTMENT OF JUSTICE

With the change of leadership in the summer of 1988, the department is likely, by early 1989, to have recovered to some degree from the severe morale and image problems that plagued it in recent years. That process will have to continue if Justice is to attract the talent that every department needs on a recurrent basis in both its career and appointed ranks. This particular department badly needs a refurbished reputation at the top; it hardly needs emphasizing that, more than ever, demonstrated integrity should be a prime credential in restoring confidence.

As the country comes slowly to grips with a drug problem whose full complexity and dimensions have only recently begun to emerge, the Justice department's heavy involvement will clearly increase. One view of this role, typified by the comments of a senior Congressional committee staff member, is that the responsible programs at Justice should be broadened beyond "straight law enforcement" to address--with other agencies--the economic and social bases of the problem.

Other immediate tasks for the incoming leadership of the department will come from the areas of immigration and of judicial appointments which may include the Supreme Court.

The ambiguity of responsibilities over the last decade between the deputy attorney general and the associate attorney general positions has left a few observers with the feeling that things ought to go back to the pre-1977 structure. They point out that the associate AG was established in that year to fill a particular and temporary need which no longer exists. To them, while the position currently carries oversight responsibility for the law enforcement and criminal sides of the department, it represents unnecessary layering.

It has always been important for the individuals in all of Justice's senior jobs to understand the policy issues the department handles, not just as academic questions but in the political and public frameworks in which the Congress, the White House and the press deal with them. It is equally important to act on that understanding in terms of the relationships established among these various positions and those other government and public institutions.

Justice comes near the end of the cabinet department list in terms of budget size--$5.4 billion in fiscal 1988--but has 72,500 employees.

DEPARTMENT OF JUSTICE

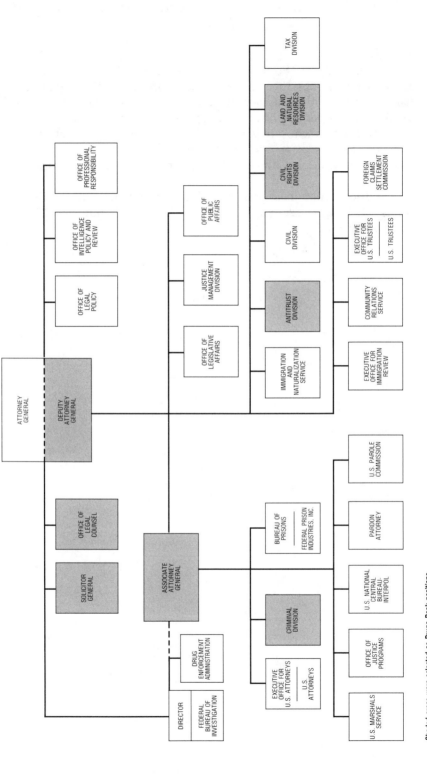

Shaded areas were selected as Prune Book positions

DEPUTY ATTORNEY GENERAL

Level II - Presidential Appointment with Senate Confirmation

Major Responsibilities

o   Assist the attorney general in overall policy formulation. Function as chief operating executive of the department. Direct all department programs and activities concerned with civil legal matters.

o   In the absence of the attorney general, act in that capacity with the same authority except where legally prohibited or delegated elsewhere. Oversee the nomination of federal judges.

o   Mediate internal differences on policy issues and operational jurisdiction. Manage preparation of the budget within the department and with the Office of Management and Budget, the support of budget-related legislation before the Congress, and the department's general legislative program.

Necessary Background, Experience, Personal Skills

Like the top job at Justice, the deputy position and most of the others in the building require practiced lawyers of varied training and experience. But, says former deputy attorney general Laurence H. Silberman (1974-75), many individuals in the number two slot "are chosen only because they are good lawyers, which is a mistake because they often are not good managers." This job clearly requires both, with previous service in the federal government a valuable additional asset. One former deputy suggests the increasing usefulness of foreign language ability, particularly Spanish, because of increasing contact with Latin American officials involved in the struggle against international narcotics traffic.

Insight

The Deputy Attorney General has always filled the day-to-day operating role that characterizes the second-ranking job in most departments. In 1977, with creation of the Associate Attorney

General position, oversight of the criminal and civil sides of the department was split between the two jobs, with the deputy AG taking specific supervision of criminal law enforcement. In 1981, emphasis was restored to the deputy AG's role as chief operating officer with department-wide responsibilities. The deputy has additional direct oversight of the civil side--anti-trust, civil, land and natural resources, civil rights, and tax divisons--and the Immigration and Naturalization Service. Criminal law activities have been the province of the associate AG, who reports to the deputy. With ultimate responsibility for both civil and criminal matters thus resting with the deputy AG, the associate AG position now really represents, not a split in duties, but an extra layer of management.

Edward C. Schmults, deputy AG in 1981-84, agrees with Silberman on the central importance of management ability in this job. While a legal background clearly helps--for general knowledge as well as credibility--he says "you could do the deputy job without being a lawyer if you were a good manager." As he points out, the department has not only hundreds of lawyers but thousands of non-lawyers, spread around the country. It requires a good deal of skill to run it coherently, develop sensible policies, get the divisions to work together, and "manage the white spaces--where people come into conflict."

The development of recommendations for appointment to the federal bench is an important duty for the deputy AG. "In one sense, there are not many things more important to spend your time on," Schmults says. Some of the processing work on this can be delegated. But final decisionmaking requires careful consultation with senior department colleagues and with the general counsel at the White House. It's a procedure in which controversial prospective nominees inevitably cause ripples, or real surf. "Whenever Senators got agitated it came up to me or higher, and the problem had to be sorted out," Schmults recalls. "And you may get people pushed on you who do not meet the requirements. You've got to try to resist that and negotiate other names. It's a wondrous process that is intensely political. If you want to do it right, you have to spend time on it." Harold R. Tyler, Jr., who had the job in 1975-77, mentions the recurrent burden of "being solicited by office seekers for appointments to the bench" and says "we developed eight different form letters to answer them." An attorney representing a public-interest legal group thinks the deputy AG, in selecting candidates for federal bench appointments, must have a broad acquaintance in the legal community and the ability to analyze legal background and experience. "They will need to know Senators, or get to know them quickly, and have the personality and interpersonal skills that will allow them to work effectively with individual Senators" and with the various organizations which affect the selection and confirmation of federal judges.

The department's principal line of daily contact with the White House--usually with the counsel to the President--runs through the the deputy's office. And, while political or previous government experience is not essential for this slot, it would be hard to overestimate its value. "It is an extremely sensitive job with intense public scrutiny," says one veteran of it. Knowing how Washington works, and "what you can and can't do" is a must, especially if the person in the top job doesn't have that kind of experience. "It would be a big mistake for both the attorney general and the deputy to be green in the Washington sense."

Former deputy AG Silberman thinks deputy jobs in departments and agencies are the most difficult in government. "You have as much responsibility as the chief but you don't have the full authority. You only gain the authority by having a close relationship with him and the respect of the President. You have to be able to walk the fine line between loyalty to one and loyalty to the other." Schmults thinks that there is nothing more important than that the attorney general and deputy be able to work closely together and trust each other.

As in every politically appointed job, gaining the confidence of the career staff and reciprocating it bears directly on effective performance. But that equation takes on added weight when one is managing an agency. "If it ever turns into a we-versus-they mentality," warns a previous deputy AG, "you can forget about it and go home. The deputy has a very big part in building confidence, because he or she has more contact with the career people than the attorney general ever has." It's a view that finds agreement in the comments of Benjamin R. Civiletti, deputy AG in 1977-79. Civiletti (who moved up to attorney general in 1980-81) thinks "it's foolish for a political appointee to believe that a few good men at the top...can galvanize an agency into a higher level of effectiveness simply by their presence. They must provide effective leadership so that career people below want to effect change. They must inspire so strength builds from the foundation up."

Key Relationships

Within the Department

Reports to: Attorney General

Works closely with:

> Associate Attorney General
> Solicitor General
> Assistant Attorney General, Office of the Legal Counsel
> Assistant Attorney General for Legal Policy

Outside the Department

> Deputies in other departments, and certain agencies such as the Environmental Protection Agency
> Associate Director, Economics and Government, Office of Management and Budget
> Equivalents in the White House domestic policy and political and intergovernmental affairs offices

Outside the Federal Government

> Minorities, especially Hispanics, blacks, Indians; minority groups, such as Congressional Black Caucus Foundation, NAACP Legal Defense and Educational Fund, Inc., Native American Rights Fund, Mexican-American Legal Defense and Educational Fund; American Bar Association; feminist organizations, such as Women's Legal Defense Fund, Women's Equity Action League; National Association of Attorneys General

Deputy Attorneys General of Justice Since 1969

Administration	Name and Years Served	Present Position
Reagan	Harold G. Christensen 1988 - Present	Nominated
Reagan	Arnold I. Burns 1986 - 1988	Partner Proskaner, Rose, Goetz & Mendelsohn New York, New York
Reagan	D. Lowell Jensen 1985 - 1986	U.S. Judge for Northern District of California San Francisco, California

Reagan	Carol E. Dinkins 1984 - 1985	Partner Vinson and Elkins Houston, Texas
Reagan	Edward C. Schmults 1981 - 1984	Senior Vice President, External Affairs GTE Corporation Stamford, Connecticut
Carter	Charles B. Renfrew 1980 - 1981	Director & Vice President of Legal Chevron Corporation San Francisco, California
Carter	Benjamin R. Civiletti 1977 - 1979	Partner Venable, Baetjer, Howard and Civiletti Washington, DC
Carter	Peter F. Flaherty 1977	Commissioner Allegheny County Pittsburgh, Pennsylvania
Ford	Harold R. Tyler, Jr. 1975 - 1977	Partner Patterson, Belknap, Webb and Tyler New York, New York
Nixon/Ford	Laurence H. Silberman 1974 - 1975	U. S. Circuit Court Judge U.S. Court of Appeals, DC Circuit Washington, DC
Nixon	William D. Ruckelshaus 1973	Senior Partner Perkins, Coie, Stone & Williams Seattle, Washington
Nixon	Joseph T. Sneed 1973	U.S. Circuit Court Judge U.S. Court of Appeals, Ninth Circuit Boise, Idaho

| Nixon | Ralph E. Erickson
1972 - 1973 | Los Angeles, California |
| Nixon | Richard G. Kleindienst
1969 - 1972 | Of Counsel
Lesher and Borodkin
Tucson, Arizona |

ASSOCIATE ATTORNEY GENERAL

Level III - Presidential Appointment with Senate Confirmation

Major Responsibilities

o   Assist the attorney general in setting federal criminal law enforcement policy. Oversee or directly supervise the work of component offices of the department with mandates in this area.

o   Integrate the department's efforts with those of other law enforcement agencies or programs within the federal government and internationally. Direct the work of the National Drug Enforcement Policy Board Coordinating Group.

Necessary Background, Experience, Personal Skills

Prior government service--preferably federal--at a senior level of law enforcement is imperative. Former associate AGs also list a thorough knowledge of law enforcement technology, trial practice or judicial experience, training in comparative evaluation or analysis, and budget and administrative background.

Insight

From its establishment in 1977, until 1981, this third-ranking position at the department had oversight of policies and programs concerned with civil justice matters. Supervision of the criminal side was handled by the deputy attorney general as part of the overall responsibilities of that position. Since 1981, however, the associate AG has had specific oversight responsibilities for all criminal law enforcement activities--investigative and prosecutorial-- for the federal government. The position reports to the attorney general through the deputy AG, who continues to have operational oversight of the entire department, including its criminal side.

For the associate AG, this means general supervision of all U.S. attorneys in criminal matters, and of the department's Criminal Division, the Bureau of Prisons, and the U.S. Marshals Service. Further, the associate AG supervises the work of the Drug Enforcement Administration and directs interagency coordination of federal drug law enforcement. The Office of Justice Programs and the Pardon Attorney's office also belong to this domain, and the associate AG is chief U.S. representative to INTERPOL.

Coordinating criminal law enforcement throughout the federal government, and with other governments, is the toughest part of this job. Much, if not most, of the serious crime in question requires--in an ideal world--carefully integrated counter measures at home and abroad. As an obvious but vivid example, take the dramatically increased burdens of drug law enforcement--now the top priority. The associate AG has to bring together, and keep together, elements of the Departments of Justice, Treasury and State, among others, in a sustained attack on drug trafficking problems which long ago took on global proportions. "There are a lot of different players and each has a slightly different agenda and perspective," says a former tenant of the job. "They are also protecting their own turf, which is a Washington problem that has always been here and always will be. So you somehow have to get them to become part of the solution instead of part of the problem."

A similar challenge, but at a different level of complexity, is found overseas--in drugs, organized crime, terrorism, gun-running, money-laundering, child pornography, tax evasion, and more. The looming menace of the narcotics trade has resulted in establishment of about 65 Drug Enforcement Agency offices in 40-odd countries. Anti-crime working-group arrangements exist with several countries whose cooperation is key. The United States is an active member of INTERPOL. This international aspect of the work "is fascinating, the most interesting part of the job," says one who has held it. "It's also one of the newest. The economy is global. If you think you can stay at home and fight crime, you're wrong."

Of the job in general, Stephen S. Trott, associate AG in 1986-88, says "first, you have to get your act together. Then that act has to survive on three levels--in the courts, on the Hill and in the press. You had better be technically competent and know what you're talking about across the board--investigating and trying cases, writing and serving search warrants, collecting evidence, and working with police and victims." He suggests a familiar rule of thumb to help shape proposed actions. "Ask yourself what it is going to look like on the front page. Because perception is part of the reality here. If you can stand that, and think it is otherwise a good idea, then go ahead....Don't let the media--who tend to pronounce everything dead on arrival--throw you." In his time in the job, he valued the power of persuasion when dealing with other agencies over which he lacked direct authority. "It should be everybody's product when you sign off. You have to be willing to be part of the solution, not the guy out in front in the headlines. The more you're in the headlines, the more people are waiting to push you off of whatever it is you're sitting on."

Trott therefore advises newcomers to the job to take time to think about it, figure out the staffing required and find competent self-starters. "The career people are exceptional," he says, "but they can either support or sink you. If they see you playing political games, they'll go after you. But if they view you as doing a good, straightforward law enforcement job, they'll be with you through whatever fires come along....Law enforcement and politics don't mix."

Key Relationships

Within the Department

Reports to: Attorney General

Works closely with:

> Deputy Attorney General
> Solicitor General
> Counselor to the Attorney General
> Director, Federal Bureau of Investigation
> Director, Bureau of Prisons
> Administrator, Drug Enforcement Administration
> Commissioner, Immigration and Naturalization
>   Service
> Director, United States Marshals Service
> Chief, INTERPOL-U.S. National Central Bureau
> U.S. Attorneys

Outside the Department

> Deputy Secretary, Assistant Secretary, International Narcotics Matters, and Legal Adviser, Department of State
> Assistant Secretary for Enforcement; Director, Bureau of Alcohol, Tobacco and Firearms; Director, U.S. Secret Service; Commissioner of Internal Revenue; and Commissioner, U.S. Customs Service, Department of the Treasury
> Commandant, U.S. Coast Guard
> Director, Central Intelligence Agency

Outside the Federal Government

Bar associations; national and international law enforcement organizations: civic groups; prison and other reform organizations, such as American Correctional Association and National Organization for Victim Assistance; state government officials; associations of state attorneys general and district attorneys, such as Federal Criminal Investigators Association, National Criminal Justice Association, National District Attorneys Association

Associate Attorneys General of Justice Since 1977*

Administration	Name and Years Served	Present Position
Reagan	Francis J. Keating 1988	Nominated
Reagan	Stephen S. Trott 1986 - 1988	U.S. Circuit Court Judge U.S. Court of Appeals Ninth Circuit Boise, Idaho
Reagan	Arnold I. Burns 1985 - 1986	Partner Proskaner, Rose, Goetz & Mendelsohn New York, New York
Reagan	D. Lowell Jensen 1983 - 1985	U.S. Judge for Northern District of California San Francisco, California
Reagan	Rudolph W. Giuliani 1981 - 1983	U.S. Attorney for Southern District of New York New York, New York
Carter	John H. Shenefield 1980 - 1981	Partner Morgan, Lewis and Bockius Washington, DC

Carter	Michael J. Egan	Partner
	1977 - 1979	Sutherland, Asbill and Brennan
		Atlanta, Georgia

* Position created by Public Law 95-139 in 1977.

SOLICITOR GENERAL

Level III - Presidential Appointment with Senate Confirmation

Major Responsibilities

o   Represent the executive branch of Government before the Supreme Court.

o   Select the cases which the government will ask the Court to review, and develop the government's positions. Oversee preparation of the government's briefs and supervise and take a leading role in oral arguments.

o   Approve all decisions to appeal to the Supreme Court cases the United States loses in lower courts.

Necessary Background, Experience, Personal Skills

A former Solicitor General, Erwin N. Griswold (1967-73), notes that in establishing this position more than a century ago, the Congress specified that its occupant must be "learned in the law." The history and present circumstances of the job make their own powerful arguments on this score. The Solicitor General should be an accomplished lawyer of integrity, balance, fairness and reputation, whose record includes substantial argument before the Supreme Court or at a minimum the appellate courts, preferably with distinction.

Insight

About 5,200 lawyers work for the Department of Justice. Only 23 of them work for the Solicitor General. It's a misleading ratio, in no way conveying the significance of the SG's mission or its impact on all three branches of the federal government. The SG is a quasi-judicial figure who operates, in effect, at the highest level of government, and whose decisions largely determine what business the executive branch brings before the Supreme Court. More than that, the experience, skill, judgment and vision of the SG--in selecting the cases for which he will ask review, and in how he exercises the singular privileges allowed him by the Court --can set priorities, create frameworks or point directions for the Justices as they address many of the cases before them.

But the Court expects more from the SG than superior substantive and technical performance by an experienced lawyer. It looks to the occupant of this position to go beyond the administration's immediate objectives or interests in given cases; to consider where the Court should and should not be heading on issues likely to come before it; and to reflect carefully on what the effect or implications of the Court's decisions will be, not only for the Constitutional principles by which cases are judged but for the enacted statutes from which they arise.

Some facts derived from statistics add meaning to these observations. The Justices, of course, grant only a small fraction of the several thousand review petitions flowing into the Court each year. But in *The New Yorker* issue of August 10, 1987, Lincoln Caplan points out that petitions brought by the Solicitor General usually rack up an acceptance rate vastly higher than petitions originating elsewhere. Moreover, he demonstrates, of the cases the Court considers on their merits each term, those in which the government participates usually constitute a majority. And the SG's winning record in the Court has almost invariably been better than those of private lawyers.

Compared with senior colleagues at Justice, the SG spends little working time outside the department and the Court. Rex E. Lee, who held the position in 1981-85, says that, "in the company of the Attorney General, there might have been about eight times during my tenure where the AG felt it better that the White House hear about a problem directly from me." Generally, he says, the Solicitor General has no problems of access to the Attorney General because of "the importance of the job to the department." The occupant has budget responsibility for his small office, but an executive assistant handles day-to-day administrative duties. Besides the SG's office at main Justice, Caplan writes, there are chambers at the Court which, among other conveniences, make it possible for the SG to don the morning coat still customary for appearances before the Court.

Through the years some debate, mostly internal, has focused on the degree of independence with which the Solicitor General should approach his responsibilities, and there have been some formal attempts to define the job's proper posture in this respect. With political reality in mind, it is clear that an SG who regularly departs from an administration's general view or interpretation of the law will probably not stay long. In a fundamental sense, as one who has held the job points out, the executive branch is the SG's client. At the same time, the central importance of that client in the life of the nation and its citizens imposes an equal-- and special--obligation which the SG must serve, as free as possible from the constraints of political pressure and the temptations of compromise. This principle seems reasonably well established by past practice in the SG post. Its essence is that an SG in basic agreement with a political philosophy must still be able to reach objective judgments and decisions about the law that may run counter to that philosophy.

But it is often not easy. As former Solicitor General Lee puts it, a chronic difficulty "was striking the right balance between my clients on the one hand and maintaining my status as an officer of the court." Griswold, looking at the job today, thinks one of its key problems is "pressure on the office from the administration."

Key Relationships

Within the Department

Reports to: Attorney General

Works closely with:

Deputy Attorney General
Assistant attorneys general

Outside the Federal Government

Most interest groups who make filings in U.S. Supreme Court cases also attempt to influence the SG. They cover an exceptionally broad section of U.S. society.

Solicitors General of Justice Since 1969

Administration	Name and Years Served	Present Position
Reagan	Charles Fried 1985 - Present	Incumbent

Reagan	Rex E. Lee 1981 - 1985	Professor Brigham Young University Provo, Utah
Carter	Wade H. McCree, Jr. 1977 - 1981	Deceased
Nixon/Ford	Robert H. Bork 1973 - 1977	Washington, DC
Johnson/Nixon	Erwin N. Griswold 1967 - 1973	Partner Jones, Day, Reavis and Pogue Washington, DC

ASSISTANT ATTORNEY GENERAL
ANTI-TRUST DIVISION

Level IV - Presidential Appointment with Senate Confirmation

Major Responsibilities

o   Encourage and maintain competitive markets through enforcement of federal civil and criminal anti-trust laws, principally the Sherman and Clayton anti-trust acts. Counsel other agencies with respect to revising anti-trust law and regulations to promote competition and take advantage of market forces.

o   Represent the department in interagency deliberations on such issues as trade policy, micro-economic concerns, corporate takeovers and industrial organization.

o   Conduct close working relationships with other governments with whom the United States shares mutual interests in anti-trust activities and laws. Represent the United States in the anti-trust concerns of international organizations.

o   Manage the Anti-trust Division--about 280 lawyers, 40 economists and 240 support staff in seven field offices dedicated to criminal enforcement, and five litigating groups in Washington.

Necessary Background, Experience, Personal Skills

Only an experienced, skilled anti-trust attorney or litigator can fill this position. Not only do the scope of the assignment and the nature of the decisions reached in it make that kind of background and training imperative, but the occupant of the job must also command the respect of the bar. Beyond that, this assistant AG should have a firm grasp of practical economics, a feel for policy, and skill in understanding the client perspective in anti-trust cases.

Insight

At Justice, the anti-trust division differs from other components of the department because the rather general statutes it enforces amount to a common law which has developed over time, rather than to a code. As a result, this division probably operates with more latitude or discretion than the others in the economic sphere where its work lies. To some extent, it has closer relationships with certain other departments and agencies than within its own. Such semi-autonomy facilitates decisionmaking in this specialized sector of the law. But it also tends to keep the division's activities away from regular attention at the top of the department. That can make it hard to enlist support from above on some issues, especially in disputes between departments at the Cabinet level.

Enforcement has grown enormously in recent years. Besides responsibilities in that area--investigating possible violations, taking anti-trust cases through indictment, trial and appeal, putting final judgments in force--the occupant of the position has the assignment of promoting competitive practices within the government. This entails a variety of committee meetings, hearings, and reports, as well as formal counsel to other agencies on the competitive implications of certain of their activities. In addition, present procedure calls for the division to share with the Federal Trade Commission the responsibility of anti-trust enforcement on the civil side, splitting with the FTC the task of reviewing proposals for corporate mergers.

Beyond these immediate fields of action, the assistant AG for anti-trust needs to keep an attentive eye on the middle distance and the horizon. Basically, that means developing or sharpening insights into how anti-trust policy and the economy are likely to shape and influence one another in the future. Charles F. Rule, the current assistant AG, says "it is important to be sensitive to the power you wield in this job and the potential cost to the economy that you can impose." And one of his predecessors thinks the job's occupant must constantly look to how policy should or can be revised as economic conditions change.

Two outside observers, one representing a broad-based industrial association and the other a leading bar association, give generally good overall ratings to the anti-trust division's recent performance. But they are critical of its track record on mergers and acquisitions. Though it's a bad idea, says the first, to restrict every merger or acquisition on the merest hint that it might damage competitiveness, "it can go the other way, too," with damage of other kinds to the work force and the economy. "Some cases have not been so well thought through," says the second. That suggests that perhaps the division could use some more staff with economic background for case analysis and preparation, which is "generally more available at the FTC."

Asked about the division's relations with the FTC in handling anti-trust matters, this source notes that the two have a "working agreement," but adds that, "as far as compatible policy orientation is concerned, there's a tension that develops over time." In fact, the division appears to question whether the FTC should have an anti-trust role at all. For its part, the American Bar Association in March, 1989 will report results of its current study of what the FTC's legitimate role should be. At the least, meanwhile, there seems to be room for a better definition of each organization's assignments in this respect, so that they don't duplicate each other's work.

Reflecting on other points for an incoming assistant AG to keep in mind, Rule warns that "it is essential to remember that anti-trust enforcement does not operate in a vacuum. Unlike the enforcement of most other statutes that are specific and detailed, the anti-trust laws themselves are general, and enforcers have substantial discretion: outside the criminal area, there are no clear and immutable lines separating the legal from the illegal. Consequently, decisions must be explained by reference to policy goals and an AAG generally cannot hide behind precedent. Any decisions must be carefully considered in advance. A number of constituencies are usually affected by a decision, and while an AAG cannot, and *should* not, try to please everyone, he or she better be prepared for the abundance of criticism that virtually any high profile decisions are likely to generate. One of the worst outcomes is to feel forced to reverse a publicly announced decision because some relevant factor or policy consideration was ignored or overlooked. An AAG can't reverse himself or herself publicly and maintain credibility."

Rule stresses the value of credibility in another direction. An AAG has to be concerned not only that the decisions are thoroughly considered and correct, but that they are effectively explained to the public. The first is easier for lawyers than the second. For example, Rule says, the division has not been particularly successful, "in explaining how much our policies have helped small businesses. As a result, some politically motivated state attorneys general have exploited that failure and tried to fill in what they claim are gaps in enforcement." There is a potential danger in the development of power there, he explains, because there are, "hints that they intend to use it to promote the parochial interest of their state and their citizens at the expense of the rest of the national economy. You have to maintain your credibility because you are not the only alternative out there."

Also looking at the future, our bar association observer says this position takes on added importance "as we realize we're going into a world market. It's essential that the assistant AG play a major role in rationalizing world competitiveness policy on the one hand and anti-trust policy on the other. It's an evolving aspect of the job."

Key Relationships

Within the Department

Reports to: Attorney General

Works closely with:

Deputy Attorney General
Solicitor General
Assistant Attorney General, Office of Legal Counsel

Outside the Department

Chairman, Federal Trade Commission
Director, Competition Bureau,
    Federal Trade Commission
General Counsel, Department of Commerce
Assistant Secretary, Communications and Information, Department of Commerce
Undersecretary, International Trade, Department of Commerce
Assistant Secretary, Economic and Business Affairs, Department of State
Administrator, Office of Information and Regulatory Affairs, Office of Management and Budget
Associate Director, Economics and Government, OMB
Senior Staff Economist, Microeconomic Issues, Council of Economic Advisors
Assistant Secretary, Economic Policy, Department of the Treasury
General Counsel, Federal Reserve Board

Outside the Federal Government

American Bar Association, Business Round Table, U.S. Chamber of Commerce, National Association of

Manufacturers; consumer advocate and international trade groups, such as American Association of Exporters and Importers, International Trade Council, National Consumer Law Center, U.S. Business and Industrial Council

Assistant Attorneys General for the Anti-Trust Division Since 1969

Administration	Name and Years Served	Present Position
Reagan	Charles F. Rule 1986 - Present	Incumbent
Reagan	Douglas H. Ginsburg 1985 - 1986	U. S. Court Judge U.S. Court of Appeals Washington, DC
Reagan	J. Paul McGrath 1983 - 1985	Partner Dewey, Ballentine, Bushby, Palmer & Wood New York, New York
Reagan	William F. Baxter 1981 - 1983	Professor College of Law Stanford University Stanford, California
Carter	Sanford M. Litvack 1980 - 1981	Partner Dewey, Ballentine, Bushby, Palmer & Wood New York, New York
Carter	John H. Shenefield 1977 - 1980	Partner Morgan, Lewis and Bockius Washington, DC
Ford	Donald I. Baker 1976 - 1977	Senior Partner Sutherland, Asbill and Brennan Washington, DC

Nixon/Ford Thomas E. Kauper Professor
  1972 - 1976 College of Law
   University of Michigan
   Ann Arbor, Michigan

Nixon Richard W. McLaren Deceased
  1969 - 1972

ASSISTANT ATTORNEY GENERAL
CIVIL RIGHTS DIVISION

Level IV - Presidential Appointment with Senate Confirmation

Major Responsibilities

o   Enforce civil rights laws barring discrimination on any of several grounds in principal sectors of American life, in federal government policies and operations, and in federally-aided programs. Develop litigation strategy to make these statutes effective.

o   Design the administration's approach or response to legislative initiatives by the Congress and coordinate its public positions on civil rights issues. Act as the administration's civil rights spokesman.

o   Direct the substantive activities of the division's seven units and 175 lawyers. Review budget and personnel matters and make hiring recommendations.

Necessary Background, Experience, Personal Skills

A successful lawyer with a sound background in litigation best fits the requirements. This individual should also demonstrate a close familiarity with the principal current issues in civil rights and with civil rights history of the past 35 years. "Exemplary" public speaking abilities, to use the word of a former occupant of the job, and some experience with the Congress will prove highly useful.

Insight

The civil rights division's various units operate in broad and basic segments of U.S. economic and political existence--among them education, employment, housing, voting, the use of public facilities, and credit. These are the major national arenas where, predictably, civil rights issues arise most frequently and where an extensive body of civil rights law requires investigation and enforcement. Most of this work is litigation-oriented, and in its various specific issue areas much of it also gets attention from other government agencies. Because the Justice Department has litigating responsibility for the entire executive branch, however, it has a much larger reach and grasp. The department thus takes the lead--sets the agenda--in civil rights matters across the board. This responsibility, explains William Bradford Reynolds, the current assistant AG, incorporates the duty to see that statutes "are consistently enforced and that the regulations each agency develops under those statutes are uniform and fit together in a coherent way."

"It's a tough job no matter how you hack it," is the comment from a legal association representative who watches this deputy AG closely. "It's tough in terms of formulating overall law enforcement policies, presenting those to the public as being fair, being able to allocate resources in a practical way, and then present that to the various publics so that they accept it as fair."

Civil rights legislation under consideration on the Hill inevitably involves the assistant AG, who must decide whether to support, oppose, or try to modify it. Here, as with policy initiatives of its own, the division has to consider its steps carefully, given the sensitivity of the subject. Addressing this aspect of the job, one of its veterans theorizes about the fickle nature of the emotion and attention aroused by a given action or proposed action. In this view, the amount of reaction depends to some extent on whether the move represents new policy and "whether it fits comfortably into the agenda of the people who are not in control--Republican or Democrat." This individual found that quiet talks with members of constituency groups about their concerns, for instance in crafting legislation, produced results. "There was not nearly the gulf that everyone anticipated and we were able to come to an agreement on what needed to be done."

For Drew S. Days III, assistant AG for civil rights from 1977 to 1980, the key "is being able to use good judgment. You need to consider not only what is intellectually the right thing to do, but also to take into consideration the right timing and the right way to do it."

Overall, Reynolds says, this position "is a huge management job. You've got a lot of litigation and a lot of legislation that is churning all the time. It's important that all of those bases are covered in a way that advances the policies of an administration, not interferes with them. It requires a lot of management just to make sure that the trains run on time, that we meet our deadlines, that briefs say what they ought to, and that there is an opportunity to coordinate with anyone else in the administration that wants to weigh in...." He adds that "it is a little like running a large law firm--only the government is an easier client to manage than having multiple clients. With the government you have one client, you shape the policy agenda, you move out in whatever direction you're going to move in, and keep on trucking." He believes incoming assistant AG's should set their goals within a few weeks or face the possibility of never being able to. These should be modest, not ambitious, he says, because "the reality is that what you can accomplish is probably best accomplished through the courts, rather than outside the court system."

"It's a challenge," Days thinks, "to see how litigation can result in new legal doctrines and have an impact after one leaves the administration." He adds: "You definitely get a lot of exposure. You certainly will be well-known in the field once you leave that job!"

Key Relationships

Within the Department

Reports to: Attorney General

Works closely with:

> Deputy Attorney General
> Assistant Attorney General, Office of Legislative
> and Intergovernmental Affairs
> Assistant Attorney General, Civil Division
> Solicitor General

Outside the Department

> Chairman, Equal Employment Opportunity Commission
> Chairman, Commission on Civil Rights
> Civil rights assistant secretaries or equivalents in
> other departments and agencies
> Director, Federal Bureau of Investigation
> Counsel to the President
> Assistant to the President for Legislative Affairs
> President's National Committee for the Handicapped
> Chairman, Architectural Transportation Barriers Com-
> pliance Board

Outside the Federal Government

A broad range of civil rights organizations, employer groups, and housing groups, such as American Civil Liberties Union, Americans for Democratic Action, Leadership Conference on Civil Rights, National Low Income Housing Coalition; state and local government leaders and state officials in education, housing and civil rights areas; National Education Association; and U.S. Conference of Mayors

Assistant Attorneys General for the Civil Rights Division Since 1969

Administration	Name and Years Served	Present Position
Reagan	Wm. Bradford Reynolds 1982 - Present	Incumbent
Reagan	James P. Turner(Acting) 1981	Deputy Assistant Attorney General for the Civil Rights Division Department of Justice
Carter	Drew S. Days III 1977 - 1980	Professor Yale Law School New Haven, Connecticut
Nixon/Ford	J. Stanley Pottinger 1973 -1977	New York, New York
Nixon	David L. Norman 1971 - 1973	Not Available
Nixon	Jerris Leonard 1969 - 1971	Not Available

ASSISTANT ATTORNEY GENERAL
CRIMINAL DIVISION

Level IV - Presidential Appointment with Senate Confirmation

Major Responsibilities

o   Direct the enforcement of all federal criminal laws, principally through supervision of the investigation and prosecution activities of U.S. attorney's offices in the nation's 94 federal judicial districts. Set general enforcement policies for the performance of this task.

o   Coordinate with other agencies of government in national and international efforts to combat terrorism and trafficking in narcotics and other illegal materials.

o   Recommend revision to federal criminal statutes as necessary or desirable, and develop and support legislation to that effect. Keep the Congress appropriately informed about federal criminal law enforcement policy and operations.

o   Advise and counsel the attorney general as requested on specific criminal matters. Manage main Justice's criminal division of about 400 lawyers in a dozen or more specialized offices.

Necessary Background, Experience, Personal Skills

This position should go to a trained lawyer with substantial work as a prosecutor and an updated grasp not only of the federal criminal code but of the major issues and problems now engaging the criminal division. An individual with prior service as a U.S. attorney and, perhaps, at main Justice in Washington probably meets those criteria. But the right candidate should also have a broad view of criminal law issues and criminal justice; the position requires the perspective that comes through outside practice, teaching or other related activity and not exclusively from work as a prosecutor. This assistant attorney general needs considerable leadership, organizational and managerial skills, and a familiarity with the Congress. The growing international dimension of the position argues for background in that area as well.

Insight

Drugs and terrorism in the last few years have meant increasing business for this assistant AG with the State Department, the Central Intelligence Agency and the National Security Council. William F. Weld, assistant AG from 1987 to early 1988, estimates spending half of his final six months in this widening field of activity--one that also includes the offshore aspects of white collar crime. He predicts that, if problems like these continue to be substantial preoccupations, then "whoever has this job in the next administration had better have some ability in the international area." He points to the sharp contrast with the 1950s, when the most frequent crime prosecuted by U.S. attorneys was car theft, and even with the early 1980s when the most prestigious trial cases were bank robberies. "Those are both street crimes. Now you have so many thorny international problems which the [state] district attorneys can't begin to cope with, that the Feds have to do it." More than that, Weld points out, Washington has to take the lead, since a U.S. attorney making an espionage arrest somewhere may not be aware of its foreign policy implications.

Except on rare occasions, the assistant AG is, de facto, the key decisionmaker on the shape and direction of individual criminal cases, setting priorities, monitoring activity and directing resources where they are needed most. This responsibility has inherent management problems. U.S. attorneys doing the front-line work around the country handle 90 percent of federal government litigation in the field. They tend to be an independent crew, says Philip B. Heymann, who ran the criminal division in 1978-81. "It's very hard to know all the quite public and newsworthy decisions people are making and for which you are responsible. You have to try to spot cases you want to keep your eye on, and get regular reports."

Weld makes some similar points about U.S. attorneys as a group--"dukes in their duchies," in his phrase. For one thing, they must perceive the assistant AG as knowing the ropes, and respect his decisions rather than appeal them over his head. Moreover, assertiveness is the style for many prosecutors, and handling them "may require more finesse than a street cop. On the other hand, you'd better understand the street-cop approach...." The scene features constant jurisdictional tugging between various sections of the criminal division and U.S. attorneys. For example, the fraud section of the division may prosecute all over the country, Weld says, "but they damn well better have the consent of the U.S. attorney before they go into his district or they're going to have a shouting match that they're going to lose."

A key task in this job should be to prevent the politicization of law enforcement or criminal justice decisions. Politicization can cut either way--pressure, say, to investigate a prominent figure in the political opposition on ill-conceived or shaky grounds, or conversely, to protect someone of the party in power who may clearly be a transgressor. "It is something that, in a well-run department, you should never have to worry about," says a qualified observer. "But if it ever comes up, it is extremely dangerous. You don't want a yes man in the criminal spot."

One former assistant AG told us he brought to this position a particular emphasis on specific goals--a sort of "programmatic impetus" beyond the basic responsibilities. "I wanted to fight white-collar crime and stop corruption. I felt that unless people push those areas, they're not going to get pushed, because they're so difficult." This veteran was at pains to stress that this kind of personal agenda is not a requisite. "You can either come with a program or come without one. You don't need a program. But it's possible to come and superimpose that on your other duties."

Key Relationships

Within the Department

Reports to: Attorney General

Works closely with:

Associate Attorney General
Deputy Attorney General
Assistant Attorney General, Office of the Legal Counsel
Assistant Attorney General, Office of Legal Policy
Assistant Attorney General, Legislative and Inter-governmental Affairs
Director, Federal Bureau of Investigation

Outside the Department

Ambassador for Counterterrorism, Department of State
Director, Counterterrorism and Narcotics, National Security Council

Outside the Federal Government

American Bar Association, American College of Trial Lawyers, Federal Criminal Investigators Association, National Association of Criminal Defense Lawyers, National District Attorneys Association, and National Legal Aid and Defender Association

Assistant Attorneys General for the Criminal Division Since 1969

Administration	Name and Years Served	Present Position
Reagan	Edward S. G. Dennis, Jr. 1988 - Present	Nominated
Reagan	William F. Weld 1987 - 1988	Senior Partner Hale and Dorr Washington, DC
Reagan	Stephen S. Trott 1984 - 1987	U. S. Circuit Court Judge U.S. Court of Appeals Ninth Circuit Boise, Idaho
Reagan	D. Lowell Jensen 1981 - 1983	U.S. Judge for the Northern District of California San Francisco, California
Carter	Philip B. Heymann 1978 - 1981	Professor Harvard University School of Law Cambridge, Massachusetts
Carter	Benjamin R. Civiletti 1977 - 1978	Partner Venable, Baetjer, Howard and Civiletti Washington, DC
Ford	Richard L. Thornburgh 1975 - 1977	Attorney General Department of Justice

Ford	John C. Keeney (Acting) 1975	Deputy Assistant Attorney General for the Criminal Division Department of Justice
Nixon/Ford	Henry E. Petersen 1972 - 1974	Not Available
Nixon	Will R. Wilson 1969 -1971	Not Available

ASSISTANT ATTORNEY GENERAL
LAND AND NATURAL RESOURCES DIVISION

Level IV - Presidential Appointment with Senate Confirmation

Major Responsibilities

o   Represent the United States in litigation, including defensive litigation, in the areas of environment, natural resources, Indian lands and claims, public lands and wildlife.

o   Take action as necessary to recommend revision of legislation applicable to the mandate under which the Land and Natural Resources Division operates.

o   Provide substantive and administrative management to the division.

Necessary Background, Experience, Personal Skills

The position requires an attorney with extensive litigation or trial background.   Candidates should also have a knowledge of environmental law.   Prior experience in government and--even better--some familiarity with the Environmental Protection Agency provide an excellent leg up.

Insight

Increasingly, the name of the game in the Land and Natural Resources Division has been environment. True, the division prosecutes and defends cases under fish and wildlife laws, and speaks for the government when the United States supports Indian land rights claims.   But the growing workload in the environmental sector flows, of course, from landmark legislation in that area of roughly the last decade.   This has established and strengthened standards for the protection and recovery of natural resources, fixed liability for improper handling of hazardous wastes and toxic substances, and provided certain forms of recourse for persons injured by such materials.   Notable among the civil and criminal enforcement cases brought by the division on environmental matters are those about clean air and water and hazardous wastes, with the Environmental Protection Agency as the largest client. The division must likewise defend the federal government--primarily, the EPA--in suits challenging agency decisions.

"The major goals," in the view of F. Henry Habicht II, who held this job in 1983-87, "should be to improve the coordination of the government agencies' positions on environmental issues, see that environmental enforcement stances are well-developed, prosecuted and explained, and ensure sound and consistently applied standards of judicial review of environmental decisions that people inevitably want to contest. Finding alternatives to litigation should also be a top priority." In this job's areas of responsibility, he also thinks it wise to pay careful attention to federal-state relationships and separation of powers among the three branches at the federal level.

"It exceeded my expectations," one of his predecessors remembers about the position. "The assistant attorney general of the land division focuses on oversight of all problems involving all environmental happenings." Another makes a different point, saying that "many people go into the job feeling they can make major changes in policy, when you just have to make minor ones day by day."

As described by those who have run the division, the typical routine of its chief includes assignment of cases, supervising subordinate attorneys, reviewing their work, making tactical and strategic decisions in individual matters, briefing higher levels of the department, recommending legislation, hiring, firing and budget.

Several former assistant AGs raise the problem of coordinating positions between agencies--the question of "what you get to do versus what they get to do." "Some agency lawyers resent the Justice Department representing them in court," one of them says, adding that teamwork counts heavily in making the work easier and faster. Negotiating skills thus come into frequent play within in the executive branch as well as with opponents on the other side of a case. Problems also stem from what two former occupants of the job describe as tensions with U.S. attorneys in individual cases around the country who "don't like outsiders telling them what to do;" and from the usual shortages of staff and resources to handle the caseload.

Key Relationships

Within the Department

Reports to: Attorney General

Works closely with:

> Deputy Attorney General
> Solicitor General
> Assistant Attorney General, Office of Legal Counsel
> Assistant Attorney General, Civil Rights Division

Outside the Department

> General Counsel, Environmental Protection Agency
> Assistant administrators of EPA for Solid Waste and
> Emergency Response, Pesticides and Toxic
> Substances, and Water
> Solicitor, Department of the Interior
> Commanding General, U.S. Army Corps of Engineers

Outside the Federal Government

> Environmental organizations, such as Council of
> Pollution Control Financing Agencies, Environmental
> Law Institute, Water Pollution Control Federation;
> chemical and petrochemical industry organizations,
> such as Chemical Manufacturers Association, National
> Association of Chemical Distributors; and state attor-
> neys general and such organizations as National
> Association of Attorneys General

Assistant Attorneys General for the Land and Natural Resources Division Since 1969

Administration	Name and Years Served	Present Position
Reagan	Roger J. Marzulla 1987 - Present	Incumbent
Reagan	F. Henry Habicht II 1983 - 1987	Partner Perkins, Coie, Stone & Williams Washington, DC
Reagan	Carol E. Dinkins 1981 - 1983	Partner Vinson and Elkins Houston, Texas

Carter	James W. Moorman 1977 - 1981	Partner Cadwalader, Wickersham and Taft Washington, DC
Ford	Peter R. Taft 1975 - 1977	Partner Munger, Tolles and Olson Los Angeles, California
Nixon/Ford	Wallace H. Johnson, Jr. 1973 - 1975	Not Available
Nixon	D. Kent Frizzell 1972 - 1973	Director, National Energy, Law and Policy Institute University of Tulsa College of Law Tulsa, Oklahoma
Nixon	Shiro Kaskiwa 1969 - 1972	Retired Circuit Judge Federal Circuit Washington, DC

ASSISTANT ATTORNEY GENERAL
OFFICE OF THE LEGAL COUNSEL

Level IV - Presidential Appointment with Senate Confirmation

Major Responsibilities

o   Assist the attorney general in his capacity as principal legal adviser to the President. Draft formal attorney general opinions.

o   Exercise the attorney general's mandate as legal adviser to the executive branch. Write the attorney general's formal opinions. Provide legal advice and opinion to heads of departments and agencies on request, to staffs of the White House and the executive departments, and within the Department of Justice. Design executive branch positions on constitutional and other government-wide legal questions.

o   Provide constitutional analysis of pending legislation. Resolve legal disputes between departments and agencies. Coordinate the department's work on international treaties, executive agreements and international organizations.

o   Manage the Office of the Legal Counsel with respect to budget and personnel matters.

Necessary Background, Experience, Personal Skills

This position calls for a lawyer of sound and substantial experience with an emphasis on constitutional, federal and administrative law. In making the selection, look for solid legal academic credentials that add credibility to the opinions the individual will write, and an intellectually curious individual given to going the extra mile to gather all evidence with a bearing on a given legal issue. This assistant AG should also work comfortably under pressure and criticism and handle media encounters without difficulty.

Insight

It would be entirely correct to view the Office of the Legal

Counsel as filling the role of constitutional lawyer to the President. Under the direction of the assistant AG, however, the office furnishes advice to the White House and the executive departments on legal issues that ranges far beyond the Constitution, spanning the entire U.S. Code and federal regulations structure. It regularly provides advice on a wide variety of international law questions. "I can't imagine another office with the breadth of legal issues that we had," says Charles J. Cooper, assistant attorney general ˎfrom 1985 to mid-1988. Among the most contentious of these in recent years have been disputes over the nature and extent of the President's obligations to the Congress in committing U.S. forces to hostilities overseas, and about the constitutionality of the independent prosecutor law.

The Presidential advisory dimension of this job clearly entails a good deal of personal interaction with the attorney general. "There's a need for a high level of confidence and trust, and frequent and ready communication with the attorney general," says Theodore B. Olson, who held the position in 1981-84. But at a different level, the office also has the duty to provide arms-length advice and opinion to the attorney general on specific proposed actions by the Justice Department, just as it would to the chief of any other executive department. The assistant AG is in one sense, therefore, closer to the attorney general than are other assistant AGs; and in another sense, more distant, because of the obligation to say "no" when necessary.

This duty--to provide objective legal advice--can have interesting and challenging links to policy. The Office of the Legal Counsel does not provide legal advice in a bell jar; rather, it usually knows and is sensitive to the policy preferences of the requesting agencies. Such knowledge many times adds a vital ingredient to the office's work. As Cooper explains, "it is important not just to provide your best unbiased legal judgment to an agency and be done with it. If an agency asked us whether it is legally authorized to do something, we usually knew there was an important policy reason for doing it. And the Office of the Legal Counsel has a responsibility, no less than any other legal adviser, to assist its client agencies in achieving their policy goals. Therefore if the agency has identified an illegitimate means to achieve a legitimate end, I believe the office should determine whether there are legitimate means available to achieve the same end. The worst thing you can do is say yes to an agency if the answer is no. If disengaged and dispassionate legal analysis leads to the conclusion that the law really isn't friendly to a given policy, the worst thing would be to blur that message to the policymakers. I place the personal firmness to say no at the very top of the list of attributes one should have coming in to this office."

Something like 90 percent of the legal matters handled by the assistant AG and staff comes at the request of the departments and agencies. It's an outside-counsel situation comparable to the use by a large corporation's own counsel of external legal help in certain matters. The office can, however, move in without invitation if it has reason to think a government department's position on an issue is questionable from a legal point of view. On legislation, the office looks at the constitutional aspects of each proposal an administration sends to the Hill, averaging about ten bill comments a week. Most legal counsel business with the Congress flows through the department's legislative office.

"It helps," a veteran of the job says, "if one brings personal skills to the job that make it easy to deal with others" in a position whose occupant deals constantly with high-level officials all over the government day in and day out, frequently telling them things they don't want to hear. "That can be unpleasant. But the ability to...minimize the friction is very much an advantage." He further suggests that hiring decisions in this job are among the most crucial. Invoking a principle applicable across the Justice department, if not the government as a whole, he warns that "no assistant attorney general will be better than his worst lawyer. If your lawyers make mistakes, you will."

Key Relationships

Within the Department

Reports to: Attorney General

Works closely with:

Deputy Attorney General
Solicitor General
Assistant attorneys general

Outside the Department

Counsel to the President
Counsel, Office of Management and Budget
General counsels or legal advisers in other departments
and agencies

Outside the Federal Government

> National and international law associations, such as American Bar Association, Inter-American Bar Association and Association of Trial Lawyers of America; International Law Institute; university law schools and centers; Association of American Law Schools; constitutional rights groups, such as American Civil Liberties Union; state attorneys general; and National Association of Attorneys General

Assistant Attorneys General for the Office of the Legal Counsel Since 1969

Administration	Name and Years Served	Present Position
Reagan	Douglas Kmiec (Acting) 1988 - Present	Incumbent
Reagan	Charles J. Cooper 1985 - 1988	Partner McGuire, Woods Battle & Boothe Washington, DC
Reagan	Ralph W. Tarr(Acting) 1984 - 1985	Solicitor Department of the Interior
Reagan	Theodore B. Olson 1981 - 1984	Partner Gibson, Dunn and Crutcher Washington, DC
Carter	John M. Harmon 1977 - 1981	Partner Graves, Dougherty, Hearon and Moody Austin, Texas
Nixon/Ford	Antonin Scalia 1974 - 1977	Associate Justice U.S. Supreme Court
Nixon	Robert G. Dixon 1973 - 1974	Not Available

Nixon	Ralph E. Erickson 1972	Los Angeles, California
Nixon	Roger C. Cramton 1972 - 1973	Not Available
Nixon	William H. Rehnquist 1969 - 1971	Chief Justice U.S. Supreme Court

16

DEPARTMENT OF LABOR

The department ranks fifth in annual budget, at $31.5 billion for fiscal 1988, and has 18,500 employees.

If this agency's function is to represent workers, the point also needs to be made that this is not the same as speaking for the AFL-CIO. Organized labor now represents about 15% of the nation's work force. The unions obviously remain a substantial constituent group, but the department's activities and interests in the labor field reach even more broadly beyond them. At the same time, its relationship with the management of business and industry has been widening. In a roughly parallel process, although more than half this agency's activity continues to lie in the area of regulation and law enforcement, it must also step up its program responses to the changing environment of the American work place.

In the 1990s, for example, the education of the U.S. worker will be even more acutely what in the last two decades it has already become--an important factor in the U.S. ability to compete in world markets. Not long ago, a study by a national manufacturers organization demonstrated that 20% of the auto industry labor force is functionally illiterate. It is difficult for such individuals to survive the unpredictable shifts in the location and composition of job markets that foreign competition imposes. At the same time, for the work force in general, the relentless thrust of high technology demands new skills, including learning skills; work processes are changing; team concepts have come into play; and workers are participating in management.

The functional illiteracy of some workers, an official of a large manufacturers organization believes, is something which American industry got away with in the past but cannot carry any longer.

Faced with it, some large companies are investing time during the work day in the remedial education of their employees. In some instances, workers are obliged to put some of their off-hours time into this as well, a practice which this observer suggests is a technical violation of the Fair Labor Standards Act. Should the department enforce the law? Or, since employees are theoretically receiving cost-free improvement of their educational skills in return for using some of their own time, should the department move to amend it?

For the Department of Labor, such issues and questions should be pointing out part of its agenda for today, tomorrow and the longer future. Industry, particularly small and medium-sized companies, needs increasing encouragement by government to provide its work force with multi-skill training and retraining. Further, because employees of the future are going to have more authority in what happens in their work areas and in the affairs of their employers and communities, industry needs additional persuasion to assist workers to acquire math skills, real literacy and the other tools of a broader citizenship.

DEPARTMENT OF LABOR

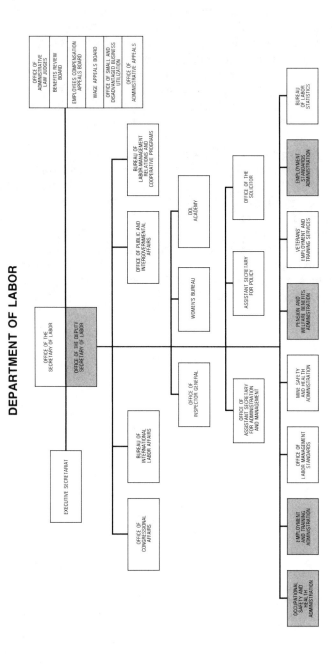

OFFICE OF THE SECRETARY OF LABOR

OFFICE OF THE DEPUTY SECRETARY OF LABOR

OFFICE OF ADMINISTRATIVE LAW JUDGES

BENEFITS REVIEW BOARD

EMPLOYEES COMPENSATION APPEALS BOARD

WAGE APPEALS BOARD

OFFICE OF SMALL AND DISADVANTAGED BUSINESS UTILIZATION

OFFICE OF ADMINISTRATIVE APPEALS

EXECUTIVE SECRETARIAT

OFFICE OF CONGRESSIONAL AFFAIRS

BUREAU OF INTERNATIONAL LABOR AFFAIRS

OFFICE OF INSPECTOR GENERAL

OFFICE OF PUBLIC AND INTERGOVERNMENTAL AFFAIRS

WOMEN'S BUREAU

DOL ACADEMY

BUREAU OF LABOR-MANAGEMENT RELATIONS AND COOPERATIVE PROGRAMS

OFFICE OF ASSISTANT SECRETARY FOR ADMINISTRATION AND MANAGEMENT

ASSISTANT SECRETARY FOR POLICY

OFFICE OF THE SOLICITOR

OCCUPATIONAL SAFETY AND HEALTH ADMINISTRATION

EMPLOYMENT AND TRAINING ADMINISTRATION

OFFICE OF LABOR MANAGEMENT STANDARDS

MINE SAFETY AND HEALTH ADMINISTRATION

PENSION AND WELFARE BENEFITS ADMINISTRATION

VETERANS' EMPLOYMENT AND TRAINING SERVICES

EMPLOYMENT STANDARDS ADMINISTRATION

BUREAU OF LABOR STATISTICS

Shaded areas were selected as Prune Book positions

DEPUTY SECRETARY

Level II - Presidential Appointment with Senate Confirmation

Major Responsibilities

o   Manage the day-to-day operation of department programs. Maintain liaison with the department's field components.

o   Advise the secretary on policy issues and in setting program priorities. Develop and manage the department's budget.

o   Oversee the department's dual role as program developer and enforcer.   Ensure that this is reflected in policy development and in the interagency policy coordination process.

o   Act as a principal senior spokesman for department policies, programs and goals to constituent groups, the public and the media.

Necessary Background, Experience, Personal Skills

Extensive, successful public- and private-sector management experience leads the recommendations for this position.   Some grounding in political science or accounting, an exposure to labor's basic concerns, and a demonstrated ability in negotiating contexts come next.   To complete the list, pencil in those qualities that add up to good personal relations in large managerial positions and are particularly necessary in this one--objectivity, a readiness to listen, a talent for persuasion, articulacy, poise and toughness.

Insight

At Labor, the deputy secretary normally functions as chief operating officer.   To that description, Ford B. Ford, deputy secretary in 1983-85, adds a familiar but apt label for these second-ranking jobs: "Alter ego" of the secretary.   "The deputy must be able to step in on all issues," he says.   "You are as accountable to the President as the secretary for the department's performance and its pursuit of the President's policy goals."   When not in the acting secretary role, the deputy's responsibility includes "maintaining an awareness of evolving issues, influencing the direction of those issues, and preventing the secretary from being blindsided."

The job carries an important role in the mediation of labor-management disputes where the department has lead responsibility. Policy responsibilities weave through the job in other ways as well--representing the department on the President's Economic Policy Council and the Pension Benefits Guarantee Corporation; supporting, modifying and sometimes opposing labor-related legislative initiatives, which involves close and regular Congressional contact; participating in the work of the Youth Employment Opportunity Wage Committee.

In addition to chairing or sitting on policy committees and working groups and executive and performance review boards, the deputy secretary takes part in coordinating meetings of the Cabinet Council on Economic Affairs. The position also has supervision of departmental grants to state-run employment and training programs. Its occupant conducts the department's relationships with the International Labor Organization. In that connection, the deputy secretary needs to make certain the department keeps those who make decisions on trade policy aware of sensitive issues concerning labor forces abroad. All of this, of course, brings the deputy secretary into frequent contact on various subjects and levels with organized labor and with civil rights groups. Special assignments have included seats on the guarantee board for the federal loan to the Chrysler Corporation, and to groups working on civil service and welfare reform.

Some of those formerly in the position emphasize the importance of experience in making encounters with interest groups and the press effective. "Overcoming misinformation" and "trying to get documented facts exposed to the general public" presented a chronic problem for one of them, who felt that "if it comes from the department it's considered self-serving and doesn't get much attention." Overcoming this meant a range of efforts--working carefully with the press, speaking to audiences embodying mixed constituent interests, keeping an open door to all interest groups, "staying informed on subjects even remotely related," running programs that keep the workshop, the factory floor and the board room informed. "There are constituents coming out of the walls," recalls Richard F. Schubert, deputy secretary in 1973-75. "You have to deal with many different groups. It's a very visible role."

In a department where regulation and enforcement comprise much of the action, the occupant of this job should keep in mind what one previous deputy secretary calls "the danger of the impact of heavy-handed enforcement activities. It's a people department," this veteran points out. "You have to project credible leadership, be durable, maintain your cool. Recognize that a lot of adverse criticism is politically motivated. Don't overreact." Or, as another reflects, "I believe you need a balance of internal insight."

Key Relationships

Within the Department

Reports to: Secretary

Works closely with:

> Assistant secretaries
> Solicitor
> Inspector General

Outside the Department

> Secretaries, deputy secretaries or undersecretaries of the departments of Commerce, Health and Human Services, Housing and Urban Development, Interior, and Transportation
> Deputy Attorney General, Department of Justice

Outside the Federal Government

> AFL-CIO and other labor organizations; state, county and city governments; industrial and business groups and individual companies; trade associations

Deputy Secretaries of Labor Since 1969*

Administration	Name and Years Served	Present Position
Reagan	Dennis E. Whitfield 1985 - Present	Incumbent

Reagan	Ford B. Ford 1983 - 1985	Chairman Federal Mine Safety and Health Review Commission Washington, DC
Reagan	Malcolm R. Lovell, Jr. 1981 - 1983	Distinguished Visiting Professor George Washington University Washington, DC
Carter	John N. Gentry 1979 - 1981	Reston, Virginia
Carter	Robert J. Brown 1977 - 1979	Mediator National Mediation Board Washington, DC
Ford	Michael H. Moskow 1976 - 1977	Vice President for Strategy and Business Development Premark International, Inc. Deerfield, Illinois
Ford	Robert D. Aders 1975 - 1976	President and CEO Food Marketing Institutes Washington, DC
Nixon/Ford	Richard F. Schubert 1973 - 1975	President American Red Cross Washington, DC
Nixon	Laurence H. Silberman 1970 - 1973	Circuit Judge U.S. Court of Appeals DC Circuit Washington, DC
Nixon	James D. Hodgson 1969 - 1970	Beverly Hills, California

* Position formerly titled Undersecretary of Labor. Title changed to Deputy Secretary of Labor by PL 99-619, signed November 6, 1986.

ASSISTANT SECRETARY
EMPLOYMENT AND TRAINING

Level IV - Presidential Appointment with Senate Confirmation

Major Responsibilities

o   Provide policy direction to component offices of the Employment
    and Training Administration (ETA) in the job training and
    employment security fields, and of other ETA offices which
    bring planning, research, financial and administrative support
    to those activities.

o   Monitor programs funded by ETA to ensure their adherence to
    provisions of law, regulatory statutes and Constitutional precepts,
    and their freedom from discrimination and fraud.

o   Advise the secretary and other officials of the government in
    matters of employment and training policy. Represent administra-
    tion policy to the Congress.

Necessary Background, Experience, Personal Skills

This assistant secretary needs a strong manpower and training
background and expertise in labor markets, should know the management side of business, and possess some accounting, budgetary and
negotiating skills. Since the ETA manages the Trade Adjustment
Assistance Program, the occupant of this job must also understand
recent world trade history, its current patterns and trends, and their
impact on domestic employment. Some familiarity with setting up
and running management information systems is helpful.

Insight

Beyond seeing to the stated duties of this position, its occupant
should "provide leadership and vision as to where the agency is
going," says Roger D. Semerad, assistant secretary in 1986-87.
The job needs someone who "cares about people and the labor
force of the United States."

But sustaining support for any particular set of goals seems prey at times to problems. Albert Angrisani, assistant secretary in 1981-83, talks about a "lack of understanding or care" in the bureaucracy and Congress about the "bottom-line result" and thinks "more emphasis should go to budget reduction and efficiency." This veteran takes a tough view of the challenge of the job--"to manage the agency in the most hostile and adverse management environment imaginable." A former occupant complains of "unrealistic demands from the White House and Congress, wanting things done by a certain date for political good looks." Another perception of the position comes from a Senate committee staff member who has seen a few assistant secretaries come and go. This observer feels that, on balance, "a career person has more to offer the Hill. There's just a more balanced agenda when someone has been there for 20 years and will be there (in the future)."

The position is critically important to industry. One of its main responsibilities is to administer the Job Training Partnership Act, which calls for a significant business contribution at the local level and sets up a system for training disadvantaged workers and retraining the dislocated. Five component sections make up the Employment and Training Administration. They focus on training, employment assistance, and unemployment insurance, and on internal support services for those programs. One office administers a nationwide block grant program providing funds for the training or retraining mostly of economically deprived youth and uprooted and seasonal workers; others make part-time employment opportunities available to low-income older workers and support the improvement and protection of employment standards for apprentices. In the job security area, ETA manages such programs as the Federal-State Unemployment Compensation Program and the U.S. Employment Service and runs the Office of Trade Adjustment Assistance. To collect and process the facts and figures used by many of these services, ETA's Office of Financial and Administrative Management operates a management information system with an extensive data base.

One of those who has held this job says "I thought the appointment would give me the opportunity to make an impact, but it turned out to be a middle manager's position." Another, however, sees it differently, calling the job an opportunity to make "a constructive contribution to society by helping the labor market work effectively." Semerad put it like this: "It's not a glory job, or one to take for the glamor. It's a constant battle. The only glory is knowing you made a contribution."

Key Relationships

Within the Department

Reports to: Secretary

Works closely with:

Deputy Secretary
Solicitor General
Assistant Secretary for Administration and Management

Outside the Department

Administrator, Family Support Administration,
Department of Health and Human Services
Assistant Secretary for Human Development Services,
HHS
Assistant Secretary for Fair Housing and Equal Opportunity, Department of Housing and Urban Development
Assistant Secretary, Elementary and Secondary Education, Department of Education

Outside the Federal Government

Labor unions, such as AFL-CIO; organizations for
senior citizens and the handicapped, such as American
Association of Retired Persons, National Council on
the Handicapped; minority training and Indian groups,
such as Americans for Indian Opportunity, National
Association for the Advancement of Colored People;
National Association of Counties; League of Cities;
National Governors Association; National Association
of Manaufacturers, U.S. Chamber of Commerce and
other business associations and firms

Assistant Secretaries for Employment and Training
Since 1969

Administration	Name and Years Served	Present Position
Reagan	Roberts T. James 1987 - Present (Acting)	Incumbent
Reagan	Roger D. Semerad 1986 - 1987	Senior Vice President Burson-Marsteller, Inc. Washington, DC
Reagan	Frank C. Casillas 1984 - 1985	Not Available
Reagan	Albert Angrisani 1981 - 1983	Consultant Arthur D. Little, Inc. New York, New York
Carter	Ernest G. Green 1977 - 1981	Senior Vice President Shearson/Lehman Brothers New York, New York
Nixon/Ford	William H. Kolberg 1973 -1977	President National Alliance of Business Washington, DC
Nixon	Malcolm R. Lovell, Jr. 1970 - 1973	Distinguished Visiting Professor George Washington University Washington, DC
Nixon	Arnold R. Weber 1969 - 1970	President Northwestern University Evanston, Illinois

ASSISTANT SECRETARY
EMPLOYMENT STANDARDS

Level IV - Presidential Appointment with Senate Confirmation

Major Responsibilities

o   Establish and supervise programs to maintain national standards of employment, carried out by the department's Employment Standards Administration. These programs cover minimum wages, overtime, wages paid under government contracts and sub-contracts, registration of farm labor contractors, workers' compensation for federal and some private employers, and nondiscrimination and affirmative action.

o   Develop legislation and regulatory reforms to support and improve these programs as necessary.

o   Direct and provide administrative supervision to the Employment Standards Administration.

Necessary Background, Experience, Personal Skills

The read-out on this position says that strong preference should go to labor lawyers with experience in public management. The job also calls for a substantial working background in the Congress, if possible with exposure to lobbying practices. In addition to these, candidates with some practical knowledge of sociology, social psychology, medicine or insurance probably have an advantage coming in.

Insight

The Employment Standards Administration divides into three sections managed by this assistant secretary--the Wage and Hour Division, the Office of Federal Contract Compliance Programs, and the Office of Workers' Compensation Programs. "Controlling the condition of the American workplace," as one veteran of the job describes it. "Wages, fairness and safety--that's the holy trinity."

Much of the work falls in the category of enforcement. In

the wages and hours area, federal minimum wage and overtime laws set the basic objectives--protection of low-wage incomes and of workers' health. This effort also covers the registration of farm labor contractors. Federal contract compliance applies and maintains non-discrimination standards in employment by federal government contractors and subcontractors and in construction programs which get federal assistance. The workers' compensation program uses three statutes in this field to provide compensation to federal workers, maritime employees and coal miners disabled by respiratory disease resulting from coal dust inhalation.

Running this operation--which has ten regional offices around the country--presents the assistant secretary with a mix of policy-making and implementation. "You have a policy, say, on what the minimum wage should be," explains Donald E. Elisburg, who held the job in 1977-81. "What is the law and what is the policy?" To work it out, "you deal with Congress, the public, business executives." Once the Congress sets the policy, he says, the question becomes "how you translate it into a manageable program. You have to figure out how to make that happen. You have to understand policy and then sell it in your system. And then you have to carry it out." "When I took over the office," recalls Arthur A. Fletcher, assistant secretary in 1969-71, "there was a rumor you couldn't collect the minimum wage. I had to see to it that they could. We set a system in motion to make it work. You have to put the Congress on it, too, so they know what's going on when the phone starts ringing."

Concerning the Congress, Robert Burns Collyer (1981-84) emphasizes the importance of "knowing the Hill staff." Given the attention which lobbyists devote to labor legislation, he advises, "it helps to know that that's the game. It's what goes on before you get there that counts. You have to get the votes in. You have to know how the underground operates." Another who served in the position estimates that his years on the Hill were probably more useful experience than his legal background.

"Whoever gets this job has to understand that it's a traveling job," Elisburg warns. "You have to visit the field, run the operation from the office, car, airplane or whatever. To manage it, you have to be there. There should be no illusions about it." Another offers this bit of advice: "Be an uncommon listener. And be able to think on your feet and on your rump, too."

Key Relationships

Within the Department

Reports to: Secretary

Works closely with:

Deputy Secretary
Assistant Secretary for Administration and Management
Assistant Secretary for Policy
Assistant Secretary for Occupational Safety and Health
Assistant Secretary for Congressional Affairs
Director, Women's Bureau
Solicitor

Outside the Department

Generally, officials in other agencies with
responsibilities in employment and procurement

Outside the Federal Government

AFL-CIO and other unions; National Association for
the Advancement of Colored People; Urban League;
federal employee groups; business and industrial
firms and associations, such as American Industrial
Health Council, American Textile Manufacturers Institute, National Association of Manufacturers, U.S.
Business and Industrial Council; campuses and think
tanks, such as American Enterprise Institute, Brookings
Institution

Assistant Secretaries for Employment Standards Since 1969

Administration	Name and Years Served	Present Position
Reagan	Fred W. Alvarez 1987 - Present	Incumbent

Reagan	Susan R. Meisinger* 1985 - 1987	Vice President American Society for Personnel Administration Alexandria, Virginia
Reagan	Robert Burns Collyer* 1981 - 1984	President The Collyer Company Ormand Beach, Florida
Carter	Donald E. Elisburg 1977 - 1981	Attorney-at-Law Washington, DC

Ford	John C. Read
	1976 - 1977
		Vice President - Small
		   Engine Business
		Cummins Engine Company,
		   Inc.
		Columbus, Indiana

Nixon/Ford	Bernard E. DeLury 1973 - 1976	Staff Vice President for Labor Relations Sealand Corporation Anderson, New Jersey
Nixon	Richard J. Grunewald 1972 - 1973	St. Michaels, Maryland
Nixon	Arthur A. Fletcher 1969 - 1971	Vice Chairman Pennsylvania Avenue Development Corporation Washington, DC

*   Held position as Deputy Undersecretary for Employment Standards
Administration.

ASSISTANT SECRETARY
OCCUPATIONAL SAFETY AND HEALTH

Level IV - Presidential Appointment with Senate Confirmation

Major Responsibilities

o Administer and enforce the provisions of the Occupational Safety and Health Act, designed to minimize or eliminate hazards from any source in six million U.S. work places in the private and public sectors. Develop and publish safety and health standards and the regulations to apply them. Oversee the conduct of inspections and investigations to determine compliance, and the citation of violators.

o Advise and assist the secretary in formulating policy for these operations. Work with other federal agencies to coordinate the process, and with the Congress to explain and seek support for policy and actions. Build and maintain informative and productive relationships with interest groups concerned with occupational safety and health issues.

o Oversee the substantive and administrative operations of the Operational Safety and Health Administration (OSHA).

Necessary Background, Experience, Personal Skills

A background in improving the safety of the work place and protecting it from health hazards is the basic credential. It assists in understanding the implications of prospective policies and the degree of acceptance they are likely to find. Business experience is clearly important, not only in grasping how OSHA affects business operations but in gaining insight into how to create consensus between labor and management in this often controversial area. Management skills honed in such a background are useful. The assistant secretary should also be able to understand scientific data, and draw on some familiarity with Congressional procedures and with the political framework in which the position operates.

Insight

This post has three basic responsibilities, according to John A. Pendergrass, assistant secretary since 1986--defining what a safe and healthy work place is, enforcing the regulations that are supposed to make it that way, and educating and training employers, employees, the public and the office's own staff. A fourth could be added: Enlarging and strengthening labor-management conciliation and cooperation in the often suspicious, sometimes incendiary atmosphere of safety and health regulation.

Comparatively speaking, OSHA is not a big agency. On a budget of $245 million, it operates with a staff of about 2,300 employees in ten regional and some 100 local offices across the land. Nearly half the states have their own occupational safety programs, and OSHA works closely with them. Small or not, Pendergrass says OSHA presents problems in "overcoming inertia," both in getting some things moving and in bringing others to a halt. He likens changing directions to "being in a canoe up against the bow of an aircraft carrier." But it can be done, and "your constituents can help." He thinks it is important to establish a dependable constituency, not one that invariably agrees with OSHA policy, but which can provide its opinions and serve as a sounding board and test bench.

The job seems to have its own share of occupational hazards. "In OSHA, you go on instinct," says Thorne G. Auchter, who headed the agency in 1981-84. "It's highly political and charged with emotion. You must make decisions based not on your own desires but on information the agency has gathered and analyzed, and you have to understand it so you can explain it to others. The challenge is to survive in the job without getting blown away." Eula Bingham, who had this post in 1977-81, found one of its chronic problems to be "agency bashing," by "people who didn't want the health and safety act to exist, attorneys trying to slow or stop enforcement." Pendergrass's comments on this aspect of the job run in a similar vein. "There are almost no friends for this agency," he agrees. "It's very visible. You have to have self-confidence." He would like to have had a better understanding when he began of how government works, and says he "never dreamed of the influence that the Congress has."

Views of what OSHA needs to do in the future vary with the vantage point, of course, but don't necessarily conflict. A representative of a manufacturer's group thinks the agency's process of standards development needs speeding up, explaining that many proposed regulations date back several years but the accompanying standards "are still not out--and that's true no matter who's in the administration." The long-term solution, in this view, "is to have performance-based standards, not prescriptive." The next assistant secretary needs to "increase the number of inspectors, develop some kind of consensus between labor and management, and examine how the Act can best be implemented to achieve its purpose." A national education organization member believes the assistant secretary should be "an advocate for the rights of employees" in OSHA matters, and "build relationships with the states to find out what the rules and regulations can actually do to offset recent rollbacks."

Auchter doesn't think OSHA goals need to change from personality to personality, however. "It has only one law to administer, and that sets up the goal," he says. "The problem has been inconsistency in personalities. OSHA needs to reduce its political image among the constituents. When you make a decision, you've got to stay with it." Pendergrass thinks the agency "has made a difference," and cites declining accident rates where people work, and increasing numbers of industrial hygienists and safety engineers. But "resources will always be the challenge. The answer is not just to keep adding more people. You have to look at the resources and see what the best ways are to use them. We can't inspect every work place. We need to rely heavily on voluntary compliance. The days of wild budgets are over."

Despite the high and tough exposure of this position, Auchter expresses a general view when he says "there isn't much that could make you feel better than knowing you've saved someone's life or reduced their risk of cancer." "There really aren't any career opportunities," he warns, but asserts that the job was "the most exciting thing I've ever done" and "I'd do it again in a second."

Key Relationships

Within the Department

Reports to: Secretary

Works closely with:

Undersecretary
Assistant Secretary for Mine Safety and Health
Assistant Secretary for Labor-Management Relations
Assistant Secretary for Policy

Deputy Undersecretary for Congressional Affairs
Solicitor

Outside the Department

Associate Director, Human Resources, Veterans and Labor, Office of Management and Budget

Director, National Institute for Occupational Safety and Health, Department of Health and Human Services

Director, Health and Environmental Review, Office of the Assistant Administrator for Pesticides and Toxic Substances, Environmental Protection Agency

Director, Health and Environmental Assessments, Office of the Assistant Administrator for Research and Development, EPA

Outside the Federal Government

AFL-CIO and other unions; National Association of Manufacturers, U.S. Chamber of Commerce, Iron and Steel Institute and other industrial, manufacturing and commercial associations and individual corporations; state government labor officials; American Industrial Hygiene Association, Organizational Resources Counselors, and other industrial health and safety advocacy groups; American Society of Safety Engineers; medical, nursing and hospital associations, and health care agencies; the insurance industry

Assistant Secretaries for Occupational Safety and Health Since 1971*

Administration	Name and Years Served	Present Position
Reagan	John A. Pendergrass 1986 - Present	Incumbent
Reagan	Patrick R. Tyson 1985 - 1986 (Acting)	Senior Partner Constangy, Brooks and Smith Atlanta, Georgia

Reagan	Robert A. Rowland 1984 - 1985	Austin, Texas
Reagan	Thorne G. Auchter 1981 - 1984	Executive Vice President The Jefferson Group Ponte Vedra Beach, Florida
Carter	Eula Bingham 1977 - 1981	Dean, Graduate Studies and Research University of Cincinnati Cincinnati, Ohio
Ford	Morton Corn 1975 - 1977	Baltimore, Maryland
Nixon/Ford	John H. Stender 1973 - 1975	Auburn, Washington
Nixon	George C. Guenther 1971 - 1973	Berwyn, Pennsylvania

*   Position created in 1971 by the Occupational Health and Safety Act.

ASSISTANT SECRETARY
PENSION AND WELFARE BENEFITS

Level IV - Presidential Appointment with Senate Confirmation

Major Responsibilities

o   Oversee the auditing of pension and welfare plans of private
    U.S. employers. Ensure compliance with the provisions of the
    Employee Retirement Income Security Act. Recommend solutions
    to problems of technique and efficiency in the auditing process.

o   Write and revise regulations covering disclosure, auditing and
    enforcement procedures under the act. Recommend necessary
    legislative adjustments to the Congress.

o   Manage the Pension and Welfare Benefits Administration (PWBA).
    Represent administration pension and welfare policy to con-
    stituent groups, the public and the Congress.

Necessary Background, Experience, Personal Skills

The position needs a broad background in the administration
of employee benefits, backed by legal training or extensive experience
in the interpretation of statutory or legislative concepts and language. An understanding of accounting and familiarity with investment management are other helpful assets. A previous occupant
of the job summed it up this way: "If you start off with nothing,
there's too much to learn to be effective."

Insight

Under the legislation which this job enforces (known, sometimes
without affection, as ERISA), administrators or managers of private
pension plans in the United States must report yearly to PWBA
about the financial operation of the plans and the legal security
of those who manage plan assets. They must meet tough trust
and custodial standards which PWBA also enforces. Further, ERISA
requires plan managers to summarize effectively for their participants
the terms and entitlements offered, and to maintain the summaries

on file with PWBA.

While supervising compliance with these provisions, working through ten field offices, the assistant secretary participates in the work of the Cabinet council on economic affairs as coordinator of administration private pension policy. Contact with the private sector to explain and discuss policy has become a key effort. As described by two former assistant secretaries, this meant "trying to (go) to the private sector by letters, speeches, whatever it took, as to what was going to be our policy" and "speaking to a myriad of groups on the interpretation of pension regulations." A third, Ian D. Lanoff, who had the job from 1977 to 1981, remembers that, other than preparing the PWBA budget, "I tried very much to leave my time free and not get involved in administrative work. I felt it was more important to set policy and make sure everyone else was managing." In fact, says a former occupant, the position currently has strict and explicit conflict of interest laws which in fact "legally prevented me from doing many of the administrative functions of the job."

The principal challenge appears to lie in exerting a greater impact, with limited resources, on the employee benefit community. One of those who served in the post thinks that amounts to "how to get things energized, especially on the enforcement side. The people and programs are there--it's just a question of getting them excited again."

But operational and other problems may get somewhat in the way. Robert A. G. Monks held the job in 1984-85 (as administrator of the former Office of Pension and Welfare Benefits Programs). He says he had "no control over the legal staff. If I wanted to bring a criminal action, my department, the Solicitor, the Department of Justice and the (appropriate) U.S. Attorney had to approve it." Further, he notes, while "the home Congress made for us was in Labor...they (Labor) have nothing to do with my particular agency. I couldn't look to them for help." He recommends establishing "a written set of guidelines" for department policy concerning PWBA. At present, he thinks, PWBA "is required to perform in an environment where they are not perceived as being a major financial organization. If it was, they'd get the kind of skills they need there ....Whenever I had a high-level vacancy, I went to the Securities and Exchange Commission to get skills not available at Labor."

Looking at the job from outside, an officer of a big constituency group says the individual in this job "needs to be able to work well with the other pension players--Treasury and the Pension Benefit Guaranty Corporation. A go-it-alone attitude wouldn't work. These have traditionally been a very difficult series of relationships, with no clear lead and inconsistent policy initiatives. The Treasury is interested in minimizing the pension loss, the Labor Department in getting as many pensions out to people as possible, and PBGC's objective is to keep itself financially sound. This is a function of each agency's only having a piece of the issue, with conflicting missions."

Key Relationships

Within the Department

Reports to: Secretary

Works closely with:

Assistant Secretary for Administration and Management
Solicitor

Outside the Department

Executive Director, Pension Benefit Guaranty
Corporation
Assistant Commissioner for Employee Plans and Exempt
Organizations, Internal Revenue Service

Outside the Federal Government

Organizations and associations in the corporate, investment, pension plan, accounting and retirement communities, such as American Association of Retired Persons, Employee Stock Ownership Association, Government Finance Officers Association, National AFL-CIO, Public Securities Association, Retired Workers Program

Assistant Secretaries for Pension and Welfare Benefits Since 1976*

Administration	Name and Years Served	Present Position
Reagan	David M. Walker 1987 - Present	Incumbent

Reagan	Dennis M. Kass 1985 - 1987	Vice President Goldman, Sachs and Company New York, New York
Reagan	Robert A. G. Monks** 1984 - 1985	President Institutional Shareholders Services, Inc. Washington, DC
Reagan	Jeffrey N. Clayton** 1981 - 1983	Partner Callister, Duncan and Nebecker Salt Lake City, Utah
Carter	Ian D. Lanoff** 1977 - 1981	Partner Bradhoff & Kaiser Washington, DC
Ford	William J. Chadwick** 1975 - 1977	Not Available
Ford	James D. Hutchinson** 1975 - 1976	President Capital Associates, Inc. Reston, Virginia

* Pension and Welfare Benefits Program established in 1976 by Employee Retirement Income Security Act.

** Held this position as Administrator, Pension and Welfare Benefit Programs, a Senior Executive Service position.

17

NATIONAL AERONAUTICS AND
SPACE ADMINISTRATION

After the tragedy of the Challenger mission in January, 1986, nothing seemed to go well for the space agency. Failures of two or three other programs followed, effectively if temporarily dropping the United States out of space. Investigation of the Challenger disaster brought disquieting disclosures about decision-making processes and relationships with contractors. The Soviet Union's space program continued to mark achievements, some of which, at least to the American public, contributed to the image of a U.S. effort which was falling far behind on the military as well as the scientific front. With uncertainty about the future and a drop in momentum and public confidence, NASA lost valuable career staff.

The agency will get a significant shot in the arm if the relaunch of the space shuttle program, which at this writing is scheduled for Fall, 1988, goes off without incident and future shuttle flights also succeed. Beyond that are plans for what an aerospace industry representative calls an "orbiting NASA facility"--a satellite space station reportedly expected to operate for 30 years as both a gravity-free laboratory and a launch platform for further deep-space probes.

But the debate continues on the larger question of what NASA's basic purpose and long-term assignments should be. On this subject, a former senior agency official feels, for example, that NASA needs an integrated, long-range plan on which everybody concerned, including the Congress, can agree, instead of the agency's current mode of going from one principal project to another. NASA is described as "a very internally motivated agency," whose desire to live up to a promised schedule that exceeded its capacities was partly responsible for Challenger's fall. A more measured and deliberate approach to the agency's overall mission could also be expected to communicate itself to individual programs like the shuttle.

A key determinant in any long-term plan, of course, will be money. Although NASA won a 15% hike in its fiscal 1989 funding and is said to need a further 20% increase in 1990, there are doubts that it will get it. Another former high-ranking agency insider predicts that the next President, of either party, will try to cut the agency's budget.

ADMINISTRATOR

Level II - Presidential Appointment with Senate Confirmation

Major Responsibilities

o   Plan and direct operations to support and conduct peaceful exploration of space and to promote research that has both practical and theoretical applications.   Create space programs with balanced scientific, engineering and operating components.

o   Manage the investigation of the problems of space flight. Oversee the design, construction and procurement of flight vehicles, and the conduct of unmanned and safe manned missions into near and distant space.   Maintain liaison with other governments on space matters. Employ NASA and other American technical resources to cooperate with other nations in peaceful space activities.

o   Advise the President on matters of U.S. space and space flight policy.   Inform the Congress on these subjects and work closely with it on agency budget and other requests.   Act as principal spokesman for U.S. space policy at home and abroad.

Necessary Background, Experience, Personal Skills

Engineering or scientific training and practice, plus a background in large-scale project development and management that features finance skills, must be the dominating--but not the only-- credentials of anyone considered for the position.   It would be helpful if this experience has developed a familiarity with the realities of federal procurement procedure, preferably in a military or space context, and to the Congressional considerations which relate to it.

Insight

In the woeful period for U.S. space programs that began with the Challenger disaster in early 1986, the watchword and rallying cry for NASA and the people running it has been a harsh one:

Get the United States back into space. For the administrator of this troubled, vital, constantly visible agency, that is the central goal--an urgent and elusive task, and one that carries the humiliating undertone of having to start again almost from square one. A successful shuttle flight in the late summer or fall of 1988 would provide an immeasurable boost for the agency, but will be only one promising step along a tough road back. That road, as defined by former NASA administrator James M. Beggs (1982-85), is "planning and operating this agency so as to gain and preserve a U.S. lead in space research."

In any such uphill battle, say the former NASA administrators we talked with, the right kind of leadership becomes not just important, but crucial. Alan M. Lovelace, who served as deputy administrator from the late Ford administration into the early Reagan months when he was also acting administrator, puts it this way: "Somebody is going to have to come into NASA and get them up out of the trenches. If you're going over the top, you're not going to do it with somebody who wants to hunker down. NASA has been through a lot of criticism, some of it justified, most of it the kind of stuff that just buys headlines. It's unjustified, but that's the perception. It becomes a reality for them and I sense they've gotten much more bureaucratic. They're afraid to take any risks."

Lovelace thinks the United States is "not the space power that we should be," not solely in military terms but with respect to "our position in the national community of scientists and engineers and scholars." Looking past the agency's current leadership to the future, he believes that, "to the degree that the administrator and the deputy provide leadership, so goes the national endeavor. You have to be sagacious enough to know when to stand up. The time is coming to stand up."

Not surprisingly, the administrator of NASA invests large amounts of time in planning and procurement for future programs, monitoring the technical and operational progress of existing projects, husbanding precious financial resources, plowing through senior interagency and White House meetings and defending NASA and its budget on the Hill. "Too much to do," is the way former administrator Robert A. Frosch (1977-80) sums it up. "Blood, sweat and tears."

But these and other regular functions on the administrator's schedule hint at only part of the job. Important as they are, they may in the long run mean less to NASA's future than efforts in other directions. The real measure of effectiveness for NASA's future chief could lie in how well that individual can deploy personal resources and talents in building public confidence in the agency, managing constituencies which can help or hinder its mission, assembling the necessary political building blocks, and encouraging staff development.

On the personnel front, for example, Beggs underlines the need to "develop executive talent to assure people are growing in their jobs and will be able to replace those who leave." Such an effort becomes all the more vital in light of what Lovelace calls "more disincentives" which have lessened NASA's attraction for "highly-qualified people" coming in from the outside. "Identify the people who can help get the job done and will make a good team," Frosch advises. "Most of them--almost all--will be civil servants. There are plenty of good ones to choose among, as well as people who can be brought into the agency."

Where constituencies are concerned, the administrator and deputy administrator must balance between several. Many interest groups are scientists--astronomers, planetary scientists and more-- and each group wants, through NASA, to do its own thing. The administrator must listen, apply independent judgment about NASA's best course on a given issue, and then explain it. If, as often happens, a constituent group doesn't like what it hears, it can and often does work politically to oppose the administrator's decision. "That," says Lovelace, "is our process and that's the one you live in. If you aren't a pragmatist and a realist about the world and how you get things done, you're going to be very frustrated."

One reality perceived by a former upper-level NASA executive is the perennial danger of "becoming a stepchild of the Defense Department, while still feeling that the agency is separate and needs to do its own things." NASA in recent years has not been viewed by any President "as an important part of what [an administration] is there to do," and therefore commands little attention from the White House. This former insider thinks the Defense Department depends less on NASA since the Challenger crash, since it has "gone back to building its own missiles," and in any event had to be "dragged kicking and screaming" into the shuttle project to begin with. "I think," he says, "NASA isn't going to grow in terms of projects or people unless some kinds of agreements are reached with the Russians for cooperative ventures, or peace breaks out and there are more civilian-type efforts like Kennedy had in mind."

Frosch thinks it essential that the administrator and deputy be able to work well together. Neither can carry the other, he warns. "It's a lean office and they must divide the load." Lovelace believes the administrator and the deputy also have to be the "translators and interpreters" to restore and increase public belief and support. "They have to tell the public what all this means. There are things you can relate in layman's language that are exciting to people." Moreover, in his view, NASA is like a publicly-held company, "paid for by the taxpayers and they own the stock. A publicly-owned company has to report to the stockholders." The agency needs to "go out and talk to people." Without intellectual curiosity, this country "isn't going to be a very nice place to live. And it is really exploration, not just of space, but exploration of any kind that is the soul of the human race."

In addition to technical credentials and management and administrative experience, some former administrators stress a third intellectual skill required by this job. "You've got to be able to deal at the political level," warns one of them. The laws of physics may flatly dictate only one way to achieve a mission and, technically, that might be the only way to go. "Politically, though, if you want to get from A to B, you may have to do it in ways that involve accommodation," he advises. "You have to listen, for example, to the Air Force. Where are they coming from and what is their motivation? How do I find a solution that serves my needs and theirs? Then you have to do that same thing in the political arena, on the Hill."

An incoming administrator should expect to testify often in Congress. Where general Congressional support for NASA was once crisp and direct, getting it has become substantially more difficult since Challenger. "The coin of the realm," Lovelace asserts, "is credibility. Congress looks at you (NASA) and says, I can trust you. Then you go off and do something that embarrasses them and they lose credibility with their constituencies. The only way they know how to recover is to come down hard on you."

Those who have had the job make some further points. "The administrator can probably do a percent or two of what obviously needs to be done," Frosch observes. "So the first task is to identify that percentage and try to stick to it." Lovelace would remind the next occupant of the position that NASA is not a cabinet agency. He agrees that the administrator does not get the kind of ready access to the President--the kind, for example, that regular staff meetings provide. "If he needs to see the President on an issue, he has to force it. He has to make it happen. You have to turn budget issues into policy issues in order to force the policy issue to the President's desk and get a hearing."

On the contentious issue of NASA's relationships with its contractors, the popular perception has been that they are perhaps too close. Lovelace thinks some of that has changed and the pendulum has swung back. "There has to be a close working relationship, but it can still be a very arm's length professional relationship."

"The serious accident" remains the agency's major problem, says Frosch. "Get the system flying as soon as possible in a safe mode," he advises. "Rebuild its scientific applications and the transportation program. Decide what you should and might accomplish and don't spend too much time doing other things if you can avoid them."

Key Relationships

Inside the Federal Government

Reports to: President

Works closely with:

> Secretary of Defense
> President's Assistant for National Security Affairs
> Science Advisor to the President
> Director, Research and Engineering, Department of Defense
> Secretary of the Air Force
> Undersecretary, National Oceanic and Atmospheric Administration, Department of Commerce
> Associate Director, Natural Resources, Energy and Science Affairs, Office of Management and Budget
> Deputy Secretary, Department of Transportation

Outside the Federal Government

> Foreign space, science, defense and diplomatic officials and their counterparts in international organizations; Aerospace Industries Association of America, Council of Defense and Space Industry Associations, other defense contractor groups and many individual aerospace engineering, construction, communications and research firms; scientific organizations in various disciplines; and academic institutions

Administrators of the National Aeronautics and Space Administration Since 1969

Administration	Name and Years Served	Present Position
Reagan	James C. Fletcher 1986 - Present	Incumbent
Reagan	James M. Beggs 1982 - 1985	Chairman Spacehab, Inc. Washington, DC
Reagan	Alan M. Lovelace(Acting) 1981	Vice President General Dynamics San Diego, California
Carter	Robert A. Frosch 1977 - 1980	Vice President Research Laboratories General Motors Corporation Warren, Michigan
Nixon/Ford	James C. Fletcher 1971 - 1976	Incumbent
Nixon	Thomas O. Paine 1969 - 1970	President Paine Associates Los Angeles, California

DEPUTY ADMINISTRATOR

Level III - Presidential Appointment with Senate Confirmation

Major Responsibilities

o   Assist the administrator in directing the operations of the agency and, where necessary, in its external relations. Serve as chief operating officer.

o   Assume direction of the agency in the absence of the administrator. Take a principal role in the conduct of its Congressional relationships in the areas of policy and operations.

o   Manage the agency's budget process--preparation, discussion and negotiation with the Office of Management and Budget, and support before Congressional budget and appropriations committees.

Necessary Background, Experience, Personal Skills

The position requires a strong technical background in the field of aeronautics or space operations and--most critical--significant experience in managing a large technical operation. Although the aerospace industry is a natural place to look, the agency itself is another. Prior service in NASA, in fact, comes close to being requisite for this job. Budget skills are important, as well as a grasp of budgetary and appropriations procedures in the Congress. These may have come through previous government service elsewhere in Washington at a management level, but a prospective appointee should also have had first-hand exposure to the private sector in areas relevant to what the agency does.

Insight

This position, and those of the administrator and the inspector general, are the only politically-appointed jobs in the space agency. There are no assistant secretary slots or other potential power centers where political appointees typically alight; NASA is a technically-based, "leanly-managed" organization, as a onetime agency official terms it, where the power resides in the top two jobs.

In the agency's history, the deputy administrator has usually run the place and the administrator has concentrated on the external, up-front responsibilities. But nothing is carved in stone. As in other such relationships, the individual strengths and personalities involved play a strong part in working out the two roles and, while the administrator is clearly the boss, the best system will result from intelligent decisions to play to, and exploit, those strong suits and talents. Alan M. Lovelace, who held the deputy job in 1976-81 (and served simultaneously as acting administrator for about half a year thereafter) estimates he spent 50 to 60% of his time on the internal management of the agency, and the rest in interagency, Congressional and other external activities.

NASA is budget-oriented, a program management agency of large and intricate projects. Some of those programs are important to the country's foreign and defense policies, but NASA is not a policy organization in the conventional sense and, in any case, its guidelines do not change much from administration to administration. The deputy administrator, who has a lot to say about how the agency's money is allocated, comes in for a great deal of budget-related activity on the Hill. Although assistant administrators testify on issues concerning their particular area of responsibility, it is the deputy--and often the administrator--who takes on the main role in testimony regarding the agency's overall budget and programs.

In fiscal 1989 the agency received a budget increase of around 15%; it will, we were told, need a 20% hike in fiscal 1990, in the first budget of the new administration. "I don't see how they're going to get that," a former associate administrator of NASA says. Unlike its earlier Apollo years, this veteran doesn't see the same "driving goals" for the agency, which has had "to scrabble to do things." In part, this was the problem with the Challenger shuttle program, he says, where NASA was "promising that it would do a lot and then trying to build it on the cheap."

Despite the concentration of management power at the top of the agency, informed and interested individuals who know the agency and have observed it over the years assert firmly that its strength is its operations in the field. These are ten diverse kinds of centers performing various missions across the country--in Texas, Florida, Alabama, Maryland, California and elsewhere. "That's where the technical abilities are, where the programs are run," says one of these sources. "The deputy administrator has got to understand he's running a complex of NASA centers. There are probably 20,000 people in NASA. Eighteen thousand are in the field," along with a large number of contractor employees. The agency's organizational structure, built around the centers, seems to have alternated between a system in which the center directors reported to the deputy administrator, and one in which management of the centers was split among center directors. The first gave the deputy an un-manageably broad control responsibility, and the other spawned overlap and confusion because most NASA projects are split among different centers, not assigned to just one of them. Either way, the deputy has a management problem of considerable magnitude.

Another NASA-watcher says the centers "have become a bureau-cracy unto themselves." Fueled by the initial U.S. attempt to rush into space, they peaked with the successes of the lunar phase of NASA history. The agency kept them nourished after that with decisions like the one to handle much of the Skylab program in-house, rather than contract it out. Similarly, with NASA now at work on the project to put a space station into a 30-year orbit, this observer says, "Congress has dictated that the work [be done by the centers]." Congressional delegations from states which are the locations of NASA centers "have a lot of clout." All of them are now "political strongholds," which will "exist and get a piece of the action irrespective of the appropriateness of that piece of action to the job to be done."

Though management is the cornerstone of this job, it seems to Lovelace that part of it is also "to look outward to the public and figure out how to get, not just more support but--how do you get kids turned on to space and science? How do you get the schools to start promoting the concept that this is important to our national development?" As one small example he points to technology, in the microlaboratory carried by the Viking lander to Mars, that has provided techniques applicable to the non-invasive analysis of infant health. "They will probably save lives," he says. "But who knows about it?"

Key Relationships

Within the Department

Reports to: Administrator

Works closely with:

Associate administrators
Space center directors

Outside the Department

Secretary of the Air Force
Undersecretary of the Air Force
Director, Research and Engineering, Department of Defense
Director, Commercial Space Transportation, Department of Transportation
Undersecretary, National Oceanic and Atmospheric Administration, Department of Commerce
Associate Director, Natural Resources, Energy and Science, Office of Management and Budget

Outside the Federal Government

Aerospace and related industries and their associations; construction, engineering and research companies; environmental groups; state and local governments

Deputy Administrators of the National Aeronautics and Space Administration Since 1969

Administration	Name and Years Served	Present Position
Reagan	Dale D. Myers 1987 - Present	Incumbent
Reagan	William R. Graham 1985 - 1986	Science Advisor Office of Science and Technology Policy Washington, DC
Reagan	Hans Mark 1982 - 1984	Chancellor University of Texas System Austin, Texas
Ford/Carter	Alan M. Lovelace 1976 - 1981	Vice President General Dynamics San Diego, California
Nixon/Ford	George M. Low 1969 - 1976	Deceased

18

DEPARTMENT OF
STATE

Established in 1789, the Department of State is the oldest of federal departments. Its budget is second smallest, at $3.7 billion in fiscal 1988, and its 26,000 employees rank it as sixth smallest. It operates almost 300 foreign posts ranging from embassies and missions to consulates general and consular agencies.

This venerable, vital department has steamed through increasingly stormy seas over recent years. Bad news has come in several varieties. A severely shrinking budget has brought the department to the threshold of a reduction in work force and further closures of diplomatic posts overseas. New foreign service legislation, designed to speed the advancement of promising middle-grade officers and prune the over-the-hill ranks, meant the loss of solid, experienced, able seniors. Terrorism has changed the expectations and operating styles of foreign policy people at home and abroad. The department has lost its foreign commercial function to another agency, and faces continuing challenges within the foreign policy community to its leadership role. Morale, suffering under these blows, isn't helped by what some department veterans view as a devaluation of the ambassadorial position and function.

But like a galleon of old, the ship of State carries treasure accumulated with great care and labor over long years, and not easily replaced. The department continues to carry out an essential, extensive mission which, even if it were conceivable, no other part of government would for years be able to do nearly as well. If the department loses significant headway and direction in the present rough weather, its considerable store of talent and high standards will dissipate and an incomparable base of experience and knowledge will decay. Indeed, some assert that those processes have already begun.

No one knows all the answers. Clearly, however, the next administration and the Congress must take the department's serious funding requirements deeply and permanently into account. State has never had the kind of domestic constituencies that other departments can energize in the Congress. Nonetheless, some of those who look at the situation from the vantage point of the Hill believe the department's management of its Congressional relationships has lost it valuable ground in the battle for resources. Some of this criticism goes to what is seen as a low level of directness and candor in testimony and a reticence about sharing information or seeking advice when the occasion calls for it. Some of it relates to a perceived recent instinct to confront the Congress with policy initiatives known to arouse Congressional concerns--or, conversely, to be unnecessarily deferential and erratic.

There seems to be some support among senior career veterans of the department for the view that part of its problem can be attacked by reorganization. One formula for this would reduce the number of undersecretaries and eliminate some of the layering in areas like economic affairs. Economic and political affairs would be grouped under one undersecretary and resources management and administrative support under another; the latter, and perhaps both, would be politically-appointed, and both would remain at the third-ranking level, under the secretary and deputy secretary. The career service would continue to handle geographic and functional responsibilities.

Another revision would concentrate control of the budget of the foreign affairs community in the hands of the secretary. In the words of a proponent of this change, the secretary, "as the principal foreign policy agent of the President, should make the decisions on how most effectively to spend the money the political process allocates for the conduct of foreign relations."

It's worth noting, finally, that the leadership positions of a number of American diplomatic missions abroad carry responsibilities which qualify them for mention. Although not described in detail here, these ambassadorial jobs should be the object of careful study in examining the skills and backgrounds of those who will fill them. Several qualified careerists who were asked about this listed Korea, the Philippines, Turkey, Pakistan, Canada, China, the Soviet Union and Mexico as foremost among the countries whose economic, political or strategic importance to the United States warrants such consideration.

DEPARTMENT OF STATE

SECRETARY

DEPUTY SECRETARY

ARMS CONTROL AND DISARMAMENT AGENCY

UNITED STATES INFORMATION AGENCY

AGENCY FOR INTERNATIONAL DEVELOPMENT

COUNSELOR

INSPECTOR GENERAL

UNDER SECRETARY FOR ECONOMIC AND AGRICULTURAL AFFAIRS

UNDER SECRETARY FOR POLITICAL AFFAIRS

UNDER SECRETARY FOR SECURITY ASSISTANCE, SCIENCE AND TECHNOLOGY

UNDER SECRETARY FOR MANAGEMENT

EXECUTIVE SECRETARY

LEGAL ADVISER

LEGISLATIVE AFFAIRS

PUBLIC AFFAIRS

POLICY PLANNING COUNCIL

PROTOCOL

EQUAL OPPORTUNITY AND CIVIL RIGHTS

COMPTROLLER

ADMINISTRATION

MEDICAL SERVICES

OFFICE OF FOREIGN MISSIONS

INTERNATIONAL COMMUNICATIONS AND INFORMATION POLICY

HUMAN RIGHTS AND HUMANITARIAN AFFAIRS

INTELLIGENCE AND RESEARCH

POLITICO-MILITARY AFFAIRS

DIPLOMATIC SECURITY

MANAGEMENT OPERATIONS

DIRECTOR GENERAL OF THE FOREIGN SERVICE AND PERSONNEL

FOREIGN SERVICE INSTITUTE

EUROPEAN AND CANADIAN AFFAIRS

AFRICAN AFFAIRS

ECONOMIC AND BUSINESS AFFAIRS

INTERNATIONAL NARCOTICS MATTERS

CONSULAR AFFAIRS

REFUGEE PROGRAMS

EAST ASIAN AND PACIFIC AFFAIRS

INTER-AMERICAN AFFAIRS

NEAR EASTERN AND SOUTH ASIAN AFFAIRS

INTERNATIONAL ORGANIZATION AFFAIRS

OCEANS AND INTERNATIONAL ENVIRONMENTAL AND SCIENTIFIC AFFAIRS

DIPLOMATIC, CONSULAR, AND OTHER ESTABLISHMENTS AND DELEGATIONS TO INTERNATIONAL ORGANIZATIONS

Shaded areas were selected as Prune Book positions

DEPUTY SECRETARY

Level II - Presidential Appointment with Senate Confirmation

Major Responsibilities

o Assist and support the secretary in the formulation, execution and enunciation of U.S. foreign policy. Act for the secretary, in his absence, on all matters, representing him at high-level interagency meetings and managing the operations of the department. Develop policy in areas of assigned geographic or functional responsibility. Operate as chief troubleshooter.

o Take a leading part in, and frequently direct, the process of identifying and recommending specific actions on a wide range of foreign policy issues, aimed at achieving stated objectives over time or to respond to developing situations requiring early U.S. attention.

o Undertake fact-finding, consultational or negotiating missions abroad as assigned by the secretary or the President.

Necessary Background, Experience, Personal Skills

No requisites exist for this position as to specific career history. To move confidently in the areas and kinds of problems most often involved, however, a deputy secretary with a good track record in the law or business seems to have a clear leg up. An experienced State Department watcher says that "management skills are primary." Negotiating and analytical experience have great value for this job, and the more that all these credentials have been acquired in an international context, the better. Prior work and residence abroad add a helpful resource, and knowledge of a world language can often speed or otherwise facilitate performance.

Insight

More than in most other departments, the stature and personal style of the Secretary of State usually define the real dimensions of the number two job. That, in turn, goes far in determining what individual abilities are most useful in the deputy's position, and who will be effective and satisfied in it. "There's no job description," asserts one former occupant. Rather, the nature of the job reflects "how the President wants to use his Secretary of State and how the secretary wants to use his deputy."

Whatever the equation turns out to be in a given administration, some key responsibilities of this job remain unchanged. Warren Christopher, who held the job in 1977-81, points out that the deputy secretary "inevitably has a direct relationship with the White House and, unless the situation is working very badly, with the President himself." When the secretary is away and the President is in Washington, which happens often, the deputy "has to be able to relate directly to the President," he says. That's important in considering candidates for the position, because a lot of people freeze in dealing with the President of the United States."

In his own right and as acting secretary--in duties that can range from running the department to testifying to the Congress to heading policy-oriented missions overseas--the deputy secretary has reasonably high public, political and diplomatic visibility. He needs an articulate personal presence and authority that can handle the television camera or speaker's rostrum, plus what a former deputy calls "a sense of the do-able, of what will fly politically." At the same time, says another, he must recognize and accept that, in many of his public and Congressional appearances, he will confront audiences which really prefer the Secretary of State. The deputy "will always be, in a sense, second best."

Even so, the occupant of this job needs a feel for Congressional propensities and sensitivities. At the Senate Foreign Relations Committee, with which the deputy has regular and frequent contact, an official thinks the Secretary of State should choose the deputy partly with the Congress in mind. The secretary, this authority says, ought to ask "how do I think this guy is going to help me deal with the Congress, whether it's on the budget issues or on the substantive foreign policy issues?"

The workload can assume desperate proportions. As a onetime deputy secretary remembers his tenure, the job means that "you're going to be thrown instantaneously into matters of high importance where you have relatively little background and have to try to catch up." This requires "somebody who is adaptable and quick, who'll be able to read the secretary and instinctively know what needs to be done. You don't want somebody who, when he gets that new assignment, immediately thinks he has to chart an entirely new course. He has to be able to pick it up and move it along."

Key Relationships

Within the Department

Reports to: Secretary

Works closely with:

Undersecretary for Political Affairs
Executive Secretary
Director of Policy Planning
Undersecretary for Management
Regional assistant secretaries
Legal Adviser

Outside the Department

President's Assistant for National
Security Affairs
Deputy Secretary, Department of the Treasury
Deputy Secretary, Department of Defense

Outside the Federal Government

Foreign policy and foreign affairs associations; think tanks; bar associations; business and trade groups; representatives of foreign governments at the most senior level

Deputy Secretaries of State Since 1969

Administration	Name and Years Served	Present Position
Reagan	John C. Whitehead 1985 - Present	Incumbent
Reagan	Kenneth W. Dam 1982 - 1985	Vice President IBM Armonk, New York
Reagan	Walter J. Stoessel, Jr. 1982	Deceased

Reagan	William P. Clark 1981 - 1982	Partner Rogers and Wells Washington, DC
Carter	Warren Christopher 1977 - 1981	Managing Partner O'Melveny and Myers Los Angeles, California
Ford	Charles W. Robinson 1976 - 1977	Chairman Energy Transition Corp. Santa Fe, New Mexico
Ford	Robert S. Ingersoll 1974 - 1976	Wilmette, Illinois
Nixon	Kenneth Rush 1973 - 1974	Manchester, Vermont
Nixon	John N. Irwin II* 1970 - 1973	Of Counsel Patterson, Belknap and Webb New York, New York
Nixon	Elliot Richardson* 1969 - 1970	Partner Milbank, Tweed, Hadley, and McCloy Washington, DC

*   Held the position as Undersecretary of State.

UNDERSECRETARY
MANAGEMENT

Level III - Presidential Appointment with Senate Confirmation

Major Responsibilities

o   Direct all management functions of the department, mobilizing and allocating department personnel and resources to support the department's policy priorities in Washington and around the world.

o   Maintain close formal and informal working relationships with the Congress on budget, resource allocation, foreign building construction and operation, and other management matters.

o   Supervise budget preparation and conduct the department's budget relationship with the Office of Management and Budget. With the deputy secretary, recommend career appointments at the ambassadorial level.

Necessary Background, Experience, Personal Skills

Views differ whether the management undersecretary should come from the career ranks of the department or from the outside. Regardless of origin, however, the consensus is that this position needs someone who knows the State Department, is familiar with how it and the Congress work, and understands the budget process and OMB. It does not permit on-the-job training.

Insight

The State Department's worst management problems in the past five years come down to three words--money, security and personnel. Serious alarm bells resounded in Washington and shook embassies abroad when the Congress seemed about to appropriate some $84 million less in salaries and operating expenses for fiscal 1988 than the department felt was the minimum necessary to continue functioning at existing levels. Plans for dramatic cutbacks in person-nel and foreign missions were announced. Only the White House-

Congressional budget summit in November, 1987 averted that particular axe. But, says Ronald I. Spiers, undersecretary since late 1983, that doesn't even represent a reprieve. "What we have is an agreement which gives us a two percent growth to cover an increase of 10.5 percent in our requirements--because of exchange rate losses and inflation differentials overseas--without any new programs. And we keep getting new programs." Since much of the department's outlay goes to personnel expenses, Spiers points out, "the handwriting's on the wall. We're going to have to shrink the work force of the State Department."

Establishing and sustaining the physical protection of U.S. diplomatic facilities at home and overseas has absorbed increased amounts of planning, time, effort and money. These demands seem unlikely to slacken in the visible future. Construction and renovation of U.S. missions abroad remain a continuing requirement; as an additional special task, the undersecretary coordinates plans to restore or rebuild the new but bug-ridden American Embassy building in Moscow (no decision at this writing).

Legislation in 1980 reorganized the senior foreign service personnel system with emphasis on an up-and-out philosophy. Seen at the time as a beneficial tonic to the service and the department, the new structure requires some decisions which "are painful for a lot of our foreign service officers," Spiers says. "Senior officers are unhappy with me because we give too few career extensions, and middle-level officers because we give too many, which tends to frustrate their promotion possibilities."

While he believes that problem "will solve itself in another couple of years," Spiers thinks the tough personnel decisions an undersecretary must share in are one argument against putting a professional career individual into the position. "This is a job where you do not make anybody happy," he explains, "and what that does is militate against your career interests. Further, he says, "you've inevitably got people on the Hill who are unhappy with you, particularly on the security front where I've had to argue against a lot of things they wanted to do which we believed didn't make sense."

The area of responsibility in this job covers a number of widely differing functions, among them budget, personnel, administration, communications, buildings, security, accounting, medical services, family liaison, and the Foreign Service Institute. Transfer payments--for such purposes as refugee and narcotics programs or United Nations dues--take half of the $4 billion budget the undersecretary manages. There is a $10 billion real estate operation to oversee. Travel overseas, to look at U.S. establishments and talk to employees at first-hand, absorbs up to a third of the time spent outside the office and can average 15-20 U.S. diplomatic missions a year. Spiers spends "a lot of time with the Congress, traveling with them, testifying, just chatting with members and staff. The Congressional dimension is very important."

Key Relationships

Within the Department

Reports to: Secretary

Works closely with:

Deputy Secretary
Undersecretary for Political Affairs
Regional and functional assistant secretaries

Outside the Department

Director, Office of Presidential Personnel, Executive Office of the President
Associate Director, National Security and International Affairs, OMB
Deputy Director for Administration, Central Intelligence Agency
Chairmen, members and staff, House and Senate Appropriations Committees, House Foreign Affairs Committee and Senate Foreign Relations Committee

Outside the Federal Government

Business Council and other business executive groups; American foreign service associations and other foreign service organizations

Undersecretaries for Management Since 1969

Administration	Name and Years Served	Present Position
Reagan	Ronald I. Spiers 1983 - Present	Incumbent

Reagan	Jerome W. VanGorkom 1982 - 1983	Chicago, Illinois
Reagan	Richard T. Kennedy 1981 - 1982	Ambassador at Large for Nuclear Proliferation Department of State
Carter	Ben H. Read* 1977 - 1981	Washington, DC
Carter	Richard M. Moose* 1977	Senior Vice President American Express Company Washington, DC
Nixon	Lawrence Eagleburger* 1975 - 1977	President Kissinger Associates Inc. New York, New York
Nixon	L. Dean Brown* 1973 - 1975	Not Available
Nixon	William B. Macomber,Jr.* 1969 - 1973	Not Available

* Served in this position when its title was Deputy Undersecretary of State for Management.

UNDERSECRETARY
POLITICAL AFFAIRS

Level III - Presidential Appointee with Senate Confirmation

Major Responsibilities

o   Oversee the day-to-day operations of the department on political matters, centering on five geographic and several functional bureaus.   Coordinate these when they involve more than a single bureau, sorting out priorities and overlapping responsibilities.

o   Review the alternatives for a wide range of daily actions which advance or sustain U.S. positions on international political issues, making decisions on many and sending others forward to the secretary or his deputy with recommendations.

o   Play a leading consultative and counseling role as a permanent member of the secretary's closest senior advisory group. Undertake special policy-making and management assignments and missions overseas as directed by the secretary.   Function as acting secretary when required.

o   Represent the department in senior inter-agency coordination and decisionmaking.

Necessary Background, Experience, Personal Skills

Established as the senior career position in the department, this job since the Nixon Administration has seen only career department officers (while of course requiring Senate confirmation).   One of the position's former occupants states flatly that appointment to it from the outside "is not a good idea."   But note carefully that he would also shun anyone who took merely a foreign service approach to the job.   In his words, "no one should be in that position without an appreciation of the political structure and the fact that the department and foreign service are part of the organization of an elected president."   In point of fact, the undersecretary operates most of the time in the busy intersection where professional service and political structure meet.   Understanding both, and the nature of the equation between them, is not optional equipment for this job; it is basic. An undersecretary also needs high-level management experience, perhaps developed by running an embassy abroad or a bureau in Washington, plus first-hand familiarity with the Congress, and expertise in one or more areas of the world.

Insight

If the Secretary of State fills the ace pitching slot on the senior department team and his deputy comes on when needed in long relief, the Undersecretary for Political Affairs operates as utility infielder. "There are no hard and fast guidelines about the assignment and permanence of responsibilities" at the top level, says David D. Newsom, who had the job from 1978 to 1981. "There is a management role on the seventh floor--the management of process. And the undersecretary is well-placed to try to get a sense of where things are on that floor and in the department generally, to be sure there is no uncertainty or overlapping of responsibilities."

An experienced Congressional source says "the idea of the undersecretary position is to focus on the major issues, making sure that what needs to be done down the line is done in terms of input and information and recommendations to the secretary. He ensures that all these issues are being addressed in a coherent way both for what the secretary sees and what flows down from him for action. The undersecretary plays to some extent a filtering and directing role in what the secretary ought to know in a critical area and what the secretary ought to be doing."

As coordinator for actions that cross bureau lines--the U.S. vote on a U.N. Security Council resolution, for example--the occupant of this position has to referee some occasionally awesome disputes over substance and jurisdiction. Three or four geographic and functional areas of the department might be involved. These and many other policy decisions, including guidance for the press spokesman, also require the undersecretary to determine whether he can act on his own authority or must consult at the highest level in the department or at the White House.

The New Yorker magazine in June, 1980 ran three articles by Robert Shaplen about this position. They still make informative reading. In them the author expresses a certain wonder at the number of daily issues facing the undersecretary, each deserving several days of study, that must often be dealt with in minutes. Between issues, however, also come the job's regular duties, such as agenda preparation for meetings between the secretaries of state and defense; and more occasional tasks, like heading an out-of-the-country negotiating mission. There are chronic problems, like the intermingling of personnel responsibilities with those of the Undersecretary for Management and the Director General of the Foreign Service; and intermittent irritations, such as senior officers who feel they can only deal directly with the secretary.

Former undersecretary Lawrence Eagleburger (1982-84) notes other problems of the chronic variety. "There's a tendency within the State Department," he says, "not to tell the seventh floor what's going on, and not to give alternatives so much as the preferred alternative." When necessary to force the development of genuine policy choices, he says, "you have to be a son of a bitch."

Key Relationships

Within the Department

Reports to:

Secretary
Deputy Secretary

Works closely with:

Executive Secretary
Regional and some functional assistant
secretaries
Director of Policy Planning
Undersecretary for Management
Undersecretary for Economic Affairs
Undersecretary for Security Assistance,
Science and Technology
Director General of the Foreign Service

Outside the Department

Deputy Secretary, Department of Defense
Undersecretary, International Security Affairs,
Department of Defense
Deputy Director of the Central Intelligence Agency
Deputy Assistant to the President for National
Security Affairs

Undersecretary, International Affairs, Department of Commerce

Outside the Federal Government

Ethnic associations; world affairs and foreign policy groups; foreign governments

Undersecretaries for Political Affairs Since 1969

Administration	Name and Years Served	Present Position
Reagan	Michael H. Armacost 1984 - Present	Incumbent
Reagan	Lawrence Eagleburger 1982 - 1984	President Kissinger Associates Inc. New York, New York
Reagan	Walter J. Stoessel, Jr. 1981 - 1982	Deceased
Carter	David D. Newsom 1978 - 1981	Director Institute for the Study of Diplomacy Georgetown University Washington, DC
Ford/Carter	Philip C. Habib 1976 - 1978	Belmont, California
Ford	Joseph J. Sisco 1974 - 1976	President Sisco Associates Washington, DC
Nixon	William J. Porter 1973 - 1974	Deceased
Nixon	Alexis V. Johnson 1969 - 1973	Washington, DC

ASSISTANT SECRETARY
ECONOMIC AND BUSINESS AFFAIRS

Level IV - Presidential Appointment with Senate Confirmation

Major Responsibilities

o   Develop short- and long-term recommendations for U.S. foreign economic policy, in consultation with the Secretary of State and with senior representatives of other government entities involved. Implement policy as approved by the Secretary and/or the President, through negotiations with other countries and by other actions. Advise the Secretary on international economic issues.

o   Provide substantive support to the Undersecretary for Economic and Agricultural Affairs and to the secretary in their own responsibilities for the department's role in foreign economic policy matters. As necessary, function as alter ego to the undersecretary in policy consultation, negotiation and implementation.

o   Direct the Bureau of Economic and Business Affairs.

Necessary Background, Experience, Personal Skills

The position requires a wide-ranging grasp of economics, with a strong substantive background in the historical development and goals of U.S. international economic policy. Familiarity with the current and imminent issues with which that policy must grapple, and the institutions and people involved, carries a large plus, especially when acquired in the private sector. Negotiating experience is important. A knowledgeable and empathetic approach to the stakes which other countries have in international trade, monetary relationships and economic development would enable the occupant to enhance both performance and results. Facility in a foreign language or two doesn't hurt, either.

Insight

The first thing to understand about this job concerns its

recently changed nature. After 1945, the State Department took much of the natural lead in formulating and applying foreign economic policy. Inevitably, this role suffered some gradual erosion as other government agencies claimed pieces of the action, and in 1979 the Congress transferred several major implementing functions elsewhere.

If some observers feel good reasons existed for these shifts, they acknowledge an unpleasant side effect--a partial diminishing of the assistant secretary's image in the foreign economic policy hierarchy. But Julius L. Katz, assistant secretary in 1976-79, says the department "does not have to have an operating role in every case. What it needs is a policy role--a major role--and it has to have a negotiating role." That, he feels, "comes about through the quality of the people doing it, not what's on an organization chart."

In any event, according to Katz, the job as it now exists "is generally and correctly perceived as one of the half dozen most difficult and demanding" headquarters posts the department has. Another who held the job cites a complicating factor--and a second point to keep in mind about the job: "Most secretaries of state understand intellectually that economic policy is an important part of foreign policy, but they can't seem to find the time...to tear themselves away from other things...."

In an important sense, that underlines the need for an efficient relationship between the assistant secretary and the undersecretary he works for. Lack of it raised problems for one former occupant of the job: "We were doing very similar things and our responsibilities were not clearly differentiated. Things would get confused --we'd be doing the same jobs." But another worked it out productively with his undersecretary: "We were alternates and tended to divide up issues--for example, he handled financial matters and I did trade, energy and resources. We didn't duplicate each other, and tried not to attend the same meetings. It's not meant to be a competitive relationship and it's important that it not be." He adds: "You need to select the undersecretary first, and he ought to have a hand in choosing the assistant secretary."

He thinks the ideal individual for the job is probably an investment (as opposed to a commercial) banker--someone who is "accustomed to dealing with multi-dimensional considerations, not just reducing everything to his own bottom line. When he's analyzing an investment he's looking at a whole number of factors. The kinds of problems we confront in this area are highly complex; we're always dealing with trade-offs. Investment bankers are used to that."

Outside relationships, including those at the White House and National Security Council, absorb large amounts of time and effort. "I had more contact with other members of the Cabinet than with the Secretary of State," Katz recalls. "You've got to be able to negotiate. You're negotiating all the time--more often with colleagues in and outside the department, and with private interests, than with foreigners. And, within certain limits, many of them are decision-making contacts." He encouraged his staff to develop balance in dealing with the private business community. "There is a tendency at State to regard the private sector as an enemy. But a second danger is to avoid getting in bed with them. You have to communicate with the private sector, understand their views, learn from them. It may just be that they're right and you're wrong."

Richard T. McCormack held the job in 1983-85, and strongly supports that view. "If you shut your door to those with an axe to grind," he suggests, "that axe is likely to reappear in part of your anatomy." McCormack says the job "requires mastery of the micropolitics of individual economic issues"--autos, energy, textiles, food policy, trade controls, maritime affairs, third-world debt-- across the full range of foreign economic policy. The micropolitics of negotiating an aviation agreement, in his hypothetical example, might oblige the assistant secretary to steer a delicate, fatiguing course between several semi-competitive interests--a foreign country, a U.S. airline, the White House, the Congress, other government agencies, and other offices within the State Department.

With such duties also comes that of running a large bureau supporting the undersecretary and secretary. Among the challenges former occupants see in this area are sagging morale and a deterioration in staff quality. One of them asserts that "the poorest bureau leaders have been those who were very strong individual players" with an affinity for the public limelight.

Finally, a previous tenant of the position raised what he sees as a major future preoccupation. "There is a view that the world has changed in some important ways that require changes in U.S. policy. Increasingly, our foreign economic policy is behaving as if we were now only a regional power and need to pursue our objectives through bilateral arrangements. The multilateral, open, non-discriminatory world we have believed was in our major interest is a proposition increasingly being challenged. It's easy to slip into such beliefs. We need to take a serious look and confirm whether they're true. This is a role for the State Department--no one else is going to do it--and the assistant secretary should be a major figure."

Key Relationships

Within the Department

Reports to:

Secretary
Undersecretary for Economic and
Agricultural Affairs

Works closely with:

Other assistant secretaries

Outside the Department

Assistant Secretary, Department of the Treasury
Other assistant secretaries in Agriculture,
Commerce, Labor, Energy, Transportation
departments
National Security Council Staff
U.S. Trade Representative

Outside the Federal Government

Most manufacturing industries and associations; airline,
communications and energy industries and associations;
financial institutions; trade associations

Assistant Secretaries for Economic and Business Affairs
Since 1969

Administration	Name and Years Served	Present Position
Reagan	Alan Larson (Acting) 1987-Present	Incumbent
Reagan	Douglas W. McMill 1985 - 1987	Not Available

Reagan	Richard T. McCormack 1983 - 1985	Permanent Representative of the Organization of American States Department of State
Reagan	Robert D. Hormats 1981 - 1982	Managing Director Goldman, Sachs and Company New York, New York
Reagan	Deane R. Hinton 1980 - 1981	Not Available
Carter	Julius L. Katz 1976 - 1979	President The Government Research Corporation Washington, DC
Ford	Joseph A. Greenwald 1976	Attorney-At-Law Washington, DC
Ford	Thomas O. Enders 1974 - 1975	Managing Director Salomon Brothers New York, New York
Nixon	Willis C. Armstrong 1972 - 1974	Not Available
Nixon	Philip H. Trezise 1969 -1971	Not Available

ASSISTANT SECRETARY
AFRICAN AFFAIRS

Level IV - Presidential Appointment with Senate Approval

Major Responsibilities

o   Work closely with the secretary in developing U.S. foreign policy toward the countries of Africa. Oversee policy implementation and articulation abroad and at home.

o   Supervise the operations of American embassies and missions in the 50-plus African countries, including their budgeting and staffing, and protection of American citizens and business and commercial interests. Play an advisory role in the selection of U.S. ambassadors to Africa.

o   Coordinate interagency activities involving African matters, such as U.S. economic assistance. Chair interdepartmental meetings concerned with decisions on African issues or with policy recommendations to the National Security Council.

o   Direct the Bureau of African Affairs. Represent it in budget questions at the Office of Management and Budget and in the Congress. Take overall responsibility for relations with African diplomatic representatives and visitors in Washington, and for the dialogue with U.S. interest groups.

Necessary Background, Experience, Personal Skills

To be effective, the occupant has to draw on a high degree of expertise and wisdom in African affairs, achieved through residence, study, or a hands-on background in business or diplomacy--preferably, all of these. Nor should one approach this job without experience in the dynamics of third world economic development and an understanding of what one veteran calls the "politics of human rights" and the phenomenon of apartheid in southern Africa. An ability to speak and understand French is important.

Insight

Sub-Saharan Africa has long suffered the brutalizing impact of two intertwined struggles which exert some domestic political effect on the assistant secretary. One of these involves racial segregation in the continent's most advanced country. The other embraces a handful of internal armed conflicts in which the factions reflect the typically opposed interests of the superpowers in a third-world context. In the United States, political and ideological frictions usually generated in debates on apartheid and the U.S.-Soviet rivalry can make the management of relevant U.S. national interests in Africa uncomfortably warm.

Beyond those quandaries lie other more conventional but equally chronic sources of trouble such as recurrent starvation in Ethiopia and the Sudan, and the spasmodic restlessness of Libya's Khadafi.

From an operational viewpoint, the job's occupant still has a two-way educational challenge which remains more characteristic of his geographic area of responsibility than those of his regional counterparts. First, secretaries of state have traditionally paid less attention to Africa than to other areas and issues. This attitude has usually been dictated by necessity, even while developments since 1986 have clearly begun to change it. But it has tended to shape approaches to Africa among other busy senior department officers. An incoming assistant secretary should understand that "Africa is not a top priority for the U.S. and that American interests are more vital in other areas," says one who held the job. "I felt it was incumbent on me to make it my responsibility to educate them. The people to whom you report still need a lot of information." If South Africa and one or two other problem areas now escape that definition, the rest of Africa does not.

Second, in this view, American attitudes need explaining to Africans. "You need historical perspective not only on Africans but also on how American society tends to view Africans....One has to understand that American cultural biases are not necessarily understandable to Africans, and vice versa. You have to make them understandable."

Like other regional assistant secretaries, this one travels a good deal. A previous occupant estimates he spent 25% of his total working time seeing African leaders and officials, in their countries and his own. The social schedule can be formidable. "Sometimes," says another, not totally in jest, "I believed stamina was more important than intelligence."

Of the complexities of the job, he adds: "One gets a bit frustrated, but that's the challenge. To realize that you are responsible for relations with that many countries should be enough to make it attractive." Newcomers to the position, he says, should always see their objectives in relation to the established emphases of the broader foreign policy picture. Above all, he counsels, "don't arrive with solutions. If you do, you'll fail."

Key Relationships

Within the Department

Reports to: Secretary

Works closely with:

Deputy Secretary
Undersecretary for Political Affairs
Other regional assistant secretaries
Assistant Secretary for Economic and
    Business Affairs
Assistant Secretary for International
    Organization Affairs
Director of Policy Planning

Outside the Department

Assistant Secretary, International Security
    Affairs, Department of Defense
President's Assistant for National Security Affairs
U.S. Permanent Representative to the United Nations
Assistant Secretary, International Economic Policy,
    Department of Commerce
Counterpart in the Central Intelligence Agency

Outside the Federal Government

Academics specializing in African affairs; African-American organizations; companies signatory to the Statement of Principles (concerning South Africa); lobbying groups such as TransAfrica; U.S. corporations with interests in Africa; and church leaders

Assistant Secretaries for African Affairs Since 1969

Administration	Name and Years Served	Present Position
Reagan	Chester A. Crocker 1981 - Present	Incumbent
Carter	Richard M. Moose 1977 - 1981	Senior Vice President American Express Company Washington, DC
Ford/Carter	William E. Schaufele,Jr. 1975 - 1977	Salisbury, Connecticut
Ford	Nathaniel Davis 1975	Hixson Professor of Humanities Harvey Mudd College Claremont, California
Ford	Donald B. Easum 1974 - 1975	President African American Institute New York, New York
Nixon	David D. Newsom 1969 - 1974	Director, Institute for the Study of Diplomacy Georgetown University Washington, DC

ASSISTANT SECRETARY
EAST ASIAN AND PACIFIC AFFAIRS

Level IV - Presidential Appointment with Senate Confirmation

Major Responsibilities

o   Advise and assist the secretary in devising and implementing
    U.S. policy towards the countries of east and southeast Asia,
    the Pacific region and Australia and New Zealand.   Manage
    the inter-agency consultations integral to that process.

o   Represent the department in multi-agency efforts to deal with
    special problems like those surrounding U.S. servicemen missing
    in southeast Asia, children in Vietnam fathered by American
    citizens, and heroin trafficking.

o   Oversee the operations of the Bureau of East Asian and Pacific
    Affairs.   Advise on the assignment of U.S. envoys and supervise
    their performance and that of two dozen diplomatic missions
    under their leadership.   Defend the bureau's budget to the
    Congress and the Office of Management and Budget.   Decide on
    key personnel appointments in the field and in the bureau.

Necessary Background, Experience, Personal Skills

"I don't mean to sound arrogant," says one who held this
job, "but there shouldn't be any surprises" for the individual coming
into this job.   "Know the ground on which you walk.   Know it
authoritatively, or you won't be very effective."   As expressed by
another former occupant, this means "it is essential to have worked
in the area" long enough to know it thoroughly.   A third: "I studied,
visited, worked on and knew a lot about the countries concerned."
All three were career diplomats with extensive service in the area
and years of working with its governments and people.   At a minimum, candidates for the position need the equivalent of a black
belt in Chinese affairs, southeast Asia, or the Japan-Korea-Taiwan-
Singapore economic and trade matrix--and close familiarity with
the other two.

Insight

Not surprisingly, the complicated and equally critical U.S. relationships with Japan and China take much of the attention and energy of the occupant of this job. The world impact of Japanese economic strength and China's currently brisk pace of economic and political change top the list of preoccupations. In managing U.S. policy toward each country day-to-day, the assistant secretary needs to move confidently amid a vast amount of up-close detail while maintaining perspective on the thrust and effectiveness of policy.

A number of related questions, important in their own right, flank these concerns both within and beyond Asia. The relevance of developments in China to directions Moscow may take, or the effect on long-range planners in Tokyo of pressure from Asia's newly-industrializing countries, are only two of the most obvious.

No less demanding of careful attention are Korea and the Philippines. There, democracy's fragile revival will require alert American counsel and support to survive and grow stronger. Resolving the fate of missing American servicemen still unaccounted for in southeast Asia--and Vietnam's continuing role in Cambodia--will present special challenges into the visible future.

Despite the focus on facts and figures, former assistant secretary John H. Holdridge (1981-83) advises, one must have "a sense of people. You're not dealing with statistics, but with people. It takes judgment and tact--I guess it's called diplomacy." It also takes an acute sensitivity to cultural differences that figure significantly in what the United States can accomplish in this part of the world. Further, says another who held the job, performance benefits from the time and patience to ensure that immediate and seemingly urgent developments don't obliterate the long-range view.

While avoiding this kind of myopia, however, the assistant secretary must regularly and personally lead the trouble-shooting effort when problems arise. When he had the job, says Philip C. Habib (1974-76), "I kept traveling to these countries until I was able to work out a solution--in other words, by working my arms and feet off. It was a seven-days-a-week job." Which is to say that the occupant of the job lives out of a suitcase much of the time, ranging across the Pacific and within this country on special missions and visits, and in general diplomatic and public affairs activity.

Key Relationships

Within the Department

Reports to: Secretary

Works closely with:

Deputy Secretary
Undersecretary for Political Affairs
Other regional assistant secretaries
Undersecretary for Management

Outside the Department

Assistant Secretary, International Security
Affairs, Department of Defense
President's Assistant for National Security Affairs
Associate Director, National Security and Inter-
national Affairs, Office of Management and Budget
Counterpart in the Central Intelligence Agency

Outside the Federal Government

Asian-American business and cultural associations;
Asian ethnic groups; Vietnam veterans; families of
missing-in-action servicemen

Assistant Secretaries for East Asian and Pacific Affairs Since 1969

Administration	Name and Years Served	Present Position
Reagan	Gaston J. Sigur, Jr. 1986 - Present	Incumbent
Reagan	Paul D. Wolfowitz 1982 - 1986	U.S. Ambassador to Indonesia Department of State
Reagan	John H. Holdridge 1981 - 1983	Bethesda, Maryland

Carter	Richard C. Holbrooke 1977 - 1981	Managing Director Shearson/Lehman Brothers New York, New York
Carter	Arthur W. Hummel, Jr. 1976 - 1977	Not Available
Ford	Philip C. Habib 1974 - 1976	Belmont, California
Ford	Robert S. Ingersoll 1974	Wilmette, Illinois
Nixon	Marshall Green 1969 - 1973	Washington, DC

ASSISTANT SECRETARY
EUROPEAN AND CANADIAN AFFAIRS

Level IV - Presidential Appointment with Senate Confirmation

Major Responsibilities

o   Advise the secretary on political, economic and military developments in European and Canadian affairs, especially as they affect U.S. relationships and objectives on subjects as diverse as
terrorism and grain sales or West Berlin and currency fluctua-
tions. With the National Security Council, coordinate the work
of the department and other elements of government in shaping
recommended initiatives which respond to such developments or
which pursue long-term policy goals in Europe and Canada.

o   Play a central policy-making and implementing role in the
U.S.-Soviet relationship, with particular emphasis on nuclear
and conventional weapons questions.

o   Manage the Bureau of European and Canadian Affairs. Make
the key decisions on budget and work load, and take a leading
part in senior personnel assignments in the field and the Bureau.
Act in an advisory role in the selection of ranking U.S. diplomats in Europe and Canada, and supervise them and the missions they lead. Maintain close ties with the European diplomatic
community in Washington.

Necessary Background, Experience, Personal Skills

Beyond a first-hand and profound understanding of Europe
and Europeans, one might next look for the ability to engage sophisticated and experienced European diplomats and leaders in a convinc-
ing and productive way. As with counterpart positions for the
other geographic regions, this is no place for novices. The occupant
of the job must take it on with a demonstrated knowledge of U.S.
goals in Europe, the policies which undergird them, and many of
the principal players. Those who have held this post over the last
two decades were career foreign service officers with long backgrounds in European affairs, or individuals whose service in other
senior executive foreign policy positions gave them similar exposure.

Conceivably, a corporate executive with lengthy on-the-ground experience in Europe and close ties to the foreign affairs and business communities there and at home could also handle the assignment effectively.

Insight

Some European nations are among our oldest friends in war, peace, and basic political and social outlook. Some, in varying degrees, have been among our oldest antagonists. Some are a little of both. Tending America's complicated, carefully nuanced and indispensable network of relationships in such an area remains one of U.S. diplomacy's toughest, most important tasks. In it, this job carries heavy responsibility.

One can argue that this position takes on further potential weight in light of emerging economic and political trends which suggest that dramatic shifts in relations with both Europes may lie ahead. Whatever direction events take, however, the hard-won lessons of U.S. foreign policy in Europe and the basic principles which drive it will continue as the essential backdrop against which the position operates.

In recent years, this assistant secretary has become a leading team member in managing the dialogue and process of arms control and reduction with the Soviet Union. It's a role that draws quantities of time and effort away from other matters and imposes greater public affairs demands than strictly regional activities do. How this responsibility evolves will depend, of course, on the particular abilities and expertise of the job's occupant and, equally, on the predilections of the secretary and the President.

Another singular dimension of the job grows out of the simple fact that Europe hosts many international institutions and activities important to U.S. policy. There are the NATO alliance, the European Community, arms negotiations, and annual economic summit meetings which four times of every seven convene in Europe--to name only a few. There is the world's only other current superpower. Together, these engage the energies and constant focus of huge segments of official Washington. They attract the attention of the President himself, offering more frequent requirements--and more tempting opportunities--for his personal participation than do other parts of the world. "It was fantastic...it exceeded my expectations," says a former assistant secretary about the occasions afforded by his job to advise the topmost officers of government. Perhaps by the same token, former assistant secretaries for Europe and

Canada seem to have found more problems than their regional colleagues in what one called "the organizational relationships with
NSC staff."

The occupant of the position should expect a grueling work
schedule, frequently seven days a week, of travel, conferences,
meetings, negotiations, and social engagements.

Key Relationships

Within the Department

Reports to: Secretary

Works closely with:

Other Assistant Secretaries of State
Undersecretary for Management
Undersecretary for Political Affairs

Outside the Department

President's Assistant for National Security Affairs
Assistant Secretary, International Security Affairs,
Department of Defense
Counterpart in the Central Intelligence Agency

Outside the Federal Government

European-U.S. cultural organizations, manufacturers
and trade associations; arms control groups; foreign
policy associations; think tanks

Assistant Secretaries for European and Canadian Affairs
Since 1969

Administration	Name and Years Served	Present Position
Reagan	Rozanne L. Ridgway 1985 - Present	Incumbent

Reagan	Richard R. Burt 1983 - 1985	U.S. Ambassador to Germany Department of State
Reagan	Lawrence Eagleburger 1981 - 1982	President Kissinger Associates New York, New York
Carter	George S. Vest 1977 - 1981	Director General of the Foreign Service Department of State
Ford/Carter	Arthur A. Hartman 1974 - 1977	Washington, DC
Nixon	Walter J. Stoessel, Jr. 1972 - 1974	Deceased
Nixon	Martin J. Hillenbrand 1969 - 1972	Director Center for Global Policy Studies University of Georgia Athens, Georgia

ASSISTANT SECRETARY
INTER-AMERICAN AFFAIRS

Level IV - Presidential Appointment with Senate Confirmation

Major Responsibilities

o   Assist in formulating and carrying out U.S. policy in Latin America. Monitor events and trends in the region, interpreting them and briefing and counseling the secretary. Develop policy recommendations adhering to U.S. objectives and foreign policy principles. Execute policy through the bureau and U.S. diplomatic missions in the area, taking a personal up-front role as required.

o   Direct the Bureau of Inter-American Affairs, which includes the U.S. Permanent Mission to the Organization of American States, and the operations of U.S. embassies in Central and South America and the Caribbean. Oversee policy dissemination to the field and day-to-day crisis management. Preside over senior personnel decisions and play a role in ambassadorial appointments.

Necessary Background, Experience, Personal Skills

Candidates for this job should have a solid working knowledge of Spanish or Portuguese and a firm grip on the fundamentals and much of the detail of Latin America's current posture and history, particularly with respect to its relations with the United States. Also required: A strong and realistic appreciation not only of Latin America's problems but of the nature of possible solutions. Diplomatic or business experience in the region, developed at least partly in residence there, is highly recommended.

Insight

Given Latin America's geographic, social and ethnic disparities, a prime skill for this assistant secretary can reasonably be defined as the "ability to break a problem down to manageable pieces that can be solved." But the former occupant of the job who makes this point also emphasizes that, to solve a piece of a problem, one must design a policy "which is realistic within the bounds of the resources available and its domestic acceptability." This normally takes place in an often-intense interagency process of debate and compromise.

Crafting policy successfully also means continuous and productive contact with the Congress. This and public and diplomatic representation and defense of U.S. positions and policies in Latin America require large investments of time and concentration. Politically, this job is currently among the most exquisitely sensitive in Washington. One recent occupant counts 47 Congressional hearings in which he testified and submitted to questions in a period of two years. The personal virtues he finds useful in these aspects of the job are "the patience and ability to communicate, to know how to use the different media."

The major preoccupations of this job? Arguably, these are Latin America's debt crisis--upwards of $300 billion at this writing; the region's struggle for continued economic growth; and, of course, the long political-military conflict in Central America towards which U.S. policy in the last decade has been as ineffective as it has been uncertain. As most people recognize, these exert a direct and profound effect on domestic political debate, on the state of U.S. relations with individual countries of the area, and on the pursuit of overall U.S. objectives. By consequence, the assistant secretary faces a bigger task across the range of his responsibilities in a variety of other matters. These can be as big and tough as the drug trade and the travails of U.S. banks holding Latin American debt, or as seemingly manageable as landing rights for U.S. airlines and the world prices of commodities like sugar and coffee.

To Latin American leaders and officials, in the region and in Washington, the assistant secretary thus must almost continuously explain, mediate and negotiate, attempting where necessary to stave off crisis and seeking to devise solutions. In the words of one who has traveled this road, the job's occupant must "suggest U.S. policy to a world in which resources are less, the U.S. has a lower capacity to affect problems, and the area is changing greatly."

Key Relationships

Within the Department

Reports to: Secretary

Works closely with:

Deputy Secretary
Undersecretary for Economic and Agricultural Affairs
Assistant Secretary for Economic and
  Business Affairs
Other regional assistant secretaries
Legal Adviser

Outside the Department

Assistant Secretary, International Affairs,
  Department of the Treasury
Undersecretary, International Trade, Department of
  Commerce
Undersecretary, International Affairs and Commodity
  Programs, Department of Agriculture
President's Assistant for National Security Affairs
Assistant Secretary, International Security Affairs,
  Department of Defense
Counterparts at the Central Intelligence Agency and
  the office of the Joint Chiefs of Staff

Outside the Federal Government

Human rights and church organizations; U.S.-Latin
American associations; U.S. Chamber of Commerce;
AFL-CIO; AID program contractors

Assistant Secretaries for Inter-American Affairs Since 1969

Administration	Name and Years Served	Present Position
Reagan	Elliot Abrams 1985 - Present	Incumbent
Reagan	Langhorne A. Motley 1983 - 1985	President L.A. Motley and Company Washington, DC
Reagan	Thomas O. Enders 1981 - 1983	Managing Director Salomon Brothers New York, New York

Carter	William G. Bowdler 1980 - 1981	Northern Neck, Virginia
Carter	Viron P. Vaky 1978 - 1979	Senior Associate Carnegie Endowment for International Peace Washington, DC
Carter	Terence A. Todman 1977 - 1978	U.S. Ambassador to Denmark Department of State
Carter	Harry W. Shlaudeman 1976 - 1977	Not Available
Ford	William D. Rogers 1974 - 1976	Partner Arnold and Porter Washington, DC
Nixon/Ford	Jack B. Kubisch 1973 - 1974	Not Available
Nixon	Charles A. Meyer 1969 - 1973	Not Available

ASSISTANT SECRETARY
NEAR EASTERN AND SOUTH ASIAN AFFAIRS

Level IV - Presidential Appointment with Senate Confirmation

Major Responsibilities

o   Play a principal part in formulating and recommending U.S. policy in the areas of diplomacy and military and economic assistance in the Middle East and South Asia, assisting the secretary in that effort.   Represent the department in senior interagency consultations and articulate administration policy on Capitol Hill.

o   Monitor and report on developments in the geographic areas of responsibility.   See that necessary decisions and responses flow in a timely and coordinated manner.

o   Supervise the activities of the Bureau of Near Eastern and South Asian Affairs, and of about 25 U.S. diplomatic missions, in the implementation of policy.   Oversee budget and personnel management.   Participate in the selection of chiefs of mission for area posts.

Necessary Background, Experience, Personal Skills

As with the other regional jobs at State at this level, nothing short of lengthy, first-hand exposure to the cultural and political history and the problems and peoples of the two areas--accompanied by a detailed grasp of U.S. policy objectives--will really meet the need.   Those in the job over at least the past 15 years have been career foreign service officers.   "Time in the field, in the missions, having lived in the region" is the way one of them sums it up. The selection process for this position should also emphasize executive experience and an ability to correctly judge and manage crisis.

Insight

Unless things change significantly before January, 1989, the conflict in the Persian Gulf will continue as the top headache facing the United States in the Middle East. In projecting that likelihood, however, Richard W. Murphy, assistant secretary since 1983, thinks the new administration will have "a second, almost equal priority:" the effort to resolve Arab-Israeli differences. Newly exacerbated by the West Bank and Gaza clashes that began in late 1987, this "is an enormously complicated problem" which, says Murphy, "is an issue with such heavy domestic political content--as well as complexities in the region--that the new team will want to take time to see what stamp they want to put on it." In this regard, he adds, "we are trying now to package things up to have them in the best possible condition for decisionmaking by the new team."

Though Soviet troops by the end of 1988 may have exited Afghanistan--the third-ranking priority for this position--the focus on the political future of that country will continue to increase. Other principal matters for attention are the ever-testy India-Pakistan relationship, in which U.S. military assistance to Pakistan has continued to stir Indian suspicions; and the direction and status of Pakistan's nuclear program--and India's.

The assistant secretary invests great amounts of time in keeping abreast of these varied, evolving and crisis-prone questions and designing and fine-tuning policy. Doing this, and developing the right responses to particular events, mean limitless rounds of guidance and policy meetings inside and outside the department and trips to the Congress. Steadying and supporting U.S. relationships and advancing American policy in the Middle East and South Asia require a taxing amount of travel and time. Those who have carried these responsibilities make it clear that nothing can substitute for on-the-ground experience, enough time for its lessons to soak in-- and specific knowledge and skills. "You've got to have a background in the conflicts of those areas," says Alfred L. Atherton, Jr., assistant secretary from 1974 to 1978, "and experience in conducting negotiations."

Murphy illustrates good preparation for the job this way: "Someone who's watched the aid programs, how they operate in the field, what the types of resources are, how you can organize and manage substantial programs, what the implications of a shift in our aid budgets are for our political relationships in the area. There is so much detail that you can't soak up purely intellectually, sitting here in this office. You can easily be oblivious to an enormous number of things that are going on and making a difference to the governments out there and to our relationships."

Like most bureaus and offices in most government agencies, this one lives with a certain number of jurisdictional and policy frictions. Effective counter-terrorism policy, for example, is a department-wide standard which all bureaus at State support and share. But shaping a consensus on that policy can involve conflicting objectives when looked at from a broad or narrow perspective. In another quarter, because this bureau tends to handle its relationships and contacts on the Hill rather independently of the Congressional affairs office, an awkward relationship has developed. Further, because the bureau handles nearly half of the department's foreign assistance funds, it attracts a certain natural envy from other regional bureaus which would like more of the action.

But the bureau can also claim a different kind of fame within the department. As Murphy points out, "we rack up 60%-plus of the department's crisis-management operations--the hijackings, killings, assassinations, and wars."

Key Relationships

Within the Department

Reports to: Secretary

Works closely with:

Deputy Secretary
Undersecretary for Political Affairs
Assistant Secretary for Economic and Business Affairs
Other regional assistant secretaries
Assistant Secretary for Legislative Affairs

Outside the Department

Senior Director, Near East and South Asian Affairs,
National Security Council
Assistant Secretary, International Security Affairs,
Department of Defense
Assistant Secretary, International Economic Policy,
Department of Commerce
Counterpart at the Central Intelligence Agency

Outside the Federal Government

Jewish-American and Arab-American organizations; business firms mainly in the defense area; foreign policy and world affairs groups; colleges and universities; think tanks

Assistant Secretaries for Near East and South Asian Affairs Since 1969

Administration	Name and Years Served	Present Position
Reagan	Richard W. Murphy 1983 - Present	Incumbent
Reagan	Nicolas A. Veliotes 1981 - 1983	President Association of American Publishers, Inc. Washington, DC
Carter	Harold H. Saunders 1978 - 1981	Visiting Fellow The Brookings Institution Washington, DC
Ford	Alfred L. Atherton, Jr. 1974 - 1978	Director The Harkness Fellowships Washington, DC
Nixon	Joseph J. Sisco 1969 - 1974	President Sisco Associates Washington, DC

LEGAL ADVISER

Level IV - Presidential Appointment with Senate Approval

Major Responsibilities

o   Serve as principal legal officer of the department. Advise the secretary on the international legal implications involved in making and executing specific policy decisions, and devise and recommend solutions. Provide regional and functional bureaus with legal input and effective and justifiable courses of action. Function where necessary as a member of negotiating teams supporting the secretary and other senior officials.

o   Serve as adviser to the executive branch on issues of international law and act as the ultimate authority on all questions of treaty law and international agreements. Oversee the department's legal advisory and implementing role in such areas as settlement of international claims and visa questions. Represent the department in matters of international criminal justice.

o   Assist the secretary in defining international issues in legal terms understandable and defendable to other cabinet departments, the Congress and constituent groups.

Necessary Background, Experience, Personal Skills

The position clearly demands an established and experienced attorney with a full legal career and an unassailable background in international law. "He ought to be a prominent lawyer," in the view of a knowledgeable authority, "not necessarily a scholar, but somebody with a first-rate reputation in the field." The value of previous service in government and/or in business at a senior level cannot be overestimated. An attractive candidate for the job would preferably also offer a knowledge of world affairs and some exposure to various aspects of other national societies--their laws, diplomacy, and approach to negotiating.

Insight

"Probably the most exciting job, legally, in the U.S. government aside from the Attorney General's," declares a formal legal adviser. "To have the U.S. government as a client is a wonderful experience," states another. But he warns that, like clients in private practice, this one may sometimes have a hard time with the fact that "lawyers always say no." The necessary but unpopular role of naysayer-- "advising what's legal and what isn't"--can be especially tough, he says, "when you want to be able to work as a member of a team."

This doubtless relates directly to a problem lamented by several previous occupants of the job: The apparently long-standing tendency not to include the legal adviser at the outset of the decision- making process. This "reluctance to consult in a timely manner," as one of them discreetly puts it, may not occur in every instance. But when it does, another legal adviser says, it results uncomfor- tably in having to justify decisions after the fact.

But the legal adviser should not allow operating difficulties like these to cloud his vision, says an observer of department decision- making. "It requires somebody of great independence and integrity to tell the emperor that he has no clothes when he doesn't, to warn the secretary and the administration when they're going to step into something that smells bad." More than simply doing the sec- retary's bidding, this source argues, "the more important thing is to give the secretary--and through him, the President--honest, unbiased and independent counsel as to what's the smart thing to do, the right thing to do, the Constitutional thing to do."

Over the last 20 years, the legal adviser's work has ranged over an increasingly broad landscape. It has notably included Constitu- tional questions about Presidential authority to commit U.S. military forces to hostilities abroad, disputes about the negotiating and legis- lative histories of arms control agreements, a role in exceptionally delicate negotiations to free Americans held hostage overseas, and extradition and enforcement efforts against international drug traf- ficking, terrorism and organized crime. This expanding territory leads some of those who have held the job to stress the "critical" importance of building "relationships of confidence" in the department and outside it, and of helping the secretary to "explain policy and justify and marshall support for it."

Key Relationships

Within the Department

> Reports to:
> Secretary
> Deputy Secretary

> Works closely with:

> Regional and functional assistant secretaries

Outside the Department

> Undersecretary, Policy, Department of Defense
> Associate Attorney General, Department of Justice
> General counsel of other departments

Outside the Federal Government

> American and other bar associations; a wide variety
> of legal counsels for corporations, foreign governments,
> and international organizations

Legal Advisers of State Since 1969

Administration	Name and Years Served	Present Position
Reagan	Abraham D. Sofaer 1985 - Present	Incumbent
Reagan	Davis R. Robinson 1981 - 1985	Partner Pillsbury, Madison and Sutro Washington, DC
Carter	Roberts B. Owen 1979 - 1981	Partner Covington and Burling Washington, DC
Carter	Herbert J. Hansell 1977 - 1979	Not Available

Ford	Monroe Leigh 1975 - 1977	Partner Steptoe and Johnson Washington, DC
Nixon	Carlyle E. Maw 1973 - 1974	Not Available
Nixon	John R. Stevenson 1969 - 1973	Partner Sullivan and Cromwell Washington, DC

19

DEPARTMENT OF TRANSPORTATION

To manage its responsibilities for how people and things move through a large, populous, mobile, industrialized and urbanized country, this heavily regulatory department divides itself into separate components for each "mode" of transportation. Atop this structure, the secretary and deputy secretary and functional supporting offices provide basic policy direction and management and administrative services.

The comments of many of those who held executive positions in Transportation reflect the view that safety will continue to be a primary concern for several of the modal agencies and for the leadership of the department. That is one of the propelling reasons for current departmental and Congressional scrutiny of proposals to reorganize the Federal Aviation Agency. An extended series of rail accidents, some of them drug-related, has also intensified the focus on safety, as have increasingly articulate campaigns around the nation against drunk driving and for the use of seat belts, and the raising of interstate speed limits in many areas.

The department will have to push most of its other priorities for the future through the perennial battle for resources and the Congressional gauntlet. The Coast Guard, for example, needs more money to engage fully in the fight against illegal narcotics import, yet has to justify the closing of almost every under-used search and rescue station. Rebuilding and repairing the aging interstate highway network is hostage to deficit reduction efforts which impound the trust fund fed by the federal gasoline tax and legally reserved for highway purposes. Especially where highways are concerned, the Congress tends to think of the innovative concept of demonstration projects primarily in terms of benefitting home districts. At sea, the U.S. maritime industry still has a long voyage back to an equal competitive footing in the world. Finally, some observers think the department should strengthen its research and development efforts on the cutting-edge of transportation technology.

Established in 1966, the department has the sixth largest budget among cabinet departments, at $27.1 billion in fiscal 1988, and 61,000 employees.

DEPARTMENT OF TRANSPORTATION

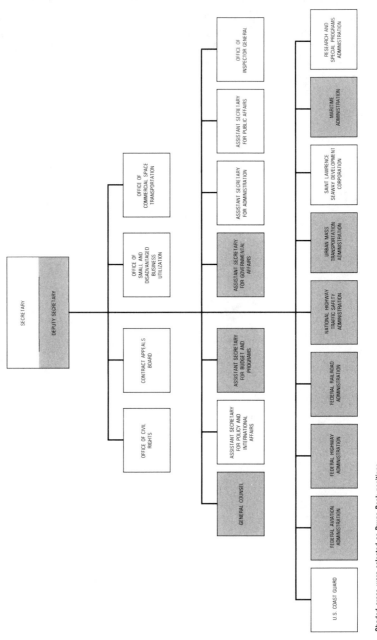

SECRETARY

DEPUTY SECRETARY

OFFICE OF CIVIL RIGHTS

CONTRACT APPEALS BOARD

OFFICE OF SMALL AND DISADVANTAGED BUSINESS UTILIZATION

OFFICE OF COMMERCIAL SPACE TRANSPORTATION

GENERAL COUNSEL

ASSISTANT SECRETARY FOR POLICY AND INTERNATIONAL AFFAIRS

ASSISTANT SECRETARY FOR BUDGET AND PROGRAMS

ASSISTANT SECRETARY FOR GOVERNMENTAL AFFAIRS

ASSISTANT SECRETARY FOR ADMINISTRATION

ASSISTANT SECRETARY FOR PUBLIC AFFAIRS

OFFICE OF INSPECTOR GENERAL

U.S. COAST GUARD

FEDERAL AVIATION ADMINISTRATION

FEDERAL HIGHWAY ADMINISTRATION

FEDERAL RAILROAD ADMINISTRATION

NATIONAL HIGHWAY TRAFFIC SAFETY ADMINISTRATION

URBAN MASS TRANSPORTATION ADMINISTRATION

SAINT LAWRENCE SEAWAY DEVELOPMENT CORPORATION

MARITIME ADMINISTRATION

RESEARCH AND SPECIAL PROGRAMS ADMINISTRATION

Shaded areas were selected as Prune Book positions

DEPUTY SECRETARY

Level II - Presidential Appointment with Senate Confirmation

Major Responsibilities

o   Assist the secretary in the comprehensive planning and direction of department activities. Manage the department on a daily basis. Assume responsibility as acting chief of the department when necessary.

o   Referee jurisdictional disputes between operating components of the department and decide a broad range of both significant and routine issues. Represent the department in interdepartmental discussions and Congressional testimony.

o   Supervise the legislative and budget functions of the department, as well as senior personnel assignments. Defend the department on budget matters at the White House and to the Congress.

Necessary Background, Experience, Personal Skills

Aspirants to this job should have sufficient background in the transportation field to know the basic issues and at least some of the players. They also should possess strong management experience, preferably at the chief operating level. Strengths in financial analysis, procurement practices, law, the Congress or foreign languages are all good additional assets.

Insight

While providing across-the-board management of an agency organized basically by transportation "modes" (air, highways, rail, maritime and others), the deputy secretary can also get involved in substantive decision-making on highly visible matters of central economic importance. During his tenure in 1981-83, Darrell M. Trent says he had a part in handling the strike of air traffic controllers, deciding government policy on car imports, the selling of a government-owned railroad company, and imposing a five-cent gasoline tax. At this writing, the current deputy secretary is deeply involved in DOT's proposed reorganization of the Federal Aviation Agency. The challenge of the job, Trent thinks, comes quite simply in "managing an agency with over 100,000 people and a very large budget, as well as in the allocation of resources and the setting of priorities."

A veteran of this job says its duties bear a strong kinship to those of the chief operating officer of a major corporation, and thinks the department's organizational structure is "unique," with the secretary, the deputy and a group of assistant secretaries perched atop the eight modal agencies. "That makes the managerial task more interesting," in this view. "It's not as if you had an assistant secretary for highways and another for aviation. Instead you have distinct organizations with their own traditions and goals, and part of the deputy's responsibility is to bring that under one umbrella." And "that works better on some days than others." Time management in such a situation may be much more difficult, "because there are so many more uncontrollables....Whether it's acquisition, personnel, policy management of an internal nature, labor-management disputes, liaison with the modal administrations--the processes of day-to-day management are the kinds of activity that eat away at your time."

In making decisions in many areas that unburden the secretary, the deputy must have, or work out, a good relationship that includes a firm understanding about how such responsibilities divide. Comments from some former occupants show the benefits of establishing such a situation. "We shared a suite of offices and both of us had an open door policy," or "we had a close personal and professional working relationship and that's why it was easy."

The job's occupant heads interagency task forces on transportation matters, sometimes confers with or reports informally to White House staff, and often has what a prior deputy secretary calls "deep involvement in significant procurement contracts." A good portion of time goes into encounters with transportation constituent groups who want to talk about their issues. "You have to be comfortable being in the limelight, before the media and large groups. You need to have that good self-confident presence," says one of those who has done it.

Former deputies tell a familiar story about too much to do with too few resources, a situation that involves the deputy secretary in some tough choices. Typical of this long-running phenomenon is a money-short Coast Guard stretched thin by the increasing need to interdict narcotics traffic.

Beefing up the Coast Guard in fact constitutes one of the chief goals for the department as seen by some of those who have helped run it from the second-ranking job. But they put even greater emphasis on modernization of air safety operations and regulations, and on transportation safety generally. For Alan Butchman, deputy secretary in 1977-79, "the biggest challenge is trying to operate in an environment with so many increasing and decreasing cross currents. You need to see it from beginning to end to have a definite impact." He offers this advice: "Don't stop and worry about reorganizing. Pick out what's important and channel your energies on those. Figure out what you want to do, put your head down, and do it."

That advice would doubtless get firm support from another veteran of the job, who tells about "pressure from the outside" in such areas as the FAA. "A Senator will tell us not to micromanage the FAA. Then they'll call next day and say, 'the FAA is doing the dumbest thing in the world. You must fix it.' So--it's don't micromanage, unless it's *my* micromanagement, something *I* need."

Key Relationships

Within the Department

> Reports to: Secretary

> Works closely with:

>> Heads of operating administrations
>> Assistant secretaries

Outside the Department

>> Counterparts at the Departments of State, Defense, Treasury, Agriculture, Interior and Housing and Urban Development; and the Environmental Protection Agency
>> Associate Director, Economics and Government, Office of Management and Budget
>> Assistant to the President for Policy Development

Outside the Federal Government

>> Transportation industry associations across the board, such as Airline Pilots Association International; American Association of State Highway and Transporta-

tion Officials; American Society of Civil Engineers; consumer groups interested in transportation issues, such as American Automobile Association; and travel organizations, such as Travel Industry Association of America

Deputy Secretaries of Transportation Since 1969

Administration	Name and Years Served	Present Position
Reagan	Mimi Weyforth Dawson 1987 - Present	Incumbent
Reagan	James H. Burnley IV 1983 - 1987	Secretary Department of Transportation
Reagan	Darrell M. Trent 1981 - 1983	Chairman & CEO Rollins Environmental Service Wilmington, Delaware
Carter	William J. Beckham, Jr. 1979 - 1981	Not Available
Carter	Alan Butchman 1977 - 1979	Managing Partner Garvey, Schubert and Barer Washington, DC
Ford	John W. Barnum 1973 - 1977	Partner White and Case Washington, DC
Nixon	James M. Beggs 1969 - 1972	Chairman Spacehab, Inc. Washington, DC

ADMINISTRATOR
FEDERAL AVIATION ADMINISTRATION

Level II - Presidential Appointment with Senate Confirmation

Major Responsibilities

o   Supervise the nationwide system of air traffic control governing the use of navigable airspace in the United States. Establish safe and efficient operating regulations for civil and military aviation in this space and require compliance with them.

o   Set standards for construction and maintenance of the national aviation system and the aircraft permitted to use it. Oversee the cost-effective design, development, procurement, maintenance and modernization of equipment the system uses. Direct the allocation of airport and air route development funds.

o   Direct the technical and management training, and the general activities, of nearly 50,000 employees throughout the United States and the world. Supervise preparation of the agency's budget and its negotiation with the Office of Management and Budget. Support the budget with the Congress.

o   Articulate and explain FAA policy to the public, the industry and the international aviation community.

Necessary Background, Experience, Personal Skills

A recent occupant of the position calls the FAA "a technical agency." He and other ex-administrators make it clear that nothing can substitute in this job for technical background and lengthy experience in aviation, and--highly critical--in the aviation industry; "I can't stress enough the importance of large-scale industry experience," one of them says. But an aviation-sector source outside the FAA stresses the importance of expertise on the operational side of air traffic control, and of a manager who has anticipated and dealt with strategic change within an organization. No appointee to this job, moreover, would be effective in its worldwide responsibilities without an extensive grasp of international aviation issues. The position carries high visibility: its occupant should be able to

handle frequent encounters with the press, the industry and the
Congress.

Insight

Most of the public attention to transportation issues in this
country probably fastens on the problem of safety in air travel.
Getting around by car, rail and bus may clearly be less safe by a
number of measures, including annual fatalities and injuries. But
the spectacular and fatality-intense nature of many air accidents
tends to unbalance the general view of the overall travel safety
picture. In no sense should any of this minimize the size and
severity of the problems that air safety managers must still overcome.
Because it unduly intensifies public focus on the FAA, however,
the administrator may labor under the most unfair handicap in the
federal transportation community.

Some of those who have held the job do express some concern
about this. They talk about "a public that doesn't understand
aviation" and "getting the media to report objectively instead of
sensationally." Such problems doubtless intensified when the FAA
in the spring of 1988 decided on an unprecedented plane-by-plane
inspection of a big national airline company. Yet, says Donald D.
Engen, FAA administrator in 1984-87, "taxpayers are entitled to
the answers." He and other previous administrators spent a lot of
time trying to provide them. "I was on every major news program,
and was interviewed by hundreds of reporters," Engen recalls. "I
was constantly selling the agency to people. I traveled throughout
every state and talked personally with state aviation officials to
achieve their support as well." Another ex-administrator describes
constant liaison with aviation communities--airlines, pilot associations,
manufacturers, air taxi carriers. In campus speeches, he encouraged
students to think about aviation careers.

Public attention to the FAA widened further in late April of
1988 with the announcement of several far-reaching reorganizing and
streamlining proposals. Some saw this as a response to efforts in
the Congress to take FAA out of the Department of Transportation,
a move which reportedly enjoys wide support among pilots and
airlines, among others. The Secretary of Transportation does apparently favor establishing the air traffic control system--with
more than 60% of FAA employees--as a separate agency. Whatever
emerges from these plans and views, some basic changes for FAA
seem clearly in store.

Certain comments from within the aviation community bear

directly on this prospect. An official of a research and development organization working on the kinds of technology used by FAA thinks most agency people understand the regulatory side of FAA. But "almost nobody understands the operational mission of the agency." That mission has long since changed, this observer reminds us, from one of managing infinite air space and relatively few aircraft to precisely the opposite. "It's like the energy shortage. Now we have a resource (air space) that needs to be managed, and failure to manage it efficiently will mean either safety problems or traffic reduction problems....The FAA has no tools for managing the capacity of the air space." That situation has developed because FAA management "is too politically motivated; they spend all their time servicing the Congress and Office of Management and Budget and all that....The FAA's problem is that the real job--the job everyone cares about--is being done at a remarkably local level." The solution? "The ideal guy for the FAA would be someone who understands operations, a guy who can put them in a new context, a guy who understands management. The political process isn't good at bringing those people forward....What you need is a modern manager, and if I were on a transition team I'd bring in some of the people who have been doing some thinking and learned that there is an experience base out there....It's got to be somebody who has relevant experience in understanding a strategic change in an organization and has managed it successfully."

"This is not a cocktail circuit job," advises a previous administrator. Once in it, there is no time to learn, he says--"you need to know it and have it." He advocates extensive management as well as technical training among the agency's staff, and suggests the administrator himself be "a rated pilot, since your main function is moving planes." Another feels an administrator should understand everything from the budget cycle and the budgets of other related departments to equipment design.

Amid the 12-hour days, constant traveling, public exposure and running a dispersed and changing organization, former administrators are unanimous that the FAA chief must not lose sight of the primary goal--the safest possible movement of air traffic. "It was the hardest job of my life," one of them asserts. "If you do it right, it's the hardest."

Key Relationships

Within the Department

Reports to: Secretary

Works closely with:

Deputy Secretary

Outside the Department

Director, Federal Bureau of Investigation
Deputy Chief of Staff for Operations,
  Department of the Air Force
Administrator, Drug Enforcement
  Administration
Director, Counterterrorism and Narcotics,
  National Security Council

Outside the Federal Government

Aerospace Industries Association of America; Aircraft
Owners and Pilots Association; International Air
Transport Association; General Aviation Manufacturers
Association; consumer groups, such as Aviation Con-
sumer Action Project; civic organizations; state and
local governments

Administrators of the Federal Aviation Administration Since 1969

Administration	Name and Years Served	Present Position
Reagan	T. Allan McArtor 1987 - Present	Incumbent
Reagan	Donald D. Engen 1984 - 1987	President Air Safety Foundation Frederick, Maryland
Reagan	J. Lynn Helms 1981 - 1984	President Consultants International Bridgeport, Connecticut
Carter	Langhorne M. Bond 1977 - 1981	Partner Santarelli and Bond Washington, DC

Ford	John L. McLucas 1975 - 1977	Chairman of the Board Questech, Inc. McLean, Virginia
Nixon	Alexander P. Butterfield 1973 - 1975	Partner Armistead and Alexander Los Angeles, California
Nixon	John H. Shaffer 1969 - 1973	Not Available

ADMINISTRATOR
FEDERAL HIGHWAY ADMINISTRATION

Level II - Presidential Appointment with Senate Confirmation

Major Responsibilities

o   Manage the Federal-Aid Highway Program of financial assistance
    to states for highway construction and improvement, and for
    research, safety and impact activities associated with the pro-
    gram.   Advise the secretary on policy issues which affect this
    and other responsibilities of the FHWA.

o   Maintain and expand standards and enforcement regulations
    for commercial motor carriers in the areas of size, weight,
    and safety.   Continue the establishment of requirements for a
    national commercial vehicle driver license.

o   Direct the Federal Highway Administration, with ten regional
    bureaus nationwide and several offices overseas. Provide required
    reports to the Congress on such matters as construction costs
    and safety. Oversee the FWHA's budget processes. Represent
    the FHWA on the Hill and to the public.

Necessary Background, Experience, Personal Skills

A sound background in transportation, banking or public management gives the individual in this job a sizeable advantage.
Congressional experience has proved highly useful but not essential.
Sensitivity to political realities and how to deal with them, however,
is important.   Candidates for the position should feel comfortable
in public speaking and other group communication situations. A
former Transportation official who knows the position well warns
that the wrong choice for this slot would produce "a lot of bad
vibes" across the country. Some Congressional experience or state-
house exposure is helpful.

Insight

This agency deals primarily in the policy area, because its

assistance is allocated by financial aid formulas to programs developed by individual states and carried out at the state and community
level. Like certain counterparts elsewhere in the department and
the government, the administrator functions as a sort of banker in
partnership with state and local authorities. Consequently, the
occupant spends much time in contact with these people in all 50
states, reviewing the construction and improvement plans they
design and keeping a steady eye on their implementation.

In brief, federal highway assistance covers construction and
maintenance of some 42,000 miles of road in the interstate and
defense system, with federal-state financing split 90-10; and another
800,000 miles of primary and secondary highways and city streets,
which the Feds and states split 75-25. Other FHWA programs in
this area focus on bridge repair and replacement, safety design,
environmental impact, land acquisition and aid to those whom this
displaces, roads damaged by natural events, and national standards
for signal lights and other traffic control machinery. The Highway
Trust Fund, fed by user taxes, supplies the federal share of all
this as appropriated by the Congress. It is FHWA's job to see
that the money flows according to a Congressionally-mandated
formula.

The biggest challenge of the highway program, a former administrator says, "is to minimize the amount of review by federal
officials and be sure the money is used the way Congress intended."
He also emphasizes the value of research "to design highways that
last longer, are built cheaper, and conserve natural resources."
Among the current problems of the program, one of his predecessors
finds, is Congressional "misuse of demonstration projects, which
are meant to be innovative but are used instead as political gifts
and favors."

The FHWA administrator has a regulatory responsibility for
commercial highway users--mainly, of course, trucks. Legislation
in 1982 instructed FHWA to designate a national truck network,
and to promulgate rules covering truck sizes and weights, and the
safe operation of motor carriers. In addition to setting rational
standards for state-issued licenses for drivers of commercial vehicles
(a task begun only in the last year or two), FHWA issues grants
to states to implement and enforce federal motor carrier laws.

An experienced interest-group official thinks "it doesn't matter
what the administrator is, or what he knows, because the professional
bureaucrats will run it anyway." But another previous FHWA chief
recalls that "people skills were especially useful in my case. My
department was 99% engineers and an administrative, people-oriented
person was needed to manage effectively." FHWA has a staff of

approximately 3,500.

Norbert T. Tiemann, who held the post in 1973-76, says "two major goals exist today" in the highway program: rebuilding the interstate system and pushing the bridge replacement program. He further stresses the need to reclassify highways because of the growth of the populations they serve. Tiemann also sees a significant problem in what he calls "illegal" impoundment practices concerning the Highway Trust Fund "to help reduce the budget deficit. Legislation protects these funds, but it is rarely enforced and they do it anyway," he says.

Ray A. Barnhart, who served as Administrator in 1981-87, has high praise for the professionalism of the staff. "Contrary to most public perceptions," he says, "the career people in FHWA are some of the most competent individuals with whom I've worked. It is the laws which they are obliged to enforce which are the cause of the program's problems and criticisms. Increasingly, the Congress writes legislation which benefits specific political jurisdictions, gives preferential treatment to politically powerful groups and products, and undermines the states' abilities to manage their highway programs. The bureaucrats get the blame."

Barnhart thinks the major challenge facing the FHWA is to define the proper federal role in highways for the post-1992 era, when the interstate highway system is scheduled for completion.

Key Relationships

Within the Department

Reports to: Secretary

Works closely with:

Administrator, National Highway Traffic Safety
Administration
Administrator, Federal Railway Administration
Administrator, Urban Mass Transit Administration

Outside the Department

Assistant Secretary, Marketing and Inspection Services,
Department of Agriculture
Transportation Command, Department of Defense

Outside the Federal Government

State governors; consumer and industry groups, such as American Road and Transportation Builders Association, American Automobile Association, American Association of State Highway and Transportation Officials, and Asphalt Institute

Administrators of the Federal Highway Administration Since 1969

Administration	Name and Years Served	Present Position
Reagan	Robert Farris 1988	Incumbent
Reagan	Ray A. Barnhart 1981 - 1987	Consultant Texas Research & Development Foundation Austin, Texas
Carter	John S. Hassell, Jr. 1980	Not Available
Carter	Karl S. Bowers 1978 - 1980	Director of Transportation Stevens and Wilkinson Columbia, South Carolina
Carter	William M. Cox 1977	Not Available
Nixon/Ford	Norbert T. Tiemann 1973 - 1976	Vice President HDR, Inc. Alexandria, Virginia
Nixon	Ralph R. Bartelsmeyer 1972 - 1973	Not Available
Nixon	Francis C. Turner 1969 - 1971	Not Available

ADMINISTRATOR
FEDERAL RAILROAD ADMINISTRATION

Level III - Presidential Appointment with Senate Confirmation

Major Responsibilities

o Develop and enforce railroad safety regulations that cover such areas as inspection, equipment and track maintenance, operating rules and employee conduct. Work with the Congress to keep the underlying legislation updated and relevant, and to explain policy, operations, and budget requests.

o Maintain balanced working relationships with the principal constituencies of the job, notably organizations representing management and labor. Provide budget and administrative supervision to the agency.

o Oversee federal administrative aspects of Amtrak and other FRA assets, including the management and sales of FRA's $500 million outstanding loan portfolio. Represent the agency to the public.

Necessary Background, Experience, Personal Skills

The position requires a detailed knowledge of the railroad industry and a grasp of the current nature of the federal regulatory role. A tough and experienced manager who can maintain a balanced view and approach to these responsibilities is essential. Prior federal service is valuable, especially if the candidate dealt regularly with the Congress and can move confidently around the Hill. The administrator should also feel at home with the press and know how to play in that arena.

Insight

The FRA has become primarily a safety agency. Understanding why is important to handling the administrator's responsibilities effectively, and requires a bit of recent history.

Until 1980, a basically healthy U.S. railroad industry operated under regulations which prevented it from adapting to a dramatically changed transportation environment. The Staggers Act, enacted in that year, lifted much of this burden and, at the same time, significantly changed the focus of the FRA. It cut almost to zero the large lending programs which had been the agency's chief activity. As the deregulation of Staggers moved the railroads from cash-poor status to the point of being able to upgrade and modernize, the FRA was better able to enforce and maintain tougher safety standards. Safety, always a concern of the FRA, is today its key focus.

Besides writing all rail transport regulations, FRA operates an inspection staff of 325, runs a substantial safety research and development center, and has about 40 people analyzing economic trends in the industry and the effect of Interstate Commerce Commission rulings on its financial health. It is currently engaged in selling off about half of its $500 million loan portfolio, a task the next administrator will have to complete. It oversees Amtrak, sits on its board, and dispenses its federal money.

In mid-1988, the agency entered another new era with passage of the Rail Safety Improvement Act. In a nutshell, that legislation gave FRA a large measure of jurisdiction over railroad employees. Until then, there were no uniform licensing requirements for engineers, no on-the-job performance standards, and no practical or punitive recourse for the agency in the face of negligent or unsafe performance. The fact of 48 accidents within 18 months involving drugs or alcohol had built support for this legislation. But the catalyst, of course, was the 1987 Amtrak collision near Chase, Maryland. That accident, says John Riley, FRA administrator since 1983, "was a tragic but definitive example both of the role employees play in rail safety and the FRA's lack of power to help prevent such accidents. It crystallized the 20-year argument over bringing employees under the FRA umbrella--a brutal battle for years."

Passage of the law, though, won't necessarily make the administrator's job easier. Implementing it is certain to be tough. Much of the FRA's new power is likely to face litigation. Consequently, Riley predicts, "the next administrator will have to continue to shape both public and Congressional opinion" by stressing the importance of enforcing correct employee behavior and of substance abuse testing of individuals who have the public safety in their hands, as well as the importance of FRA's traditional role in monitoring rules compliance by railroad companies.

The other genuinely difficult dimension of the new law and of safety issues generally is the continuing struggle between railroad management and labor. This fight about safety is "old, passionate and entrenched," Riley says, because the issue is the vehicle for the basic economic battle between the two sides, with each claiming to have the answer. In an example of this, with the railroad work force dropping heavily in recent years, the unions eye every safety measure for its potential to increase employment. Hindered by a "mind-set" that relies on government to resolve every decision and driven by each party's belief that it's worth the struggle to get the FRA on its side, management and labor don't work issues out between themselves. This throws the agency into the middle of every dispute, pulls its chief in many directions, and makes the administrator's perspective and judgment a key factor in the outcome of every dispute. Each side, Riley notes, claims the agency "is in the pocket of the other, which is exactly as it should be. The challenge for future administrators will be in maintaining that balance."

Asked what kind of FRA chief would turn in the best performance, Riley says the next administration should choose an individual "who will be vigilant in keeping management and labor from capturing the agency," someone who takes on the job "with the public interest in mind." That obviously means, he warns, not selecting the president of the American Association of Railroads or the chief counsel of the Railway Labor Executives Association. At the same time, the job cannot go to someone "who does not know the industry cold," because "you can get conned in this job too easily. You can't take much of what you hear from the parties at face value."

As for advice and suggestions to those who will run FRA in the future, Riley has these to pass on:

"Spend the necessary time to learn technical issues in depth, such as the minutia of how brakes function. Ultimately, you'll be in a position to sort out a technical issue and will have to make the final decision based on your judgement."

"Aggressively seek the counsel of everyone involved--management, labor, and your staff. But in the end, decide what is in the public interest and go with it."

"Don't simply seek compromise between competing entities, or you'll end up with a mish-mash of regulations that don't make sense because the primary contenders merely trade concessions."

"Make good use of the press. It is an important tool in

the arsenal of public policymaking and is essential to accomplishing your legislative goals."

"Don't duck any issue. Don't underestimate the depth of the conflict between management and labor or its effect on your job. If you stand firm for what you truly believe is right, you'll succeed."

"If you can't say no, don't take the job. You have to be willing not to care how you look day to day, but how your accomplishments will look over two or three years. This is not a job where you can expect to make friends and be effective. It is a public interest job, not a jumping-off place for future employment."

Key Relationships

Within the Department

> Reports to: Secretary
>
> Works closely with:
>
>> Deputy Secretary
>> Assistant Secretary for Governmental Affairs
>> Assistant Secretary for Public Affairs
>> General Counsel

Outside the Department

>> Assistant Attorney General, Anti-trust Division, Department of Justice
>> Chairman, National Railroad Passenger Corporation (Amtrak)
>> Associate Director, Economics and Government, Office of Management and Budget

Outside the Federal Government

>> Association of American Railroads, Institute of Transportation Engineers, Brotherhood of Railway Signalmen and many other rail labor and management groups; passenger advocate organizations; and individual railroad companies

Administrators of the Federal Railroad Administration Since 1969

Administration	Name and Years Served	Present Position
Reagan	John Riley 1983 - Present	Incumbent
Reagan	Robert W. Blanchette 1981 - 1983	Attorney Washington, DC
Carter	John M. Sullivan 1977 - 1981	President Haug Die Casting Corp. Kenilworth, New Jersey
Ford	Asaph H. Hall 1975 - 1977	Vice President, Data Systems Division General Dynamics St. Louis, Missouri
Nixon	John W. Ingram 1971 - 1974	Not Available
Nixon	Reginald N. Whitman 1969 - 1970	Not Available

ADMINISTRATOR
MARITIME ADMINISTRATION

Level III - Presidential Appointment with Senate Confirmation

Major Responsibilities

o   Administer programs providing subsidies to bridge the gap between specified costs of operating merchant ships under the U.S. flag and foreign flags, and between ship construction and renovation costs in U.S. and foreign shipyards.

o   Supervise programs to develop and improve U.S. ports and harbor facilities, to raise the performance of the U.S. merchant marine, and to increase its use by American industry.

o   Negotiate maritime issues with foreign governments to ensure the participation of United States flag vessels in U.S.-foreign commerce and to secure the removal of barriers to the efficient operations of U.S. flag vessels in such trade.

o   Act as administration spokesman on maritime issues. Represent policy in this area to the Congress, press and public. Manage the War Risk Insurance Program for American ship operators and seamen. Oversee the operation of the U.S. Merchant Marine Academy, and of assistance programs for six state merchant marine academies. Supervise development of the agency's budget document and defend it within the administration and to the Congress.

Necessary Background, Experience, Personal Skills

It's easy to see that "experience in ships and shipping," in the words of a former administrator, makes all the difference in this job. The present maritime administrator served in the U.S. Coast Guard; his predecessor spent 42 years in the U.S. Navy, rising to flag rank. Knowing one's way around the Congress can be helpful. At the same time, "this is not a job for a politician," declares a veteran of the position.

Insight

The maritime administrator's essential mission these days is to sustain the long effort to keep the U.S. merchant marine in business and support American builders of merchant ships. Pushed hard for years by foreign flag fleets and shipyards, the U.S. maritime industry continues to need greater efficiency and economy in order to remain, or become, truly healthy and competitive--whether around the world and in the U.S. coastal trade. The importance of this turns not just on commercial benefits, but on the ability of the merchant marine fleet to perform vital functions in conditions of generalized or local warfare. That reflects a dual nature of the administrator's responsibilities. They run from managing the crucial subsidies programs and helping develop markets for the U.S. merchant marine to maintaining and--when necessary--operating the National Defense Reserve Fleet.

"I knew it was in terrible shape," says Adm. Harold E. Shear (USN-ret.), administrator from 1981 to 1985. "I wasn't asking for the job, I did it as a public service. It's a massive job, a total massive, thankless, tough, critical job." As he saw things at the time, "the industry had been going down hill since the end of World War II. We had to get labor under control first. Some progress has been made, but not enough. Second, the ships were old. We had to replace them with new, competitive ships if we were to be able to compete on the high seas....It's better now, but the industry has a long, long way to go." An administrator with a former military career, Shear asserts, should not be penalized by having to forego his entire military retired pay while serving in this position. Such a situation imposes "a very heavy burden" and essentially means "working for nothing, which I did for four years." Its effect is "to keep good people from accepting government jobs."

Among the many regular duties that the administrator handles are once-weekly meetings of the Maritime Subsidy Board, public speaking appearances which average twice a month, and testimony before about a dozen Congressional hearings a year.

Anyone coming into the job, describes John A. Gaughan, administrator since 1985, "had better like contact sports. Often it appears nothing is easy. There's a lot of pushing and shoving going on. You have to be able to operate within the agency's environment, out in the public, before Congress." Moreover, he adds, "If you have a President with specific fundamental changes to make in the way the U.S. supports its maritime industry, this job offers the opportunity to have your fingerprints all over it. We have tried to make radical changes in an industry that wasn't prepared for radical changes."

Key Relationships

Within the Department

Reports to: Secretary

Works closely with:

Deputy Secretary
Chiefs of the nine other component administrations
of the department
Assistant Secretary for Budget and Program

Outside the Department

Chairman, Federal Maritime Commission
Assistant Secretary for Shipbuilding and Logistics,
Department of Defense

Outside the Federal Government

Shipping and maritime construction groups, such as
Shipbuilders Council of America; American Society of
Naval Engineers; National Ocean Industries Association; maritime, shipbuilding, and stevedore unions,
such as AFL-CIO Maritime Committee; pilots and
ship owners groups; port authorities; transportation,
navigation and oceanographic institutes, such as
Water Transport Association; and Propeller Club of
America

Administrators of the Maritime Administration Since 1969

Administration	Name and Years Served	Present Position
Reagan	John A. Gaughan 1985 - Present	Incumbent

Reagan	Harold E. Shear 1981 - 1985	Groton Long Point, Connecticut
Carter	Samuel B. Nemirow 1979 - 1981	Partner Garvey, Schubert and Barer Washington, DC
Nixon/Ford/ Carter	Robert J. Blackwell 1972 - 1979	Partner Dow, Lohnes and Albertson Washington, DC
Nixon	Andrew E. Gibson 1969 - 1971	Not Available

ADMINISTRATOR
NATIONAL HIGHWAY TRAFFIC SAFETY
ADMINISTRATION

Level III - Presidential Appointment with Senate Confirmation

Major Responsibilities

o   Recommend to the secretary decisions on automotive safety regulations and oversee their enforcement.

o   Administer highway safety grant programs to states.

o   Serve as administration spokesperson on highway safety, and as policy adviser to the secretary in this area.

o   Direct the work of NHTSA's staff of 650 at headquarters, ten regional offices and the agency's vehicle research test center. Supervise budget preparation and review, and see it through its Office of Management and Budget and legislative phases.

Necessary Background, Experience, Personal Skills

Former administrators give strong priority to a good understanding of the federal regulatory environment and how it affects private industry; and of the Washington political arena, especially the Congress. It helps to know the industry associations and consumer groups which watch NHTSA closely and constantly, and to have negotiating experience. A legal or engineering background raises an administrator's credibility in certain situations, but isn't essential.

Insight

As with the leadership of other regulatory agencies, NHTSA's chief lives in a glass house, one in which the stones come hurtling from the outside in. Almost inevitably, many of the decisions the administrator hands down will raise hackles in one quarter or another--the Congress or public interest groups or the affected manufacturing sector. The recent heated attention to the issue of speed limits on the interstate highway system provides a good example. A given constituent group's support for the work of the agency is inconsistent at best, changing with the direction a decision takes.

But, says the current administrator, Diane K. Steed, "I don't think there is another position in government in which you see the effects of your job every day and get the satisfaction of watching the work get done." To her, the position currently has two equal focuses--not only regulating vehicle safety, but shaping public attitudes to support and advance highway safety measures. Once "mostly vehicle regulators," agency people are now also "human behavior specialists. We look at new ways to solve problems. Such as, is it really possible to solve the drunk driving problem with a new device on the car? No, you have to change people's behavior." To this end, the agency provides federal matching grants which assist state programs in driver, pedestrian, and motor vehicle safety.

Whatever the approach on this particular front, the administrator must face the permanent requirement to justify and defend the agency's actions to the auto industry and keep the safety issue before the public. Among other consequences, failure to deal effectively and equitably with industry and interest groups and the press can produce problems of morale and intellectual fatigue inside NHTSA.

A former administrator, who emphasizes the regulatory mandate of the job, found it difficult to hire "the proper people;" says the agency "is losing some talented staff;" and sees the main problems then and now as insufficient funding and lack of support from the Congress. In this view, the job fares best with a "thick-skinned and aggressive" individual at home on the Hill and with the media.

Coming up with a balanced regulatory policy amid these difficulties, according to Steed--"one that is sound from a legal, economic, and engineering standpoint--is a major management challenge. The person coming into this job ought not to have a predetermined or political agenda, but have thought pretty hard about what bottom line they would like to see. Are there areas that you are really interested in, places you'd like to make changes? I don't know of another thing that touches every single person in this country more than the automobile. You really can make a difference here."

Key Relationships

Within the Department

Reports to: Secretary

Works closely with:

> Deputy Secretary
> Administrator, Federal Highway Administration
> Assistant secretaries
> General Counsel

Outside the Department

> Assistant Administrator, Air and Radiation, Environmental Protection Agency
> Assistant Secretary, Conservation and Renewable Energy, Department of Energy
> Chairman, National Transportation Safety Board

Outside the Federal Government

> Motor Vehicle Manufacturers' Association, National Safety Foundation, American Automobile Association, Mothers Against Drunk Driving

Administrators of the National Highway Traffic Safety Administration Since 1969

Administration	Name and Years Served	Present Position
Reagan	Diane K. Steed 1983 - Present	Incumbent
Reagan	Raymond A. Peck, Jr. 1981 - 1983	Not Available
Carter	Joan Claybrooke 1977 - 1981	President Public Citizen Washington, DC
Ford	John W. Snow 1976 - 1977	President & COO CSX Corporation Richmond, Virginia

| Ford | James B. Gregory
1973 - 1976 | Not Available |
| Nixon | Douglas W. Toms
1970 - 1973 | Not Available |

ADMINISTRATOR
URBAN MASS TRANSPORTATION ADMINISTRATION

Level III - Presidential Appointment with Senate Confirmation

Major Responsibilities

o   Administer an annual multi-billion dollar program of formula and discretionary grants to state, regional and city government bodies and other public authorities to assist in acquisition and improvement of urban mass transportation equipment and facilities, as well as in operations and planning.

o   Consult and work with state and local authorities on their transportation objectives.   Act as the administration's chief spokesperson on public transportation and urban mobility issues.

o   Develop, secure approval for, and defend the agency's overall budget and programs. Manage the agency's staff of 500.

Necessary Background, Experience, Personal Skills

A good resume for this job would reflect a combination of direct experience in public management with urban planning and real estate development.   Backgrounds in transportation management or engineering are also extremely useful.   Political skills are important, including the ability to work with the Congress.   Some exposure to the corporate world will help an administrator in contacts with private transit operators and the equipment suppliers and design and construction firms with which transportation agencies deal.

Insight

The administrator operates exclusively in the grant-making business.   Most of the funds approved by UMTA assist public transit authorities and states in handling their urban mass transportation requirements.   The rest goes to research, technical studies, managerial training and non-urban areas.   Grants in the first category cover many sectors--bus and rail system operations, equipment, maintenance, and planning. Currently, the administrator signs 90% of them. Eight or nine years ago, this job was largely discretionary in the projects it funded. Now the Congress earmarks much of the money for grants it desires, and others are handed out by formula--controlled by factors such as population of the community under consideration. In this situation, "you serve as a shield to make sure the process doesn't get too political. That is a very important duty," says a previous administrator.

Cities and their populations who depend on good transit are clearly the central consideration in this job. It is important to recognize that transportation systems and infrastructure are but one part of the urban mosaic. A background in urban planning and development is therefore an advantage in making judgments, say, about the merits of fixed rail or road transportation in a given situation. Theodore C. Lutz, administrator from 1979 to 1981, makes two further points about the nature of the work. First, as a financial assistance agency, "you don't 'run' anything. You're not making the train go. You're the banker, not the boss. But there's a philosophy in Washington that he who has the gold rules. And, as a result, you are held accountable for what the guys in the street are doing--frequently on operational issues over which you have no control." Second, the supplier companies in the transportation sector "are a key area. You have to have a thoughtful approach to the impact your decisions will have on suppliers, try to structure programs that ensure a healthier supplier community. It's easy to ignore their needs, but it's important to understand their position intellectually."

Away from the office, the administrator leads a hectic official life. "It's incredible, the external demands of this job," says one who had it. "Members of Congress, mayors, state officials, academics--it's a big transportation community. There are volumes of mail from the outside. Everyone writes about this or that grant. And the ceremonial part of the job wouldn't quit."

Earlier administrators list a number of points and goals to keep in mind. They include provision of timely advisories to the secretary on where money is going and when; and the need for constant effort to review and reform the regulations governing grants and for greater UMTA support of research and development in areas like safety. "Recognize that urban transportation has moved to the suburbs," one veteran of the job says. "It has an impact on many people and cannot be mishandled." In another area--staff support for the administrator--he feels that "not enough data came up from below. It was there but it had to be extracted. There is much too rigid a reporting relationship, and you cannot correct it with a flow chart. Help had to be asked for."

From the vantage point of an interest group which follows Department of Transportation actions closely comes another pointer from an observer familiar with UMTA's recent approach to the Congress. "They were following a game plan that was opposite to what the committees thought was appropriate," this individual says. "Everything they said was right, but they pushed it so strongly that they couldn't win."

As for challenges in running UMTA, a former administrator finds one of the biggest simply in "making good decisions on priorities for the use of resources and getting the best value for the money in a timely manner--getting affordable public transportation." The job also has its rewards: "A tangible product in the end. You see something that got built. You get to know a lot about America. You see the relationship between transportation and urban development. Things like this put you in the forefront of urban America."

Key Relationships

Within the Department

Reports to: Secretary

Works closely with:

Federal Highway Administrator
Federal Railroad Administrator
Assistant Secretary for Budget and Programs
Assistant Secretary for Governmental Affairs

Outside the Department

Assistant Administrator, Air and Radiation, Environmental Protection Agency

Associate Director, Government and Economics, Office of Management and Budget

Assistant Secretary, Community Planning and Development, Department of Housing and Urban Development

Outside the Federal Government

> American Public Transportation Association, Advanced Transit Association and other industry groups; business and urban development organizations, such as National League of Cities, U.S. Conference of Mayors; and taxpayer and environmental associations, such as Consumer Energy Council of America

Administrators of the Urban Mass Transportation Administration Since 1969

Administration	Name and Years Served	Present Position
Reagan	Alfred A. DelliBovi 1987 - Present	Incumbent
Reagan	Ralph L. Stanley 1983 - 1987	Vice Chairman Municipal Development Corporation New York, New York
Reagan	Arthur E. Teele, Jr. 1981 - 1983	Partner Sparber, Shevin, Shapo and Heilbronner Miami, Florida
Carter	Theodore C. Lutz 1979 - 1981	Business Manager The Washington Post Washington, DC
Carter	Richard S. Page 1977 - 1979	President Washington Roundtable Seattle, Washington
Carter	Charles F. Bingman 1977 (Acting)	Visiting Professor The George Washington University Washington, DC
Ford	Robert E. Patricelli 1975 - 1977	President Value Health, Inc. Avon, Connecticut

Nixon/Ford	Frank C. Herringer 1973 - 1975	President Transamerica Corporation San Francisco, California
Nixon	Carlos C. Villarreal 1969 - 1973	Not Available

ASSISTANT SECRETARY
BUDGET AND PROGRAMS

Level IV - Presidential Appointment with Senate Confirmation

Major Responsibilities

o   Prepare the department's annual budget request and defend it in Office of Management and Budget review and before the Congress. Reconcile intradepartmental budget needs with available resources and program priorities.

o   Advise the secretary, and provide recommendations, on resource allocation questions.

o   Monitor program activities of the department for their effectiveness and consistency with departmental objectives.

Necessary Background, Experience, Personal Skills

This staff position calls for extensive skills in handling the budget of a large and complex organization--analysis, review with requesting divisions, and management of the end product. Familiarity with these procedures in a federal government context is extremely desirable. Also recommended: A knowledge of the federal transportation sector and of related private business and industry.

Insight

Each year, says Janet Hale, who has held this position since 1986, "we negotiate for two weeks with OMB on a budget for a period which is 18 months in the future. We spend the next 50 weeks defending that budget on the Hill." Like most federal budget managers, the assistant secretary spends a high proportion of time riding herd over the department's budget process. Doing so requires not only shepherding the impending budget on the Hill, but also overseeing the two that flank it on either side--the current budget, and the one for the following fiscal year. The job is complicated somewhat by the independent nature of Transportation's several "modal" agencies which operate with strong budget officers and a measure of autonomous budget management. While retaining overall budget authority, the assistant secretary must contend with fairly strong internal forces in negotiating the department's final budget numbers, as well as doing battle with OMB and Congress.

The program oversight function of the job--which is as important if not equally as time-consuming as handling the budget--involves examining such program aspects as effectiveness, policy, and legislative development. According to Hale, it complements the budget responsibility by providing a comprehensive understanding of the agencies' needs. The more the assistant secretary knows about the characteristics, goals and requirements of the programs, the easier it is to translate program demands into budget dollars.

Dividing ever-scarcer resources among the competing priorities of nine operating agencies takes ability on several levels within the department. "Know the structural make-up of the department," a former occupant of the job advises, "and communicate effectively with the players who constantly critique the budget." Another says that "if you're innovative in resource allocation and can get program managers to rethink the way they do things, significant funding solutions can be devised."

One of the biggest current challenges in this area is the conflict in priority between the exigencies of deficit reduction and the urgent need for greater funding for two of the department's most visible agencies. One of these is the Federal Aviation Administration. The other is the Coast Guard, which needs more money to do the job it has been assigned in combatting international traffic in narcotics.

In these duties, the assistant secretary functions as the secretary's main adviser. A previous tenant of the job recommends, "you need to be open and honest in your recommendations. Don't simply report what you think the secretary wants to hear. I was responsible for advising the secretary and deputy secretary on major budget and legislative recommendations. If you kept that responsibility up front, there were no problems from a management point of view."

In the challenge and opportunity department, those who have held the job talk about the chance to achieve change. "Transportation issues in this country are massive, the problems are diverse and stimulating," says Hale, who is currently active in problem-solving concerns ranging from the National Drug Policy Board to the Pennsylvania Avenue Development Corporation. "The challenge is the reality that you can effect change on a grand scale." "If you communicate effectively with state and local governments, change results," adds another.

Problems: "The chronic frustration of program managers who don't get the dollars they want," says one former assistant secretary. "I had to fight this battle over and over. How many ways do you say no?" Donald A. Derman, assistant secretary in 1981-85, mentions a "we-they syndrome between political appointees and careerists." And, since this is a job sometimes filled by careerists, he offers a suggestion for improvement. "I urge more senior careerists to accept presidential appointments, become exposed to political appointees. They will be surprised how adaptive and sharp the appointees really are."

Key Relationships

Within the Department

Reports to: Secretary

Works closely with:

Deputy Secretary
Heads of operating administrations of the
    department
Assistant Secretary, Governmental Affairs
Other assistant secretaries

Outside the Department

Associate Director, Economics and Government, Office
    of Management and Budget
White House domestic policy staff

Outside the Federal Government

Transportation industry associations, such as Aerospace Industries Association of America, Motor Vehicle Manufacturers Association, National Air Transportation Association, Travel Industry Association of America; state and local government representatives and groups, such as National Governor's Association, U.S. Conference of Mayors

Assistant Secretaries for Budget and Programs Since 1969

Administration	Name and Years Served	Present Position
Reagan	Janet Hale 1986 - Present	Incumbent
Reagan	Donald A. Derman 1981 - 1985	Consultant SYNETICS Washington, DC
Carter	Mortimer L. Downey III 1977 - 1980	Executive Director Metropolitan Transportation Authority New York, New York
Ford	Michael Brown* 1976	Not Available
Nixon/Ford	Theodore C. Lutz* 1973 - 1976	Business Manager The Washington Post Washington, DC
Nixon	John P. Olsson* 1970 - 1972	Not Available
Nixon	Charles D. Baker* 1969 - 1970	Professor of Business Administration Northeastern University Boston, Massachusetts

*   Served as Deputy Undersecretary for Budget and Programs.

ASSISTANT SECRETARY
GOVERNMENTAL AFFAIRS

Level IV - Presidential Appointment with Senate Confirmation

Major Responsibilities

o   Manage the department's Congressional relations and maintain close personal contact with members and staffs of relevant committees. Coordinate presentation of the department's legislative program.

o   Act as outreach to state and local governments in explaining DOT programs, and consulting about state and local transportation plans, projects and problems.

Necessary Background, Experience, Personal Skills

Given the nature of this job's principal duties, Congressional experience and prior federal or state government service are the most valuable resources. A candidate will be significantly better qualified if that background came in the transportation field, provided specific knowledge of the issues in one or more of the transportation areas, or--at the federal level--developed expertise in liaison with state and city governments and constituency groups.

Insight

The key responsibilities of this job, as described by a recent incumbent, are really three-fold. First comes constant and heavy-duty Congressional contact across the entire range of DOT programs and operations. Next, the job requires close work with state and local legislatures, governors, mayors and other elected and appointed officials, and other public as well as private groups on transportation plans, projects and problems across the board at those levels. These efforts cover a lot of ground. Typical examples are the department's current proposals to reorganize the Federal Aviation Administration; issues connected with management of the highway and airport construction trust funds; funding decisions in the broad range of state and local transportation projects supported by DOT grants; and important transportation-related goals like getting drinking-age or seat belt laws through state legislatures. "So much of what that office deals with is information," a former assistant secretary points out, "and getting it correct both ways--from inside the administration out, and from outside in."

That doubtless applies in equal measure to the third important task--the consumer affairs function relating to air travel, which the government affairs office inherited from the now-extinct Civil Aeronautics Board. This involves investigating and trying to deal with the underlying causes of such common complaints as inefficient or unacceptable baggage handling or ticket refunds. Among other requirements, this assignment means continuous and heavy contact with consumer and constituency groups and the population at large.

The governmental affairs office also takes the lead in substantial amounts of general contact with constituency groups representing the entire transportation industry, from airlines to trucking companies. The office acts only in a liaison capacity with the various modal administrations on technicalities like the varying consistency of asphalt used in road-building in cold and warm climates. But, it is probably the first office someone would contact if they were worried, say, about the huge problem Alaska has with roads buckling in the winter and what solutions can be considered.

Key Relationships

Within the Department

Reports to: Secretary

Works closely with:

Deputy Secretary
Assistant secretaries
Administrators of DOT component agencies

Outside the Department

Counterparts and transportation officials in certain other departments (i.e., Defense, Agriculture, Interior)

Outside the Federal Government

Safety and consumer groups; state and local transportation officials; American Association of State Highway and Transportation Officials, National Governor's Association, U.S. Conference of Mayors; urban affairs associations; transportation technology firms; and transportation industry associations, such as Air Transport Association of America, Motor Vehicle Manufacturer's Assocation, National Association of Air Transportation Specialists, Travel Industry Association of America

Assistant Secretaries for Governmental Affairs Since 1971*

Administration	Name and Years Served	Present Position
Reagan	Edward Hamberger 1988 - Present	Incumbent
Reagan	Rebecca G. Range 1985 - 1987	Deputy Assistant to the President & Director for Public Liaison The White House
Reagan	Charles G. Hardin 1983 - 1985	Not Available
Reagan	Lee L. Verstandig 1981 - 1983	Chairman Verstandig & Associates Washington, DC
Carter	Susan J. Williams** 1980 - 1981	Partner Bracy Williams and Co. Washington, DC
Carter	Terrence L. Bracy** 1977 - 1979	Chief Executive Officer Bracy Williams and Co. Washington, DC
Ford	Roger W. Hooker, Jr.** 1975 - 1977	Palisades, New York

| Nixon | Robert T. Monagan**
1973 - 1974 | Not Available |
| Nixon | Laurence J. Burton**
1971 - 1972 | Not Available |

*   Position created in 1971 by a departmental reorganization.

**   Served as Assistant Secretary for Congressional and Inter-governmental Affairs.

GENERAL COUNSEL

Level IV - Presidential Appointment with Senate Confirmation

Major Responsibilities

o   Serve as chief legal officer of the department. Advise the secretary on questions of law relevant to department programs and activities. Coordinate the activities of chief counsels of the component agencies.

o   Speak for the department in regulatory agency deliberations. Evaluate the legal implications of its legislative proposals. Coordinate the department's legal interests as necessary with counterparts in other areas of government.

Necessary Background, Experience, Personal Skills

The position calls for an experienced lawyer with a background in litigation. A knowledge of federal regulatory policy, including anti-trust law, is helpful but not essential. The appointee should move confidently around the Hill as a result of previous exposure to Congressional ways and means.

Insight

"This is very much a policy job," says one of those who has filled it. "And he or she will be chosen as someone who can support, understand and advance the secretary's policy in whatever areas the secretary wants to address--deregulation, reorganization, budgeting, privatization, and so on." In this as in other respects, the general counsel should be politically sensitive to the likely sources of outside opposition and support for a particular proposal or program or piece of legislation. Equally good inside antennae are important --inside the administration and the department itself--"because there is a great deal of interface with other government agencies." Most of the big issues that come up in the department have relevance to other agencies which may be working in the same area with similar or different objectives. The Federal Aviation Administration's activities on the international aviation front for example, might or might not mesh with concerns at State or Commerce.

This department's heavy regulatory activity generates a sizeable legal workload. If, say, highway plans call for a right of way through federal park land, the secretary must come up with a finding that considers whether any statutory requirement or existing regulation forbids it. And in a regulation-writing agency, says John W. Barnum, general counsel in 1971-72, "there's a constant tension between engineers on the one hand and lawyers on the other. You can tell when a regulation was written by a lawyer and when by an engineer. In the FAA, for instance, you're writing regulations that take a mix of aviation expertise and lawyering to produce something which is comprehensible. And that's true throughout the department."

As for legislative work, the department's general program can also keep the general counsel's office busy. The general counsel does not often testify on the Hill. But in preparation of legislation and comments on it to the Office of Management and Budget, in drafting supporting testimony and briefing the department's witnesses, the "real work on the department's position is done in the general counsel's office," according to one veteran of the job. This is so even though a given bill affects only the FAA or one of the other "modal" administrations.

There are some complaints about the amount of time absorbed by meetings to deliberate on and coordinate decisions. Jim J. Marquez, who held the job in 1984-86, says "the time it took to make decisions always delayed policy implementation. The long, simmering discussions were rather frustrating." But former general counsel Linda Heller Kamm (1977-80) feels that, "decision meetings with a tight agenda can often greatly reduce the amount of time which would otherwise be spent in an 'on paper' coordination process."

It's probably useful to glance at the legal structure of this many-lawyered department and the relationships within it. In the early 1970s, DOT considered whether to bring all of its lawyers under the general oversight of the general counsel, a pattern one can find in other departments. It's a system, Barnum thinks, that doesn't work in the Department of Transportation, "where you have administrators of the various modes who have quite specific missions to perform, require specific expertise and ought to have a counsel of their own and the confidence that they can (take an action) without having to talk to the secretary's lawyer." Consolidating the department's several hundred lawyers, including those working for the Coast Guard, into a reporting relationship to the general counsel would enable the latter "to do nothing but count sheep," he says. What the basic organizational decision not to do so means, he adds, "is that you do have this sort of dotted line responsibility from the six or seven chief counsels of the modal administrations to the general counsel of the department. That works depending on who's sitting in the chair. It doesn't work as an institutional matter simply because you draw the dotted line. So one problem the general counsel always has in dealing with any of the modal administrations is the kind of relationship to have with the people sitting in the positions of chief counsel or regulatory counsel or legislative counsel in the various modes."

Key Relationships

Within the Department

> Reports to: Secretary

> Works closely with:

> > Deputy Secretary
> > Assistant Secretary for Governmental Affairs

Outside the Department

> General counsel of other departments

Outside the Federal Government

> > Regulatory law groups; American Bar Association; insurance industry groups, such as American Insurance Association; consumer advocate groups such as Center for Auto Safety, Public Citizen

General Counsels of Transportation Since 1969

Administration	Name and Years Served	Present Position
Reagan	B. Wayne Vance 1987 - Present	Incumbent

Reagan	Jim J. Marquez 1984 - 1986	Partner Condon and Forsythe Washington, DC
Reagan	James H. Burnley IV 1983	Secretary Department of Transportation
Reagan	John M. Fowler 1981 - 1982	Vice President Commercial Credit Corporation Baltimore, Maryland
Carter	Thomas G. Allison 1980	Partner Preston, Thorgrimson, Ellis and Holman Seattle, Washington
Carter	Linda Heller Kamm 1977 - 1980	Of Counsel Foley & Lardner Washington, DC
Ford	John Hart Ely 1976	Professor Stanford University School of Law Stanford, California
Ford	Rodney E. Eyster 1974 - 1975	Vice President, Law Association of American Railroads Washington, DC
Nixon	J. Thomas Tidd (Acting) 1973	Not Available
Nixon	John W. Barnum 1971 - 1972	Partner White and Case Washington, DC
Nixon	James A. Washington, Jr. 1969 - 1970	Not Available

20

DEPARTMENT OF
THE TREASURY

Third largest federal department in current annual budget ($199 billion in fiscal 1988) and second largest in personnel (152,000), the Treasury department enjoys a good name in Washington. Some people speak of its professionalism, others of the virtues of flexibility, direct access to the top and fast decisions and action. Treasury, says one of its former officials who now represents a national business association, has clout. In his view, that is a function of assertive people and a very strong career service that doesn't change much and gives this agency an organizational nucleus and memory that other institutions don't have. A former Treasury secretary describes it as the premier department. Whatever their political persuasion is, he says, senior Treasury officials are basically sound money managers and the department is run in a very consistent, conservative fashion.

One reason behind its generally favorable reputation may lie in the fact, as some see it, that Treasury's early organizational structure and operation remain largely intact. While administrations have been stirred over the years by the yen to create, eliminate, split up or otherwise make over various agencies, they have seen fit to leave Treasury--created in 1789--mostly alone. No one seems certain whether this is due to an alert self-defense of department turf or simply to the advice of the sage famous for muttering something about not trying to fix things that already work.

Tax collection plus the department's diverse enforcement responsibilities--customs, secret service, alcohol, tobacco and firearms-- make it what one of its former senior officials calls the largest law-enforcement agency in the world. But tax policy, debt management, and international economic policy will continue as leading

A number of competent observers, including several who have served in senior Treasury positions, raise questions about the effective day-to-day management of U.S. foreign economic policy, in which the department is centrally involved. Three who share this concern are Paul A. Volcker and Beryl W. Sprinkel, both former Undersecretaries for Monetary Affairs; and C. Fred Bergsten, former Assistant Secretary for International Affairs. They think the department should become, or de facto already is, the lead agency in managing the nation's international economic affairs. But they doubt the adequacy of the department's present superstructure to sustain that role. To handle it, at a time when domestic and international economic matters grow increasingly interlocked, Volcker feels Treasury "should be organically interlinked."

Traditionally, the former Undersecretary for Monetary Affairs job generally carried the most senior department responsibilities in two areas--for domestic debt management and financial institutions policy, and for monetary, trade and other key issues on the international side. When it was eliminated in 1985, its senior domestic duties went to a newly-created Undersecretary for Finance, and day-to-day management of international affairs devolved onto the existing assistant secretary in that area. But the latter position seems to suffer badly from insufficient rank and authority.

As a remedy, Volcker and Sprinkel separately favor reviving the Undersecretary for Monetary Affairs job at the same level, whatever its title. Bergsten would leave in place the present Undersecretary for Finance, establish a new position level with it--or a step higher--and assign to it the senior international affairs portfolio. All three would retain the present Assistant Secretary for International Affairs.

DEPARTMENT OF THE TREASURY

SECRETARY

DEPUTY SECRETARY

Office of Intelligence Support

Executive Secretary

General Counsel
- Deputy General Counsel

Inspector General

Assistant Secretary (Tax Policy)
- Deputy Asst. Sec'y (Tax Policy)
- Office of Tax Legislative Counsel
- Office of International Tax Counsel
- Deputy Asst. Sec'y (Tax Analysis)
- Office of the Analysis

Assistant Secretary (International Affairs)
- Senior Deputy Asst. Sec'y (International Economic Policy)
- Deputy Asst. Sec'y (International Monetary Affairs)
- Deputy Asst. Sec'y (Developing Nations)
- Deputy Asst. Sec'y (Trade & Investment Policy)
- Deputy Asst. Sec'y (Arabian Peninsula Affairs)

Assistant Secretary (Legislative Affairs)
- Deputy Asst. Sec'y (Legislative Affairs)

Assistant Secretary (Public Affairs & Public Liaison)
- Deputy Asst. Sec'y (Public Liaison)
- Deputy Asst. Sec'y (Public Affairs)

Assistant Secretary (Management)
- Deputy Asst. Sec'y (Departmental Management)
- Deputy Asst. Sec'y (Administration)
- Deputy Asst. Sec'y (Departmental Information Systems)
- Deputy Asst. Sec'y (Departmental Finance and Planning)

Under Secretary for Finance

Treasurer of the United States
- Deputy Treasurer of the United States
- U.S. Savings Bonds Division
- United States Mint
- Bureau of Engraving & Printing

Assistant Secretary (Domestic Finance)
- Deputy Asst. Sec'y (Federal Finance)
- Deputy Asst. Sec'y (Financial Institutions Policy)
- Deputy Asst. Sec'y (State & Local Finance)
- Office of Revenue Sharing

Assistant Secretary (Economic Policy)
- Deputy Asst. Sec'y (Economic Forecasting)
- Office of Financial Analysis
- Office of Special Studies
- Applied Econometric Staff
- Monetary Policy Analysis Staff

Fiscal Assistant Secretary
- Deputy Fiscal Asst. Sec'y
- Financial Management Service
- Bureau of the Public Debt

Comptroller of the Currency
- Office of the Comptroller of the Currency

Commissioner of Internal Revenue
- Internal Revenue Service

Assistant Secretary (Enforcement)
- Deputy Asst. Sec'y (Enforcement)
- Office of Financial Enforcement
- Office of Foreign Assets Control
- Deputy Asst. Sec'y (Operations)
- Bureau of Alcohol, Tobacco and Firearms
- U.S. Customs Service
- U.S. Secret Service
- Federal Law Enforcement Training Center

Indicates bureaus

Shaded areas were selected as Prune Book positions

DEPUTY SECRETARY

Level II - Presidential Appointment with Senate Confirmation

Major Responsibilities

o   Act as chief operating officer for the department, managing its day-to-day operations. Take leadership of the department as acting secretary when required.

o   Manage specific projects and undertake specific missions as directed by the secretary. Develop or oversee development of policy as circumstances warrant in any area of Treasury responsibility.

Necessary Background, Experience, Personal Skills

One of those who held this position asserts flatly that candidates for it must have previous Treasury service. Most of the others emphasize the ability to manage a government bureaucracy, suggesting strongly the necessity--at a minimum--that this be at the Federal level. Candidates should also possess such other assets as experience with the Congress and the media, knowledge of economics, and good relationships within the business community.

Insight

In a department described by former deputy secretary Robert Carswell (1977-80) as "a conglomerate, not a single-purpose agency," the occupant of this job should expect to handle a little bit of everything. What kind and how much seems to depend partly--but importantly--on the operating style of the secretary; in that sense, this position resembles others at the same level elsewhere in government. And, like them, the best approach to this job lies in establishing an effective working relationship with the secretary and a clear mutual understanding of the deputy's specific tasks and duties. Whether or not any such agreed framework like this exists, however, some of the deputy's work inevitably falls in the ad hoc and short-notice category.

Whatever their origin, however, the deputy's assignments have in the past covered varying terrain--everything from a crucial role in arranging a hostage-release agreement with Iran to handling the day-to-day "crunch" negotiations with Canada on a free-trade agreement. At least one recent deputy had overall charge of Treasury's international trade, monetary, and third-world debt responsibilities while also assisting in the formulation of landmark tax revision and the corresponding legislative proposals. In the absence of the secretary, the deputy steps into the full range of substance and ceremony at that level as well.

As operating manager of the department, the deputy faces routine chores--consulting with Congressional members and staff, interviewing and recommending candidates for senior-level jobs, seeing representatives of interest groups. Other tasks, such as overseeing the enforcement arms of the department, may occasionally exceed mere routine; William E. Simon, a former secretary of the Treasury who also served in the deputy slot in the mid-1970s, points out that Treasury ranks as "the largest law-enforcement agency in the world," embracing the Bureau of Alcohol and Firearms, the U.S. Secret Service, the U.S. Customs Service and the Internal Revenue Service, among other functions.

The problems encountered in this position really mirror those of the department as a whole. A former deputy secretary says that "the problems never change, it's the magnitude of the problems that change," such as, budget deficits and the defense of stable international exchange rates. Another talks about the ability to overcome a large number of interlocking obstacles, such as the department, Congress, public interest groups. How? "Compromise, send memos, pass it to someone else, educate the people, anything that works."

Still, "the challenges are manifold," recalls Simon. "There isn't an area that Treasury doesn't deal with. It's a very diversified, satisfying day. You have an opportunity to make decisions that help and beneficially change people's lives, and that's the enjoyable part."

Key Relationships

Within the Department

Reports to: Secretary

Works closely with:

Assistant Secretaries for Tax Policy, Domestic
Finance, Economic Policy, International Affairs,
Legislative Affairs, and Public Affairs
Commissioner, Internal Revenue Service
General Counsel

Outside the Department

Deputy Secretary, Department of State
Deputy Secretary, Department of Defense
Deputy Secretary, Department of Energy
Deputy Secretary, Department of Justice

Outside the Federal Government

American Bankers Association, Independent Bankers
Association of America

Deputy Secretaries of the Treasury Since 1972*

Administration	Name and Years Served	Present Position
Reagan	M. Peter McPherson 1987 - Present	Incumbent
Reagan	Richard G. Darman 1985 - 1987	Managing Director Shearson/Lehman Brothers Washington, DC
Reagan	R. T. McNamar 1981 - 1985	Partner Edgar, Dunn and Conover Los Angeles, California
Carter	Robert Carswell 1977 - 1980	Senior Partner Shearman and Sterling New York, New York
Ford	George H. Dixon 1976 - 1977	Long Lake, Minnesota

Ford	Stephen S. Gardner 1974 - 1976	Deceased
Nixon	William E. Simon 1973 - 1974	Chairman WSPG International, Inc. Morristown, New Jersey
Nixon	Charls E. Walker 1972 - 1973	President Charls E. Walker Associates, Inc. Washington, DC

*   Position established in 1972.

COMMISSIONER
INTERNAL REVENUE SERVICE

Level III - Presidential Appointment with Senate Confirmation

Major Responsibilities

o   Administer and enforce federal internal revenue laws and related statutes. Interpret changes enacted in the laws and revise tax rules and regulations accordingly.

o   Work to motivate and maintain a high rate of voluntary taxpayer compliance. Direct education programs designed to support this effort, and assistance programs which improve taxpayer understanding of rights and obligations and improve collection.

o   Speak publicly for the administration on tax collection issues. In an advisory capacity, assist the policymakers at Treasury and in the Congress in formulating legislation to improve the tax code and collection system.

Necessary Background, Experience, Personal Skills

Some of those who have run IRS say it can't be done by anyone lacking a detailed understanding of the federal internal revenue laws and collection system. One says the job demands a top tax lawyer. Two others cite only a background in tax law. Most stress the slightly less obvious requirement of a successful record in managing a large, dispersed organization. While strictly techni-cal know-how doesn't seem as mandatory, former commissioners wouldn't sneeze at skills in accounting, financial management, and information systems. The agency's responsibility in administering tax treaties with other countries probably makes some familiarity with international affairs desirable.

Insight

A recent commissioner points out that the IRS collects about 92 cents of every dollar of federal government tax revenue. To do so, another adds, the chief of IRS runs a staff of 100,000 fulltime employees all over the country; their number grows by some 20,000 during the tax filing season. These statistics suggest two dimensions of this position not immediately apparent to those concerned with filling it.

First comes the public image of the federal tax collector and how it affects taxpayer attitudes. Randolph W. Thrower, commissioner in 1969-71, says "the efficiency of the administration of the revenue system depends on acceptance by taxpayers and their compliance with the tax laws. Support of the system from business and the general public is an essential element. The commissioner has to be the principal communicator with the public and the Congress in this regard."

Second, "most people think of the job as being a super tax accountant or tax lawyer, sitting in that chair and wielding power," says Roscoe L. Egger, Jr. who led the IRS from 1981 to 1986. "To me, it is much more like being the CEO of a large, spread-out company. It's a large management job. In a big organization as decentralized as this one, it becomes extremely difficult to maintain control of what is going on." Among other correctives, that means the commissioner travels frequently to talk with staff at the regional offices. Like Thrower, Egger puts considerable emphasis on communicating in both directions. "It's a very critical need, because you are the senior in the top office and people tend to listen to you and do what you say. (And) if you don't have the ability to listen, you'll make mistakes." Or, as Thrower recalls, "a lot more depended on administrative ability, personnel relationships and stimulation of morale than I contemplated."

Meanwhile, of course, the commissioner faces the daily substantive challenges of tax collection. "When I accepted I knew the job was large and complicated but I don't think I conceived its scope," acknowledges one who held it. Complex or dramatic revision of the tax laws, such as that enacted in 1986, clearly makes life more hazardous for the IRS. It must struggle first to interpret the full intent of the changes and then draft tax return forms and instruction language which corporate accountants and individual citizens alike can understand. In this latter effort, IRS has had something less than unbridled success. The chore has not become any easier under the impact of what a former commissioner labels "the rapid changing of tax laws and their lack of consistency and constancy." Apart from big tasks like this, says a onetime commissioner, "you're responsible for approving every published ruling and regulation that deals with substance and interpretation of the law. You obviously have counsel to advise you, but the ultimate substantive decisions rest with the commissioner. The policy-making role is very important."

Other duties fall in the areas of Congressional testimony, a frequent task; there is also regular contact with the chief of staff of the Joint Committee on Taxation and staff directors of the Senate Finance and House Ways and Means committees and relevant subcommittees. The commissioner oversees the budget process and the selection and training of executive-level personnel; one veteran views such training as critically important. This job also operates on a high speech-making frequency--estimates vary widely, from 40 to more than 100 a year--much of it part of a broad public affairs effort to improve the public view of IRS and increase respect for what it does.

Beyond the whirlwind of adapting to and enforcing frequent tax law changes, previous commissioners list IRS' other chief problems as "insufficient resources to provide adequate tax administration and taxpayer assistance," "keeping the good career people there," "trying to persuade the press to tell the complete story instead of grabbing a headline," and "the administration of sensitive cases and embarrassing instances of the conduct of people in the field."

General agreement exists about the goals of future commissioners. They should "continue to refine the tax code, increase its fairness, eliminate special interest provisions, and make it fairer;" "run the tax system impartially;" "reduce non-compliance and increase respect;" and establish "a culture of excellence and quality" within the agency.

Key Relationships

Within the Department

> Reports to: Secretary

> Works closely with:

>> Deputy Secretary
>> Assistant Secretary for Tax Policy
>> Assistant Secretary for Management
>> General Counsel

Outside the Department

>> Comptroller General, General Accounting Office, U.S. Congress

Assistant Attorney General, Tax Division, Department of Justice

Chief of Staff, Joint Economic Committee, U.S. Congress

Staff directors, Senate Finance Committee and House Ways and Means Committee

Outside the Federal Government

American Bar Association, American Institute of Certified Public Accountants, National Association of Tax Administrators; tax executives and financial executives organizations

Commissioners of the Internal Revenue Service Since 1969

Administration	Name and Years Served	Present Position
Reagan	Lawrence B. Gibbs 1986 - Present	Incumbent
Reagan	Roscoe L. Egger, Jr. 1981 - 1986	Tax Partner Price Waterhouse Washington, DC
Carter	Jerome Kurtz 1977 - 1980	Partner Paul, Weiss, Rifkind, Wharton and Garrison Washington, DC
Nixon/Ford	Donald C.Alexander 1973 - 1977	Partner Cadwalader, Wickersham and Taft Washington, DC
Nixon	Jonnie M. Walters 1971-1973	Partner Leatherwood, Walker, Todd & Mann Greenville, South Carolina
Nixon	Randolph W. Thrower 1969 - 1971	Partner Sutherland, Asbill and Brennen Atlanta, Georgia

COMPTROLLER OF THE CURRENCY

Level III - Presidential Appointment with Senate Confirmation

Major Responsibilities

o   Implement laws governing the operations of 5,000 U.S. national banks to provide a secure national banking system. Participate in formulation of legislation in support of that goal.

o   Supervise the periodic examination of national banks to assess their financial soundness, the integrity of their operations, and their adherence to banking laws.

o   Approve the chartering of newly-organized national banks, alteration of bank status from state to national, and similar changes involving national banks.

Necessary Background, Experience, Personal Skills

A previous comptroller thinks "a lawyer who works for a bank would be ideal" in this position. Candidates need extensive experience in the financial system, with legal and management background a plus. Clearly, hands-on bank experience is a minimum requirement. Performance in the job also gains from a knowledge of accounting and a bent toward analysis. A veteran comptroller-watcher reports never having seen anyone in this job who was not "very well qualified."

Insight

Simply put, the comptroller has the main responsibility to see that individual national (as opposed to state-chartered) banks run safely, soundly, and honestly. Generally, this means that they operate in the best interests of their individual and corporate customers, in compliance with applicable law, and without endangering the security of the banking system. When this is not the case, the comptroller takes corrective action to the degree necessary. To exert this kind of regular supervision of some 5,000 banks, the comptroller manages a nationwide examination apparatus with a staff of about 2,000.

In addition to this implementing side of the job, one of those who served in it says "you have the right to deal in policy issues you believe will strengthen and protect the banking system." Some comptrollers have basically stuck to implementation and remained silent on policy, he reflects, and "some combine the two."

As for preparation for the post, a former comptroller believes that no one who takes it on "really knows what he's getting into." Another believes some solid homework helps, but "there is no substitute for knowledge gained by being in the chair." Wide agreement exists on the high quality of staff--"dedicated, career-oriented, hard-working professionals" and on an insufficient salary scale that drives people toward higher compensation not only in the private sector but in other agencies.

Of the several federal agencies which oversee the activities of the nation's financial sector, the comptroller's office stands as the only single-person regulator. Further, the occupant of this job sits as one of the three members of the Federal Deposit Insurance Corporation. In the view of at least one who held it, the position represents something of an anomaly, "free of any control from the executive branch" and accountable to the Congress "to some degree" but "not the same as most of the other agencies." As such, he says the job "offers you a chance to bring about change, serving your country without any interference."

Different views exist on this point. Another who held the job agrees that it has "major impact on one of the nation's most important industries in a very significant way." But he says "you don't manage things any differently than you do anywhere else--keep people informed, give loyalty to your boss and demand loyalty from your staff." An informed Congressional staff member points out that the comptroller "technically is an employee of the Treasury, and he's supposed to be independent. It is a regulatory body, it hands out enforcement actions, it penalizes people....But at the same time, he does report to (the Secretary of the Treasury) and when he testifies up here he has to go through the same Treasury clearance process."

At the same time, a previous occupant notes, "the nature of the job--the process of examining a bank--is highly confidential. The law is very specific on that. The hard part was making sure that the relevant parties knew what was happening on an extremely confidential basis." In this, he adds, the key lies in the relationship with the Congress. The comptroller must establish lines of communication such that "you can share with them information you can't share with anybody else. It is a personal relationship and it's based on trust."

This former comptroller makes a further point: "The position is apolitical, so the comptroller must be apolitical. Once he is seen to favor one party over another he cannot be effective. Any sense of partiality destroys the credibility of the agency." None of that, however, seems to rule out the need for political antennae in good working condition, "so he can know what he can accomplish."

Key Relationships

Within the Department

Reports to: Secretary

Works closely with:

Deputy Secretary
Undersecretary for Finance

Outside the Department

Chairman, Federal Reserve Board
Chairman, Federal Deposit Insurance Corporation
Chairman, Federal Home Loan Bank Board

Outside the Federal Government

State banking and securities industry associations, such as American Bankers Association, National Associationn of Securities Dealers, Public Securities Association, Securities Industry Association; consumer organizations; low- and moderate-income housing groups, such as League of Cities, National Association of Housing and Redevelopment Officials

Comptrollers of the Currency Since 1969

Administration	Name and Years Served	Present Position
Reagan	Robert L. Clarke 1985 - Present	Incumbent

Reagan	C. T. Conover 1981 - 1985	Partner Edgar, Dunn and Conover San Francisco, California
Carter	John G. Heimann 1977 - 1981	Vice Chairman Merrill Lynch Capital Markets New York, New York
Nixon/Ford	James E. Smith 1973 - 1976	Vice President Chamber Associates, Inc. Washington, DC
Nixon	William B. Camp 1966 - 1973	Deceased

ASSISTANT SECRETARY
DOMESTIC FINANCE

Level IV - Presidential Appointee with Senate Confirmation

Major Responsibilities

o   Formulate and recommend financing and debt management policy for the federal government, and coordinate its execution among all federal agencies and programs involved. Work with financial markets which set interest rates at which the government borrows and invests.   Establish and maintain guidelines and standards for federal credit programs such as loan guarantees.

o   Take a leading part in developing legislative proposals affecting financial institutions and the federal agencies which regulate them.

o   Supervise federal revenue sharing.   Shape federal government positions and actions in matters involving state and local government financing.

Necessary Background, Experience, Personal Skills

Good performance in this job depends on prior, practical exposure to U.S. financial markets and an updated understanding of how the regulation of banks and other financial entities works. "Being an economist isn't enough. The job needs hands-on experience," says one of those who held it. Specifically, that means the incoming assistant secretary should have worked at the management level in a bank, bond house or other institution closely tied with markets operations. Working contacts in this field, and some career background in an area of government relevant to it, are other qualifications to look for. The job's occupant should feel comfortable with the Congress, the press and the financial community, all of which absorb large amounts of time.

Insight

This is a technical job.   It operates at the front line in the federal government's permanent battle to finance its mountainous debt at the least possible cost. And it has a central role affecting the behavior of financial institutions, especially in the crafting and support of legislation affecting federal entities which regulate them, such as the Federal Deposit Insurance Corporation.

Day-to-day management of federal debt and credit policy is exerted through a number of interagency groups and Treasury Department functions which this assistant secretary chairs, takes part in, or directs. These interlocking activities, says a previous tenant, make the job "the Treasury's eyes and ears into the financial markets." The occupant monitors the credit markets daily; attends weekly decision meetings on debt issuance and oversees the weekly Treasury debt auction; supervises the Federal Financing Bank and co-chairs the Cabinet council on federal credit policy.

He heads a similar Cabinet group concerned with financial institutions and directs the Securities Investor Protection Corporation. The job has oversight of the department's responsibilities with respect to the Pension Benefit Guaranty Corporation and of projects bequeathed by the former Synthetic Fuels Corporation.

In the financial institutions area, issues centering on their status and stability represent part of the current agenda of this position. These notably include the question of long-debated legislation--passed by the Senate in March, 1988 and, at this writing, awaiting House action--to revise existing law (four titles of the Bank Act of 1933) to allow banks to go into the securities business. Thomas J. Healey, who held the position in 1983-85, says the key objective in this field "is to create a financial institutions regulation policy more rational than the one we have now, and to re-establish the stability of the deposit insurance funds."

Finally, the assistant secretary has a contribution to make in defining the more constructive, more finely-tuned federal role called for by the frequent turbulence and potentially disruptive impact of the financial marketplace. One of those formerly in the job supports the view that events like the October, 1987 stock market crash have given both federal financial managers and financial market authorities an important challenge: To take a broader view of what constitutes the responsibility of each in market behavior.

Key Relationships

Within the Department

Reports to: Undersecretary for Finance

Works closely with:

> Secretary
> Deputy Secretary
> Undersecretary for Finance
> Assistant Secretary for Legislative Affairs
> Assistant Secretary for Tax Policy
> Assistant Secretary for Economic Policy

Outside the Department

> Deputy Director, Office of Management and Budget
> Associate Director, Economics and Government, Office
> of Management and Budget
> Chairman, Federal Reserve Board
> Assistant to the President for Domestic Affairs

Outside the Federal Government

> American Bankers Association, National Association
> of Home Builders, United States League of Savings
> Institutions, Securities Industries Association

Assistant Secretaries for Domestic Finance Since 1976*

Administration	Name and Years Served	Present Position
Reagan	Charles O. Sethness 1985 - Present	Incumbent
Reagan	Thomas J. Healey 1983 - 85	Vice President, Real Estate Department Goldman Sachs and Co. New York, New York
Reagan	Roger Mehle 1981 - 1983	Partner Royer, Shacknai & Mehle Washington, DC

Carter	Roger C. Altman 1977 - 1980	Partner Blackstone Group New York, New York
Ford	Robert A. Gerard 1976 - 1977	Managing Director Morgan Stanley Inc. New York, New York

*   Position established in 1976.

ASSISTANT SECRETARY
INTERNATIONAL AFFAIRS

Level IV - Presidential Appointment with Senate Confirmation

Major Responsibilities

o   Assist in guiding the development and proper direction of U.S. international economic policy, principally in monetary affairs, trade and investment, and Third World debt. Consult in this process with the secretary and deputy secretary. Coordinate policy formulation with other departments and agencies.

o   Lead and direct the execution of department policy responsibilities in the above and related fields, including the conduct of diplomacy with countries of the developed and developing worlds and U.S. participation in multilateral development institutions.

o   Monitor and analyze events and trends in international exchange and interest rates, balances of payments, energy prices and investment.

Necessary Background, Experience, Personal Skills

The pace and responsibilities of this job allow little or no time to learn. Candidates should already know and have thought about the policy issues. An economist or investment banker with a knowledge of international markets probably best matches the demands of the position. But real-world private and, if possible, public sector experience, with demonstrated negotiating skill, is in any case imperative. "If you bring a reputation in as somebody who's known, respected and knowledgeable, it's just an enormous difference," a former assistant secretary asserts. "It is really helpful when the crunch is on to be able to go to corporate CEOs, either the head of a bank or the person who runs the international side, and talk turkey with him." Further, some public visibility, especially in the media, and skill in conveying abstruse subject matter can often help carry the day. And, advises a veteran of the job, don't underestimate physical stamina.

Insight

This job staggers under vital responsibilities and great work load without sufficient rank to handle them effectively. That's the strong view of two qualified observers whose prescriptions for cure vary somewhat, but with the same objective. C. Fred Bergsten, who held the position in 1977-81, and Paul A. Volcker, former Federal Reserve Board chairman, think that leadership of U.S. economic policymaking belongs with the Treasury Department, especially in the international area. They believe the logic of events increasingly confirms that judgment. And--as examined in the introductory discussion of Treasury--they would do some reorganizing at the top of the department to enable it to operate more effectively in what has become an interdependent global economy. Specifically, though with slightly differing blueprints, they would upgrade senior stewardship of Treasury's international affairs responsibilities to the undersecretary level or higher.

Volcker, who also once held the now-eliminated job of Undersecretary for Monetary Affairs, describes it as the only economic position in government at that level which combined international and domestic responsibilities and "that's the world we live in." A restructuring, he suggests, would reflect the reality of "an era in which international and domestic economic issues are increasingly tied together and are often the same thing where policymaking is concerned."

Whatever its precise formula, such a move would hardly leave the assistant secretary for international affairs with nothing to do. And without some solution, the matter of rank will continue to pose one of the central obstacles confronting the important mission of this position. At its current level, the occupant "doesn't have as much rank as most of his foreign counterparts and people at other agencies he's dealing with," Bergsten explains. "The job is not high enough, doesn't have enough authority, to handle the monetary affairs and international financial negotiating responsibility on behalf of the U.S. government," Volcker says. The current structure means, moreover, that the deputy secretary--who does have the clout--cannot give full attention to the international side as the former undersecretary for monetary affairs once did. Yet perversely, when the deputy secretary (or secretary) does get involved and attendance at high-level meetings and other activities is restricted, the assistant secretary might be left out. "The poor guy who's negotiating day to day isn't even in the key meetings because the deputy is there," Bergsten points out.

The sheer quantity and range of work present the other big

operational challenge in this job's present configuration. Monetary, trade and third-world debt issues crowd the agenda in a 60- to 80- hour week. For example, a Congressional source who watched the development and presentation of the Baker plan to deal with third-world debt says the assistant secretary for international affairs "is the point man" in that effort. "The whole day was like a dentist's office," recalls Marc E. Leland, assistant secretary in 1981-84, "people in and out." The job requires regular travel across many latitudes and longitudes. "You've got to go around the industrial world working out exchange rate arrangements or monetary system reforms," Bergsten says, "and to Argentina, Brazil, Mexico and so on to work on debt. You've got to treat Paris flights like shuttles--fly overnight, go to the meeting, fly right back, be in the office next morning without being zonked."

Efforts with the Congress take upwards of 25 percent of total time. In recent years the issues covered in this job have become more difficult to negotiate with the Congress. With tighter budget constraints, for example, the Congress has felt less comfortable than ever grappling with requested U.S. funding levels for the several multilateral development banks toward which the assistant secretary has policy responsibility. Some of this Congressional work takes place behind the scenes, greasing wheels that must turn favorably for upcoming legislation. Some goes simply to holding Congressional hands "when they want to bitch about the dollar or foreign investment or something," remembers one of those who did it.

The assistant secretary also invests considerable time and energy in contacts and relationships with constituency groups. Here the financial community comes foremost, along with foreign government and private sector officials whose understanding and cooperation are frequently essential assets. As with any international issue, the tenant of this job must mediate between foreign and domestic interests and pressures. When the matters at hand involve exchange rates, interest rates, trade and debt--pocketbook issues which can also bring down markets and governments alike--the pitch and intensity rise. A former assistant secretary says "you have to be able to understand where both (foreign and domestic interlocutors) are coming from, what their concerns are, what their constraints are, what their irrationalities are."

As for the consequences of failure, Bergsten uses third-world debt as an illustration. Mishandle it, he says, and "a few big banks could go bust and the whole financial system would be at risk. This was more true five years ago than now, but we're still not out of the woods....I would really stress picking a team that you have confidence in, because you can't do it all yourself. You must have deputies out there working the different components. If you don't do that, you're not going to succeed, even if you work an 80-hour week yourself."

Key Relationships

Within the Department

> Reports to: Secretary

> Works closely with:

>> Deputy Secretary
>> Assistant secretaries for Economic Policy and
>> Domestic Finance

Outside the Department

> Undersecretary, Economic Affairs, Department of State
> Assistant Secretary, Economic and Business Affairs,
> Department of State
> Senior Director, International Economic Affairs,
> National Security Council

Outside the Federal Government

> Financial and business communities, domestic and foreign, such as American Bankers Association, Bankers Association for Foreign Trade, International Economic Policy Association, U.S. Council for International Business; investor groups, such as New York Stock Exchange, Securities Industry Association; economic associations

Assistant Secretaries for International Affairs Since 1969

Administration	Name and Years Served	Present Position
Reagan	David C. Mulford 1984 - Present	Incumbent

Reagan	Marc E. Leland 1981 - 1984	President Marc Leland & Associates Washington, DC
Carter	C. Fred Bergsten 1977 - 1981	Director Institute for International Economics Washington, DC
Ford	Gerald Parsky 1974 - 1977	Partner Gibson, Dunn & Crutcher Washington, DC
Ford	Charles A. Cooper 1974 - 1977	Not Available
Nixon	John M. Hennesey 1972 - 1974	Chairman and CEO Credit Suisse First Boston London, England
Nixon	John R. Petty 1968 - 1972	Chairman and CEO Marine Midland Banks New York, New York

ASSISTANT SECRETARY
TAX POLICY

Level IV - Presidential Appointment with Senate Confirmation

Major Responsibilities

o   Counsel and assist the secretary in devising and implementing domestic and international tax policy. Formulate and recommend changes in policy, taking into account changes proposed by the Congress or advocated elsewhere in the executive branch.

o   Assist in the analysis and development of tax legislation. Oversee the interpretive aspects of the Internal Revenue Service's tax regulation function. Prepare revenue estimates for the administration's yearly budget presentation.

o   Supervise and participate in negotiation of tax treaties and agreements with other nations.

Necessary Background, Experience, Personal Skills

Candidates who haven't practiced or taught tax law shouldn't apply. Substantial expertise in this field, however acquired, plus familiarity with the history and philosophy of American tax policy, are basic requisites. It helps to have some general economics background or training and to understand the operation of the Internal Revenue Service. Note also that this assistant secretary puts in much time on the Hill and on public speaking platforms, in support and explanation of administration tax proposals and programs.

Insight

This position needs a knowledgeable tax lawyer who can closely watch the operation of a complicated federal revenue structure, judge its economic and social impact, and interpret the findings in terms of what tax changes might prove necessary or beneficial. Such calculations must take account of other key factors which continuously influence the direction of the national and international economy. In recommending tax law changes, moreover, the assistant secretary in this job needs to consider their political practicality and--in a political as well as a substantive light--the tax actions and inclinations of other government entities and of the Congress. John E. Chapoton, who held the post in 1981-84, supplies this realistic definition of its central mission: "To maintain a sound and objective analysis of the tax laws, somewhat devoid of political influence."

The most notable--though probably not the most typical-- recent illustration of these functions came with the long tax revision effort of the mid-1980s. Treasury set the basic process in motion, spending many months on different versions of legislation that reflected principles and goals viewed as generally acceptable and desirable, such as the idea of revenue neutrality. Ultimately, the Congress produced the dramatic Tax Reform and Simplification Act of 1986. On the long road to this result, the Assistant Secretary for Tax Policy had an important day-to-day conceptual, drafting and Congressional role in a top-echelon Treasury effort led by the secretary. As the new law's provisions continue to take effect and work their way into the economy, the occupant of this job will remain a key monitor of its progress. This explains the con- tinuous dialogue with legislators, the business, accounting and tax law communities and interest groups maintained by the assistant secretary as a regular and important part of the assignment.

Other facets of the job involve its tenant in consultations with the chief and staff of the Internal Revenue Service, a source of practical data and assessment on tax law application; in inter- agency meetings on domestic economic policy; in the issuance of tax regulations and rulings; and in frequent contacts with foreign tax officials. In addition, a former assistant secretary says, "there were plenty of speeches, some television interviews, and ceremonial events in other countries."

Those who have held the job give good marks to the staff support they received, citing "high-caliber lawyers" with a "great sense of professional responsibility" in an "exceedingly productive office." However, one mentions a jurisdictional problem involving the office of the General Counsel, which has administrative control of the lawyers in the tax policy office.

Key Relationships

Within the Department

Reports to: Secretary

Works closely with:
> Assistant secretaries for Domestic Finance, Economic Policy, International Affairs, and Legislative Affairs
> Commissioner, Internal Revenue Service

Outside the Department

> Associate Director, Economics and Government, Office of Management and Budget

Outside the Federal Government

> U. S. Chamber of Commerce, National Association of Manufacturers, Distilled Spirits Council of the United States, Motor Vehicle Manufacturers Association; taxpayer and public policy groups, such as Citizens for Tax Justice, Federation of Tax Administrators, National Taxpayers Union

Assistant Secretaries for Tax Policy Since 1969

Administration	Name and Years Served	Present Position
Reagan	O. Donaldson Chapoton 1987 - Present	Incumbent
Reagan	J. Roger Mentz 1985 - 1987	Tax Partner Cadwalader, Wickersham and Taft Washington, DC
Reagan	Ronald A. Pearlman 1984 - 1985	Chief of Staff Joint Committee on Taxation
Reagan	John E. Chapoton 1981 - 1984	Partner Vinson and Elkins Washington, DC
Carter	Donald C. Lubick 1977 - 1981	Resident Partner Hodgson, Russ, Andrews, Woods and Goodyear Washington, DC

Carter	Laurence N. Woodworth 1977	Deceased
Ford	Charles M. Walker 1975 - 1977	Partner Paul, Hastings, Janofsky and Walker Santa Monica, California
Nixon/Ford	Frederick W. Hickman 1972 - 1975	Senior Partner Hopkins and Sutter Chicago, Illinois
Nixon	Edwin S. Cohen 1969 - 1972	Senior Partner Covington and Burling Washington, DC

GENERAL COUNSEL

Level IV - Presidential Appointment with Senate Confirmation

Major Responsibilities

o   Provide legal counsel to the secretary and other principal officers on all matters relating to Treasury activities.

o   Act as chief legal officer of the department. Represent the department within the administration, before the Congress, and outside the government on relevant legal issues and policy initiatives with strong legal dimensions.

o   Direct the activities of the legal staff of the Office of the Secretary (about 45 lawyers). Oversee the work of the chief counsels of individual department divisions.

Necessary Background, Experience, Personal Skills

Consideration for the position should go to a lawyer with a strong financial law background that includes banking, securities, tax, and corporate law, and familiarity with financial institutions. A knowledge of the legal aspects of government fiscal, budgetary and monetary operations also ranks high.

Insight

A chief operational concern in handling this job seems to center on bringing all significant decisions at Treasury under legal review before they become final. Although one might assume general recognition within the department of such a necessity, Peter J. Wallison, general counsel in 1981-85, says "the key problem is assuring that officials within the department understand the necessity for lawyers' review of the issues presented to the secretary or deputy secretary for resolution. These issues generally have legal aspects which must be reviewed by the department's lawyers before decisions are made."

One obvious answer, he thinks, lies in requiring "a sign-off by the general counsel on all matters involving actions by the secretary or deputy secretary," a procedure not adequately followed during his time in the job. He dealt with the problem by "jaw-boning," and by encouraging the department's lawyers to respond effectively and imaginatively to requests for advice. "That," says Wallison, "had the effect of increasing the degree to which they were consulted when policies were being developed."

The same considerations are echoed in the comments of Robert H. Mundheim, who held the position from 1977 to 1980. He lists one of its responsibilities as ensuring "that the legal staff is brought into problems at the right time." To him, that means "early in the problem" and includes giving the legal staff "all the facts." He advises future occupants to "get people to understand that the legal staff is there to help, not hinder," and "take the job only if you can have an open, steady relationship with the secretary or deputy secretary."

Running Treasury's legal functions involves an expectable routine of regular meetings at senior levels as well as within the legal office and with the chief counsels of the department's various bureaus. The occupant of the job has appointment authority for the legal staff and chief counsels, approves promotions, and oversees other administrative operations. There are frequent public affairs duties.

Key Relationships

Within the Department

> Reports to: Secretary

> Works closely with:

>> Deputy Secretary
>> Assistant secretaries

Outside the Department

>> General Counsels and legal advisors in the White House and in other departments and agencies

Outside the Federal Government

>> American Bankers Association, Association of Bank Holding Companies, Securities Industry Association; banks, thrifts, investment bankers; law firms

General Counsels of the Treasury Since 1969

Administration	Name and Years Served	Present Position
Reagan	Mark Sullivan III 1988 - Present	Incumbent
Reagan	Robert M. Kimmitt 1985 - 1987	Partner Sidley & Austin Washington, DC
Reagan	Peter J. Wallison 1981 - 1985	Partner Gibson, Dunn and Crutcher Washington, DC
Carter	Robert H. Mundheim 1977 - 1980	Dean University of Pennsylvania Law School Philadelphia, Pennsylvania
Ford	Richard R. Albrecht 1974 - 1976	Executive Vice President Boeing Commercial Airplane Company Seattle, Washington
Nixon	Edward C. Schmults 1973 - 1974	Senior Vice President, External Affairs GTE Corporation Stamford, Connecticut
Nixon	Samuel R. Pierce, Jr. 1970 - 1973	Secretary Department of Housing and Urban Development
Nixon	Paul W. Eggers 1969 - 1970	Partner Eggers & Greene Dallas, Texas

21

VETERANS
ADMINISTRATION

ADMINISTRATOR

Level II - Presidential Appointment with Senate Confirmation

Major Responsibilities

o   Direct the activities of the Veterans Administration (VA) in providing medical, surgical, pension and death benefits to veterans of U.S. military service.

o   Articulate veterans affairs issues within the administration and, especially on budget issues, to the Congress. Similarly, act as public spokesman for veterans' interests.

Necessary Background, Experience, Personal Skills

Almost by definition, the manager of the federal government's responsibilities to those entitled to benefits through military service must be a veteran. "Whether it's a career military person is relatively unimportant," according to the current administrator, Thomas K. Turnage. "But the fact that the person is a veteran is quite important." He and others underline the importance of an ability to represent VA positions and views convincingly to the country as a whole and to veterans, and of principled decisionmaking and administration of the agency. The position also requires some management background, with an emphasis on budgetary experience.

Insight

At this writing the chances seem better than ever that the Congress will establish federal management of veterans affairs as a Cabinet department. The move would of course elevate the occupant of this position to the secretary level. Would this make a substantial difference in the professional or personal credentials necessary to do the job? "I see no difference," says Turnage, who has run the VA since 1986. "We find ourselves in a dialogue now on whether this agency should be a Cabinet office. In trying to compare, we point out that the agency is bigger than four of the other Cabinet departments combined, which probably assists in answering that question. But the sensitivity of it, the scope and depth of it, would not change one iota." For fiscal 1989, the VA's budget request comes in at $30.1 billion, and there are 240,000 employees; Turnage notes that, "if you count the number of people we paid last year, it was about 322,000 because of attrition and turnovers."

The administrator runs this agency through three main departments: medicine and surgery, veterans benefits, and memorial affairs. They provide services ranging from disability and death compensation payments, pensions and education assistance, to health care in 172 medical centers, and burial and cemetery benefits. These departments operate within policy guidelines set by the administrator, who sees that they are followed throughout the system. For the administrator, most of the time actually spent on the Hill comes during the budget season, but there is a good deal of telephone contact. Other senior officials of the agency visit the Congress regularly and frequently; on the day we interviewed Turnage, the deputy administrator and the medical and benefits directors testified at three separate hearings.

Turnage puts a premium on "political sensitivity" to the role played by the administrator in handling the sometimes conflicting interests and views of the veterans constituency, the administration and the Congress. An administrator, he thinks, must establish credibility with all three to do the job effectively. This, he says, "can be a very delicate thing," with the veterans "opting for more" and, on the other side, the need to operate in a "constrained resource environment" and "follow the objectives of the administration to try to hold that within reason."

On this point, another recent administrator emphasizes the

value of "a sense of personal integrity. If you get caught being cute you will die by your own sword. Communication skills are extremely important." Although when he took on the job, "I expected to be tarred and feathered and run out of Washington," he says "it was exhilarating and gratifying and one of the highlights of my life."

Like their predecessors, future administrators will face the problem of limited resources and the need to improve the management of the VA to squeeze as much value as possible out of available funds. This will become harder as veterans, whose average age as a group exceeds that of the populace as a whole, require greater medical attention. There have been special issues of high visibility and deep emotion, like the controversies over federal responsibility for death and injury to veterans in early post-war nuclear testing and through the use of defoliating agents in Vietnam. Such situations will doubtless continue to put the VA chief to increasingly tough tests, not just of agency leadership, but of credibility with veterans organizations. At the same time, says Turnage, these groups "have responsible people out there and they understand the art of the possible....They provide voluntary help that we couldn't buy. From the standpoint of moral support and dollar support and other things, they are big adjuncts to our budget process."

Key Relationships

Within the Agency

Reports to: President

Works closely with:

Chief Benefits Director
Chief Medical Director
Chief Memorial Affairs Director

Outside the Agency

Assistant Secretary, Health, Department of Health and Human Services
Director, National Institutes of Health, HHS
Assistant Secretary, Special Education and Rehabilitative Services, Department of Education
Assistant Secretary, Pension and Welfare Benefits, Department of Labor

Medical officials of the three military services

Outside the Federal Government

Veterans organizations, medical and nursing associations, health care agencies, insurance companies

Administrators of the Veterans Administration Since 1969

Administration	Name and Years Served	Present Position
Reagan	Thomas K. Turnage 1986 - Present	Incumbent
Reagan	Harry N. Walters 1982 - 1986	President & CEO Great Lakes Carbon Corp. Briarcliff Manor, New York
Reagan	Robert P. Nimmo 1981 - 1982	Atascadero, California
Carter	Max Cleland 1977 - 1981	Secretary of State State of Georgia Atlanta, Georgia
Ford	Richard L. Roudebush 1974 - 1977	Not Available
Nixon	Donald E. Johnson 1969 - 1974	Executive Director National Credit Union Administration Washington, DC

APPENDIX I

The Toughest Management and Policy Making Jobs in Washington

In selecting the 116 jobs included in this volume, the Principals of The Center for Excellence reviewed nearly 650 key positions throughout the federal government. In making their choices, each team faced many "close calls"--positions that fell only a little short of meeting the prescribed criteria. They concluded that there are 69 such positions which also deserved attention. A list of these positions follows.

DEPARTMENT OF AGRICULTURE

Assistant Secretary for Science and Education (Level IV, Presidential Appointment with Senate Confirmation)

Inspector General (Level IV, Presidential Appointment with Senate Confirmation)

Administrator, Farmers Home Administration (Level V, Presidential Appointment with Senate Confirmation)

Administrator, Food and Nutrition Service (Senior Executive Service)

Administrator, Foreign Agricultural Service (Senior Executive Service)

Deputy Undersecretary for International Affairs and Commodity Program (Senior Executive Service)

Deputy Undersecretary for Small Community and Rural Development (Senior Executive Service)

DEPARTMENT OF COMMERCE

Deputy Secretary (Level II, Presidential Appointment with Senate Confirmation)

Undersecretary for Economic Affairs (Level III, Presidential Appointment with Senate Confirmation)

CONSUMER PRODUCT SAFETY COMMISSION

Chairman (Level III, Presidential Appointment with Senate Confirmation)

DEPARTMENT OF DEFENSE

Department of the Air Force

Assistant Secretary for Acquisition (Level IV, Presidential Appointment with Senate Confirmation)

Department of the Army

Assistant Secretary for Financial Management (Level IV, Presidential Appointment with Senate Confirmation)

Assistant Secretary for Research, Development and Acquisition (Level IV, Presidential Appointment with Senate Confirmation)

Department of the Navy

Assistant Secretary for Research, Engineering and Systems (Level IV, Presidential Appointment with Senate Confirmation)

Assistant Secretary for Financial Management/Comptroller (Level IV, Presidential Appointment with Senate Confirmation)

Office of the Secretary

Assistant Secretary for Command, Control, Communications, and Intelligence (Level IV, Presidential Appointment with Senate Confirmation)

Assistant Secretary for Legislative Affairs (Level IV, Presidential Appointment with Senate Confirmation)

DEPARTMENT OF EDUCATION

Assistant Secretary for Educational Research and Improvement (Level IV, Presidential Appointment with Senate Confirmation)

General Counsel (Level IV, Presidential Appointment with Senate Confirmation)

Deputy Undersecretary for Planning, Budget and Evaluation (Level V, Presidential Appointment with Senate Confirmation)

DEPARTMENT OF ENERGY

Assistant Secretary for Fossil Energy (Level IV, Presidential Appointment with Senate Confirmation)

Director, Office of Civilian Radioactive Waste Management (Level IV, Presidential Appointment with Senate Confirmation)

Assistant Secretary for Environment, Safety, and Health (Level IV, Presidential Appointment with Senate Confirmation)

Assistant Secretary for Nuclear Energy (Senior Executive Service)

Chairman, Federal Energy Regulatory Commission (Level III, Presidential Appointment with Senate Confirmation)

ENVIRONMENTAL PROTECTION AGENCY

Assistant Administrator for Air and Radiation (Level IV, Presidential Appointment with Senate Confirmation)

Assistant Administrator for Pesticides and Toxic Substances (Level IV, Presidential Appointment with Senate Confirmation)

Assistant Administrator for Policy, Planning and Evaluation (Level IV, Presidential Appointment with Senate Confirmation)

Assistant Administrator for Research and Development (Level IV, Presidential Appointment with Senate Confirmation)

Assistant Administrator for Water (Level IV, Presidential Appointment with Senate Confirmation)

EXPORT-IMPORT BANK OF THE UNITED STATES

President and Chairman (Level III, Presidential Appointment with Senate Confirmation)

FEDERAL COMMUNICATIONS COMMISSION

Chairman (Level III, Presidential Appointment with Senate Confirmation)

FEDERAL DEPOSIT INSURANCE CORPORATION

Chairman of the Board of Directors (Level III, Presidential Appointment with Senate Confirmation)

FEDERAL ELECTION COMMISSION

Chairman (Level IV, Presidential Appointment with Senate Confirmation)

FEDERAL HOME LOAN BANK BOARD

Chairman (Level III, Presidential Appointment with Senate Confirmation)

FEDERAL TRADE COMMISSION

Chairman (Level III, Presidential Appointment with Senate Confirmation)

DEPARTMENT OF HEALTH AND HUMAN SERVICES

Family Support Administration

Administrator (Senior Executive Service)

Office of Civil Rights

Director (Senior Executive Service)

Office of Human Development Services

Assistant Secretary for Human Development Services (Level IV, Presidential Appointment with Senate Confirmation)

Commissioner, Administration on Aging (Level V, Presidential Appointment with Senate Confirmation)

Commissioner, Administration for Children, Youth and Families, (GS 18, Presidential Appointment with Senate Confirmation)

Public Health Service

Administrator, Alcohol, Drug Abuse and Mental Health Administration (Level IV, Presidential Appointment with Senate Confirmation)

Surgeon General (Level IV, Presidential Appointment with Senate Confirmation)

Director, National Cancer Institute, National Institutes of Health, Public Health Service (Presidential Appointment)

Director, Indian Health Service (Senior Executive Service)

DEPARTMENT OF THE INTERIOR

Director, Bureau of Land Management (Level V, Presidential Appointment with Senate Confirmation)

Director, Minerals Management Service (Senior Executive Service)

Director, Fish and Wildlife Service (Level V, Presidential Appointment with Senate Confirmation)

INTERSTATE COMMERCE COMMISSION

Chairman (Level III, Presidential Appointment with Senate Confirmation)

DEPARTMENT OF JUSTICE

Assistant Attorney General, Office of Legal Policy (Level IV, Presidential Appointment with Senate Confirmation)

Assistant Attorney General, Office of Legislative and Intergovernmental Affairs (Level IV, Presidential Appointment with Senate Confirmation)

DEPARTMENT OF LABOR

Solicitor (Level IV, Presidential Appointment with Senate Confirmation)

NATIONAL AERONAUTICS AND SPACE ADMINISTRATION

Associate Administrator for External Relations (Senior Executive Service)

Associate Administrator for Policy and Planning (Senior Executive Service)

Associate Administrator for Space Flight (Senior Executive Service)

Director, George C. Marshall Space Center (Senior Executive Service)

Director, Lyndon Johnson Space Center (Senior Executive Service)

NUCLEAR REGULATORY COMMISSION

Chairman (Level II, Presidential Appointment with Senate Confirmation)

SECURITIES AND EXCHANGE COMMISSION

Chairman (Level III, Presidential Appointment with Senate Confirmation)

DEPARTMENT OF TRANSPORTATION

Administrator, Saint Lawrence Seaway Development Corporation (Level IV, Presidential Appointment with Senate Confirmation)

Deputy Administrator, Federal Aviation Administration (Level IV, Presidential Appointment with Senate Confirmation)

Administrator, Research and Special Programs Administration (Senior Executive Service)

Commandant, Coast Guard (Appointed by Secretary of Transportation)

DEPARTMENT OF THE TREASURY

Undersecretary for Finance (Level III, Presidential Appointment with Senate Confirmation)

Deputy Assistant Secretary for Legislative Affairs (Senior Executive Service)

U. S. ARMS CONTROL AND DISARMAMENT AGENCY

Director (Level II, Presidential Appointment with Senate Confirmation)

UNITED STATES INFORMATION AGENCY

Director (Level II, Presidential Appointment with Senate Confirmation)

UNITED STATES INTERNATIONAL DEVELOPMENT CORPORATION

Director (Level II, Presidential Appointment with Senate Confirmation)

UNITED STATES INTERNATIONAL TRADE COMMISSION

Chairman (Level III, Presidential Appointment with Senate Confirmation)

APPENDIX II

The Prune Book Interviewees

The Center for Excellence in Government would like to thank the nearly 400 individuals who consented to be interviewed for this project. Without their cooperation and support, the book would not have been possible.

Those interviewed include present and former occupants of the positions described in the book (Part 1) and individuals with detailed knowledge of the positions through close observations and/or past association with them (Part 2). Part 1 lists these interviewees by name. Part 2 lists the private-sector organizations and congressional committees represented by those interviews.

Part 1: Present and Former Occupants

Henry Aaron
The Brookings Institution

Philip Abrams*
Philip Abrams and Associates

Donald C. Alexander*
Cadwalader, Wickersham and Taft

Robert F. Allnutt*
Pharmaceutical Manufacturers
Association

Alvin L. Alm*
Alliance Technologies Corporation

James R. Ambrose
Atherton, California

Annelise Anderson
Hoover Institution

Albert Angrisani
Arthur D. Little, Inc.

Roy L. Ash
Ash Capital Corporation

Alfred L. Atherton, Jr.
Washington, DC

Thorne Auchter
The Jefferson Group

Charles D. Baker
Northeastern University

Vincent P. Barabba
General Motors Corporation

A. James Barnes
Environmental Protection Agency

Robert T. Barnett
Barnett, D'Amours, Sivon and
Shay

Ray A. Barnhart
Texas Research and Development
Foundation

John W. Barnum
White & Case

Morton A. Baruch
Morton A. Baruch & Associates

William F. Baxter
Stanford Law School

James M. Beggs
Defense Group, Inc.

C. Fred Bergsten
Institute for International
Economics

Eula Bingham
University of Cincinnati

Robert W. Blanchette
Robert W. Blanchette Associates

Danny J. Boggs
U.S. Judge, 6th Circuit Court
of Appeals

Jack R. Borsting
University of Southern California

Karl S. Bowers
Stevens & Wilkinson

Albert A. Bowker
Research Foundation for City
University of New York

Charles A. Bowsher
General Accounting Office

Lawrence J. Brady
Hill and Knowlton

Robert N. Broadbent
Clark County Department of
Aviation

Cynthia Brown
Council of Chief State School
Officers

June Gibbs Brown
Department of Defense

Robert J. Brown
National Mediation Board

George M. Browning
Burdeshaw Associates, Ltd.

Charles E. Buckingham
Great Falls, Virginia

Hamer Budge
Palm Desert, California

Alan A. Butchman*
Garvey, Schubert & Barer

Charles M. Butler III
Kidder Peabody

John V. Byrne
Oregon State University

Anthony J. Calio
Planning Research Corporation

Howard H. Callaway
Crested Butte Mountain Resort

Alan K. Campbell*
ARA Services, Inc.

Gerald Cann
General Dynamics

James B. Cardwell
Blue Cross & Blue Shield

Gerald P. Carmen
Federal Asset Disposition
Association

Robert Carswell
Shearman and Sterling

Richard E. Carver
Department of Defense

C. Hale Champion
Commonwealth of Massachusetts

John E. Chapoton*
Vinson and Elkins

Dicken Cherry
National Center for Municipal
Development

Jed D. Christensen
Department of the Interior

Warren Christopher*
O'Melveny & Myers

Fred T. Cioffi
Department of Education

Benjamin R. Civiletti
Venable, Baetjer, Howard &
Civiletti

Joan Claybrooke
Public Citizen

Jeffrey M. Clayton
Callister, Duncan & Nebeker

W. Graham Claytor
National Railroad Passenger
Corporation

William C. Clohan
Clohan, Adams & Dean

John F. Cogan
The Hoover Institute

Robert Collyer
The Collyer Company

Terry Coleman
Department of Health and Human
Services

Robert H. Conn
Department of Defense

C. T. Conover
Edgar, Dunn & Conover

David S. Cook
Buckeye Federal Savings & Loan

Michael B. Cook
Environmental Protection Agency

Charles J. Cooper
McGuire, Woods, Battle and
Boothe

Robert S. Cooper
Atlantic Aerospace

Theodore Cooper*
Upjohn Company

Robert B. Costello
Department of Defense

Douglas M. Costle
Vermont Law School

Chapman B. Cox
Sherman, Howard

Carol T. Crawford
Office of Management and Budget

Malcolm R. Currie
Hughes Aircraft Company

Charles B. Curtis
Van Ness, Feldman, Sutcliffe &
Curtis

Eliot R. Cutler
Cutler and Stanfield

M. Rupert Cutler
Population Environment Balance

Larry H. Dale
Fannie Mae

Kenneth Dam
IBM Corporation

LeGree S. Daniels
Department of Education

C. Marshall Dann
Dann, Dorfman, Herrell &
Skillman

Carolyne K. Davis
Ernst & Whinney

Nathaniel Davis
Harvey Mudd College

Randall E. Davis
Jones, Day, Reavis & Pogue

W. Kenneth Davis
Bechtel Corporation

Drew S. Days III
Yale Law School

Silvio J. DeBartolomeis
Winn Group

Richard D. DeLauer*
Orion Group

Bernard DeLury
Sea-Land Corporation

Bohdan Denysyk
Global USA, Inc.

Donald A. Derman
SYNECTICS

Donald J. Devine
Citizens for America

Gerald P. Dinneen
Honeywell, Inc.

Thomas R. Donnelly
The Pagonis-Donnelly Group

Mortimer L. Downey, III
Metropolitan Transportation
Authority

Herbert Doyle
National Association of Letter
Carriers of USA

Hans H. Driessnack
United Technologies

Lawrence S. Eagleburger*
Kissinger Associates, Inc.

Donald B. Easum
African-American Institute

Charles C. Edwards
Scripps Clinic and Research
Foundation

Michael J. Egan
Sutherland, Asbill & Brennan

Roscoe Egger
Price Waterhouse

Donald E. Elisburg*
Washington, DC

Frank B. Elliot
North Garde, Virginia

Edward M. Elmendorf
Policon Corporation

Robert C. Embry, Jr.
Abell Foundation

Donald D. Engen
Air Safety Foundation

William W. Erwin
Bourbon, Indiana

Mark B. Feldman
Washington, DC

Michael J. Fenello
Eustis, Florida

C. William Fischer
University of Colorado

Guy W. Fiske
Fiske Associates

Ray V. Fitzgerald
Falls Church, Virginia

Arthur Fletcher
Pennsylvania Development
Corporation

William H. Foege
Carter Presidential Center of
Emory University

Sylvester R. Foley
Foley Associates

Ralph Forbes
Canton, Massachusetts

Ford B. Ford
Federal Mine Safety and Health
Review Committee

Carol Tucker Foreman
Chevy Chase, Maryland

Richard A. Frank
Population Services International

Donald S. Frederickson
National Institutes of Health

Paul Freedenberg
Department of Commerce

Robert W. Fri
Resources for the Future

D. Kent Frizzell
University of Tulsa

Robert F. Froehlke
IDS Mutual Fund Group

Robert A. Frosch*
General Motors Corporation

H. Lawrence Garrett
Department of Defense

John A. Gaughan
Department of Transportation

John N. Gentry
Reston, Virginia

Forrest J. Gerard
Gerard & Byler

Kenneth A. Giles
Department of Agriculture

Richard P. Godwin
Defense Group, Inc.

Herman R. Goldberg
Ergo Associates, Inc.

Richard W. Goldberg
Department of Agriculture

Harold P. Goldfield
Strategic Resources, Inc.

Edwin Gray
Chase Federal Savings & Loan

Marshall Green
Washington, DC

Joseph A. Greenwald
Washington, DC

J. Steven Griles
Department of the Interior

Erwin N. Griswold
Jones, Day, Reavis & Pogue

Philip C. Habib
Belmont, California

F. Henry Habicht II
Perkins, Coie, Stone and Williams

Janet Hale
Department of Transportation

Herbert J. Hansell
Washington, D. C.

Edwin L. Harper*
Campbell Soup Company

James R. Harris
Dick Harris and Associates

Dale E. Hathaway
The Consultants International
Group

Teresa A. Hawkes
State of California

Arthur Hull Hayes, Jr.*
EM Pharmaceuticals, Inc.

Thomas J. Healey*
Goldman Sachs & Company

George H. Heilmeier
Texas Instruments, Inc.

John Heimann
Merrill Lynch Capital Markets

Walter N. Heine
Walter N. Heine Associates

Benjamin W. Heineman, Jr.
General Electric Company

Richard Helms
Safeer Company

J. Lynn Helms
Consultants International Ltd.

Robert E. Herzstein*
Arnold and Porter

Philip B. Heymann
Harvard Law School

Frederick Hickman
Hopkins and Sutter

Donald A. Hicks
Hicks & Associates, Inc.

Edward Hidalgo
Vorys, Sater, Seymour & Pease

Martin J. Hillenbrand
University of Georgia

Roderick Hills
The Manchester Group

John H. Holdridge
Bethesda, Maryland

Kenneth N. Hollander*
Ford Aerospace Corporation

Robert D. Hormats
Goldman Sachs & Company

Constance J. Horner
Office of Personnel Management

Lawrence R. Houston
Washington, DC

Phillip S. Hughes
Port Republic, Maryland

Fred C. Iklé
Bethesda, Maryland

Robert S. Ingersoll
Wilmette, Illinois

B. R. Inman*
Westmark Systems, Inc.

John N. Irwin
Patterson, Belknap and Webb

Jay Janis
Gibralter Savings

Mary C. Jarratt
Jarratt & Associates

Edward R. Jayne II
McDonnell Douglas Astronautics
Company

D. Lowell Jensen
U. S. District Court

Donald E. Johnson
National Credit Union
Administration

Gary L. Jones
Trinity IV

James A. Joseph
Council on Foundations

Linda Heller Kamm
Foley & Lardner

Julius L. Katz
The Government Research
Corporation

John G. Keane
Department of Commerce

James D. Keast
Carmody, McDonald, Hilton and
Wolf

Donald Kennedy
Stanford University

Donald M. Kerr*
EG&G, Inc.

Ray Kline
National Academy of Public
Administration

John J. Knapp*
Powell, Goldstein, Frazier &
Murphy

E. Henry Knoche
Denver, Colorado

Robert W. Komer
The RAND Corporation

John E. Krings
Department of Defense

Jerome Kurtz*
Paul, Weiss, Rifkind, Wharton &
Garrison

Stephen Kurzman
Nixon, Hargrave, Devans and
Doyle

Richard P. Kusserow
Department of Health and Human
Services

Ronald Lamont-Havers
Massachusetts General Hospital

Bert Lance
Calhoun, Georgia

Ian D. Lanoff
Willkie, Farr & Gallagher

Donald C. Latham
Computer Sciences Corporation

Rex E. Lee
Brigham Young University
School of Law

Monroe Leigh
Steptoe and Johnson

Marc E. Leland*
Marc Leland & Associates

Michael Leonard
Department of Defense

Daniel B. Levine
National Academy of Sciences

Alan M. Lovelace
General Dynamics

Donald Lubick
Hodgson, Russ, Andrews, Woods
& Goodyear

William R. Lucas
Huntsville, Alabama

Stephen J. Lukasik
Northrop Corporation

Theodore C. Lutz*
The Washington Post

Lawrence H. Lynn, Jr.
University of Chicago

Frederick Y. Malek*
Marriott Corporation

Daniel Marcus*
Wilmer, Cutler and Pickering

Peter A. Marino*
Lockheed Electronics Company

Jim J. Marquez
Condon & Forsythe

Robert G. Marston
University of Florida

James O. Mason
Centers for Disease Control

Stephen May
Washington, DC

Robert P. Mayo
Chicago, Illinois

Terence E. McClary
Ft. Lauderale, Florida

Richard T. McCormack
Department of State

James F. McGovern
Department of Defense

J. Paul McGrath
Dewey, Ballantine

Jack W. McGraw
Environmental Protection Agency

John R. McGuire
Falls Church, Virginia

James T. McIntyre
McNair Law Firm

Robert H. McKinney
Jefferson Corporation

C.W. McMillan
McMillan and Farrell

Edward L. Meador
Springfield, Virginia

Thomas P. Melady
Connecticut Public Expenditure
Council

Alex P. Mercure
Hicks, Mercure and Associates

Robert H. Meyer
La Jolla, California

J. William Middendorf II
Middendorf, Ansary and Company

Daniel N. Miller, Jr.
I.W.O. Exploration

Steven A. Minter
The Cleveland Foundation

Robert Monks
Institutional Shareholders
Services, Inc.

James W. Moorman
Cadwalader, Wickersham & Taft

Robert C. Moot
Annandale, Virginia

Alfred C. Moran
Barrett, Montgomery and Murphy

William A. Morrill*
Mathtech, Inc.

Thomas D. Morris
Bethesda, Maryland

Gerald J. Mossinghoff*
Pharmaceutical Manufacturers
Association

Langhorne A. Motley
L.A. Motley and Company

Robert Mundheim
University of Pennsylvania

Richard Murphy
Department of State

Russell Murray II
House Committee on Armed
Services

Frank W. Naylor, Jr.
Farm Credit Administration

Howard N. Newman*
Powell, Goldstein, Fraser and
Murphy

David D. Newsom
Institute for the Study of
Diplomacy

Mark Novitch*
Upjohn Company

Raymond J. O'Connor*
Citibank Corporation

Donald G. Ogilvie*
American Bankers Association

Theodore B. Olson
Gibson, Dunn & Crutcher

Walter J. Olson
Walter J. Olson & Associates

Paul H. O'Neill*
Aluminum Company of America

John J. O'Shaughnessy
Greater New York Hospital
Association

Verne Orr
Pasadena, California

Don Paarlberg
Purdue University

Richard S. Page*
Washington Roundtable

Clarence D. Palmby
Marcell, Minnesota

John Pendergrass
Department of Labor

William J. Perry
H&Q Technology Partners

R. Max Peterson
Fairfax, Virginia

Steffen W. Plehn*
CH2M Hill

Manuel D. Plotkin
M.D. Plotkin Research &
Planning Company

James W. Plummer
Jacksonville, Oregon

J. Winston Porter
Environmental Protection Agency

David S. Potter
Santa Barbara, California

J. Stanley Pottinger
New York, New York

Richard T. Pratt
Merrill Lynch Mortgage Capital,
Inc.

Everett Pyatt
Department of Defense

Donald Quigg
Department of Commerce

Aaron J. Racusin
Quinn & Racusin

Rebecca G. Range
The White House

Everett Rank
Fresno, California

Eberhardt Rechtin*
Palos Verdes Estates, California

Thomas C. Reed
River Oaks Agricorp

Charles B. Renfrew
Chevron Corporation

Stanley R. Resor
DeBevoise & Plimpton

William Bradford Reynolds
Department of Justice

Julius B. Richmond
Harvard University

John Riley
Department of Transportation

Charles W. Robinson
Energy Transition Corporation

Davis R. Robinson
Pillsbury, Madison and Sutro

William D. Rogers
Arnold and Porter

Edward M. Roob
Daiwa Securities America, Inc.

Herman E. Roser
Albuquerque, New Mexico

Stanford G. Ross*
Arnold and Porter

Robert J. Rubin
Health and Sciences Research,
Inc.

William D. Ruckelshaus*
Perkins, Coie, Stone and Williams

Charles F. Rule
Department of Justice

Donald H. Rumsfeld
William Blair and Company

Arthur F. Sampson*
Falls Church, Virginia

George A. Sawyer
Laguna Beach, California

Leonard D. Schaefer
Blue Cross of California

William E. Schaufele, Jr.
Salisbury, Connecticut

Alexander M. Schmidt
University of Illinois

Edward C. Schmults
GTE Corporation

James E. Schoenberger
Department of Housing and
Urban Development

Richard F. Schubert*
American Red Cross

Harry K. Schwartz
Lane & Edson

Roger D. Semerad
Burson-Marstellar

David J. Sencer
Management of Sciences for
Health

Harold E. Shear
Groton Long Point, Connecticut

Joseph H. Sherick
Annandale, Virginia

Deanne C. Siemer*
Wilmer, Cutler and Pickering

Laurence Silberman
U.S. Court of Appeals
District of Columbia Circuit

Daniel B. Silver
Cleary, Gottlieb, Steen and
Hamilton

William E. Simon
WSGP International, Inc.

Lawrence B. Simons*
Powell, Goldstein, Frazier &
Murphy

Bruce Smart
Upperville, Virginia

Kenneth L. Smith
Ken Smith Associates

Anthony Solomon
S.G. Warburg USA, Inc.

Ronald I. Spiers
Department of State

Robert H. Spiro, Jr.
Sports 2000, Inc.

Stanley Sporkin
Federal District Court for the
District of Columbia

Irvine H. Sprague
Great Falls, Virginia

Beryl Sprinkel
Council of Economic
Advisors

Ralph L. Stanley
Municipal Development
Corporation

Diane K. Steed
Department of Transportation

Debra Steelman
Epstein, Becker and Green

John R. Stevenson*
Sullivan and Cromwell

Jack R. Stokvis
Department of Housing and
Urban Development

Leonard Sullivan, Jr.
Systems Planning Corporation

John A. Svahn
Severna Park, Maryland

Ross O. Swimmer
Department of the Interior

Peter R. Taft
Munger, Tulles and Olson

William H. Taft IV
Department of Defense

Arthur E. Teele, Jr.
Sparbur, Slevin, Sharpo
and Heilbroner

Lee M. Thomas
Environmental Protection Agency

Morris Thompson
Doyon Limited Corporation

Richard L. Thornburgh
Department of Justice

Randolph Thrower
Atlanta, Georgia

Norbert T. Tiemann
HDR

Alair Townsend
City of New York

Russell E. Train*
World Wildlife Fund

Darrell M. Trent
Rollins Environmental Services

Stephen S. Trott
U.S. Court of Appeals
Ninth Circuit

Richard H. Truly
National Aeronautics and Space
Administration

Thomas K. Turnage
Veterans Administration

James P. Turner
Department of Justice

Harold R. Tyler, Jr.
Patterson, Belknap, Webb &
Tyler

Viron P. Vaky
Carnegie Endowment for
International Peace

George S. Vest
Department of State

Paul A. Volcker
James D. Wolfensohn, Inc.

Charls E. Walker*
Charls E. Walker Associates

Peter J. Wallison*
Gibson, Dunn & Crutcher

Harry N. Walters
Great Lakes Carbon Corporation

Richard Warden
United Auto Workers

Charles K. Watt
Georgia Tech Research Institute

Arnold R. Weber
Northwestern University

Frank A. Weil*
Abacus and Associates, Inc.

William F. Weld
Hale and Dorr

Togo D. West, Jr.
Patterson, Belknap, Webb & Tyler

Robert M. White
National Academy of Engineering

John P. White*
Interactive Systems Corporation

Madeleine C. Will
Department of Education

Frank Wille
Greater New York Savings Bank

James H. Williams
River Groves, Inc.

Ewen M. Wilson
Department of Agriculture

R. James Woolsey
Shea and Gardner

Suzanne H. Woolsey*
Coopers & Lybrand

Don I. Wortman
National Academy of Public
Administration

John D. Young
Falls Church, Virginia

James W. Ziglar
Department of the Interior

* Principal of The Center for Excellence in Government.

Part 2: Private Sector Organizations and Congressional Committees

Private Sector Organizations

Aerospace Industries Association
of America

Air Transport Association

American Association of Retired
Persons

American Automobile Association

American Bar Association

American Farm Bureau Federation

American Hospital Association

Edison Electric Institute
Grocery Manufacturers of
America

Housing Assistance Council, Inc.

Mitre Corporation

National Association of
Manufacturers

National Education Association

National Security Industrial
Association

Pharmaceutical Manufacturers
Association

Sierra Club

U.S. Chamber of Commerce

W.R. Grace and Company

Congressional Committees

House Post Office and Civil
Service Committee

Senate Agriculture, Nutrition,
and Forestry Committee

Senate Appropriations Committee

Senate Banking, Housing, and
Urban Affairs Committee

Senate Energy and Natural
Resources Committee

Senate Environment and Public
Works Committee

Senate Foreign Relations
Committee

Senate Judiciary Committee

Senate Labor and Human
Resources Committee

APPENDIX III

Members of The Prune Book Departmental Teams

DEPARTMENT OF AGRICULTURE

Team Captain

Dale Hathaway is Vice President of The Consultants International Group, Washington, D.C. Mr. Hathaway served as an Under-secretary of Agriculture from 1979 to 1981.

Team Members

Lynn Daft is Vice President of Abel, Daft, & Earley, Alexandria, Virginia. From 1977 to 1981, Mr. Daft served in the White House as Associate Director for Domestic Policy. Mr. Daft also served as an Assistant Deputy Administrator in the Department of Agriculture.

James H. Williams is President, River Groves, Inc., Ocala, Florida. Mr. Williams served as a Deputy Secretary of Agriculture from 1979 to 1981.

DEPARTMENT OF COMMERCE

Team Captain

Stanley J. Marcuss is Partner, Milbank, Tweed, Hadley & McCloy, Washington, D.C. From 1977 to 1980, Mr. Marcuss served as a Deputy Assistant Secretary for Industry and Trade in the Department of Commerce. Mr. Marcuss also served as Counsel to the Senate Committee on Banking, Housing, and Urban Affairs.

Team Members

Joseph E. Kasputys is President and Chief Operating Officer, Primark Corporation, McLean, Virginia. Prior to his present position, he served as Executive Vice President, Development, McGraw-Hill, Inc. Mr. Kasputys served as Assistant Secretary for Administration in the Department of Commerce. He also served as Assistant Administrator of the Maritime Administration and Assistant to the Controller, Department of Defense.

Gerald J. Mossinghoff is President, Pharmaceutical Manufacturers Association, Washington, D.C. Mr. Mossinghoff served as Assistant Secretary of Commerce and Commissioner of Patents and Trademarks from 1981 to 1985. Mr. Mossinghoff also served as Deputy General Counsel of the National Aeronautics and Space Administration.

Paul T. O'Day is President, Man-Made Fiber Producers Association, Inc., Washington, D.C. From 1959 to 1984, Mr. O'Day held numerous positions within the Department of Commerce, including Deputy Assistant Secretary for Foreign Commercial Operations, International Trade Administration.

DEPARTMENT OF DEFENSE / NATIONAL AERONAUTICS AND SPACE ADMINISTRATION / CENTRAL INTELLIGENCE AGENCY

Team Captain

Philip A. Odeen is Regional Managing Partner, Coopers & Lybrand, Washington, D.C. Mr. Odeen served as Director of Program Analysis for the National Security Council and Principal Deputy Assistant Secretary for Systems Analysis in the Department of Defense.

Team Members

Norman R. Augustine is President and Chief Operating Officer of Martin Marietta Corporation, Bethesda, Maryland. Mr. Augustine served as Undersecretary of the Army from 1975 to 1977. Mr. Augustine also served as Assistant Secretary of the Army (Research and Development) and Assistant Undersecretary of Defense for Research and Engineering.

Robert A. Frosch is Vice President of General Motors Corporation in charge of the Research Laboratory, Warren, Michigan. Mr. Frosch served as Administrator of the National Aeronautics and Space Administration and Assistant Secretary of the Navy for Research and Development.

B.R. Inman is President and Chief Executive Officer, Westmark Systems, Inc., Austin, Texas. He retired from the Navy with the permanent rank of Admiral in 1982. Between 1974 and 1982, Admiral Inman served as the Director of Naval Intelligence, Vice Director of the Defense Intelligence Agency, Director of the National Security Agency, and Deputy Director of the Central Intelligence Agency.

Joseph E. Kasputys is President and Chief Operating Officer, Primark Corporation, McLean, Virginia. Prior to his present position, he served as Executive Vice President, Development, McGraw-Hill, Inc. Mr. Kasputys served as Assistant Secretary for Administration in the Department of Commerce. He also served as Assistant Administrator of the Maritime Administration and Assistant to the Controller, Department of Defense.

Vincent Puritano is Vice President, Government Affairs and International Trade, Unisys Corporation, Washington, D.C. From 1981 to 1984, Mr. Puritano served as Assistant Secretary of Defense (Comptroller) and Executive Assistant to the Deputy Secretary of Defense. Mr. Puritano has also served in the Department of State and Office of Management and Budget.

Ivan Selin is Chairman of the Board, American Management Systems, Rosslyn, Virginia. Mr. Selin served as Assistant Secretary for Systems Analysis in the Department of Defense.

John P. White is Chairman and Chief Executive Officer, Interactive Systems Corporation, Santa Monica, California. Mr. White served as Deputy Director of the Office of Management and Budget from 1978 to 1980. Mr. White also served as Assistant Secretary of Defense, Manpower, Reserve Affairs and Logistics.

DEPARTMENT OF EDUCATION

Team Captain

Christopher T. Cross is President, University Research Corporation, Chevy Chase, Maryland. Mr. Cross formerly held several senior positions in the Department of Health, Education and Welfare and served as minority Staff Director of the House Committee on Education and Labor.

Team Members

William C. Clohan, Jr. is member of Clohan, Adams and Dean, Washington, D.C. Mr. Clohan served as Undersecretary in the Department of Education.

Edward M. Elmendorf is President of Policon Corporation, Washington, D.C. He served as Assistant Secretary for Postsecondary Education in the Department of Education.

Patricia G. McGinnis is Vice President and Director, Francis, McGinnis & Rees, Inc., Washington, D.C. Ms. McGinnis served as a Deputy Associate Director of the Office of Management and Budget. Ms. McGinnis also served in the Department of Commerce and the Department of Health, Education and Welfare.

Elizabeth R. Reisner is Principal and co-owner, Policy Studies Associates, Inc., Washington, D.C. From 1972 to 1979, Ms. Reisner served as an education policy analyst in the Office of Education, Department of Health, Education and Welfare.

DEPARTMENT OF ENERGY / ENVIRONMENTAL PROTECTION AGENCY

Team Captain

Alvin L. Alm is President, Alliance Technologies Corporation, Bedford, Massachusetts. Mr. Alm served as Deputy Administrator of the Environmental Protection Agency from 1983 to 1985. Mr. Alm also served as Assistant Secretary for Policy and Evaluation in the Department of Energy.

Team Members

John M. Deutch is Provost, Massachusetts Institute of Technology, Cambridge, Massachusetts. Mr. Deutch served as an Assistant Secretary of the Department of Energy from 1979 to 1980.

William N. Hedeman, Jr. is Partner, Beveridge & Diamond, Washington, D.C. From 1981 to 1986, Mr. Hedeman served as Director of the Office of Emergency and Remedial Response in the Environmental Protection Agency. Mr. Hedeman also served as Assistant General Counsel in the U. S. Army Corps of Engineers.

James R. Janis is Chief Operating Officer of ICF, Inc., Fairfax, Virginia. Mr. Janis served as Deputy Assistant Secretary for Planning and Evaluation in the Department of Energy. Mr. Janis also served in the Environmental Protection Agency and the Department of Health, Education, and Welfare.

DEPARTMENT OF HEALTH AND HUMAN SERVICES

Team Captain

Suzanne H. Woolsey is Partner, Coopers & Lybrand, Washington, D.C. From 1976 to 1980, Ms. Woolsey served as Associate Director for Human Resources, Veterans, and Labor in the Office of Management and Budget. Ms. Woolsey also served as a Deputy Assistant Secretary in the Department of Health, Education, and Welfare.

Team Members

Edward N. Brandt, Jr. is Chancellor of the University of Maryland at Baltimore, Baltimore, Maryland. Dr. Brandt served as Assistant Secretary for Health in the Department of Health and Human Services from 1981 to 1984.

Howard N. Newman is Partner, Powell, Goldstein, Frazer & Murphy, Washington, D.C. He served as Administrator of the Health Care Financing Administration in the Department of Health and Human Services. Mr. Newman also served as Commissioner of Medical Services Administration in the Department of Health, Education, and Welfare and as a White House Fellow in the Bureau of the Budget.

Stanford G. Ross is Partner, Arnold & Porter, Washington, D.C. From 1978 to 1979, Mr. Ross was Commissioner of the Social Security Administration in the Department of Health and Human Services. Mr. Ross also served in the Department of Transportation, the Department of Treasury, and the White House.

DEPARTMENT OF HOUSING AND URBAN DEVELOPMENT

Team Captain

John K. Freeman is Principal, The Investment Group Capital Corporation, Washington, D.C. Mr. Freeman served as Deputy Assistant Administrator of Energy Projects in the Federal Energy Administration from 1975 to 1977. Mr. Freeman also served in the Department of Housing and Urban Development and the Office of Management and Budget.

Team Members

John K. Knapp is Counsel, Powell, Goldstein, Frazer and Murphy, Washington, D.C. Mr. Knapp served as General Counsel of the Department of Housing and Urban Development from 1981 to 1986.

Lawrence B. Simons is a Partner, Powell, Goldstein, Frazer & Murphy, Washington, D.C. Mr. Simons served as Assistant Secretary for Housing/Federal Housing Commissioner in the Department of Housing and Urban Development from 1977 to 1981.

H. Ralph Taylor is a retired real estate developer in Washington, D.C. From 1966 to 1969, Mr. Taylor served as Assistant Secretary for Model Cities and Government Relations in the Department of Housing and Urban Development.

DEPARTMENT OF THE INTERIOR

Team Captain

Heather L. Ross is Vice President, Corporate Planning, BP America, Cleveland, Ohio. From 1977 to 1981, Ms. Ross served as Deputy Assistant Secretary, Policy, Budget, and Administration in the Department of the Interior. Ms. Ross also served as Senior Economist for the Senate Budget Committee.

Team Members

H. Theodore Heintz served as a senior official in the Department of the Interior.

James A. Joseph is President, Council on Foundations, Washington, D.C. Mr. Joseph served as Undersecretary of the Department of the Interior from 1977 to 1981.

DEPARTMENT OF JUSTICE

Team Captain

Robert A. McConnell is Vice President, CBS Washington, CBS Inc., Washington, D.C. From 1981 to 1984, Mr. McConnell served as Assistant Attorney General for Legislation in the Department of Justice.

Team Members

Julian S. Greenspun is Partner, Stroock and Stroock, Washington, D.C. From 1970 to 1986, Mr. Greenspun served in the Department of Justice. Mr. Greenspun served as Deputy Chief for Litigation in the Criminal Division from 1979 to 1986.

Jonathan C. Rose is Partner, Jones, Day, Reavis and Pogue, Washington, D.C. Mr. Rose served as Assistant Attorney General, Office of Legal Policy in the Department of Justice.

Jared Stamel is an Attorney-at-Law, New York, New York. From 1973 to 1975, Mr. Stamel served as Counsel to the House Committee on the Judiciary. Mr. Stamel has also served in the Department of Justice.

DEPARTMENT OF LABOR

Team Captain

William H. Kolberg is President, National Alliance of Business, Washington, D.C. From 1973 to 1977, Mr. Kolberg served as Assistant Secretary of Labor and Administrator of the Employment Training Administration. Mr. Kolberg also served in the Office of Management and Budget.

Team Members

Michael H. Moskow is Vice President, Strategy and Business

Development, Premark International, Inc., Northbrook, Illinois. Mr. Moskow has served as Undersecretary of the Department of Labor, Director of the Council on Wage and Price Stability, and Assistant Secretary in the Department of Housing and Urban Development.

Weldon J. Rougeau is Vice President, Central Region, American Express Travel Related Services, Chicago, Illinois. Mr. Rougeau served as Director of the Office of Contract Compliance in the Department of Labor from 1977 to 1980.

DEPARTMENT OF STATE

Team Captain

John R. Stevenson is Counsel to Sullivan and Cromwell and President and a Trustee of the National Gallery of Art, Washington, D.C. From 1973 to 1975, Mr. Stevenson served as Ambassador, the President's Special Representative, and Chief of the Delegation for the Law of the Sea Conference. From 1969 to 1972, Mr. Stevenson served as Legal Advisor in the Department of State.

Team Members

Lawrence S. Eagleburger is President, Kissinger Associates, New York, New York. From 1957 to 1984, Mr. Eagleburger served as a Foreign Service Officer in the Department of State. He served as Undersecretary of State for Political Affairs from 1982 to 1984. He also served as Assistant Secretary of State for European Affairs and Ambassador to Yugoslavia.

Ted Elliott is Executive Director, Center for Asian Pacific Affairs, Asia Foundation, San Francisco, California. Mr. Elliott served as a senior official in the Department of State.

Charles F. Meissner is Vice President, Chemical Bank, New York, New York. From 1980 to 1983, Mr. Meissner served as an Ambassador and United States Special Negotiator for Economic Matters in the Department of State. Mr. Meissner also served as a Staff Member of the Senate Committee on Foreign Relations from 1973 to 1977.

John B. Rhinelander is Partner, Shaw, Pittman & Trowbridge, Washington, D.C. From 1975 to 1977, Mr. Rhinelander served as Undersecretary of the Department of Housing and Urban Development. Mr. Rhinelander also served as General Counsel of the Department of Health, Education and Welfare. He also worked in the Departments of Defense and State.

DEPARTMENT OF TRANSPORTATION

Team Captain

Theodore C. Lutz is Business Manager, *The Washington Post*, Washington, D.C. Mr. Lutz has served as Administrator of the Urban Mass Transportation Administration and General Manager of the Washington Metropolitan Area Transit Authority.

Team Member

John W. Snow is Chief Operating Officer of the CSX Corporation, Richmond, Virginia. Mr. Snow served as Administrator of the National Highway Traffic Safety Administration and as Deputy Undersecretary and Assistant Secretary in the Department of Transportation.

DEPARTMENT OF THE TREASURY

Team Captain

Thomas J. Healey is Vice President, Real Estate Department, Goldman Sachs, New York, New York. Mr. Healey served as Assistant Secretary of Treasury for Domestic Finance.

Team Members

John E. Chapoton is Managing Partner, Vinson & Elkins, Washington, D.C. From 1981 to 1984, Mr. Chapoton served as Assistant Secretary for Tax Policy of the Department of the Treasury. He also served as the Tax Legislative Counsel for the Treasury Department.

John E. Schmidt is a Managing Director, First Boston Corporation, San Francisco, California. From 1979 to 1981, Mr.

Schmidt served as Deputy Assistant Secretary in the Office of the Secretary of the Treasury.

EXECUTIVE OFFICE OF THE PRESIDENT / CENTRAL MANAGEMENT AGENCIES

Team Captain

Edward G. Sanders is President and Chief Operating Officer, International Planning and Analysis Center, Washington, D.C. Mr. Sanders has served as Staff Director of the U.S. Foreign Relations Committee and as an Associate Director of the Office of Management and Budget.

Team Members

Philip A. Odeen is Regional Managing Partner, Coopers & Lybrand, Washington, D.C. Mr. Odeen served as Director of Program Analysis for the National Security Council and Principal Deputy Assistant Secretary for Systems Analysis in the Department of Defense.

Paul H. O'Neill is Chairman and Chief Executive Officer, Aluminum Company of America, Pittsburgh, Pennsylvania. Prior to his present position, Mr. O'Neill was President of International Paper Company. Mr. O'Neill served in the Office of Management and Budget from 1967 to 1977, and was Deputy Director of OMB from 1974 to 1977.

INDEX OF NAMES